IMAGES OF THE WOMAN READER
IN VICTORIAN BRITISH AND AMERICAN FICTION

Copyright 2003 by Catherine J. Golden. This work is licensed under a modified Creative Commons Attribution-Noncommercial-No Derivative Works 3.0 Unported License. To view a copy of this license, visit *http://creativecommons.org/licenses/by-nc-nd/3.0/*. You are free to electronically copy, distribute, and transmit this work if you attribute authorship. *However, all printing rights are reserved by the University Press of Florida (http://www.upf.com). Please contact UPF for information about how to obtain copies of the work for print distribution.* You must attribute the work in the manner specified by the author or licensor (but not in any way that suggests that they endorse you or your use of the work). For any reuse or distribution, you must make clear to others the license terms of this work. Any of the above conditions can be waived if you get permission from the University Press of Florida. Nothing in this license impairs or restricts the author's moral rights.

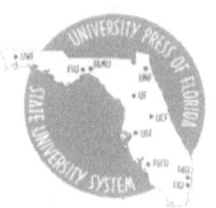

Florida A&M University, Tallahassee
Florida Atlantic University, Boca Raton
Florida Gulf Coast University, Ft. Myers
Florida International University, Miami
Florida State University, Tallahassee
University of Central Florida, Orlando
University of Florida, Gainesville
University of North Florida, Jacksonville
University of South Florida, Tampa
University of West Florida, Pensacola

UNIVERSITY PRESS OF FLORIDA

Gainesville · Tallahassee · Tampa · Boca Raton

Pensacola · Orlando · Miami · Jacksonville · Ft. Myers

Images of the Woman Reader in Victorian British and American Fiction

CATHERINE J. GOLDEN

Copyright 2003 by Catherine J. Golden

All rights reserved

08 07 06 05 04 03 6 5 4 3 2 1

Library of Congress Cataloging-in-Publication Data
Golden, Catherine.
Images of the woman reader in Victorian British and American fiction /
Catherine J. Golden.
p. cm.
Includes bibliographical references and index.
ISBN 978-1-61610-119-0
1. English fiction—19th century—History and criticism. 2. Women—Books and reading—Great Britain—History—19th century. 3. Women—Books and reading—United States—History—19th century. 4. Women and literature—Great Britain—History—19th century. 5. Women and literature—United States—History—19th century. 6. American fiction—19th century—History and criticism. 7. Books and reading in literature. 8. Women in literature. I. Title.
PR878.W6G65 2003
8 3'.809352042—dc22   2003057914

The University Press of Florida is the scholarly publishing agency for the State University System of Florida, comprising Florida A&M University, Florida Atlantic University, Florida Gulf Coast University, Florida International University, Florida State University, University of Central Florida, University of Florida, University of North Florida, University of South Florida, and University of West Florida.

University Press of Florida
15 Northwest 15th Street
Gainesville, FL 32611-2079
http://www.upf.com

For my parents,
Nancy and Lawrence Golden,
who nurtured my love of reading

Contents

List of Illustrations ix

Preface xi

Introduction 1

PART I. A HISTORICAL OVERVIEW

1. Women Readers and Reading in Victorian Britain and America 17

PART II. FICTIONAL REPRESENTATIONS OF THE WOMAN READER

2. Transatlantic Representations of the Woman Reader: Charlotte Brontë's *Jane Eyre* (1847), Henry James's *The Portrait of a Lady* (1881), Louisa May Alcott's *Little Women* (1868, 1869), and Emily Brontë's *Wuthering Heights* (1847) 51

3. Prophetic Reading: Maggie Tulliver of George Eliot's *The Mill on the Floss* (1860) 79

4. Romance Consumers: Gustave Flaubert's *Madame Bovary* (1857) and Mary Elizabeth Braddon's *The Doctor's Wife* (1864) 96

5. The Case for Compatibility: Jane Austen's *Mansfield Park* (1814), George Eliot's *Middlemarch* (1872), and Mona Caird's *The Daughters of Danaus* (1894) 117

PART III. ILLUSTRATIONS OF THE WOMAN READER

6. An Illustrative Gallery of Victorian British and American Women Readers: The Illustrated Fiction of Charles Dickens, Louisa May Alcott, Henry Wadsworth Longfellow, Mark Twain, Frances Hodgson Burnett, and Anthony Trollope 139

7. The Book as Portal: Depictions of the Mind Traveler in Lewis Carroll's *Alice's Adventures under Ground* (1864) and Charlotte Perkins Gilman's "The Yellow Wall-Paper" (1892) 187

8. "What Is the Use of a Book?" Becky Sharp as Revolutionary Reader in William Makepeace Thackeray's *Vanity Fair* (1848) 202

Conclusion 225

Notes 233

Bibliography 265

Index 279

Illustrations

1. George Cruikshank, "My Wife Is a Woman of Mind" 2
2. Eastman Johnson, *Bo-Peep* 25
3. James Gillray, "Tales of Wonder!" 33
4. Winslow Homer, *The New Novel* 38
5. Thomas Bewick, tailpiece to "Razor-Bill" 56
6. Thomas Bewick, tailpiece to "Black-Throated Diver" 57
7. G. M. Brighty, "Ducking a Witch" 83
8. Hablot Knight Browne, "Uriah Persists in Hovering Near Us, at the Dinner Party" 144
9. Hablot Knight Browne, "A Stranger Calls to See Me" 145
10. Hablot Knight Browne, "Our Housekeeping" 147
11. Hablot Knight Browne, "The Shadow in the Little Parlour" 149
12. George Cruikshank, "Rose Maylie and Oliver" 150
13. Hablot Knight Browne, "Under the Plane Tree" 151
14. E. A., "'But Fit with Their Tongues, Fearful'" 154
15. Charlotte Harding, "Algy" 155
16. Frank T. Merrill, "They All Drew to the Fire, Mother in the Big Chair, with Beth to Her Feet" 158
17. Jessie Willcox Smith, "They All Drew to the Fire" 159
18. Jessie Willcox Smith, "A Rainy Day" 161
19. Frank T. Merrill, "Reading That Everlasting Belsham" 163
20. Reginald B. Birch, "The Villagers Did Not Stand in Awe of Her" 165
21. F. O. C. Darley, "But Evangeline Knelt by His Bedside" 166
22. E. W. Kemble, "Learning about Moses and the 'Bulrushers'" 169
23. Worth Brehm, "Then She Told Me about the Bad Place, and I Said I Wished I Was There" 171

24. True Williams, "Aunt Polly Seeks Information" 172
25. Hablot Knight Browne, "Traddles and I, in Conference with the Misses Spenlow" 175
26. Hablot Knight Browne, "The Momentous Interview" 176
27. Howard Chandler Christy, "She Was a Woman Now" 179
28. Henry Sandham, "She Spent Most of Her Time in the Library Reading Her Papa's Big Books" 180
29. Sir John Everett Millais, "The Angel of Light" 182
30. Frank T. Merrill, "Curling Herself Up in the Big Chair" 184
31. Lewis Carroll, chapter 1 headpiece, *Alice's Adventures under Ground* 190
32. Jo. H. Hatfield, "I Am Sitting by the Window in this Atrocious Nursery" 194
33. Jo. H. Hatfield, "She Didn't Know I Was in the Room" 195
34. William Makepeace Thackeray, pictorial capital for chapter 64, from *Vanity Fair* 203
35. William Makepeace Thackeray, "Rebecca's Farewell" 207
36. William Makepeace Thackeray, "It Was the Death-Warrant" 210
37. William Makepeace Thackeray, "Miss Sharp in Her Schoolroom" 212
38. William Makepeace Thackeray, "She Took Up the Black-Edged Missive" 214
39. William Makepeace Thackeray, "Becky in Lombard Street" 218
40. William Makepeace Thackeray, "The Letter before Waterloo" 221
41. William Makepeace Thackeray, "Lieutenant Osborne and His Ardent Love-Letters" 223
42. Franz Robert Richard Brend'amour, "In the Library" 226

Preface

I come from a long line of reading women. My most vivid memory of my maternal grandmother, Elsie Cohen Posmantur, is of her reading a novel with a box of chocolates by her side. The candy box came with a directory, but Grandma Elsie read less discriminatingly than she chose her chocolates. A member of the Book of the Month Club from its earliest days, Elsie sampled classics, best-sellers, mysteries, and romances along with chocolate creams, a regular part of her diet. When Grandma Elsie died, my mother and I sorted through her large collection of books, some of which I own today. Not only Elsie's books but also her love of reading are a legacy my grandmother left for her children and her grandchildren.

Not surprisingly, my mother, Nancy Posmantur Golden, is an avid reader, a passion kindled in childhood. Growing up, my mother spent summers at the beach in Fort Erie, Canada, across from her home in Buffalo, New York. Most fine mornings at low tide, she set off to read for the day. Carrying a bag filled with books and a sack lunch, she spent hours reading on the rocky Canadian shoreline. Only with the rise of the tide did she break her literary reverie to return home. If I close my eyes, I can see her now: a skinny girl with long red braids trailing down her back, wearing glasses against her father's wishes (he thought glasses would spoil her looks), eagerly consuming books—a trope I consciously borrow from the Victorian period.

My mother's most beloved childhood books are classics: L. Frank Baum's *Wizard of Oz* series and Lewis Carroll's *Alice* books. Sometimes Grandma Elsie used a scary voice when she read Baum aloud to my mother, and my mother cried. The world of fiction seemed that real to my mother, as it still does to me today. My mother, in turn, read me *The Little Engine That Could, Charlotte's Web, Heidi, My Friend Flicka,* and *Rascal.* Even now, in her seventies, my mother audits courses at the University of Buffalo. The ideal student, Nancy always keeps up with her reading and passes along reading suggestions to me and my father. On my visits home, I often find my mother, like her mother before her, absorbed in the lives of those existing solely within the pages of a book.

My mother presented me with a copy of *Alice's Adventures in Wonderland* that her nanny, called "Nursie," gave her when she was a child. It bears the inscription still. Of course, she gave me the book long before I discovered my passion for Lewis Carroll or dreamed of spending my life immersed in rare books. Today, when I show that version of *Wonderland* to students at Skidmore College in a course I designed on the Victorian illustrated book, I feel a connection to my mother and to "Nursie," whom I never met. Nursie's inscription records a special time, a feeling of closeness that she and my mother shared. Like Nursie, I make a habit of inscribing books that I give to my husband, children, parents, and friends. In my own collection of children's books, some of which I, in turn, have passed along to my sons, I come across inscriptions from long forgotten chums and old boyfriends—some of whom I would prefer not to remember, some of whom I blush over when my curious sons inquire. Books reawaken my childhood, connect me to my past, and record my lifelong journey as a reader.

My own passion for reading began with a contest. My fifth-grade elementary school teacher, Mrs. Schunack, organized a reading competition that started the summer before I entered fifth grade. The contest continued into the fall of that school year. I always loved books, but my mother tells me that I did not become hooked on fiction until I became determined to win that reading contest. I read more than any other student in my fifth-grade class. I felt superior to the second- and third-place winners who had read, in my estimation, easier and shorter books.

Mrs. Schunack gave us a choice for our prize: dinner at a nice restaurant, or movie and dessert. An ardent movie goer even at that age, I voted for the movie. Now I am glad that the other children chose a dinner out. We went to a country inn called the Lion's Tea Room. The event remains vivid in my memory and senses: I can still smell the aroma wafting from the basket of flavorful cinnamon buns served before our meal. On a recent visit to Buffalo, I asked my parents if we might go to dinner at the Lion's Tea Room. I wanted to take my children to the restaurant where I celebrated my childhood reading contest. Regrettably, it had just closed down. It is never closed in my mind, however; it marks an event that opened a door in my self-perception as a reader.

My family members and close friends are all readers. They dive into current fiction, passing along suggestions to rouse me from my rootedness in the Victorian era. Books of the past captivate me. I spend countless hours reading nineteenth-century novels for pleasure and teaching. I savor biographies about my favorite Victorian British and American authors—the Brontë sisters, George Eliot, Louisa May Alcott, and Charlotte Perkins Gilman. Although I enjoy reading contemporary fiction, I now appreciate what my graduate school mentor, Martha Vicinus, told me about her life as a historian and literary scholar: some of her closest friends are dead. Mine, too. In fact, I confess I have a circle of fictional friends.

I count Maggie Tulliver and Jane Eyre as two of my closest fictional friends. I am not sure how many times I have read *The Mill on the Floss, Jane Eyre, Tess of the D'Urbervilles, David Copperfield,* or *Little Women*. Every time I read of Maggie Tulliver's death by drowning in *The Mill on the Floss*, I weep hysterically. I rejoice with Jane as she proclaims, "Reader, I married him." I cry when Beth languishes in *Little Women*, Dora dies in *David Copperfield*, and Tess hangs in *Tess of the D'Urbervilles*, even though I know these events are going to happen. I become so involved with these characters—many of whom are avid readers themselves—that they seem absolutely real to me.

I have always been curious about what books inspired my favorite authors and what novels my Victorian sisters—real and fictional—read. I jotted a note to this effect in a graduate school prelim that I took at the University of Michigan in the mid-1980s. Martha Vicinus checked it as one among a number of interesting ideas to pursue for future research. I did not explore the topic of fictional women's reading until many years later, after I had formed a personal library of Victorian illustrated books.

I savor original illustrations to Victorian novels, although I appreciate later editions of works that originally appeared without illustration (or without professional images in the case of *Little Women*). In this study, I privilege original illustrations to works currently taught in the college classroom, available in paperback editions or affordable facsimiles. The dates I cite in parentheses following first mention of a work refer to the original publication date (or dates if a work came out in separate volumes as *Little Women* did). Examining both sides of a heated transatlantic debate over women's reading, I include British fiction by Jane Austen, Charles Dickens, William Makepeace Thackeray, Lewis Carroll, George Eliot, Anthony Trollope, Charlotte and Emily Brontë, and Mona Caird alongside American works by Henry James, Mark Twain, Louisa May Alcott, Henry Wadsworth Longfellow, Marietta Holley, and Charlotte Perkins Gilman. I also bring together important British and American illustrators, principally Sir John Everett Millais, Hablot Knight Browne (Phiz),

George Cruikshank, Thackeray, E. W. Kemble, True Williams, F. O. C. Darley, Frank T. Merrill, Charlotte Harding, and Jessie Willcox Smith. I incorporate children's literature and lesser known British and American fiction to show a wider range of illustrative examples envisioning the woman reader.

Writing this book has made me reflective about myself as a consumer of books as well the reading habits of my Victorian sisters. Like my grandmother before me, I take pleasure in owning books. We have twelve bookcases in our Victorian home, which, to my delight, includes a library/music room. That number does not include the many bookshelves in my office at Skidmore College. I take pleasure in reading and perusing books, many of which are illustrated and rare. Not only the pleasure but the easy access I, as a woman born in the late 1950s, always have had to books makes me sensitive to the fact that such freedom in book selection was not necessarily the case for my grandmother born in 1900 and certainly not for her grandmother before her. For the long line of reading women who have come before me, and for those who follow, I offer this book.

ACKNOWLEDGMENTS

I wish to thank those who inspired and supported me as a reader and a writer. Foremost, I thank my parents, Nancy Jeanne Posmantur Golden and Dr. Lawrence Herbert Golden to whom I dedicate this book. They fostered my love of reading from childhood; taught me to think "I can" (just like the little engine that could); tirelessly applauded my academic achievements; and modeled the importance of reading by being lifelong readers themselves. My sister Pam, my brother Grant, my sisters-in-law Deborah and Judy, and my brothers-in-law Craig and Keren all suggest titles to me and buy me new and rare books. I particularly thank my sister for buying me books from the Lord Randall Bookshop in Marshfield, Massachusetts, and for introducing me to her friend Gail Wills, owner of the bookstore. From Gail, I purchased fine first editions of many of the volumes included in my book. I am sorry that my beloved late mother-in-law, Barbara Sharon Marx, did not live to see the publication of my book. She shared my love of reading and was a major supporter of all my academic endeavors.

I had two important mentors in my journey as a reader—one in the fourth grade and the other in graduate school. My fourth-grade teacher, Rosalie Gleason, of Eggert Road Elementary School in Buffalo, New York, was pivotal in my development as a reader. She made me believe I was the smartest girl in her classroom. I thank her for giving me the confidence to shine academically and to go on to win my fifth-grade reading contest, and much more. In graduate school at the University of Michigan, I was mentored by Martha Vicinus, who became my professor and my dissertation advisor. A leading scholar in Victorian literature and history as well as women's studies, Martha taught me the importance of exploring primary materials including popular culture to immerse myself fully in the Victorian era. I date my passion for the Victorian period and the germination of this book to my graduate school studies with Martha on Victorian literature and illustration, popular culture, and children's literature.

Friends and colleagues also shaped my book. I am indebted to my friend Debbie Bernnard, a librarian at SUNY Albany, who helped me locate a number of the illustrated editions for my book. I also thank my close friends for their support and insights into literature. My love of Victorian novels has led my friends Lollie Abramson Stark, Daria Sviatyla Schewe, Jeanne O'Farrell Eddy, Marilyn Sandberg, Fay Bell, and Ellen Sheets—all avid readers—to enter into the world of Victorian literature and even attend my classes. Their responses to Victorian literature have added new dimensions to the way I read and teach fiction. I have been blessed with the support of women colleagues—Susan Kress, Charlotte Goodman, Sarah Goodwin, and particularly Linda Simon—all of whom served as a sounding board for this project, lending advice and cheer. I thank Susan for her insights on Twain and Phelps, shaping chapter 6, Charlotte for her response to Gilman in chapter 7, Sarah for her insights on Emily Brontë in chapter 2, and Linda for her expert editorial advice on James's *The Portrait of a Lady* in chapter 2. Linda provided unfailing encouragement and excellent advice from the very inception of my book and sustained me from the first. Words simply cannot express my appreciation and esteem for Linda, Susan, Charlotte, and Sarah, women colleagues and friends.

I would also like to thank Greg Pfitzer of the American Studies Department. He helped me to conceptualize my project and discussed all the stages of bringing a book to completion. Susan Zappen, associate librarian and head of technical services of Skidmore College, offered expert advice on copyright issues. Ellen Fladger, head of special collections, Schaffer Library, Union College assisted me during my visit to Union and made scans of *Tom Sawyer* for this book. I also particularly thank Erin Budis, curator of the Hyde Collection, who was an excellent resource for this entire project. Erin asked me to serve as consulting humanities scholar for the Hyde's Fall 2000 "Picturing Gentility" show, which she curated. Lecturing on this topic at the Hyde and writing an essay for the accompanying catalogue proved invaluable to the creation of my book.

I particularly appreciate the expertise of Hunt Conard, consultant in media services. He personally scanned most of the images for this book to ensure quality reproductions. I am also especially grateful to Skidmore College for funding several research grants, which helped me to establish a personal library of illustrated books and cover the cost of permissions fees. The Norman M. Fox Collection, on loan to the Lucy Scribner Library, proved invaluable to the conception of this book. John Cosgrove, access services librarian, Amy Syrell, interlibrary loan supervisor, and Marilyn Sheffer, reference assistant, of the Lucy Scribner Library at Skidmore College helped me to locate primary and secondary sources and bibliographical information essential to my research. I thank Kristina Fennelly, Skidmore class of 2002, and foremost Nicole Zuckerman, Skidmore class of 2004, for offering assistance with minor and major tasks ranging from photocopying to proofreading.

I extend real appreciation to the University Press of Florida. Amy Gorelick, acquisitions editor, responded enthusiastically to my project from the first. With cheer, Amy guided me from the prospectus stage through to the acceptance of my manuscript. Gillian Hillis, project editor, skillfully assisted me through to the publication of my manuscript. I extend my gratitude to art historian Linda J. Docherty of Bowdoin College and Victorianist Emma Liggins of Edge Hill College, United Kingdom, for providing helpful and astute comments as readers for my manuscript. The final version of this book reflects their insights into art and literature, as well as their close reading and enthusiasm for a project dear to my heart.

Lastly, I thank my family for support and patience as I devoted countless hours to this book. My husband, Michael Steven Marx, offered me endless love and encouragement throughout this entire project. I have come to value Michael's astute editorial advice. His close reading and careful attention to language have shaped my own reading and writing processes. My twin sons, Jesse Benjamin and Emmet Gabriel Golden-Marx, are appreciative readers and listeners. Together, we participated in Junior Great Books and a parent-teen book club at the Saratoga Springs Public Library. From birth, Jesse and Emmet kindled my love for reading aloud, an important dimension in my development as a reader. And where would a reader be without a cat? Our family cats, Lee and Rose, curled up close to my computer and purred contentedly as I researched, wrote, and revised my book.

Introduction

At the same time that reading became a mark of gentility and a means to promote family unity, intellectual pursuits for the nineteenth-century woman were to be gained only in context of traditional domesticity. George Cruikshank's "My Wife Is a Woman of Mind" (1847) demonstrates this point (fig. 1). Typical of midcentury political cartoons, Cruikshank's caricature from *The Comic Almanack*, a predecessor of *Punch*, rekindles the Victorian controversy over women's rights for education.[1] Cruikshank's "woman of mind" wears thick, dark glasses, symbolically designating her a thinker. This was a time when the popular pseudoscience of phrenology held sway; her hairstyle exposes a high forehead and two pronounced intellectual bumps: "ideality," the faculty to conceive ideals; and "causality," the ability to trace an effect to its cause. Her forehead marks the intelligence and curiosity of a woman who has seemingly traded her femininity and domesticity—as well as her eyesight—for knowledge. Potent objective signifiers, the volumes that line the bookcases and surround the table where she is writing reveal her active engagement in print culture and her easy access to books.

Cruikshank's "woman of mind" caricatures a prevailing male attitude toward intellectual women. The accompanying poem declares that this woman loves not her own family but, rather, "the whole human fam'ly. For *she* is a woman of mind."[2] Intellectual, she is not domestic; in fact, the caricature suggests she is not domestic because she is intellectual, a false dichotomy that worked to maintain the status quo and keep women in their place. Amid the clutter on the floor—a testimony to her poor housekeeping abilities—lies an open book at her feet. The off-center picture, cracked window panes, torn shades, crumpled curtains, and knocked-over work basket exaggerate a lack of order in the Victorian home and the deterioration of the Victorian family. Other details confirm this. The overwhelmed husband awkwardly holds a wailing baby while a younger

Fig. 1. George Cruikshank, "My Wife Is a Woman of Mind," from *The Comic Almanack*, 1847. (Courtesy of Norman M. Fox Collection, Skidmore College.)

daughter cries over a plate of spilled food. Presumably the oldest daughter just barely manages to save her baby brother from tumbling into the fire. But still the "woman of mind" ignores her maternal duties. Surrounded by books, perhaps composing a book of her own, she waves her left hand toward her husband with an expression that speaks loudly, "do not disturb."

Cruikshank's caricature, albeit comical to readers today, illuminates the controversy over the rise of the woman reader. In the nineteenth century, a period of presumed hostility to fiction, the novel grew in popularity as a genre on both sides of the Atlantic and raised common fears. The market for secular and juvenile literature also flourished in this period in which many novels were written, published, and read. The woman reader in the Victorian period became a topic of a debate in a wide range of contexts, including periodicals and magazines, advice manuals, novels, verse, paintings, photographs, book illustrations, and educational and religious tracts. Most under attack was the novel, then a relatively new, "low" genre, which formed a major part of women's reading.[3]

The novel has become such a staple in contemporary society that we must reestablish two pivotal points from the outset. First, the reactionary response to romance and sensation fiction anticipates the fears surrounding the use of controlled substances that peaked, for example, during prohibition and 1930s antidrug campaigns. Debates over novel-reading also prophesy controversies surrounding developments in media and technology of the twentieth century: radio in the 1920s, comic books in the 1940s and 1950s, television in the 1960s, and R-rated movies and the World Wide Web today. Although Victorians recognized reading as a symbol of learning and gentility, they considered certain types of fiction as addictive as nicotine and thus hazardous to a woman's health. Second, while the media today presents television violence, R-rated movies, and unregulated websites as predominately psychological threats, in the nineteenth century romance and sensation fiction were perceived dangers to the reproductive health as well as the moral development of young women. Medical authorities made convincing, at times damning, arguments against excessive and unsupervised reading of popular fiction, linking it to early menstruation, painful menses, and infertility, as well as nervousness, insanity, and even premature death.[4]

Literary critics, social historians, and art historians have investigated the rise of the woman reader largely in Britain or America, typically from the 1830s to the start of World War I. Kate Flint's *The Woman Reader, 1837–1914* (1993), as well as Carla L. Peterson's *The Determined Reader* (1986), Michael Wheeler's *The Art of Allusion in Victorian Fiction* (1979), and Patrick Brantlinger's *The Reading Lesson* (1998) offer meaningful insights into the history of reading and the rise of the woman reader in Victorian Britain. Cathy N. Davidson's *Revolution and the Word* (1986), Nina Baym's *Novels, Readers, and Reviewers* (1984), and scholarship by Barbara Sicherman, David D. Hall, and Linda J. Docherty also provide important insights about the nineteenth-century American woman reader and reading in America.[5] This past scholarship, particularly the work of Kate Flint, has direct bearing on my examination of the woman reader in Victorian British and American fiction and book illustration.

Flint's *The Woman Reader* examines the cultural debate surrounding the woman reader in Britain between the accession of Queen Victoria and the First World War. Reconstructing the reading debate in the Victorian and Edwardian periods, Flint offers a rich analysis of women's reading to illuminate issues of mind, body, text, and culture. As Flint observes, "notions about reading fed off attempts to define women's mental capacities and tendencies through their physical attributes, and, in turn, appeared to contribute to the validation of these very definitions."[6] The circularity of this reasoning shows why certain notions about the woman reader, some of which the Victorians inherited, took root in a Victorian culture noted for its conservative gender politics and, in some cases, extended beyond the

Victorian and Edwardian ages. Flint's comprehensive examination of a range of nineteenth-century periodicals advances this book, as does her apt conclusion: "It is impossible to speak of the woman reader as though she ever held a consistent, stable identity: she is herself fragmented both into many sets of rhetorical patterns, each serving particular ideological ends, and into an endless variety of actual reading practices" (322).

I concur with Flint that the dominant ideologies current throughout the Victorian age, evident in fiction and illustration, show not a stable identity of the woman reader but "sets of rhetorical patterns" and varied practices. Building from Flint's study, my book explores the woman reader as a recurrent and multifaceted theme in fiction and book illustration to popular novels. In part 4 of her examination, Flint covers fictional depictions of the woman reader and devotes a chapter each to sensation fiction and "New Woman" fiction, although her fictional examples are more numerous and typically briefer in development than those I raise in part 2. Flint engages visual culture, opening and closing her study with an analysis of period paintings of women readers, but she does not discuss book illustration, which I introduce as a vehicle for illuminating issues of gender. Moreover, my book examines how Victorian authors and illustrators on both sides of the Atlantic envision women's reading practices.

Scholars of literature, focused as we often are on conventional literary periods and national cultures, may lose sight of a profound transatlantic connection at a time when women made great strides in reading and education. Industrialization transformed print culture in Britain and America, endorsing the logic of a joint examination of the Victorian woman reader. This study encompasses the Victorian period in Britain and the pre– and post–Civil War periods in America. Such a sweep across Western society necessarily limits the number of examples I draw from either British or American fiction and illustration, and I encourage readers to apply my arguments to other texts which stand behind them. What I may sacrifice in comprehensiveness, I hope to compensate for in coherence in my examination of what I perceive to be a transatlantic development.

During the nineteenth century, British print culture influenced American culture and, in turn, the American reader. As David D. Hall asserts, "In the centuries that lead up to our own, learned culture in America depended on books that Europeans wrote and published."[7] Among American reading preferences until the 1890s, a marked penchant for British fiction exists—notably works by William Makepeace Thackeray, Charles Dickens, and George Eliot—although we should not overlook the importance of the

New England literary tradition to many intellectual families. Moreover, as Davidson points out in *Revolution and the Word*, "in the critique of fiction, one sees how readily aspects of the British class system were transported to the New World and translated into terms consistent with the looser social structures of the young Republic."[8] In *Novels, Readers, and Reviewers*, Baym concurs: "expressed hostility to fiction was no less strong in England than in America; much of what Americans wrote and said about novels was derived from English sources."[9]

British and Scottish philosophers influenced American thinkers and teachers in their conservative censure of the novel. Numerous advice books and tracts that condemned women's reading found their way to America. In some cases, publishers reprinted British advice books in the New World. In books created and disseminated on both sides of the Atlantic, we find the woman reader as a prime object of interest, fascination, suspicion, and attack. In Britain and America, we observe the same dichotomous views regarding the novel. On the one hand, socially improving literature socialized women and maintained the status quo in gender relations. More forcefully, novels empowered women by offering fictional role models or exposing women to worlds beyond their own life and culture. On the other hand, commentators feared that fiction portraying illicit sexual relations, discontent with domestic duties, or desire for upward mobility would seduce unsophisticated readers into a state of discontent and destabilize society. To some, women's popular reading became synonymous with vice, corruption, illicit sexuality, unhappiness, and depravity. We also find similarities among literary and illustrative representations of the woman reader in Victorian British and American texts.

Previous scholars have set a precedent for comparative study. Carla L. Peterson offers fruitful parallels between reading protagonists in French and British novels in *The Determined Reader*. I include some of the novels that Peterson examines in her study of the fictional reader. Whereas Peterson pairs "determined" male and female readers in French and British novels to discern the male and female reading experience, I focus exclusively on the woman reader in British and American fiction and illustration. Baym includes the American response to British and American fiction in *Novels, Readers, and Reviewers*. Likewise, Elizabeth K. Helsinger, Robin Lauterbach Sheets, and William Veeder explore the debate fueling the "woman question" on both sides of the Atlantic in their three-volume *The Woman Question* (1983). Sandra Gilbert and Susan Gubar discuss American and Victorian texts in their groundbreaking *The Madwoman in the Attic* (1979). In my treatment of American and British fiction, I follow the format of Glennis Stephenson's *Nineteenth-Century Stories by Women* (1993); this anthology includes short stories written by British, American, and Canadian women writers. In parts 2 and 3, I have paired female reading protagonists in Victorian British and American novels to highlight the transatlantic connection, established in part 1. However, I make an occasional excursion outside these demarcations of period and culture. Chapter 5 begins with Jane Austen's *Mansfield Park* (1814). If Austen's text reflects late-eighteenth-century debates about female education and reading, it also introduces the notion of reading and compatibility, essential to the Victorian British and American novel, as illustrated later in the chapter, for example, in George Eliot's *Middlemarch* (1872). In chapter 4, Gustave Flaubert's *Madame Bovary* (1857) supremely illustrates antifiction critics' fears surrounding romance novels and also serves as a model for Mary Elizabeth Braddon's *The Doctor's Wife* (1864), a work that challenges these very concerns.

Certain parameters of gender and class are implicit in the nature of the material I am studying. The prominent ideologies and practices surrounding women's reading were primarily targeted at a white middle- and upper-class readership. Likewise, these are the very theories and practices that resonate or are debated within Victorian British and American fiction produced by and designed for a white middle- and upper-class readership. While my focus is on the woman reader, I have made an effort to examine texts and images created by male and female authors and artists whose works reinforce ideal visions of gentility or offer alternative interpretations of female reading practices. Authors and illustrators who break from traditional views of femininity associated with male mainstream culture are not exclusively female, as might be expected. Thackeray's representation of Becky Sharp as a revolutionary reader in his self-illustrated *Vanity Fair* (1848) offers a fine case in point.

During the nineteenth century, the representation of the reading woman in historical, literary, and visual sources did not follow a single path; accordingly, my methodology borrows from literary criticism, social history, and art history, with an eye to theory and history. My methodological approach corresponds to what David D. Hall describes as "Reading as 'represented' in texts" in his 1994 article titled "Readers and Reading in America"; this is the third of six categories of investigation Hall cites. Hall places in this category Wolfgang Iser, Stanley Fish, and fellow theorists of "reader-response" theory and "reception theory" who have turned to printed texts to draw out assumptions about the practice of reading encoded within them (Hall 347–51). I share the concerns of literary critics who focus on problems of interpretation and authorial production. I also recognize, as Hall does, that the production and consumption of books, central to the work of social historians, is essential to an understanding of the reading woman and the history of the book, and I raise these concerns in part 1.

Since Victorians had multiple representations and ideologies about the woman reader available to them, I have organized this three-part book to make this same variety of representations available to readers today. Part 1 offers a historical overview of women's reading in Victorian Britain and America. My aim here is two-fold: first, to offer a concise analysis of the controversy surrounding what was widely referred to as the reading habit; second, to establish a critical context for investigating representations of the woman reader in fiction and illustration presented, respectively, in parts 2 and 3. Rather than highlight historical development, the opening chapter showcases dominant ideologies current throughout the nineteenth century to underscore the many possible, and often conflicting, notions regarding women's reading.

As Hall points out, "in any given period of time, readers had available more than one representation or ideology of reading, texts, and writing; and the proper history of reading should thus be arranged around the multiple possibilities and perhaps the conflicts that existed within a particular frame of time rather than exclusively around the transition from one mode to another" (355–56). Moreover, at times a text makes available to readers several prevailing representations. In *Victorian Heroines* (1993), Kimberley Reynolds and Nicola Humble raise the idea of reading a novel through lenses "existing side by side."[10] They suggest a Victorian woman reading *Jane Eyre* or *Wuthering Heights* might, in effect, read the book with "bifocal lenses":

> When imagining the woman reader, and perhaps to a lesser extent the woman writer, of a hundred years ago it is useful to think of her as wearing bifocal lenses: sometimes she read and understood the large, outside lens as a general member of the Victorian reading public; sometimes through the lens which was more and more focused on 'women's issues'; and sometimes she was aware of the two lenses existing side by side, but offering very different views of the world. Thus the woman reading *Jane Eyre* or *Wuthering Heights* was likely to respond on a variety of levels, one of which would certainly evoke general social concerns. (27)

Reynolds and Humble's point becomes relevant to an examination of the woman reader in books by the Brontë sisters and their contemporaries on both sides of the Atlantic.

Antifiction critics targeted most concern on the reading practices of young women, considered most vulnerable to popular fiction, so I have centered my discussion on women's reading prior to marriage. My focus on fiction responds to the increased publication of popular novels in the Victorian era, which sparked fears about women's obsessions with novels and over consumption of them. However, I discuss mainstream texts, such as the Bible and *Pilgrim's Progress,* and in part 3, I include Henry Wadsworth Longfellow's *Evangeline* (1847) for its narrative, not its lyrical value. Although I have organized the ideology section in chapter 1 under two broad categories for and against women's reading, subheadings reveal the multiple ideological possibilities available to Victorians. Subheadings under each side of the debate also give direction to later chapters, which examine how authors and illustrators weigh, endorse, or challenge these very notions of women's reading in fiction and book illustration.

Parts 2 and 3 call upon the historical and theoretical material of part 1 to investigate how authors and illustrators debated women's increased access to knowledge during a period which reveals a marked rise in women's education. Methodologically, I agree with Docherty in her 1998 article "Women as Readers: Visual Interpretations" that "works of art"—which I define as fiction, painting, and book illustration—"possess historical value not as documents of fact but as windows on ideology. Regardless of whether paintings accurately describe female reading practice, they are reliable indicators of ideas surrounding, and sometimes controlling, this activity."[11] Throughout I acknowledge a fine line between fiction and history, taking care not to treat the book as a historical document or to misconstrue fiction for life. Nonetheless, I recognize that novels and the visual arts—if read in context of contemporary ideas about reading that extend beyond the covers of a book or a canvas—have historical value as "windows on ideology," speaking to the cultural ambivalence surrounding the rise of women's reading and education. Novels and illustration record conflicting notions about the middle- and upper-class woman reader, and countless authors and illustrators cast girls and women in Victorian British and American novels as readers. The very act of reading and the works these female protagonists read reveal their natures, the thematic intentions of these works, the connotations and associations held by contemporary readers about reading, and the cultural ambivalence surrounding the rise of the woman reader.

Readers of the period read mimetically; women readers often perceived literature as a reflection of life and fictional characters as role models (Davidson, *Revolution and the Word* 72).[12] Further, as Steven Mailloux explicates, works of interpretation must be seen in a political context, for they construct a reality that is inevitably charged with power relations of gender, class, race, family, or nation.[13] The works women read and women's reading habits serve as indicators of thoughts surrounding and, at times, influencing and even curbing women's reading practice in nineteenth-century Britain and America. The examples in this book, which invite complex interpretations from readers, respond to specific ideas raised, for example, in advice books, periodical articles, and medical texts of the period that form an essential part of the history of reading at that time.

My aim in part 2 is to show how fiction variously functions as a reflection of prevailing notions of domesticity and as a testimony for social change by disarming mainstream tradition. In some cases, texts straddle both sides of a hotly contested reading debate. While I do not treat fiction as a factual document, I perceive novels as indicators of Victorian British and American culture, respond to them in light of contemporary ideas, and prize them, in fact, for their historical value. I have organized examples of fictional women readers into four chapters that cover literary representations of the woman reader: transatlantic pairings of women readers approximating visual art; prophetic reading; women as romance consumers; and reading taste as an indicator of marital compatibility. Each chapter aims to demonstrate how, in the fictional arena, authors dramatize and debate dominant ideologies about women's reading in Victorian British and American culture as presented in part 1, particularly the argument for empowerment; the socialization and gentility arguments; the moral argument; the biological argument; and the pervasive tropes of consumption and addiction. For example, Louisa May Alcott (chapter 2) presents reading improving literature in *Little Women* (1868, 1869) as a socialization tool. Mary Elizabeth Braddon (chapter 4), in her depiction of reading addiction in *The Doctor's Wife*, initially endorses but ultimately confronts the moral and addiction arguments against women's novel-reading.

Specific chapters also analyze how books that women protagonists do or do not read reflect the reading practices of their creators and shape our understanding of their characters and the thematic intentions of the works. Part 2 thus responds to a claim that Sally Mitchell makes in her chapter on "Reading Feelings" in *The New Girl* (1995): "A continuous thread connects the daydreams of some girls who grew up to become authors, the fictions they wrote (as adults) for a new generation of girls to read, and the (subsequent) daydreams that provided expressive codes for the new girls as they grew to womanhood."[14] While I cannot attempt to determine the impact Victorian British and American fiction had on the daydreams of young girls, I give consideration, at points, to how the books women writers read reappear as influential literary companions of their fictional creations. Some chapters explore the adolescent and childhood reading of women who became authors alongside the daydreams and reading feelings of heroines these authors vividly created for a new generation of women readers.

Furthermore, in part 2 I am interested in what happens when a book is introduced into another work of fiction. Such a concern recalls issues raised in the literary representation of art or "ekphrasis." James A. W. Heffernan defines ekphrasis as *"the verbal representation of visual representation"* in *Museum of Words* (1993); however, he recognizes that some critics would like to extend the term to incorporate literature about texts as well as literature about pictures.[15] Heffernan fears that such an extension of the term "ekphrasis" could negate the essentially gendered struggle between the rival modes of silent (feminine) painting and expressive (masculine) writing. Nonetheless, I argue that the concept of "verisimilitude" has bearing on writing about texts as well as writing about pictures. The "narrative impulse" that "makes explicit the story that visual art tells only by indication" (Heffernan 5) affects, as well as transforms, literature reintroduced in a literary context, as some of the chapters in part 2 demonstrate.

Part 3 explores the complex role of illustration in books created by author-illustrators and authors with outside illustrators. The examination of the woman reader as she appears in nineteenth-century popular novels adds originally to the existing scholarship on representations of womanhood in the area of visual culture studies, particularly Docherty's "Women as Readers: Visual Interpretations," Susan Casteras's *Images of Victorian Womanhood in English Art* (1987), and Elaine Shefer's *Birds, Cages, and Women in Victorian and Pre-Raphaelite Art* (1990).[16] Docherty explores patterns in visual representations of women readers in colonial portraiture through turn-of-the-century American impressionism. During this time period, women steadily gained increased education and freedom in their opportunities for reading. Using a methodological approach akin to David D. Hall's third category of representation, "Reader as 'represented,'" Docherty examines eight pictorial types of women readers in American painting. Several of these types—interrupted, isolated, and venerable—

inform my examination of illustrative depictions of the woman reader in Victorian British and American fiction, which I discuss in chapter 6.

The methodology and organization of part 3 dovetail part 2. I have organized part 3 into three chapters: an illustrative gallery of Victorian British and American women readers; readers as mind travelers; and the revolutionary reader. Building upon parts 1 and 2, chapters 6–8 analyze book illustration of different types of women readers in terms of the concurrent dominating nineteenth-century ideologies governing women's reading practices, particularly arguments of gentility, socialization, and empowerment favoring women's reading, as well as medical, moral, and addictive arguments maintaining why women should not read. For example, the interrupted woman reader in Charles Dickens's novels (chapter 6) lays aside her book to attend to others in her circle and thus represents social refinement and duty, notions essential to the gentility and socialization arguments. In contrast, the isolated woman reader (chapter 6), who sequesters herself, chooses desire over social responsibility and risks ruination. Concerns central to the addiction and moral arguments become vivid in the illustrated book.

Illustrated literature for adults reached its peak of popularity during the nineteenth century. The wedding of literature to the visual arts in Victorian Britain created an important art form which grew out of the *ut pictura poesis* tradition and eighteenth-century (Hogarthian) graphic satire and caricature.[17] In the Victorian illustrated book, descriptive texts join with telling pictures for mutual enhancement. Designed for a visually literate, adult audience, nineteenth-century book illustration, like genre and narrative painting, is given to storytelling: illustration, at times, tells a moral, conveys a stage of a narrative, or speaks to the condition of the Victorian age.

Illustrations to popular novels were important to the Victorians, who relished the random pictures in popular broadsides, advertisements, signs, serial publications, novels, and later annuals and "keepsakes." In his poem "Fra Lippo Lippi" (1855), Robert Browning eloquently presents the Victorian privileging of the image. Art makes us attentive to our surroundings. "Fra Lippo Lippi" pronounces, "First when we see them painted, things we have passed / Perhaps a hundred times nor cared to see; / And so they are better, painted—better to us, / Which is the same thing. Art was given for that" (lines 301–4). Even Henry James, a virulent critic of the illustrated book, comments in *A Small Boy and Others* (1913) that Cruikshank's pictures accompanying *Oliver Twist* (1838) impressed him more than Dickens's text.[18] The views of Browning and James among others speak collectively of a time when illustrations for serial novels were studied "with passionate interest," as author-illustrator George Du Maurier has put it, "before reading the story, and after, and between."[19]

Nineteenth-century American literature often appeared without illustration, as Longfellow's *Evangeline* demonstrates. Publishers issued numerous illustrated editions of this and other works once they determined popularity and secured a clear market. By the 1870s and 1880s, important American works, such as Mark Twain's *The Adventures of Tom Sawyer* (1876) and *Adventures of Huckleberry Finn* (1885), came out with illustrations by, respectively, True Williams and E. W. Kemble. Other prominent male American illustrators of the mid- to late nineteenth century include F. O. C. Darley, Frank T. Merrill, and Howard Pyle. In American art, critics refer to the period of 1890–1920 as the golden age of illustration, and many important women illustrators, including Charlotte Harding, Elizabeth Shippen Green, Violet Oakley, and Jessie Willcox Smith, also gained stature by illustrating important British and American books.

Illustrations on both sides of the Atlantic formed a vital part of the reading experience of Victorians. The Modern Language Association "Statement on the Significance of Primary Records" argues for the importance of primary materials as artifacts for scholarship and teaching. It reads: "artifacts provide the standard for judging the reproductions; they also contain, in their physicality, unreproducible evidence that readers (scholars, students, and the general public) need for analyzing and understanding, with as much historical context as possible, the writings that appeared and reappeared in them."[20] Primary materials must be preserved, but they must be placed in a historical context if they are to be understood by a new generation of readers. By promoting the importance of "reading" nineteenth-century images before, during, and after reading a story or serial originally conceived with illustration, I hope to broaden the ongoing examination of the woman reader.

As Docherty rightly notes, "Although scholars of American history and literature have contributed extensively to our knowledge of women as readers, the visual arts remain a largely untapped source of information on this theme" (339). In its focus on women readers in book illustration, part 3 explores an even more "untapped" aspect of visual imagery, in part owing to its status as a stepchild art. The rich tradition of the British and American illustrated book leaves no heirs except in children's literature. Even canonical nineteenth-century works brought forth serially with illustration are not always accessible today in the form authors and author-illustrators conceived them. Certain editions retain all or some of the original plates, but even careful exclusion transforms the reading experience of a work designed to be told through and with a substantial number of images.[21] Although Dickens's illustrated fiction has been explored,[22] much else in the field of illustration remains in need of recovery. In recent years, critics have given attention to book illustration, and more editions increasingly include all of the original plates so that we may approach a work as it was designed and first appreciated.

Illustrations included in part 3 form part of a visual culture that spoke to the controversy over women's reading in the Victorian age. Idealized representations of women with books, such as Hablot Knight Browne's depictions of Agnes Wickfield for Dickens's *David Copperfield* (1850), preserve the Victorian model of a receptive female embracing social codes, values, and etiquette; even if such images portray ideal rather than real life, we can appreciate them as visual testimonies of fundamental Victorian sentiments and values, including duty, the domestic family circle, and woman's angelic role as companion to manhood. In contrast, illustrations of reading women transgressing gender codes could be seen as distorting mirrors to safeguard women from going astray. Some illustrations of women readers, such as Merrill's depiction of Alcott's Jo March alone in a library in *Little Women*, allow us to glimpse alternative models of womanhood: women are thinking, broadening their minds, and imagining. Illustrations of fictional women cast as various types of readers within a given book, such as Merrill's depictions of Jo March, reveal how a woman negotiates personal choice and duty in a hierarchical society with rigidly defined gender roles. Illustrations of the Victorian British and American woman reader allow us to see how gender dynamics play out within Victorian visual culture; reading illustrations, in turn, will hopefully kindle an appreciation for book illustration as a vehicle for illuminating gender issues of the Victorian era.

To tease out the full complexity of the woman reader, I conceive of literacy more inclusively to consider book equivalents—principally, pictures and letters. The reading of pictures taps into the rich visual literacy skills of nineteenth-century British and American readers. Illustrators, like artists, used books and their equivalents to make comments about learnedness, gentility, and morality. Representations of women reading letters within nineteenth-century novels pay homage to a more common eighteenth-century product, the epistolary novel, in which letters by one or several characters develop a narrative. Using Charlotte Perkins Gilman's "The Yellow Wall-Paper" (1892) and *Little Women,* I explore a woman writing—and thus creating—her own book or diary, or, in the case of Emily Brontë's *Wuthering Heights* (1847), writing in a book. While I recognize the differences between the related acts of writing and reading, I include Alcott's Jo March's writing of sensation fiction, since she reads and falls prey to it; Catherine Earnshaw's writing in the Bible, because she remakes it into her own book in *Wuthering Heights;* and the writing of a diary in the case of "The Yellow Wall-Paper," since the text the narrator is writing is arguably the very text we are reading. In "The Yellow Wall-Paper," the narrator's reading of the patterns of an untraditional text, the ubiquitous wallpaper, resembles the way her fictional Victorian British and American sisters pore over book illustrations to derive meaning from them.

Behind this book rests the conviction that fiction and book illustration are indicative of the Victorian way of seeing the world. The Victorian vision is not narrow or uniform but richly diverse. In nineteenth-century novels and visual culture, we do not find a strict historical development or demarcated transitions among dominant viewpoints, although women undeniably experienced greater opportunities for reading and education as the century progressed. In fact, in chapter 8, I argue that the most progressive image of a woman reader, Becky Sharp of *Vanity Fair* (1848), dating to the middle of the nineteenth century, anticipates developments in later Victorian British and American culture.

Like the Victorians, we must read fiction and book illustration of the period with "bifocal lenses." Together, fiction and illustration offer a verbal and visual collage of diverse viewpoints in a cultural context. It is my hope that in examining concurrent competing visions of the woman reader, this investigation will spark further scrutiny of the complexities of our own reading habits as well as those of the Victorians. Verbal and visual representations of the Victorian woman reader are not only our pictorial legacy: they are a portal into reading ideologies pervasive on both sides of the Atlantic, influential to our present reading practices.

I

A Historical Overview

1

Women Readers and Reading in Victorian Britain and America

I begin with history. My aim is not to recover ground but rather to provide a three-part summary of a rich and multifaceted debate, raising critical notions that Victorians held and inherited about women's reading dating from the sixteenth, seventeenth, and eighteenth centuries, some of which exist even today.[1] To underscore David D. Hall's seminal point in "Readers and Reading in America," "the proper history of reading should thus be arranged around the multiple possibilities and perhaps the conflicts that existed within a particular frame of time rather than exclusively around the transition from one mode to another" (356). Central to the debate surrounding the rise of the woman reader in Victorian Britain and America, such "multiple possibilities" and "conflicts" emerge in reading practices (I), ideologies about reading (II), and reading selections (III).

I. READING PRACTICES

Looking back at a time when many feared the consequences of women reading and pursuing education, we find countless examples of women and books: women reading books, holding books as props, and, in some cases, prizing the symbolic meaning of the book as an emblem of learning and authorship.[2] Titles of periodical articles—such as "What Girls Read," "Do Our Girls Take an Interest in Literature? The Other Side of the Question," and "The Novel-Reading Habit"[3]—speak to the debate surrounding the rise of the woman reader and what was widely referred to in the nineteenth century as the reading habit.

Educators, doctors, literary critics, and writers of advice manuals offered their opinions on what, when, where, why, and if a woman should read. At the same time, Victorian Britain and America witnessed a dramatic growth in literacy and many firsts in the education of women. While not addressing the woman reader per se, pioneering studies by Richard Altick and Louis James offer important insights into the rise of literacy and the dissemination of print matter within the working and lower middle classes.[4] For example, Altick points out in *The English Common Reader* (1957) that by 1900, 97 percent of those signing the marriage registry in England (presumably between ages 16 and 25) were able to write their names; we must remember, as Altick cautions, that a significant number of older men and women of this time were presumably still illiterate (172). Industrialization, the growth of the lending library, popular reading clubs in Britain and America, as well as utilitarianism and opportunities for self-improvement promoted the spread of literacy, print culture, and secular literature. With the rising middle class and the cheap-book movement, spurred on by the Society for the Diffusion of Useful Knowledge, publishers began to target the middle class as a prime publishing market and produce literature for a female readership.

Women played a key role in the culture of reading and were influenced by developments in its history. Historians of the book have commonly suggested patterns of reading established by the late nineteenth century: reading transforms from a public activity to a private one, promoting individuality and isolation; intensive reading of a few books gives way to an extensive reading of many books, making reading presumably more superficial or passive (Sicherman, "Sense and Sensibility" 206). Mid- to late-nineteenth-century readers were not limited to intensive reading of a few religious texts, such as the Bible. An increasing number of readers consumed a greater amount of books, replacing one volume after the other, thus reading extensively.[5] Still, some critics have suggested that there was greater diversity in reading habits than has conventionally been assumed, and they have questioned the claims that reading became superficial and private for women given the social importance, for example, of reading aloud in the family circle.[6]

Reading and Women's Education in Victorian England

The nineteenth century is known for public schooling of the masses, the reformation of boys' schools, and the emergence of schools for girls and young women, ranging from boarding schools to universities. Reading was an important consideration in a girl's education whether learning took place in the home, a private girls' academy, or a state-run school. In Victorian Britain, most schools were created for girls of the new middle class. Daughters of upper-middle-class and aristocratic families tended to receive their lessons at home, which remained the center of female education for the higher reaches. *Jane Eyre* (1847) illustrates this point well. Jane—an unloved orphan born of a clergyman father and a mother who marries beneath her—attends Lowood Institution, where she is trained to become a governess; securing a position, Jane teaches Mr. Rochester's ward, Adèle, in the grandeur of Thornfield Hall.

As *Jane Eyre*, *Agnes Grey* (1847), *Amy Herbert* (1844) and other nineteenth-century novels reveal, the position of governess offered a way for a respectable, unwed, slightly impoverished middle-class woman to remain in the domestic circle and thus maintain her gentility while still earning a livelihood.[7] Females of the upper middle class who were educated at home often had governesses. But the models varied. In some families, fathers taught a favorite subject or a range of studies; in other families, mothers and older sisters supervised basic education. In the Victorian climate of Evangelicalism, girls typically focused on the "Good Book"—catechism and Bible studies—as well as spelling, reading, writing, history, mathematics, drawing, and language instruction. Most Victorian girls could also play the piano "A little," as Jane admits to Mr. Rochester.[8] While not universally approved of, lectures became an important avenue for informal education and reading a gateway for self-education. For example, in Charlotte Mary Yonge's first novel, *Abbey Church* (1844), a dispute over King Arthur's Court leads the spirited Lizzie Woodbourne to attend a lecture at the secular Mechanics Institute; she repents her folly through the rest of the book, which dramatizes a pious middle-class Victorian life. Independent reading also emerges as an important route for self-education of both sexes.

Emily Davies, a tireless proponent of higher education for women, complained that education for Victorian girls outside the domestic circle prepared them for "elegant leisure" without appreciating "that an inquiring spirit, a love of reading, and an increasing interest in high and worthy subjects are of infinitely greater importance."[9] Writing about girls' secondary education in 1864, Davies describes women's habitual reading, aside from religious literature, as limited, often "confined to novels, and of novels not the best."[10] But the educational system was not without its merits or supporters. In *Family, Love, and Work in the Lives of Victorian Gentlewomen* (1989), M. Jeanne Peterson acknowledges that a Victorian woman's piecemeal style of education (part parental or hired tutor supplemented by self-education) could be "chaotic" or "haphazard," but it offered freedom, flexibility, and adaptability.[11] Peterson also refutes the notion that Victorian upper-middle-class girls were badly educated and raised to lead useless lives as gentlewomen. To Peterson, the education of the upper-middle-class Victorian girl "was regular, it was serious, and it mattered" (35). Moreover, lifelong reading, a habit which many began early and continued throughout their married lives, emerged as a positive byproduct of the independent and unstructured education typical for girls of the era. Also advancing the important role reading played in Victorian women's lives, Sally Mitchell, in an influential 1977 article titled "Sentiment and Suffering: Women's Recreational Reading in the 1860s," argues that reading offered women "vicarious participation, emotional expression, and the feeling of community that arises from a recognition of shared dreams."[12]

Reading and Women's Education in Victorian America:
A Transatlantic Connection

During the colonial period in America, particularly in New England, girls read religious texts, principally the Bible. Following the American Revolution, growth in literacy and the rising concept of a Republican motherhood gave women more opportunities for learning to rear the future leaders of America, though without granting women greater participation in the political sphere.[13] By the early nineteenth century in New England, American academies and seminaries also began to spring up with the focus on teacher training, much as in Britain. Such institutions were far from common, however.[14] In America and Britain, the role of teacher allowed women to extend their nurturing role outside the family circle while alleviating financial burdens. Likewise, self-study was common in America, particularly in the later nineteenth century. Even those who attended college often had an informal secondary education at home. Some women received instruction in a subject, such as a foreign language; this was the case of the daughters of the extremely literate Hamilton family whom Barbara Sicherman documents in her case study of late-Victorian American reading women titled "Sense and Sensibility: A Case Study of Women's Reading in Late-Victorian America" (1989). Other girls principally learned by recitation, under the guidance of parents, or by reading books in the family library. By the late nineteenth century, with a lessening of religious fervor in Victorian America, many began to regard desirable fiction as a source of culture and authority. A gendered activity, reading became an essential part of a woman's education, as numerous women's testimonials convey. Akin to their Victorian British sisters, some Victorian American women who were avid readers remarked that the reading done independently, outside of their studies, absorbed them most (Kelley 410–11).[15]

The profusion of print along with increased opportunities for learning and education created a demand for the book, particularly the novel. The Bible, psalm books, and devotional works still sold regularly and formed an essential part of the literary diet of the Victorian American and British woman, particularly in the first half of the period. Considered the most significant work in a girl's education, the Bible offered an ethical standard against which to compare all other reading. But the nineteenth-century woman was more widely read, dabbling in biography, history, and travel literature, as well as popular and canonical novels (Kelley 404; Flint, *The Woman Reader* 80). Moreover, as Mary Kelley notes in her examination of reading women in antebellum America, "In giving books to reward accomplishment, in sponsoring literary societies, in using reading to forge bonds with students, and in sharing personal libraries, teachers at female academies and seminaries defined reading as a *female* enterprise" (410).

While differences naturally exist in women's reading practices in Victorian Britain and America, a transatlantic connection emerges. Women were actively seeking opportunities for higher learning and reading—turning to books not merely for escapism, but solace, fancy, laughter, inspiration, friendship, and self-fashioning (Kelley 402–3, 414–15; Flint, *The Woman Reader* 81; Sicherman, "Sense and Sensibility" 202). The rise of reading clubs and literary societies for women made reading a collective practice (Kelley 419–20). Women's reading emerges as a continuous theme in novels, the most contested genre, as well as women's autobiographies, letters, diaries, journals, autograph albums, and commonplace books.

II. IDEOLOGIES ABOUT READING

As women made great strides in reading and education, commentators offered a bewildering array of arguments about reading fiction, pro and con. Polarized ideologies surrounding the woman reader fueled a transatlantic reading debate. Reasons for and against women's reading were wide ranging in scope. On the one hand, regulated and carefully supervised reading was a vital part of a woman's education, improving knowledge, confidence, social grace, as well as intellect and imagination. To the conservative advocate, it was a mark of gentility and a socialization tool supporting the ideology of the middle-class home. To the more enlightened, it was also a means for empowerment and uplifting education, ushering in social change for women. On the other hand, some feared reading could have damning effects. Critics presented a range of arguments against women's reading that tapped into biology, medicine, and morality. From an antifiction vantage point, a book of romance, sensation fiction, or sentimental fiction could arouse a female's sexual impulses, drain her vital energies, damage her mental and reproductive health, divorce her attention from her maternal and domestic duties, undermine her self-control, and rot her mind, leading to ruination. Although arguments fueling the polarized ideologies appear interrelated, there are four main subjects on each side of the reading debate that showcase the variety and multiplicity of viewpoints.

Why Women Should Read

The Gentility Argument

In *Culture and Anarchy* (1869), Matthew Arnold advocates that the right kind of secular reading is essential to culture, which he considers a spiritual ideal of human perfection.[16] The concept of Arnoldian "culture" fosters not discontent but a natural acceptance of the existing class system to promote class reconciliation while still advocating the notion of literacy as a means to become one's best self. If Arnoldian "culture" offers a solution to class conflict by encouraging the working class to emulate the respectable and well-spoken, equally it offers the upper reaches a way to preserve gentility. The concept of the genteel Victorian British and American lady embodies not only respectability and good conversation but decorum, breeding, sensibility, morality, and taste. Right reading was an important consideration in a girl's education and a Victorian woman's life. In *Orley Farm* (1862), Anthony Trollope even confides that a "course of novel-reading ... has become necessary for a British lady."[17] As Martha Banta sums up in her discussion of turn-of-the-century women's reading in *Imaging American Women* (1987), "Reading meant having 'culture.'"[18]

Books, often read aloud in the sacrosanct family circle, were considered appropriate companions for the cultivated Victorian British and American female. In fact, the rhetoric of the period often likens books to "companions," "people," and even "intimate friends" or "best friends."[19] A literary companion brought more than a break from boredom or loneliness. As James Mason advises in his two-part 1881 article titled "How to Form a Small Library," "A girl becomes a reflection of the graces of her favourite authors, and though she may have no wealthy or aristocratic friends, if she moves at home in the society of Shakespeare and Milton, she can never be commonplace, and will always make herself respected" (1: 7). Here the rhetorical notion of book as companion connects to issues of social propriety and refinement. Reading becomes a means to receive correct etiquette and social refinement essential to maintaining Arnoldian "culture" and the status quo. The reading woman "at home" in the literary company of Shakespeare, Milton, Dryden, and Pope augments her genteel nature and gains respect and admiration in her social circle. To combine the views of Arnold, Trollope, Mason, and Banta, reading becomes necessary to a woman's education and the cultivation of social graces because it is indelibly tied to the prevailing nineteenth-century notions of gentility.

Moreover, if we equate reading with the receiving of etiquette and the strictly structured social rituals of the upper reaches that Leonore Davidoff describes in *The Best Circles* (1973), then reading can be seen as one means of giving a woman admittance to the highly demarcated access rituals of high society that the young lady will eventually enter. From the ideological viewpoint of gentility, a woman's reading in the private home is a mark of culture, polish, grace, and refinement. Akin to those who espoused the socialization argument, gentility advocates agreed that a sound book might well raise the morals and purity of a woman, much as good society would, and keep her contented in the private home.

The Socialization Argument: Maintaining the Status Quo in Gender Relations

The reading woman received more than rituals and etiquette. Reading was an effective socialization tool to maintain the status quo in gender relations and promote marital compatibility. Pervasive in popular culture are the Victorian British ideal of the "angel in the house" and its nineteenth-century American equivalent, the self-sacrificing "mother-woman." Tending to husband, children, home, and community remained woman's true mission in the prevailing consciousness of Victorian Britain and America, and this notion supported the socialization argument (and also fostered manifold arguments against women's reading).

As Lee F. Heller notes in her cultural criticism of *Frankenstein*, "Books, it seemed, could shape people's lives."[20] The century accordingly witnessed a proliferation of self-help books and advice manuals geared for readers of the rising middle class as well as newly literate readers, many of them designed to guide young women to make effective choices in life. For example, Lucy Soulsby, the advice book writer of *Happiness* (1899), sees good reading habits as essential to guard against ennui and ensure contentment. She advocates following a system of rules about reading (for example, reading something sensible each day, avoiding novels in the morning, and taking notes about reading) to deter idleness and ultimately to prepare a young woman for the responsibilities of married life (Flint, *The Woman Reader* 99). Trollope recognizes the need for literary recreation among young women and points out in "Higher Education of Women" (1868) that novel-reading can provide some "good" if women "will take some little trouble in the choice of your novels, the lessons which you will find taught in them are good lessons. Honour and honesty, modesty and self-denial, are as strongly insisted on in our English novels as they are in our English sermons."[21] Novel-reading, to Trollope, becomes a means to inculcate norms and values. Likewise, in *Woman's Work and Worth in Girlhood, Maidenhood, and Wifehood* (1884), W. H. Davenport Adams suggests that his readers emulate fictional characters who make socially acceptable choices, such as Eliot's preacher Dinah Morris of *Adam Bede* (1859).[22]

To socialize young women and support the ideology of the middle-class home, traditional voices favored reading with discrimination and in moderation.[23] Social responsibility necessarily limited a woman's reading, as Eastman Johnson's *Bo-Peep* (1872) illustrates (fig. 2).[24] This nineteenth-century American genre painting shows a solicitous mother in a comfortable home putting aside an open book to entertain her playful baby. Johnson uses hands as a telling symbol to promote domesticity: the mother's right hand drapes over her open book, and the baby's two hands cover the mother's eyes as they play "bo-peep." In the painting, the mother assumes an active role as nurturer, not as reader. While she holds one book of unspecified type, the Bible on the prie-dieu (with a cross on its cover) speaks to her worthy character and establishes her as a reader of multiple texts as well as a virtuous mother.

Mothers also assumed an active role in reading to their children. Commentators believed reading aloud in the domestic circle would check the dangerous thrill an adolescent girl might find reading alone or in secret (fears central to the arguments of addiction and morality against women's reading). Reading aloud would also promote family unity, aiding closeness and boosting the familial bond. Reading worthy literature together, the family could have virtuous ideas to discuss. Social reading in the home was also a means to introduce children to literature considered wise and good. The conservative Sarah Stickney Ellis in *The Mothers of England* (1843) could not "imagine a scene of much greater enjoyment, than is presented by a thoroughly united and intelligent family, the female members of which are busily at work, while a father or brother reads aloud to them some interesting book approved by the mother, and delighted in by her

Fig. 2. Eastman Johnson, *Bo-Peep*, 1872. Oil on paperboard.
(Courtesy of Amon Carter Museum, Fort Worth, Texas, 1980.21)

daughters."[25] Ellis believes that "In the choice of books to be read for the instruction or amusement of her daughters, a mother should always be consulted" (196).

Mothers transmitted ideals and duties to their daughters. In fact, Gilman ridicules this point in her turn-of-the-century poem "The Mother's Charge" (1894) in which a dying mother instructs her daughter on household duties and thus passes onto her daughter the limitations of her gendered world.[26] However, to those who valued reading for socialization, it came to be seen as a means to transmit important values from one generation of women to the next. To the eyes of a conservative like Ellis, the mother's selection of reading led to the development of a dutiful, obedient, receptive daughter, who would raise, in turn, a daughter with similar values. Ellis's idea is not entirely onerous: a reading habit among girls need not be shunned, in her view, just trained. Moreover, the girl raised to be a judicious reader would be more prepared for her responsibilities as wife and mother. No doubt for reasons of self-promotion, editorials in women's magazines, a growing market in Victorian Britain and America, attest that the reading of these very magazines in no way conflicts with the cult of domesticity. In fact, editorials in *Godey's Lady's Book* frequently make claims that a husband whose wife reads *Godey's* would find her "no less assiduous for his reception, or less sincere in welcoming his return."[27]

In the eyes of many moderates entering the debate, the perfect Victorian British and American wife and mother needed to be educated, although her reading interests should be tailored to match her husband's. A woman's character, it was thought, could be judged by the books she possessed in her library; reciprocally, a man's literary taste and attitude toward books might help a young man or woman judge the worth of a potential mate and their future compatibility (Mason 2: 123; Flint, *The Woman Reader* 82). According to one mid-nineteenth-century American education manual, the ideal woman must "give a correct and elevated literary taste to her children, and to assume that influential station that she ought to possess as the companion of an educated man."[28] The woman who was an intellectual companion for her husband, experts argued, could also exercise improving influence on her father, brothers, and children. As Edward Salmon notes in "What Girls Read," "Boys' literature of a sound kind ought to help to build up men. Girls' literature ought to help to build up women. If in choosing the books that boys read it is necessary to remember that we are choosing the mental food for the future chiefs of a great race, it is equally important not to forget that we are choosing mental food for the wives and mothers of that race."[29] A woman must read, according to Salmon, to provide stimulating conversation for her husband and to raise her son. Salmon's reasoning, which introduces the trope of consumption, is undeniably riddled with stereotypes of gender and nation, but he identifies literature as a socialization tool that can positively affect character development, a notion still recognized today.

The Educational Argument

To some advocates, reading was essential for a woman's soul and intellect. In *The Victorians and Their Reading* (1935), an important but underutilized study, Amy Cruse explores what Victorians read during the first fifty years of Victoria's reign. She argues that Victorian women were attuned to intellectual nuances of topics ranging from evolution and religion to education and sexuality. Cruse devotes a chapter to "The New Woman," a term which, to Cruse, should not carry a derogatory meaning: rather, a New Woman is one "who, courageously and hopefully, stepped off the beaten, easy track and forced a way through the thick growth of prejudice and established custom to the open regions where development was possible."[30] In this chapter, Cruse cites Sophia Jex-Blake's enchantment with *Jane Eyre* and Davies's confession of loving novels such as Elizabeth Gaskell's *Ruth* (1853) and Sir Walter Scott's *Quentin Durward* (1823). Cruse explores how New Women "read widely and eagerly. They were keenly interested in the scientific and theological questions raised in those stirring days, and were not content to take their opinions on *The Origin of Species* and *Essays and Reviews* from their menfolk, as most women were" (349). Some Victorian women tackled intellectually challenging material, although, she cautions, they were not encouraged to read indiscriminately.

A strong Victorian voice for women's learning reverberates in the writings of Frances Power Cobbe, who opposed women's subjection and supported anti-vivisection. In her controversial, influential essay "What Shall We Do with Our Old Maids?" published in *Fraser's Magazine* in 1862, Cobbe argues that "popular prejudice against well-educated women is dying away. It is found they do *not* 'neglect infants for quadratic equations,' nor perform in any way less conscientiously the various duties of life after reading Plato or Kant."[31] Her reasoning runs counter to the argument against women's higher education crystallized in Cruikshank's comical 1847 caricature "My Wife Is a Woman of Mind" (fig. 1) where the wife neglects home and family for learning.

Another article published anonymously in the *Westminster Review* titled "The Higher Education of Women" (1888) quotes Cobbe's sarcastic lambasting of the medical profession for trying to keep women out of medicine. Cobbe's argument equally applies to the larger notion of women's education: "Women, beware!" the article cries; "beware! You are on the brink of destruction. You have hitherto been engaged only in crushing your waists; now you are attempting to cultivate your minds! You have been dancing all night in the foul air of ball-rooms; now you are beginning to spend your mornings in study. You have been incessantly stimulating your emotions with concerts and operas, with French plays and French novels; now you are exerting your understanding to learn Greek and solve propositions in Euclid! Beware, oh beware! Science pronounces that the 'woman who *studies*—is lost!'"[32] The author goes on to argue that "Through many generations, women have been kept intellectually in swaddling clothes. Just as the Chinese cramp up the feet of their girls and get ridiculed for their pains, so do we, with more enlightenment, and therefore with more sin, circumscribe the mental growth of our girls, thereby earning, if not receiving, the ridicule that is properly our due" ("The Higher Education of Women" 157).

"The Higher Education of Women" promotes education and reading to enlighten women and expand their "cramped" minds. The author concludes that the well-read, educated woman will not only elevate herself but the race "by giving us mothers whose cerebral development will be such that their children will be more easily taught, and capable of much more than the children of less able mothers" who succumb to neurasthenia out of ennui—rather than too much mental stimulation—and "fill the consulting rooms of medical men" (162). Gilman makes similar claims about a woman's need for meaningful work in her internationally acclaimed *Women and Economics* (1898). Still others who advocated women's education, as Elizabeth Garrett Anderson did, argued that the stimulus of attending balls and theaters was far greater than that of competing for literary and scientific honors; in fact, education for women, in prolonging chastity and asexuality in her view, gave young women a period for much needed self-development to gain emotional and intellectual independence.

The Argument for Empowerment, Real and Imagined

Independent reading outside the family circle, which opponents of women's reading labeled isolated and solitary, gave women an opportunity not only to learn but to think and imagine. As Sicherman notes in "Sense and Sensibility," "Reading provided space—physical, temporal, and psychological—that permitted women to exempt themselves from traditional gender expectations, whether imposed by formal society or by family obligation" (202). Reading on her own, a woman could experience a life free from duties and rigid gender expectations. If such independent reading offered women "space—physical, temporal, and psychological," then some nineteenth-century women readers no doubt experienced, if only fleetingly, what Virginia Woolf considers most essential for a woman—"a room of her own."[33]

In *Reading the Romance* (1984), Janice Radway argues that the act of reading romances puts women creatively in the center of their own lives. Her argument has bearing on nineteenth-century women readers who read mimetically. Women found empowering role models in the books they read and in the lives of the female authors who wrote them. Some

Victorian women, at times, projected themselves into works of fiction without identifying with a particular character. Others related to heroines' lives and incorporated the fictive worlds into their own. Likewise, Elaine Showalter advances in *A Literature of Their Own* (1977) that women writers in many cases projected aspects of themselves onto their imagined heroines, but were challenged in creating male companions for them: "If he is to be redeemed and to rediscover his humanity, the 'woman's man' must find out how it feels to be a woman."[34] Showalter also speculates that sensation fiction had great popular appeal with women readers because, in its plots of violence and domestic crimes, it voiced women's repressed emotions and fantasies.

Books exposed women readers to worlds beyond the restrictions of Victorian gentility. In other cases, reading enabled women vicariously to imagine and prepare for their futures: books introduced women to social situations common in the Victorian drawing room, warned them of dangers to avert, and offered alternative models of selfhood, which their fictional sisters had fashioned. In some instances, reading engendered an imaginative rather than an actual response. An article on "Novel-reading," appearing in *Saturday Review* in 1867, makes this point precisely, arguing to read Trollope "is only to most girls 'coming out' a season or two earlier than they would have done, and 'coming out' under the auspices of a careful drawing-room chaperon, who will not introduce them to more objectional characters than he thinks unavoidable."[35] As Flint confirms in her analysis, "At this level, reading is seen as operating in a socially mimetic way, ... ensuring that she experiences imaginatively what it would be like to move in certain circles which lie outside the range of her probable circumstances" (*The Woman Reader* 81).

In autobiographical accounts, women also attribute the reading of specific books to momentous action—the dissolution of a marriage, the pursuit of a professional career path, a change in faith, and the launching of a new endeavor (Sicherman, "Sense and Sensibility" 214).[36] For example, in her essay "Reading Little Women: The Many Lives of a Text," Sicherman notes that in 1872, the five Lukens sisters of Brinton, Pennsylvania, began their own home newspaper called "Little Things" after reading about the March sisters' magazine, "The Pickwick Portfolio," in *Little Women*.[37] Reading independently, some women even attempted to liberate themselves by broadening the prevailing cult of domesticity—favoring careers over motherhood and marriage. Participating in reading circles and clubs, women on both sides of the Atlantic shared their daydreams; they gained confidence, a sense of community, and the encouragement to fashion their own identities.

Why Women Should Not Read

While women made gains in education and received more opportunities and choices in learning, intellectual pursuits for Victorian British and American women were not to detract from domesticity. The concept of the home as a haven for wife and mother to raise her children grew out of the division of home and production accompanying industrialization. Fervently opposed by early feminists, including Mona Caird and Charlotte Perkins Gilman, the doctrine of separate spheres remained entrenched in Victorian Britain and America. A rhetoric that made women "queens" of their respective domestic hearths placated some women. This pervasive discourse supporting the cult of domesticity persisted into the early twentieth century, as Dr. W. J. Truitt's advice book *Know Thyself* (1911) attests: "The queen that sits upon the throne of home, crowned and sceptered as none other ever can be, is—mother. Her enthronement is complete, her reign unrivaled, and the moral issues of her empire are eternal. 'Her children rise up, and call her blessed'" (35). Writing more realistically about domestic womanhood in an earlier advice book called *Ladies Wreath* (1850), Helen Irving cautions that "If the necessities of her position require these duties at her hands, she will perform them nonetheless cheerfully, that she knows herself capable of higher things."[38]

Woman's mission to perform duties cheerfully for husband, children, home, and community fired the reading debate and fostered arguments against women's reading. During an era, to recall Flint, when girls, as readers, had a "privilege of choice which would have been undreamed of by their grandmothers" (*The Woman Reader* 47), the scope and comprehensiveness of reasons against women's reading cannot but impress us, even if some of the arguments appear ludicrous today.

The Biological Argument

In the Victorian era, reasoning, critical inquiry, and disinterested reflection were inherently masculine traits, although many women strove to acquire them to make themselves learned (Kelley 411). It was also believed that women read differently than men because they possessed greater morality, sensibility, sensitivity, intuition, piety, and empathy (Kelley 411; Welter 152–53). The nineteenth-century consciousness not only recognized the reproductive differences between the sexes, but believed that women's and men's brains were distinctly constituted. Moreover, throughout the nineteenth century, the functioning of the mind was connected to the brain (Flint, *The Woman Reader* 53). These commonly held theories regarding women's and men's biological differences fueled concern particularly about young women's reading.

The now forgotten but then influential Scottish biologist Patrick Geddes, along with his pupil J. Arthur Thomson, advances in *The Evolution of Sex* (1889) that natural laws determine men's superior and women's inferior social positions. The female, with an "anabolic" as opposed to a "katabolic [sic]" constitution, needs to conserve energy for survival and reproduction. The notions of cell metabolism and resulting sex differences in habits of body scientifically supported gender distinctions under fire as critics debated the "woman question." Biological differences between the sexes had social implications, as Jill Conway notes: "Male intelligence was greater than female, men had greater independence and courage than women, and men were able to expend sustained bursts of physical or cerebral activity."[39] With conviction, S. Weir Mitchell, the noted physician whom Gilman indicts in "The Yellow Wall-Paper," compatibly proclaims in *Doctor and Patient* (1887): "With the intellectual differences between man and woman I have here little to do. That there is difference, both quantitative and in a measure qualitative, I believe, nor do I think any educational change in generations of women will ever set her, as to certain mental and moral qualifications, as an equal beside the man."[40] Mitchell also believes that a girl trying to achieve the educational training of her brother can anticipate the physical and emotional consequences of "broken health" (149).

Geddes and Mitchell were among many Victorian British and American medical experts who advanced a widely held belief that women had limited energy resources.[41] A woman's entrance into the work force and higher education—traditionally male spheres—appears, from this standpoint, to sabotage her vital metabolic economy, as defined by nature. These outdated notions justified the myth of female frailty, as well as notions of domesticity and separate spheres while it also fueled the medical argument against women's reading.

The Medical Argument

The medical argument appears akin to the biological model. Reading was damned because it was thought to damage a woman's nervous system and reproductive health. Medical authorities linked excessive, unsupervised reading to a host of female reproductive ailments (for example, early menstruation, painful menses, infertility, etc.), insanity, and premature death. A woman's biological differences—her greater sensitivity and sensibility—made her more susceptible to effects of a novel. Countless experts pronounced sensation novels, mysteries, and horror tales stimuli to avoid strenuously for physical well-being. This prescription for health derives, in part, from the common belief that brain and heart were directly linked in the "feminine nature," as George Henry Lewes advances in "The Heart and the Brain."[42] To Lewes, a woman's physiology made her prone to shock: an excited feeling generated while reading a racy novel could stun a woman's heart.

Such an idea was ripe for caricature even at the onset of the 1800s. James Gillray's early-nineteenth-century satirical print titled "Tales of Wonder!"(1802) is, in Gillray's words, an "attempt to describe the effects of the Sublime & Wonderful" literature on women readers (fig. 3). The billowing fire, the ghoulish figurines on the mantelpiece, as well as the lone candle lighting the reading of the four ladies clustered around a parlor table set a mood of mystery and excitement. The woman reading the book to her friends looks so engrossed in its contents that she is unaware of the exaggerated responses of her listening companions. A visual prop of melodrama, the raised hands of the woman on the left—whose eyes pop out of her head—register shock and fascination. Equally telling is the body language of the woman alongside her: in alarm, she grasps her friend's back as they lean forward to listen. Worse, the unopened volume on the table suggests that this reading séance will continue well into the night, no doubt compounding the physical effects already evident in "Tales of Wonder!"

While we can appreciate the humor in Gillray's satire, more dire and disturbing repercussions fueled the medical argument against women's novel-reading on both sides of the Atlantic. Reading a sensation novel or romance was believed to endanger a young woman's reproductive cycle. Romance novels with vivid love scenes and sensation fiction brimming with sexual scandal might overstimulate a girl's still dormant sexual and emotional instincts and bring on early menstruation or encourage masturbation, then considered a cause of insanity. Victorians generally believed the young to be asexual; extending latency could postpone maturational problems. It was important to protect an impressionable female from reading romances that could stimulate her physical development.[43]

Dr. Mary Wood-Allen speaks directly to these points in her discussion of the "evils of novel-reading" in a respected advice book titled *What a*

Fig. 3. James Gillray, "Tales of Wonder!" 1802, frontispiece to Amy Cruse, *The Englishman and His Books in the Early Nineteenth Century*, n.d.

Young Woman Ought to Know (1899).[44] With the weight of medical authority behind her, she proclaims: "the descriptions of love-scenes, of thrilling, romantic episodes, find an echo in the girl's physical system and tend to create an abnormal excitement of her organs of sex, which she recognizes only as a pleasurable mental emotion, with no comprehension of the physical origin or the evil effects. Romance-reading by young girls will, by this excitement of the bodily organs, tend to create their premature development, and the child becomes physically a woman months, or even years, before she should" (124). Wood-Allen backs her claim that reading romance triggers a physiological response with an anecdote: an eleven-year-old female, an "omnivorous reader of romances" (124), showed early signs of development and nervousness, which diminished when she followed Wood-Allen's advice. She gave up romance reading for rigorous athletics and nature study, delaying the onset of menstruation by three years, at which point it was "painlessly established" (125). Targeting the ages of twelve to eighteen as a period of crisis in a girl's development, Wood-Allen cautions that a girl inclined toward sensation fiction who is not properly guided "may be easily led into flirtation or conduct that later in life may make her blush to remember" (108). In a chapter on "Some Causes of Painful Menstruation," she cites novel-reading (along with taking a chill and overexertion) as a cause of painful menses.

The outdated notion of forsaking novels for relief from menstrual cramps holds allure, even if it riles a feminist readership today. It is possible the girl who traded romance reading for athletics channeled her energies so completely that she induced an amenorrheic state, which we find among women athletes today. Wood-Allen's book was, nonetheless, a title in a well-respected "Self and Sex" series. Endorsements and photographs of eminent Victorian American and British educators, authors, philanthropists, and clergy appear in the front of the book. Her advocates include suffragist Elizabeth Cady Stanton as well as Helen Campbell, Gilman's "adopted mother," who wrote about the experiences of poor urban working-class women whose lives she had investigated.

Some proponents of women's education, such as Garrett Anderson and Emily Davies, argued the opposite of Wood-Allen: using the mind postponed rather than incited sexuality. But the medical objections to women's education ran to the very core of assumed differences in male and female constitutions. Experts voiced concerns that reading diverted needed energy from a woman's reproductive organs as well as her nervous system. Owing to the biological view of woman's finite energy, commentators linked novel-reading to headaches, hysteria, insanity, and fertility issues (Flint, *The Woman Reader* 56–58). Some argued that a woman should not read novels in the morning, after first waking, or during or just following any meal, since the brain needed to rest while the body was awakening or digesting. Striking terror in her readers, Charlotte Mason concludes in *Home Education* (1886), "the girl who sits for hours poring over a novel to the damage of her eyes, her brain, and her general nervous system, is guilty of a lesser fault of the nature of suicide."[45]

Nineteenth-century scientific theories backed these claims. Dr. Edward H. Clarke, a retired professor from the Harvard Medical School, voiced his concern over the rise of women's higher education, using scientific reasoning to curtail women's intellectual progress. *Sex in Education* (1873), an influential and widely read book, dramatizes the medical concerns of excessive study for women, endangering her essential biological function to bear children. To Clarke, a girl who goes to school and pursues a range of studies could not expect to "retain uninjured health and a future secure from neuralgia, uterine disease, hysteria, and other derangements of the nervous system, if she follows the same method that boys are trained in."[46] Clarke provides testimonials and damning case studies of girls who fed their brains with the same intellectual fare as boys and, as a result, starved their bodies of vital energy. Girls who studied during their menses and the onset of sexual development subsequently suffered from a host of ailments, including menorrhagia, dysmenorrhea, hemorrhage, amenorrhea, headache, dyspepsia, invalidism, neuralgia, hysteria, intense insanity, and premature death. Clarke scorns women who "graduated from school or college excellent scholars, but with undeveloped ovaries. Later they married, and were sterile" (Clarke 39). Moreover, no educated woman, in his view, is free from risk of infertility, nor is society, as a result. Clarke took book learning out of the realm of an individual woman's choice to ensure the future good of society. The stamp of science validates that book learning is not conducive to a woman's—or society's—mental and physical health.

Building upon the biological model, the nineteenth-century medical model presents body and mind as indelibly linked. The commonly prescribed treatment for nervous exhaustion or neurasthenia, the rest cure, illustrates the late-nineteenth- and early-twentieth-century belief that treating a woman's body helped her recover from a breakdown in the nervous system. Too much social activity, sustained or severe domestic trials (such as nursing a sick family member), and strain brought on by intellectual pursuits allegedly caused neurasthenia in women.[47]

This medical model met opposition. In *Sex and Education. A Reply to Dr. E. H. Clarke's "Sex in Education,"* editor Julia Ward Howe calls Clarke's work a "polemic" and notes his gender bias in her introduction: "Boys as well as girls break down under severe study, men as well as women, and at least as often."[48] Howe asserts that Clarke's book "has neither the impartiality of science, the form of literature, the breadth of philosophy, nor the friendliness of counsel" (13). In her reply to Clarke, she assembles a range of essays by important men and women of her day, who, though respectful of Clarke's rank and expertise, question his limited findings, the tone of his work, and the sweeping force of his statements. More convincing than the essays themselves is a section titled "Testimony from Colleges" about women who pursued intellectual studies at Antioch, Michigan, Lombard, Oberlin, and Vassar (an institution Clarke criticizes). These testimonies include statistics of the number of children of graduates from Antioch College and a letter from Vassar College Resident Physician Alida C.

Avery, noting Vassar's attention to create a healthy learning environment in which "no day shall find her overtaxed, even if that day has borne the added periodic burden" (Howe 194).

Heightened concern for how university education might affect the health of women also gave rise to British studies such as Eleanor Mildred Sidgwick's *Health Statistics of Women Students of Cambridge and Oxford and of Their Sisters* (1890). By the 1890s, the growing number of women in Britain and America who pursued higher education and reproduced helped to debunk the now discredited notions that reading caused physical and neurological damage and infertility (Flint, *The Woman Reader* 64). In her book, Sidgwick uses survey research to document the individual health, familial health, and marriage and childbearing patterns of college-educated women in comparison to women who did not pursue higher education. Although she takes care to qualify her results, Sidgwick reports that those attending college have a higher standard of health than their non-educated counterparts. Moreover, she finds no support for what she perceives to be unfounded concerns that higher education negatively affects motherhood. Like Howe's work, Sidgwick's is a reply to those who preached against woman's intellectual education. She quotes, for example, the conservative voice of a Mr. Grant Allen, who claims in an article in the *Pall Mall Gazette:* "You educate your women at the expense of their reserve fund; and after all you find they marry, and make very unsatisfactory and physically inefficient mothers."[49] Sidgwick concludes diplomatically that "The facts available on which to form a judgment are, as I have already said, as yet small in amount, but so far as they go they afford no support whatever to generalisations such as Mr. Grant Allen's" (66). If it took "facts" to refute mistaken "generalisations," these generalizations about inadequate intellectual mothers were pervasive and drove the ubiquitous medical model.

Tropes of Consumption and Addiction

The tropes of consumption and addiction can be seen as a logical extension of the biological and medical arguments. Commentators frequently compared books to mental food. While improving literature comprised part of a well-balanced diet, advice writers like Lady Laura Ridding in "What Should Women Read?" (1896) likened excessive consumption of novels to a "surfeit of sugar-plums."[50] Opponents feared that the practice of turning to fiction for pleasure or escape from the realities of domestic life was in itself addictive.

In *The Ladies' Guide in Health and Disease* (1882), Dr. John Harvey Kellogg presents the dual tropes of reading consumption and addiction, calling novel-reading "one of the most pernicious habits to which a young lady can become devoted. When the habit is once thoroughly fixed, it becomes as inveterate as the use of liquor or opium. The novel-devotee is as much a slave as the opium-eater or the inebriate."[51] Kellogg uses his medical backing to pronounce novel-reading deadly and equate a woman hooked on books with a drug addict and a drunkard. Florence Nightingale, in her unpublished *Cassandra* (1852 rev. 1859), also relates the reading habit to opium abuse as she argues against the ennui of middle-class women: "They are exhausted, like those who live on opium or on novels, all their lives—exhausted with feelings which lead to no action."[52] No doubt the fear of novel addiction prompted Mary Bell, author of *A Book of Counsels for Girls* (1888), to advise those overly fond of story books to deny themselves fiction during Lent (Flint, *The Woman Reader* 93). Even at the end of the nineteenth century in "The Novel-Reading Habit" (1898), George Clarke dramatically equates the "effects of novel-reading ... with those of indulgence in opium or intoxicating liquors,"[53] suggesting that as the century progressed, fears surrounding addiction to fiction remained deeply ingrained in Victorian British and American cultural consciousness.

Winslow Homer's well-known watercolor *The New Novel* (1877) offers a visual response to the dangers of reading addiction while introducing a related moral argument against women's novel-reading (fig. 4).[54] This painting shows a woman apart from her daily domestic routine, luxuriating in the latest fiction of the day. The setting is the pleasurable outdoors. Homer's self-contained and isolated reader seems deaf and blind to the natural world that frames her relaxed physique, itself an outward manifestation of her mental liberty.

The nature of the novel, declared in its title, influences the way we read the painting. The red-haired reader hugs the novel closely; her lowered gaze intimates its racy nature. The book is likely sensation fiction, an 1860s literary phenomenon "devoured by women" and characterized by "the presence of sexual desire and sexual energy" (Flint, *The Woman Reader* 274). Homer's captivated reader is no doubt reading about love, her own secret passions, and what she might hope to find in a lover. While her intense engagement in the book excludes the reader from her gaze, her physical appearance and body posture speak volumes, particularly to a Victorian viewer. Her vulnerable position could be seen as titillating. Lying

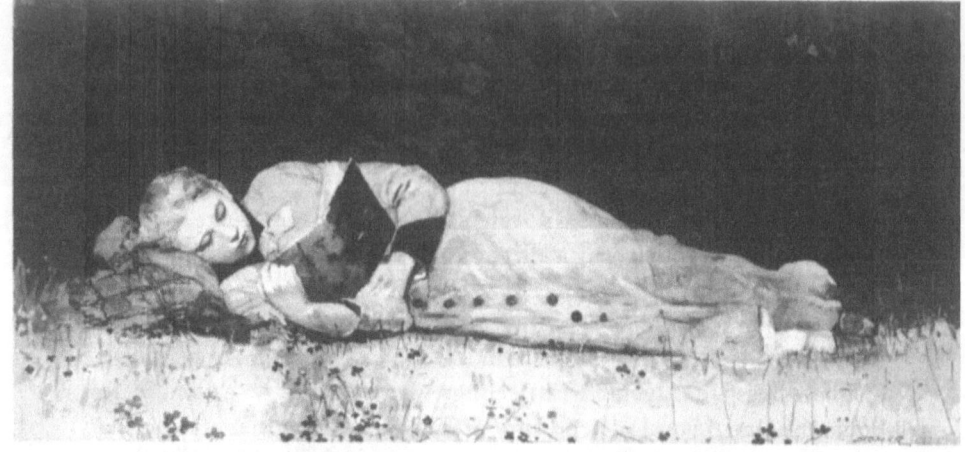

Fig. 4. Winslow Homer, *The New Novel*, 1877. (Courtesy of Horace P. Wright Collection, Museum of Fine Arts, Springfield, Mass.)

down, she is on the same plane as those who observe her. As the model reads her book, we read her body. The buttons of her dress, placed prominently down the front, call attention to her form and invite undressing as well as judgment. The figure's bold red locks associate her with a fallen woman, as exemplified in Dante Gabriel Rossetti's *Found* (1853, never completed). Her fitted bright orange dress drapes over her curving body. Her ripe red lips also suggest seductiveness and sexual availability, if not promiscuity.[55]

The Moral Argument

If we view Homer's painting in context of prevailing reading ideologies of morality as well as consumption and addiction, reading a provocative book can be interpreted as a dangerous indulgence. Sensation fiction stirs sexual impulses. Personal pleasure supersedes social duty. The woman's singular enrapture in the book, which has likely seduced her own romantic imagination, suggests why those who touted the evils of novels feared addiction and its moral repercussions.

American and British strongholds, such as Catharine Beecher and Harriet Beecher Stowe and Ellis, worried that access to sexual knowledge promoted a false view of life and immoral ways, leading women to discontent or, worse, to ruination. To many antifiction critics, novel consumption led to addiction and, naturally, to moral decline. As Heller cautions, "if books could provide guidance, they could also lead readers astray" (327). On the list of the most objectionable were racy French novels, inexpensive "blue books" or "shilling shockers" also called "horror Gothic" (Gothic tales of supernatural horrors and violent crimes), Newgate novels (which sentimentalized vice and crime), romances, and sensation fiction (which stunned the readers with domestic poisoning, sexual scandal, crime, and kidnapping). Recalling the tropes of consumption and addiction, opponents to women's reading targeted such fiction for its ability to corrupt and its addictiveness, inducing a druglike dependence. "Trashy" works were particularly dangerous to susceptible readers—namely, middle-class schoolboys, newly literate laborers, and young women. Advice books of the period overflow with stories about girls ruined by novels consumed too freely. Indiscriminate reading crippled a woman morally and weakened her mind. Girls who consumed too much fiction—it was believed—did not think enough. If she must read novels, commentators argued, then she should read edifying works by moral, upstanding authors. One advice writer, R. C. Waterston, recommended history and religious biography as the safest reading choices for women.[56]

In an era where a woman's place was in her home, novel-reading was believed to raise false expectations about love and marriage and, in turn, bring about dissatisfaction with domesticity and upset the status quo. In the words of Wood-Allen, "novel-reading engenders false and unreal ideas of life" (124). Novel-reading could interfere with piety (Welter 165) and distract the female reader from the realities of her world. "The Fatalist," appearing in *Godey's Lady's Book* in 1834, illustrates this very point; the female protagonist, Catherine, reads perilous books until life to her seems like "a bewildered dream.... O passion, what a shocking perverter of reason thou art!"[57] Most feared was solitary reading: free rein of the lending library exposed an innocent female to murder, vice, and sexual scandal. If she read in secret for escapism, the number of objectionable books she consumed remained unchecked.

"An Essay on the Modern Novel," published in *Port Folio* in 1802, declares that "Novels ... are the powerful engines with which the seducer attacks the female heart" (Davidson, *Revolution and the Word* 45). Likewise, an 1802 article titled "Novel Reading, a Cause of Female Depravity" printed in *New England Quarterly* pronounces: "Without the poison instilled [by novels] into the blood, females in ordinary life would never have been so much the slaves of vice" (Davidson, *Revolution and the Word* 45). The latter article, presumably reprinted from a British periodical titled

The Monthly Mirror, reinforces how censure of the novel in British print culture disseminated in American culture. It goes on to describe how a young lady, "poisoned" by novel-reading, becomes a "serpent" who tempts her best friend's husband. The addicted immoral reader sends her dishonored and "disconsolate parents" into "premature graves," creating wounds "never to be healed" (Davidson, *Revolution and the Word* 46).

Similar messages about the moral consequences of unsupervised reading abound in numerous evangelical periodicals, such as the British journal *The Wesleyan-Methodist Magazine;* in one 1855 article titled "What Is the Harm of Novel-Reading?" by an anonymous writer called "S," a young woman left at liberty to choose her reading from her father's library succumbs to an early death, all from reading too many novels: "Golden dreams of sinful pleasure—the creation of novel-reading—ended in disgrace, ruin, disease, a broken heart, and an untimely grave!"[58] Likewise, in *The Wedding Ring* (1886), Rev. T. DeWitt Talmage places blame for immorality squarely on the "modern novel": "In many of the cases of escapade the idea was implanted in the hot brain of the woman by a cheap novel, ten cents' worth of unadulterated perdition" (46). In exposing a woman to corruption and sexual indiscretion, the "cheap novel"—whether a historical romance, a sensation novel, sentimental fiction, or "New Woman" fiction—becomes the cause of moral impropriety, stimulating sexual drives and leading a woman to stray from the rigid morals of the proper Victorian British and American home.

Arguments in Combination

Some contemporary thinkers linked ideologies to make a case about women's reading. For example, in *The American Woman's Home* (1869), Gilman's great-aunts, Catharine Beecher and Harriet Beecher Stowe, join arguments of socialization, biology, medicine, addiction, and morality to place women's reading in context of traditional domesticity, considered crucial and valuable. They defended a woman's capacity as teacher, an extension of her domestic responsibilities. In fact, the frontispiece to their book shows a mother teaching her young child; the open book before her confirms that education is a maternal function. Still, in their chapter on "Health of Mind," Beecher and Beecher Stowe caution that excessive intellectual activity can lead to mental disease and serious health problems for women. They offer examples, including a firsthand testimonial, of industrious and promising female students "on the verge of derangement" about to "sink to an early grave" due to vigorous intellectual study.[59]

Seemingly buying into the notion of women's finite energy, they posit too much education as a cause for disease and death. They also warn against overindulgence in novel-reading for stirring discontent and damaging mental health. According to Beecher and Beecher Stowe, "Under the head of excessive mental action, must be placed the indulgence of the imagination in novel-reading and 'castle-building.' This kind of stimulus, unless counterbalanced by physical exercise, not only wastes time and energies, but undermines the vigor of the nervous system" (259). In her active pursuit of self-education and novel-reading, Gilman broke from the Beecher mold, a heritage she much coveted.

The notion of women reading within the home actually straddles both sides of the ideological debate. To antifiction critics, forbidding reading seemed the perfect solution to control women's desires. Nonetheless, advocates espousing the gentility and socialization arguments recognized the value of keeping women contentedly reading within the confines of the private home, the institution that Gilman lambasted as the source of women's oppression. Banta points out a paradox in *Imaging American Women* (1987): the act of reading for women of all classes can be interpreted as a victory (for in reading, a woman gains the time to stop, reflect, and think), yet the reading woman might also "demonstrate one of the subtle forms by which females are enslaved to the bourgeois, essentially masculine notion that women's desires are best kept under control within the walls of the home and the covers of a book, rather than being released as action in the world of public affairs" (358). Banta notes that the manifold images of women readers, appearing on nineteenth-century commercial posters, sheet-music covers, and magazine and book illustrations, can be read negatively: women arguably "shut themselves off from the actual world by entrapping their minds within bookish abstractions and irresponsible fantasies" (357).

This view held force in New England from the seventeenth through the nineteenth century and fueled the moral argument against higher education for women. The reading of fiction in the private home also makes a class statement. Here Banta crystallizes the argument: "Is reading unsupportable because it separates women who 'have' from those who 'have not' in terms of what all women ought to possess—the leisure to read? Or is the point that all women are better off, even under improved economic conditions, when they are not reading but doing?" (358). A servant in a grand home might neglect her duties to peer into a book, as William McGregor Paxton captures in his painting *The House Maid* (1910). A woman forced to work in a factory or in a seamstress shop simply did not have the time to read or dream over a book, as a woman of privilege did. The class issue Banta raises testifies how reading increasingly became a mark of leisure in Britain and America by the turn of the century.[60]

III. READING SELECTIONS

The polar ideologies that fueled the reading debate form a collage of women readers. Dire images of girls consuming novels in secret and dying with diseased minds appear alongside inspiring pictures of women reading independently, in clubs, or in the family parlor, gaining confidence and valuable life lessons. To add another layer to this collage, on both sides of the Atlantic, we witness a prismatic effect in the creation of literature for specific audiences: girls, boys, adolescents of both sexes, as well as young men, and mothers, to name a few prime markets.[61] If girls were actively reading, some critics thought it wise that they read safe or improving literature designed specifically for them. Gillian Avery suggests that gender-specific fiction arose because "The writers of juvenile fiction recognized at an early stage that in the boy they had an entirely different animal" (138).[62] Charlotte Mary Yonge makes this very point in an 1887 essay: "The mild tales that girls read simply to pass away the time are ineffective with them [boys]. Many will not read at all. Those who will read require something either solid, droll, or exciting."[63]

A comparison of two British periodicals from the later nineteenth century, the extremely popular *The Boy's Own Paper* (beginning in 1879) and *The Girl's Own Paper* (beginning in 1880), suggests boys read epic adventures, conquests of foreign lands, and jungle stories. Girls, in contrast, read school stories, poetry, information on morals and manners, and anecdotes about Queen Victoria's girlhood.[64] Sponsored by the Religious Tract Society, *The Girl's Own Paper* appealed to girls between eleven and nineteen; despite the society's aim to keep the publication free of overt didacticism, it is not surprising that its fiction is laden with socially approved values to convey a moral.[65] However, as Salmon notes in "What Girls Read" (1886), "*The Boys'* [sic] *Own Paper* is studied by thousands of girls. The explanation is that they can get in boys' books what they cannot get in the majority of their own—a stirring plot and lively movement" (524). He concludes that "Probably nearly as many girls as boys have read *Robinson Crusoe, Tom Brown's Schooldays, Sandford and Merton,* and other long-lived 'boys" stories. Nor is this liking for heroes rather than heroines to be deprecated. It ought to impart vigor and breadth to a girl's nature, and to give sisters a sympathetic knowledge of the scenes wherein their brothers live and work" (524). Salmon recognizes that Victorian girls, like their brothers, benefited from tales of adventure and travel and likely preferred the selections on their brothers' bookshelves to the preachy, "goody-goody" (515) girls' books in their personal libraries.

Mild or pious girls' tales, an outgrowth of an earlier undifferentiated didactic literature given to adults and children, did not pacify all Victorian British and American girls. Many at the turn of the century craved the freedom allotted boys, longed to be like their brothers, and indulged their daydreams through books. As Sally Mitchell notes, "Leading boy lives in fantasy let them try on alternate roles, voices, attitudes, and experiences, and enfold boyish traits in their self image. 'Hundreds of girls,' as an essayist in *Girl's Realm* put it, would 'read their brothers' books and leave their own untouched'" (*The New Girl* 111). Girls gravitated to works with active male characters and heroic friendships: historical novels (generally approved of for girls), empire adventure tales, and sea stories. G. A. Henty, a leading writer for boys at the turn of the century, also had a strong girl readership.

This point validates a notion raised under the argument of reading for empowerment: reading provided compensation to female readers, offering experiences missing in a girl's life or denied her due to gender. As Sally Mitchell notes in a chapter in *The New Girl* titled "To Be a Boy," action-packed novels with male and female characters performing daring deeds—for example, F. Marryat's *Masterman Ready* (1841), Henty's *A Soldier's Daughter* (1906), Robert Louis Stevenson's *The Black Arrow* (1888) and *Treasure Island* (1883)—sparked the daydreams of the Victorian girl who possessed an active imagination. Testimonials from girl readers suggest some identified with boy heroes. They imagined themselves shooting and wielding daggers, swimming in swift-flowing rivers, riding fast, and adventuring all the way. In the words of Helen Corke, one avid "new girl" reader, "Do I want friends? Perhaps—of the pattern supplied by Lyndall in *The Story of an African Farm*, by Hawkeye and Uncas in *The Last of the Mohicans*, by other proud and free spirits who look at me from the world of print. Reading is becoming a drug."[66] Corke buys into the pervasive notion of reading as addiction. Likewise, Agnes Hamilton, the most moral daughter of the literary Hamilton family of Fort Wayne, Indiana, admits her attempt to curb her addiction to British novels after reading Dickens's *Our Mutual Friend* (1865) and Edward Bulwer-Lytton's *My Novel* (1853):

"I have resolved not to read another novel for a week, at least, and consequently I feel like a reformed drunkard."[67] Of importance, however, Corke notes that her reading fixation is owing to the "proud and free" companions these books offer her.

Favorite Authors and Titles

It is hard to gather accurate information on the exact British and American titles and authors most popular with the Victorian British and American girl. Some books were standard in the Victorian library: histories of England, France, Greece, and Rome; improving tales and school stories, such as Thomas Day's *The History of Sandford and Merton* (1783–89), Mary Martha Sherwood's *The History of the Fairchild Family* (1818, 1842, 1847), and Thomas Hughes's *Tom Brown's Schooldays* (1857); domestic fiction, such as Alcott's *Little Women* (1868, 1869) and works still considered classics today, including John Bunyan's *Pilgrim's Progress* (1678, 1684), Daniel Defoe's *Robinson Crusoe* (1719), and Jonathan Swift's *Gulliver's Travels* (1726) (Cruse, *The Victorians and Their Reading* 286–309). In "What Girls Read" (1886), Salmon cites a study that Charles Welsh conducted on favorite authors of one thousand girl readers between ages eleven and nineteen. In a table, Salmon lists the authors' names with the number of mentions in parentheses. Those most frequently noted are: Charles Dickens (330); Sir Walter Scott (226), Charles Kingsley (91), Charlotte Mary Yonge (91), William Shakespeare (73), E. Wetherell [Susan Warner] (54), Mrs. Henry Wood (51), George Eliot (41), Edward Bulwer-Lytton (41), Henry Wadsworth Longfellow (31), Hesba Stretton (26), and William Makepeace Thackeray (18). Other sources confirm the popularity of these most-named authors. Girls frequently wrote into a "Books to exchange" column in magazines such as *Girl's Realm*, so they might swap novels by Dickens, Scott, and even Yonge for Meade's school stories written for girls, set in boarding and day schools. And in "How to Form a Small Library" (1881), Mason recommends a young woman have fifty selections in her personal library, including works by important nineteenth-century authors, such as Scott, Dickens, and Thackeray (2: 123).

Other British and American authors who received a number of mentions in the Welsh survey are Louisa May Alcott (12), Mary Elizabeth Braddon (11), John Bunyan (11), William Harrison Ainsworth (10), Lucy Maud Montgomery (9), Daniel Defoe (8), Mark Twain (8), Thomas Carlyle (6), Maria Edgeworth (6), Lewis Carroll (5), R. M. Ballantyne (5), Charlotte Brontë (5), Elizabeth Gaskell (5), and F. Marryat (5). Salmon posits that the availability of Dickens and Scott in school and home libraries, as well as the passing familiarity of these authors' names as household words, may have influenced some girls to favor some of these authors over others who wrote exclusively for girls. Using this table to drive his argument that girls need less "goody-goody" fiction, Salmon concludes that "Allowing, therefore, that the table now given at all represents the degrees of record in which various authors are held by girls, it should induce those who especially aspire to write for girls to think twice before giving to the world another story on the usual lines" (529). Salmon also notes in "What Girls Read" that fewer young ladies read works by Yonge and Elizabeth Missing Sewell than earlier in the century, suggesting a shift away from didactic or improving fiction.

With no international copyright law, many American publishers found it more profitable to reprint British and European fiction than to encourage American authorship. As a consequence, in the antebellum period, American readers had access to cheap editions of works by British writers popular among Victorian girl readers—notably, Dickens, Thackeray, the Brontës, Scott, Caroline Norton, and Bulwer-Lytton—as well as works by Continental writers and American writers, including Nathaniel Hawthorne, Herman Melville, and Edgar Allan Poe. Of American domestic fiction, *Little Women* and books by the Warner sisters (for example, Susan Warner's *The Wide, Wide World* [1850]) held a special place in American girls' reading. An 1853 reviewer for the *North American* notes that "As far as we know the early history of *The Wide, Wide World*, it was, for some time, bought to be presented to nice little girls. . . . Elder sisters were soon found poring over the volumes, and it was very natural that mothers next should try the spell. . . . After this, papas were not very difficult to convert. . . . We are much mistaken if *The Wide, Wide World*, and *Queechy*, have not been found under the pillows of sober bachelors. . . . They were found on everybody's table, and lent from house to house."[68] *Little Women*, likewise, shared a larger readership than its intended market. Long classified a rite of passage for American girls, *Little Women* attracted male readers including Theodore Roosevelt, who admitted a liking for it "at the cost of being deemed effeminate."[69] Interestingly, the youthful Alcott idolized a popular male British author: Dickens (Saxton 289).

The favorites among girl readers continued to evolve if we look beyond the Victorian era to compare Salmon's 1886 findings to those appearing in two 1906 articles in *Nineteenth Century* on the subject of preferred reading of the modern British girl and the Colonial girl.[70] Florence Low, surveying two hundred British schoolgirls, ages fifteen to eighteen, found Edna Lyall, Henry Seton Merriman, Marie Corelli, L. T. Meade, and E. E. Green to be favorites; Dickens is the only "classic" author included on the list, and only three percent of the elder girls surveyed mentioned reading *David Copperfield* (1850). Thackeray, Gaskell, Austen, and Yonge were known to only a few respondents. Low laments in her article that authors she herself adored as a girl—Margaret Oliphant, Alcott, and Juliana Ewing —were not read at all. The other 1906 article on the Colonial girl by Constance N. Barnicoat includes survey results from British and Colonial girls. Barnicoat notes that Colonial girls of ages fifteen to eighteen were easily influenced by the reading of their peers and tended to read adventure books, historical fiction, history, and works dealing with their particular colony. She lists some favorite novelists of Colonial and Indian girls: Edna Lyall, Louisa May Alcott, Mrs. Henry Wood, Charlotte Mary Yonge, Marie Corelli, L. T. Meade, Edward Bulwer-Lytton, and G. A. Henty, for example. For British girls' favorites, Barnicoat places Edna Lyall on the top of her list, with Henry Seton Merriman, Robert Louis Stevenson, Elizabeth Gaskell, Marie Corelli, and Bulwer-Lytton, among others, also noted.[71]

In *The New Girl*, Sally Mitchell offers another variation on girls' favorites, indicating that Victorian American novels also had impact on the Victorian British girl as well as vice versa. The books that British girls most frequently mention as childhood favorites include *Little Women* and Susan Warner's *The Wide, Wide World*, along with Charlotte Brontë's *Jane Eyre* (1847), Hesba Stretton's *Jessica's First Prayer* (1867), and Olive Schreiner's *The Story of an African Farm* (1883). Other British and American titles often mentioned include Anna Sewell's *Black Beauty* (1877), Beecher Stowe's *Uncle Tom's Cabin* (1852), Frances Hodgson Burnett's *The Secret Garden* (1911), Mrs. Henry Wood's *East Lynne* (1861), and Yonge's novels: *The Heir of Redclyffe* (1853), *The Daisy Chain* (1856), and *Heartsease* (1854) (Sally Mitchell, *The New Girl* 143).

Critics today may dismiss many of these works as overly sentimental and moral, but we cannot deny that this fiction had multiple attractions for girl readers that simply cannot be overlooked. For example, Alcott and Yonge create large happy families that Victorian girls coveted. Spirited Jane of *Jane Eyre* and lively Jo March of *Little Women* still engage readers today, at least in the first half of each novel, as does outspoken Lyndall in *The Story of an African Farm*. In the 1860s, Jane Eyre and Jo March join with other inquisitive girl heroines like Carroll's Alice of

Alice's Adventures in Wonderland (1865), who tumbles into a virtual wonderland.

Reading Selections of Fictional Women

Along with changes in reading selections of girl readers come changes in what girls in nineteenth-century fiction are reading. The girls in Yonge's morally improving *Abbey Church* read Sarah Trimmer's conservative, didactic Georgian children's book *Fabulous Histories*, later titled *The History of the Robins* (1786). Trimmer's robin family could easily be a human one: the adventures of the little robins named Pecksy, Flapsy, Robin, and Dick instruct children about proper behavior, morals, and benevolence to animals, a common Georgian theme. In aligning her work with Trimmer's, Yonge places it in a class of conservative fiction. In *Amy Herbert*, another book published in 1844, Elizabeth Missing Sewell's heroine reads fairy tales, common only in liberal households. Amy's fairy tale reading softens the moral tone of Sewell's novel about a girl who finds joy visiting the rectory and keeping close to her mother's side. Two decades later, Carroll's Alice recites satirical versions of didactic poems that were strongholds in the Victorian era.[72] Carroll's work intimates the gradual shift from didactic to entertaining literature for children that occurs over the course of the nineteenth century. Moreover, at the end of the nineteenth century, Kenneth Grahame celebrates creativity and invention in *The Golden Age* (1895): his fictional children read *Alice* and imaginatively follow Carroll's curious Alice down a rabbit hole.[73]

The journeys that fictional girls take as readers and the literary companions who accompany them spark this investigation. Literary and visual representations of the woman reader reveal diverse practices and ideologies for and against women's reading pervasive throughout the Victorian age. The act of reading and the very texts heroines read or reject reveal their characters and the thematic intentions of books written during an era when authors and illustrators envision women's reading as a genteel and a subversive act.[74]

II

Fictional Representations of the Woman Reader

2

Transatlantic Representations of the Woman Reader

Charlotte Brontë's *Jane Eyre* (1847), Henry James's *The Portrait of a Lady* (1881), Louisa May Alcott's *Little Women* (1868, 1869), and Emily Brontë's *Wuthering Heights* (1847)

An artist captures on one canvas what an author, alternately, describes through a series of events and actions. To recall Henry James's phraseology from his 1884 essay "The Art of Fiction," at times an author acts akin to "his brother the painter,"[1] creating representations of daily life analogous to the domestic scenes in nineteenth-century genre painting. The figure of the woman reader captured the imagination of Victorian British and American authors who created vivid images of women readers absorbing a book, longing for it, or subverting its power. Charlotte Brontë, Henry James, Louisa May Alcott, and Emily Brontë fix our attention on what and how a woman reads. Like their sister and brother artists, they use the novel as a forum to weigh choices available to women who recognize the potency of a book.

Other nineteenth-century authors demonstrate how a writer, to varying degrees, approximates a painter's art. However, this conscious pairing of authors teases out the complexity of a transatlantic development that cuts across traditional boundaries of nationality and gender. Male and female authors on both sides of the Atlantic raise and, in some cases, challenge central concerns and ideologies fueling the debate over women's reading while revealing perceived vulnerabilities and delights of independent reading. Despite their seeming dissimilarities, Charlotte Brontë's *Jane Eyre* (1847), a mid-nineteenth century novel by a British woman, and James's *The Portrait of a Lady* (1881), a late-nineteenth-century novel by an American man, arguably offer the most stunning representations of a Victorian woman reader. Both portrayals respond to dominant ideologies informing the controversy—the arguments of gentility, education, and empowerment in favor of women's reading as well as the moral argument against women's ready access to books. A second transatlantic pairing —the March sisters of Alcott's *Little Women* (1868, 1869) and Emily Brontë's Catherine Earnshaw and Catherine Linton of *Wuthering Heights* (1847)—reveals polarized ideologies of women's reading that reverberated in, respectively, Victorian America and Britain. Affirming the arguments of socialization and gentility, the book, in Alcott's domestic fiction, emerges as a spiritual and moral guide that confirms cultural assumptions while in Emily Brontë's Gothic, Romantic novel, it is a patriarchal force that obliges women to act out in the margins to find their own voices. Brontë, however, shows reading as a means for empowerment and gentility in her second generation of women. Independently, these four nineteenth-century representations have historical value; collectively, they confront us, as readers, with coexisting and competing ideologies surrounding women and books and invite us to consider our own interpretive strategies.

THE WOMAN READER AND THE POWER OF THE IMAGINATION

Charlotte Brontë and Henry James offer representations of women readers that rival visual art. Brontë opens *Jane Eyre* with an image of Jane musing over pictures in Thomas Bewick's *History of British Birds* (1797, 1804) in a secluded window seat of Gateshead Hall.[2] Likewise, James introduces Isabel Archer reading a book about German philosophy in an isolated room of her Albany home in *The Portrait of a Lady*. Family members interrupt Jane's and Isabel's reading. James sweeps Isabel away from her cloistered world where she discovers the limitations of her book knowledge. James's depiction of the room Isabel reads in, "a region of delight or of terror,"[3] also describes where Jane Eyre reads furtively in the window seat, even as it appears to the adult Jane. These opening images fix a picture of a determined woman reader and the power of the female imagination for British and American audiences.

"There was no possibility of taking a walk that day," Brontë informs us in the opening line of *Jane Eyre* (5). Brontë describes the rain as "penetrating," the wind "cold," the clouds "sombre" on this particular dreary November afternoon (5). Akin to an artist, Brontë carefully positions Jane in a sequestered corner of an ancestral hall and even notes the color of the curtains that surround her; Jane recalls, "I mounted into the window-seat: gathering up my feet, I sat cross-legged like a Turk; and, having drawn the red moreen curtain nearly close, I was shrined in double retirement" (5).[4] The landscape captivates the observer's—though not the reading woman's —gaze. Brontë depicts "a scene of wet lawn and storm-beat shrub" and "ceaseless rain sweeping away wildly before a long and lamentable blast" outside the windowpanes that "protect" but do not "separate" Jane from the natural elements (5). Sandra Gilbert and Susan Gubar note how Brontë uses opposing images of ice and fire to characterize this opening scene and Jane's entire pilgrimage, which they compare to Bunyan's *Pilgrim's Progress* with elements of traditional fairy tales: "For while the world outside Gateshead is almost unbearably wintry, the world within is claustrophobic, fiery, like ten-year-old Jane's own mind."[5] The intensity of the wintry landscape matches the vividness of the scarlet drapery enfolding Jane and the passion of her reading.

Jane indulges in independent reading, a delicious but dangerous act that incensed those espousing the moral argument against women's reading. "A novel read in secret is a dangerous thing" (338), so cautions Sarah Stickney Ellis in *The Mothers of England* (1843). Orphaned, Jane has no mother to select reading material from her Uncle Reed's bookshelves that might inculcate traditional values, as Ellis prescribes. Nor can we deny the element of escape in this opening reading scene that Brantlinger notes in *The Reading Lesson:* "reading in chapter 1 of *Jane Eyre* is represented as an escape from the exclusions visited upon Jane by Mrs. Reed and the Reed children."[6] Simultaneously, Brontë cautiously raises the possibility of Jane reading for empowerment. To recall Sicherman, "Reading provided space —physical, temporal, and psychological—that permitted women to exempt themselves from traditional gender expectations, whether imposed by formal society or by family obligation" ("Sense and Sensibility" 202). Jane's independent reading in the window seat provides her space free from "family obligation" to read, think, and imagine.

Brontë calls attention not only to what and where Jane reads but also to how she reads. The raging winds and rain draw her attention "At intervals" (5), but Thomas Bewick's *History of British Birds* captivates her. The curtains, which Gilbert and Gubar call "oppressively scarlet" (340), shield her only momentarily from the harshness of the Reed family members— some of whom torment her, all of whom do not love her—as well as from our gaze. However, Brontë does not exclude her dear "reader" from Jane's literary moment for long. "Each picture told a story;"—Jane tells us— "mysterious often to my undeveloped understanding and imperfect feelings, yet ever profoundly interesting: as interesting as the tales Bessie sometimes narrated on winter evenings, when she chanced to be in good humour" (6). Bessie tells stories that blend old fairy tales and ballads with passages from Samuel Richardson's *Pamela* (1740) and John Wesley's *The History of Henry, Earl of Moreland* (1781). Jane is privy to them only when Bessie is in "good humour." She finds Bewick's natural history book equally stimulating to her imagination.

Jane's reading of Bewick requires us to become active readers, a point Robert Scholes makes in *The Rise and Fall of English* (1998). Recalling Walter Benjamin's ideas from "The Work of Art in the Age of Mechanical Reproduction," Scholes argues that "In the age of mass media, literature has, as Walter Benjamin put it, lost its aura.... This is the chance, this is the moment, to change reading from a passive to an active process ... to replace priestly exegesis and passive coverage with attention to reading as a process."[7] To read a textual passage fully, the reader must "look for the intertextual twigs and leaves from which it hangs" (Scholes 165) and ponder the life and reading of the author that influences, in turn, his or her literary creation.

With Jane, we return to a source that influenced the life of Charlotte Brontë as well as Jane Eyre. The Brontë family owned an 1804 edition of Bewick's *History of British Birds*. This two-volume nonfiction work inspired the early drawings of Charlotte, as well as her siblings, all of whom imitated Bewick's drawings (for example, Branwell, the snapping farmyard dog; Charlotte, a water bird on a stormy sea; Anne and Emily, bird studies, including Emily's vignette of a peasant herding geese).[8] In 1832, Charlotte wrote a poetic eulogy to Bewick. In "Lines on Bewick," Charlotte re-creates Bewick's vignettes as she reveals her enchantment with his work. In a letter dated July 4, 1834, Charlotte also recommends this natural history book to her dear friend Ellen Nussey.[9] Moreover, both Anne and Charlotte include Bewick in their respective fictions: young Arthur Huntingdon fetches his copy of Bewick in *The Tenant of Wildfell Hall* (1848), giving his mother and Gilbert Markham a private moment to come to an understanding; Jane Eyre's estimation of Bewick differs from young Arthur's recommendation of this "natural history with all kinds of birds and beasts in it, and the reading as nice as the pictures."[10]

Jane shares her author's fascination with Bewick's images. As a child, Jane shows interest in Bewick's descriptions of the solitary coast of Norway and the barren, "death-white realms" (6) of Iceland, Greenland, Lapland, and Siberia, but she favors the "vignettes" (6) over the text. Those who read *Jane Eyre* and *History of British Birds* side by side notice Jane's descriptions of Bewick's pictures of desolate ships, phantoms, thieves, ghastly moons, and a solitary graveyard correspond to the small black-and-white woodcuts (approximately 2" by 3") positioned as tailpieces to Bewick's chapters on various water birds. That Bewick's woodcuts loom large in our imaginations as readers suggests that Jane, in describing them, also re-creates them.

As Jane Stedman notes in "Charlotte Brontë and Bewick's 'British Birds,'" Bewick's pictures cluster naturally into two groups: birds in their natural habitats, and a variety of small detailed vignettes unrelated to the birds described in the chapters they accompany.[11] Bewick created many attractive images of birds in their natural surroundings,[12] but Jane ferrets out vignettes in the volume on water birds akin to the wild, at times desolate, landscape of the moors, home of Charlotte Brontë. Seemingly overlooking beautiful pastoral images of a peacock or a swan, Jane lingers over pictorial moments that speak to her sense of isolation while living amongst the Reeds at Gateshead. The vein of popular culture that Bewick presents in vignettes with foul and turbid weather, supernaturalism, death, and violence fascinates Jane.

The dual aspect of Brontë's narration—the mature Jane reflecting upon and rekindling the power these images held for her as a child—resonates in these graphic descriptions:

> I cannot tell what sentiment haunted the quite solitary churchyard, with its inscribed headstone: its gate, its two trees, its low horizon, girdled by a broken wall, and its newly-risen crescent, attesting the hour of eventide. The two ships becalmed on a torpid sea I believed to be marine phantoms. The fiend pinning down the thief's pack behind him I passed over quickly: it was an object of terror. So was the black, horned thing seated aloof on a rock, surveying a distant crowd surrounding a gallows. (6)

In Jane's accounting of Bewick, we glimpse her alienation and despair, leading her to seek physical and psychological space in a moment of reading enjoyment: "With Bewick on my knee, I was then happy: happy at least in my way" (7).

The graveyard image that sparks Jane's fancy is easily identifiable. It appears as a small tailpiece to the chapter on "Razor-Bill" in volume 2 of the 1804 Newcastle edition, "Containing the History and Description of Water Birds" (fig. 5). A few details Jane does not describe strengthen the

Fig. 5. Illustration by Thomas Bewick, tailpiece to "Razor-Bill," for Thomas Bewick, *History of British Birds*, vol. 2, 1804.

haunting sentiment of the scene as narrated. The words on the "inscribed headstone" read forebodingly, "Good Times & Bad Times & all Times get over." The tombstone casts a long and dark shadow, and the "newly-risen crescent" throws an eerie light on the solitary trees, broken wall, and gate, as well as the tombstone. Although Jane admits, "I cannot tell what sentiment haunted the quite solitary churchyard," the scene exudes a weird air.

Jane is haunted by another easily identifiable Bewick image of a fiend pinning down a man's pack.[13] It forms a tailpiece to a chapter titled "Black-Throated Diver" in Bewick's second volume on water birds in the 1804 edition (fig. 6). Again, no connection exists between this woodcut and the text describing the black-throated diver, which may explain why these two images appear in different places in later editions.[14] Perhaps the piercing look and sharp antennae-like horns of the winged fiend make this illustration an "object of terror" to Jane, who quickly passes over it even in her "autobiographical" reflections. The bird-footed fiend has a menacing arrow-shaped tail. The fiend's sharp spear restrains the man whom Jane interprets to be a thief. The lumpy shape of the pack on the "thief's" back suggests it contains a body, presumably a dead one (Stedman 38). To compound the terror, the thief seems unaware of the fiend pinning him from behind.

Ignorance to a horror behind one's back likely made this image disturbing to Jane Eyre, forever unsure of her next encounter with an unsympa-

Fig. 6. Illustration by Thomas Bewick, tailpiece to "Black-Throated Diver," for Thomas Bewick, *History of British Birds*, vol. 2, 1804.

thetic servant, a cruel aunt, or a menacing cousin. In the Red Room incident, Brontë conveys the terror of being caught unaware from behind. Jane recounts, "Four hands were immediately laid upon me, and I was borne upstairs" to the Red Room (9). The phantom that Jane hallucinates while locked in the room possesses the glittering eye of the fiend in the Bewick vignette.

Absorbed by her own stories sparked by Bewick's pictures, Jane fears interruption. Interruption comes in the form of her tyrannical fourteen-year-old cousin, John Reed, who perceives the Bewick book as his material possession: "You have no business to take our books; you are a dependent, mamma says; you have no money; your father left you none; you ought to beg, and not live here with gentlemen's children like us, and eat the same meals we do, and wear clothes at our mamma's expense" (8). The book here functions as a potent objective signifier of gender and social class. John reminds Jane that all her other favorites on the shelves are his: "they *are* mine; all the house belongs to me, or will do in a few years" (8). As disreputable a character as John Reed becomes, he is—as he declares—the heir of Gateshead. Chameleon-like, the book that Jane prizes changes meaning when John pronounces, "Now, I'll teach you to rummage my book-shelves'" (8), and flings it at his dependent female cousin to "teach" her a lesson. Jane falls against the door and cuts her head, which is filled with the power of stories usurped from John Reed's bookshelves.

Jane is not defeated but aroused. She verbally retaliates: "Wicked and cruel boy! . . . You are like a murderer—you are like a slave-driver—you are like the Roman emperors!" (8). Jane's adult reflection on this moment of rage seems equally telling: "I had read Goldsmith's 'History of Rome,' and had formed my opinion of Nero, Caligula, &c. Also I had drawn parallels in silence, which I never thought thus to have declared aloud" (8). Here Stefan Morawski's point that "Quotes are a proof if not a badge of learning" lends insight into Jane's verbal retaliation.[15] Although Jane is not actually quoting Goldsmith, she refers to the contents of *History of Rome* and reveals her desire to "read widely and eagerly" for self-education (Cruse, *The Victorians and Their Reading* 349). That Jane hurls book references at John in a retaliation that she never dreamed of verbalizing can also be read as an attempt to claim her intellectual place in a household where she is not on equal terms with her cousins following the death of her uncle, her sole protector.

Jane's attempt to claim rank fails. The representation of Jane reading Bewick's *History of British Birds* first becomes bloodied and then vanishes, only to reappear unexpectedly in a much later chapter. Summoned to Gateshead at Aunt Reed's deathbed, a now grown Jane Eyre enters the breakfast room where she, as a child, read in the window seat. Her eyes immediately move to the bookcases: "I could distinguish the two volumes of 'Bewick's British Birds' occupying their old place on the third shelf" (200). Time, for these volumes, has stood still. The shelf just above the Bewick books contains two other childhood favorites that offered Jane psychological space: Jonathan Swift's *Gulliver's Travels* (1726), a "cherished volume" (17) Jane turns to after her terror in the Red Room;[16] *The Arabian Nights*, the text Jane reads for "nourishment" following her insufferable first interview with Mr. Brocklehurst.[17] In *The Art of Allusion in Victorian Fiction* (1979), Michael Wheeler suggests that "Jane's responses to her favourite books are directly attributable to obsessions and anxieties which are engendered in a hostile environment" (30). To take Wheeler's point further, these volumes and Gateshead Hall preserve Jane's childhood traumas, leading her to read for empowerment or arguably escape. The adult Jane confirms: "There was every article of furniture looking just as it did on the morning I was first introduced to Mr. Brocklehurst: the very rug he had stood upon still covered the hearth. . . . The inanimate objects were not changed" (200).

On her visit to Aunt Reed, Jane also draws imaginative pictures seemingly inspired by her and Charlotte Brontë's childhood reading (Stedman 36). Jane sketches "a glimpse of sea between two rocks; the rising moon, and a ship crossing its disk; a group of reeds and water-flags, and a naiad's head crowned with lotus-flowers, rising out of them; an elf sitting in a hedge-sparrow's nest, under a wreath of hawthorn-bloom" (204–5). In creating vignettes of water, moon, sprite, and rock, Jane rekindles the inhospitable environment that she experienced as an unloved child at Gateshead. In this later scene, we recall how Jane attempts to empower her imagination through solitary reading, risking social disapproval and punishment by seeking refuge in Bewick in a curtained window seat.

Akin to a nineteenth-century genre painter, Henry James, like Charlotte Brontë, creates an immediate, rich representation of a woman reader in *The Portrait of a Lady*. In this work, James explores the role of modern novelistic portraiture. Isabel Archer eventually struggles against Gilbert Osmond, who endeavors to make life like a work of art and turn Isabel into an object in his portrait collection. As Dorothy Van Ghent observes, "The title, *The Portrait*, asks the eye to see. And the handling of the book is in terms of seeing."[18] Much discussed is the open-endedness of the novel, giving a sense, in some critics' eyes, that the total portrait remains incomplete. However, my interest in *The Portrait of a Lady*, as in *Jane Eyre*, lies in its depiction of heroine as reader in the first part of the novel.[19] While Charlotte Brontë allows us to glimpse the empowerment gained in independent reading and the repercussions of such an act, James pokes fun at the gentility argument in Isabel's attempt to gain culture and also reveals the ways novel-reading colors one's experience of life. Offering a window into the moral argument against women's reading, *The Portrait of a Lady* suggests that a woman who spends countless hours reading unguided and alone may be ill-prepared for and disappointed in the realities of domestic life.

James constructs his representation over several chapters. Before her father's death, Isabel returns after a ten year's absence to the ancestral home of her grandmother where she lived at various times as a child. Although Isabel is already in England when James provides this flashback, James, nonetheless, allows us to see Isabel "alone with a book," just as her aunt finds her: "One wet afternoon, some four months earlier than the occurrence lately narrated, this young lady had been seated alone with a book. To say she was so occupied is to say that her solitude did not press upon her; for her love of knowledge had a fertilizing quality and her imagination was strong" (23). James positions his imaginative reader in a rain-swept ancestral setting that rekindles the wetness of shrub and lawn Jane sees outside her window at Gateshead. The piercing rain and wind keep each imaginative reader within the home, focused on her reading; Jane notices the weather only "At intervals" (5), and Isabel gives "cosmic treacheries" (25) little thought. Equally, the pelting rain could be seen to disconnect each reader from the outside world that, in its penetration and coldness, does not seemingly approve the reader's occupation and intensifies her passion for reading in seclusion.

That Isabel Archer finds her grandmother's "large, square, double house" (23) "romantic" (24) says something about her character, as does her favorite reading room. Akin to a Gothic novel such as A. Radcliffe's *The Mysteries of Udolpho* (1794), Isabel's reading chamber is a "mysterious apartment which lay beyond the library and which was called, traditionally, no one knew why, the office" (25). A door from the clandestine office opens up to the street, but Isabel prefers not "to look out, for this would have interfered with her theory that there was a strange, unseen place on the other side" (25). The room has more dilapidated furnishings than the rest of the house, a musty smell, and a mysterious past (evident in the way the door is secured by bolts and sidelights and is covered with green paper). Like Jane Eyre's window seat, Isabel's reading sanctuary, which removes her from the likelihood of interruption, is arguably a retreat into the deep recesses of her own strong and active imagination.

James divulges in these opening pages how Isabel selects her books, why she reads, and the way she reads: "The foundation of [Isabel's] knowledge was really laid in the idleness of her grandmother's house, where, as most of the other inmates were not reading people, she had uncontrolled use of a library full of books with frontispieces, which she used to climb upon a chair to take down. When she found one to her taste—she was guided in the selection chiefly by the frontispiece—she carried it into a mysterious apartment" (24–25). While Jane seemingly reads to liberate herself from her oppressive reality, Isabel reads to escape from idleness, although both read pictures.[20] Having had no real education, Isabel experiences free run of a library that presumably belonged to her grandfather. Since her companions are largely nonreaders, she, like Jane, has no one to supervise her self-education in a man's library—a source of concern to one with a conservative Victorian frame of mind.

James does not provide us with particular titles as Charlotte Brontë does, but he reveals the types of books Isabel reads: classic authors in translation (49), Browning's poetry, George Eliot's prose, romantic novels, *The*

Spectator, as well as the "latest publications" (36) and German philosophy (26). The choices are not arbitrary. Isabel's reading material allows us to characterize her and discern James's own reading preferences and biases. Isabel's reading reflects an abiding theme in James's novels—the uncultured American lacks the cultivation of his or her European contemporaries. Isabel may be attempting to bridge that gap, though she is hindered since she must read continental authors in translation. James does not specify which classic authors Isabel reads, but we can presume Ivan Turgenev, Honoré de Balzac, and Gustave Flaubert, whose works James prized. James does not define "latest publications," but tells us Isabel reads *The Spectator*, a London periodical founded in 1828 and known for its reviews and essays on politics, economics, and literature. That Isabel is reading what was considered a serious and moderately conservative journal suggests her fervent desire to acquire knowledge and views of mainstream British culture.

James includes in Isabel's list two British authors whose works James read, admired, and owned. George Eliot is known for her fiction, which sets compelling psychological portraits of ordinary lives in social contexts to dramatize the unavoidable pressures and social condition of her age. Eliot was at the pinnacle of her fame in the 1870s when James favorably reviewed *Middlemarch* (1872) and *Daniel Deronda* (1876); he had both volumes in his personal library.[21] James discussed them at length in letters to his friends and family, and he drafted a possible beginning for *The Portrait of a Lady* just after *Daniel Deronda* appeared.[22] James also mentions Eliot's fiction in the preface to *Portrait* (xi). Critics have suggested James's characterization of Isabel seems indebted to her fictional sisters, Dorothea Brooke of *Middlemarch* and Gwendolyn Harleth of *Daniel Deronda* (Long 106); how fitting it is that Isabel—akin to her creator—is reading Eliot. While Dorothea Brooke gains a measure of happiness in her second marriage to Will Ladislaw, Eliot had a predilection for disappointed heroines like Gwendolyn Harleth and Maggie Tulliver of *The Mill on the Floss*, a book which James also owned (Edel and Tintner 31). Isabel's reading of Eliot's disillusioned heroines arguably forecasts her own fate: following her marriage to Osmond, she finds no consolation in her life.

James does not specify whether Isabel reads the poems of Robert or Elizabeth Barrett Browning. Given James's predilection for his characters to read the classics, Isabel could be reading the poems of Elizabeth Barrett Browning; her *Aurora Leigh* (1857) was published in nineteen editions by 1885, suggesting its popularity when *The Portrait of a Lady* appeared. It might have warned Isabel Archer about the biting realities of bourgeois Victorian marriage to which she falls prey. However, James's library contains eight works by Robert Browning, and none by Elizabeth, so Isabel is likely reading the poetry of Robert Browning (Edel and Tintner 23–24). Included in James's library is *The Ring and the Book* (1869), a complex and demanding twelve-book poem about a seventeenth-century murder trial set in Rome. It secured Robert Browning's reputation and showcases his interests in psychology, theology, philosophy, thought, and expression. Given its range and complexity, this work might have attracted Isabel Archer in her eagerness to improve her mind.

We observe Isabel reading an unnamed "history of German Thought" (26): "she kept her eyes on her book and tried to fix her mind. It had lately occurred to her that her mind was a good deal of a vagabond, and she had spent much ingenuity in training it to a military step and teaching it to advance, to halt, to retreat, to perform even more complicated manoeuvres at the word of command. Just now she had given it marching orders and it had been trudging over the sandy plains of a history of German Thought" (25–26). German philosophy seems an unusual choice for a young woman, suggesting Isabel's naivete as a reader. James also seems to be intimating Isabel's pretentiousness in thinking she can understand the nuances of complex movements in the European Enlightenment, the German idealist school, and the writings of important thinkers—Kant, Hegel, Schiller, and Schopenhauer—some of whom James read himself (Edel and Tintner 56). Immanuel Kant's attempt to define rational understanding with precision had a major impact on Western thought and no doubt carries into James's playful description of Isabel attempting to be clever in training her mind in the manner Kant presents his philosophical writings on the role of reason in understanding the world. James's word choice reveals her effort is futile: Isabel does not march lightly over the "sandy plains" of history but "trudges" over this sophisticated ground. James's characterization of Isabel as a reader shows a woman's fruitless attempt at self-education to gain gentility.

The choice of German thought—as opposed to French or British philosophy—may be more revealing of James than Isabel Archer. German idealistic philosophy was a source for transcendentalism, a school associated with Ralph Waldo Emerson which influenced James and is evident in *The Portrait of a Lady*. Robert Long suggests that "It is against the background of Emerson and the New England Transcendentalists that Isabel's ideals and striving have been sketched" (120). Isabel's optimistic Emersonian ideals—which she voices, for example, when rejecting Lord Warburton; or follows by marrying a fortune-hunter, believing her inheritance is somehow apart from her "self"—might account for her poor judgment and disappointment with concrete reality. Even in this scene of Isabel reading German philosophy situated early in the novel, Isabel seems keenly aware of her shortcomings and is dissatisfied with the scattered way her mind works. Is it to her credit that she chooses a book about a school of philosophy characterized by precision and objectivity? These are qualities she seemingly lacks, but not ones that James endorses for her. Rather, James interrupts her futile attempt to discipline her mind: "Suddenly she became aware of a step very different from her own intellectual pace" (26)—the arrival of her Aunt Touchett.

Lydia Touchett recreates the opening image of Isabel reading when she tells her son, Ralph, why she has taken up her niece: "I found her in an old house at Albany, sitting in a dreary room on a rainy day, reading a heavy book and boring herself to death. She didn't know she was bored, but when I left her no doubt of it she seemed very grateful for the service" (42). Dreariness pervades the room where Isabel reads, much as it colors the weather, the book itself, and our view of Isabel's reading. The tome of German thought that trains Isabel's "vagabond" mind now appears "heavy," corresponding to the pelting of the "crude, cold rain" (25), isolating Isabel from the real world that she has attempted to know through books. In James's first description of Isabel as a reader, "her solitude did not press upon her" (23). Isabel's "love of knowledge" and "strong" imagination vanish from the image, which now bares Isabel's pretensions of superiority. Seen through the eyes of a nonreader, Isabel is "boring herself to death," not disciplining or cultivating her mind. If Isabel can be so easily distracted, perhaps she really is bored.

Known as the "'intellectual' superior" (30) of the three Archer sisters, Isabel is "a prodigy of learning" (49) in her uncultured American circle. She also possesses an active imagination and thinks life in England will be "just like a novel!" (17). She is destined to be a disappointed heroine.[23] Isabel's exuberance in connecting novels to life crystallizes the moral argument in the debate against women's unsupervised reading: domesticity cannot possibly match a heroine's life as glamorized in fiction.[24] Even James likens his own fictional creation to a goddess in a narrative poem when he notes that "Her reputation of reading a great deal hung about like the cloudy envelope of a goddess in an epic. . . . The poor girl liked to be thought clever, but she hated to be thought bookish; she used to read in secret and, though her memory was excellent, to abstain from showy reference" (35). That Isabel reads in secret to avoid the reputation of being too "bookish" and refrains from exhibiting her learning reveals that her sense of self is contradictory. On the one hand, she is pulled toward the male library and reads important works of philosophy and literature, showing off perhaps to herself. Simultaneously, she is keenly aware that these "masculine" inclinations do not conform to society's construction of domestic femininity; this she has no doubt gleaned from reading novels and listening to her married sisters who want to see her "safely married" (30). Another contradiction emerges in Isabel when James tells us, "She had a great desire for knowledge, but she really preferred almost any source of information to the printed page" (35). Why, then, does Isabel continually turn to reading to learn about the world? Why does she even think that novels and books will tell her at all about reality?

Arriving at her aunt and uncle's early Tudor home called Gardencourt, Isabel promptly asks her uncle all about British life, manners, customs, and politics, but then is curious to know if his ideas match descriptions she has read in books. Her uncle feigns ignorance of books and proclaims, "well, I don't know much about the books.... I've always ascertained for myself—got my information in the natural form" (56). Isabel's incessant turning to an implied "unnatural" form (reading) to sate her curiosity hangs around her like a "cloudy envelope of a goddess in an epic" and becomes a reflection of her boring, cloistered life.

In "The Art of Fiction," James argues that the highest aim of the novel is to provide a realistic record of life: "The only reason for the existence of a novel is that it does attempt to represent life. When it relinquishes this attempt, the same attempt that we see on the canvas of the painter, it will have arrived at a very strange pass" (662). In *The Portrait of a Lady*, Isabel naively believes that the novel represents life. Her characterization as a reader offers a window into reasons fueling the moral argument condemning a woman's free access to books: consuming novels will raise false expectations about love and marriage and, in turn, bring about dissatisfaction with conventional domesticity.

Isabel queries whether English people are as they seem in novels: "I don't believe they're very nice to girls; they're not nice to them in the novels" (57). We cannot be sure what novels she reads beyond those by Eliot since James notoriously leaves novels unnamed in his fiction. Adeline Tintner speculates that many of James's characters are reading novels that "sound as if they were written by James himself" (Edel and Tintner

87). Isabel, like countless Americans, could be reading other popular English choices by Charlotte Brontë and Charles Dickens that also lined James's bookshelves (Edel and Tintner 23, 30). Novels by Eliot, Brontë, and Dickens could easily have provided Isabel with ample examples of patriarchal males—Eliot's Grandcourt, Brontë's Rochester, and Dickens's Steerforth—who break or compromise a young woman's spirit, trust, and virtue. If Isabel looks to novels as a reflection of reality to guide her in the drawing room, then the heroines she models do not seem to have taught her what to expect or fear from a lover (to prepare for her future), nor how to fashion her destiny (as advocates of reading for empowerment recognized that Trollope's heroines might do). Akin to the heroines she reads about, Isabel learns to behave in a passive manner and falls victim to Osmond, who is not "very nice" to her.

During Isabel's conversation with her uncle, James shifts our attention away from Isabel's searching of the novel for life's lessons to the inaccuracy of the novel—a major theme of James's: "I believe the novels have a great deal of ability, but I don't suppose they're very accurate" (57). As this paragraph proceeds, Uncle Touchett recalls how a visiting novelist erroneously caricatures him as an American gentleman and twice more repeats the notion that novels are not always "accurate" (57). To James, the novel is not a substitute for real life but an artifice. The clever but fervently non-"bookish" Isabel does not gain gentility, valuable knowledge, a realistic expectation of life, or empowerment from books. However, I would argue that in his attention to detail, James, like Charlotte Brontë, creates a representation of a searching and self-divided woman reader that captures the "air of reality," as he describes it in "The Art of Fiction," and "competes with his brother the painter in *his* attempt to render the look of things, the look that conveys their meaning, to catch the color, the relief, the expression, the surface, the substance of the human spectacle" (665).

POLAR VISIONS: THE WOMAN AND THE BOOK

American and British authors focus not only on the woman reader but also on the book a woman reads, writes, subverts, or utilizes to reveal dominant ideologies of women's reading and illuminate theme and character. The March sisters' reading of Bunyan's *Pilgrim's Progress* (1678, 1684) in Alcott's *Little Women*, Jo March's decision to stop writing sensation fiction, Catherine Earnshaw's writing in the Bible in *Wuthering Heights*, and Catherine Linton's teaching Hareton to read all present competing images of the woman reader responding to a text. These literary examples also illuminate ideologies current throughout the period: the moral argument against reading certain types of fiction, and several arguments favoring women's reading—socialization and gentility as well as empowerment. Alcott's and Emily Brontë's representations of the woman reader may be less visually immediate than Charlotte Brontë's and James's, but I have chosen descriptive passages throughout Alcott's and Emily Brontë's novels that invite contemporary readers to bring associations to bear on these texts which envision women's reading choices and practices.

Alcott presents reading as a means to gain respect and admiration in one's social circle (gentility argument) and to promote family unity and conformity (socialization argument). It was commonly believed that reading in the Victorian domestic circle would guide the development of young children and curb the habit of independent reading, which we witness in *Jane Eyre* and *The Portrait of a Lady*. Alcott's classic that brought her instant international fame fosters gentility in two ways. The March sisters faithfully read their copies of *Pilgrim's Progress* that Marmee gives them as guidebooks on that cheerless Christmas when Father March is away at war. Reading improving literature, the March sisters embrace goodness, duty, and selflessness; gain respect and admiration in their family circle; and assume their places as model wives, mothers, and homemakers—a path Alcott herself resisted.[25] In turn, contemporary women readers who made the March sisters their "intimate friends" vicariously gained mainstream values from them. In fact, critics still consider *Little Women* a rite of passage for American girlhood and praise it because, as Nina Auerbach claims, it "is a deathless book, one that contains its author's best self. Its hopes and defeats are those of all women."[26]

The March sisters dutifully read a book that exerted great influence in nineteenth-century British and American culture, though not on ours today. While Charlotte Brontë arguably sets Jane Eyre on a pilgrimage, Alcott consciously uses *Pilgrim's Progress* as a framing device to develop the pilgrimages of Meg, Jo, Beth, and Amy March in part 1, "Little Women" (1868), and part 2, "Good Wives" (1869).[27] Translated into well over 100 languages and dialects, *Pilgrim's Progress* appealed to uneducated and intellectual nineteenth-century readers and was the most widely read and appreciated book next to the Bible.[28] While certainly not a children's book, this two-part allegory imbued with Bunyan's Puritan theology was one of several adult books commonly given to children before the market for gender-specific literature blossomed in the mid-nineteenth century. From the opening chapter of part 1, Alcott recognizes the socialization potential of *Pilgrim's Progress* to mold her characters into "little women,"[29] as Father March calls them.

Pilgrim's Progress permeates chapter 1 of *Little Women* titled "Playing Pilgrims," a direct invocation of Bunyan. Other chapter titles, such as "Amy's Valley of Humiliation," "Meg Goes to Vanity Fair," and "The Valley of the Shadow," recall Bunyan's work. Marmee also invokes Bunyan to rally the girls out of their personal "Slough of Despond." She reminds her daughters how, as children, they play acted *Pilgrim's Progress;* carrying bags on their backs to symbolize their burdens, they imitated Christian as they traveled from the "City of Destruction" (the cellar) to the "Celestial City" (the top of the house). While the youngest, Amy, fears she is too grown up to play act the story, Marmee reminds them of the role this inspirational book should still play in their lives: "We never are too old for this, my dear, because it is a play we are playing all the time in one way or another. Our burdens are here, our road is before us, and the longing for goodness and happiness is the guide that leads us through many troubles and mistakes to the peace which is a true Celestial City. Now, my little pilgrims, suppose you begin again, not in play, but in earnest, and see how far on you can get before Father comes home" (11). Through Marmee's eyes, Bunyan's drama transforms into the play of life: the road is the metaphorical path the girls travel as they await the end of the Civil War; their burdens are the sacrifices they make, such as forgoing Christmas presents "when our men are suffering so in the army" (3); the end of the war is "the peace which is a true Celestial City" (11). Marmee's inspirational message becomes literal when she gives each of her daughters the Bunyan book. On this cheerless Christmas, with no stockings hanging in the fireplace, Marmee has scraped together enough money to buy each girl her own copy of *Pilgrim's Progress* to inspire her pilgrimage toward adulthood. Alcott vividly describes how each sister finds a brightly colored "guidebook" (11), as Marmee calls it, under her pillow on Christmas morning. Meg vows, "Mother wants us to read and love and mind these books, and we must begin at once.... *I* shall keep my book on the table here and read a little every morning as soon as I wake, for I know it will do me good and help me through the day" (13). The other girls promise to follow her example: "'Thank you for our books; we read some, and mean to every day,' they cried, in chorus" (15). Their socialization instantly goes into effect: the March sisters become little pilgrims in chapter 2. At Marmee's request, they willingly give their Christmas breakfast to a poor family, offering those in need "A Merry Christmas," the title of chapter 2.

The four March sisters are very different in the beginning of the book, but they become increasingly more alike in "Good Wives." Alcott responded to commercial pressure from her publisher and fans in finding suitable matches for her fictional women. In the first book, Jo pronounces, "I can't get over my disappointment in not being a boy" (5). Unlike James's Isabel Archer who "hated to be thought bookish" (35), Jo seems content to be known as a "bookworm" (3). She relishes playing the male roles in the family theatricals and cuts off her locks to take her part in the war effort. The most intellectual of the sisters, Jo, as companion to Aunt March, reads Oliver Goldsmith's *The Vicar of Wakefield* (1766) when her aunt falls asleep, writes thrillers for "penny dreadfuls," and quotes Harriet Beecher Stowe's *Uncle Tom's Cabin* (1852) to her sisters. In her way, Jo enjoys "playing mother" (39) to sweet, shy, angelic Beth while Meg monitors and "mothers" the vain, pretty Amy. At first it seems that Marmee offers Jo the freedom to remain in the March family circle: "Right, Jo; better be happy old maids than unhappy wives, or unmaidenly girls, running about to find husbands" (93). Jo welcomes these words; she wants to be a writer and turns down a match to Laurie to pursue her career, but she ultimately conforms to convention.

The eldest, Meg, whom we discover eating apples and crying over Charlotte Mary Yonge's popular success *The Heir of Redclyffe* (1853), always reminds Jo to be more genteel. Described as a "womanly little woman" (363) and a "little mother" (372), Meg follows the most traditional path of the sisters. Her pilgrimage leads her first to the "Celestial City" of marriage and motherhood, finding "a woman's happiest kingdom is home, her highest honor the act of ruling it not as a queen, but as a wise wife and mother" (373). Meg's pilgrimage affirms mainstream values and the goodness that Bunyan's work preaches. Likewise, Amy marries Laurie, finding her own happy "kingdom" as a wife and mother. We witness Beth reading *Pilgrim's Progress* on her deathbed, her soul growing stronger as her body dwindles. In "The Valley of the Shadow," Beth tells Jo her own secret: she is not long destined for this earth. Unlike her sisters, Beth has no burden to carry on her pilgrimage. With Beth's death in chapter 40, Jo renounces her ambition to be a writer, a main theme of the novel.

In chapter 27, "Literary Lessons," Jo is writing her first novel and publishing "very mild romances in *The Spread Eagle*" (252) when she comes across a "penny dreadful" akin to *Frank Leslie's Illustrated Newspaper* (in the mid-1860s, Alcott wrote regularly for this paper, which published gossip and murder trials as well as sensation fiction). Jo boldly decides to write a sensation story and win the $100 prize advertized in the fictional *Blarneystone Banner* (Alcott won the $100 prize for her first sensational story, "Pauline's Passion and Punishment" [1863], published in *Frank Leslie's*). Not surprisingly, Jo earns the prize, and her thrillers with racy titles like "A Phantom Hand" and "Curse of the Coventrys" augment the dwindling March family income, just as Alcott's sensation fiction kept the Alcott family financially afloat. Alcott's representation of Jo writing sensation fiction possesses historical and biographical significance. Alcott's heroine publishes sensation fiction under a pseudonym and reads what she writes, mirroring Alcott's secret writing career and double literary life during the 1860s. Leona Rostenberg's 1940s discovery of Alcott's writing under the pseudonym A. M. Barnard as well as Stern's 1950 autobiography and 1970s collections of Alcott's thrillers forever influenced the Alcott reevaluation. While Alcott gained the attention of feminist critics because of her anonymous and pseudonymous sensational writing for which she, at least for a time, had a true passion, Jo's realization of the addictive and moral evils of the trashy literature she writes bolsters Alcott's presentation of reading as a means to socialize her "little women" and maintain the boundaries of Victorian convention that she privately overstepped.[30]

Through the censure of Professor Bhaer, the middle-aged man Jo marries, Alcott advances a moral argument against a genre that weaves secrets, poison, drugs, bigamy plots, adultery, scandal, impersonations, and murder into seemingly respectable domestic settings.[31] Although it raised the ire of nineteenth-century antifiction critics on both sides of the Atlantic, this subgenre of British fiction, as John Sutherland notes, was enormously popular in the 1860s. It "carried a primary meaning of 'electrical stimulus.' This was fiction that jolted the reader's nerves."[32] During a decade when the demand for this type of fiction was high, sensation fiction becomes a vehicle for Alcott to present a conservative ideology she struggled to follow despite her ambivalence toward domesticity, as Martha Saxton argues in her feminist biography *Louisa May* (1977).

Although Alcott initially calls this sort of writing "that class of light literature in which the passions have a holiday" (251), her criticism becomes scathing in chapter 34, "A Friend." Living in New York as a writer and teacher, Jo, for a time, makes a career out of writing trash, "for in those dark ages, even all-perfect America read rubbish" (324). Jo submits a pseudonymous thriller to the *Weekly Volcano*, which she passes off as the work of a friend. Alcott paints a vivid picture of a blushing and blundering Jo March, attempting to conceal her secret literary life from her editor, Mr. Dashwood.

Akin to diatribes against sensation fiction such as Reverend Francis Paget's *Lucretia* (1865), Jo quickly grows addicted to the lurid material in the stories she researches, writes, and ultimately reads. We see Jo pillaging records to learn about crime and vice that ultimately affect her character: "Mr. Dashwood rejected any but thrilling tales, and as thrills could not be produced except by harrowing up the souls of the readers, history and romance, land and sea, science and art, police records and lunatic asylums, had to be ransacked for the purpose" (327–28). Next we learn that Jo "unconsciously . . . was beginning to desecrate some of the womanliest attributes of a woman's character. She was living in bad society, and imaginary though it was, its influence affected her, for she was feeding heart and fancy on dangerous and unsubstantial food" (328). To advance a moral message, Alcott employs pervasive nineteenth-century tropes of the book as mental food and a companion. Jo has left her genteel circle for the "bad society" of sensationalism. Ingesting the unwholesome food of thrillers, she is "desecrating" what was considered sacred in her Victorian American world. To recall the arguments of Beecher and Beecher Stowe and Ellis, sensational literature read in secret has no place in a woman's well-balanced reading diet.

When Jo witnesses Professor Bhaer's negative reaction to an illustrated "penny dreadful," she blushingly betrays her clandestine writing career. Here likening sensational stories to liquor, Bhaer speaks straight from the advice books of the day: "There is a demand for whisky, but I think you and I do not care to sell it" (333). Worse, the thriller becomes "poison in the sugarplum": "They haf no right to put poison in the sugarplum, and let the small ones eat it" (333). His words dovetail those of Lady Ridding, who compares overconsumption of novels to a "surfeit of sugar-plums" in "What Should Women Read?" (1896) (29); Florence Nightingale, who equates reading addiction to opium abuse in *Cassandra* (1852, rev. 1859); and Dr. Kellogg, who compares reading to liquor and drug addiction in *The Ladies' Guide in Health and Disease* (1882).

Jo feels "as if the words *Weekly Volcano* were printed in large type on her forehead" (333). Alcott creates a vivid picture of an ashamed woman writer and reader. The "penny dreadful" becomes her personal scarlet letter.[33] Jo buys into the ideologies of consumption and addiction and becomes conscience-stricken by her own "immoral" writing and the connotations it carries. As Alcott herself did in the 1860s, Jo stops writing sensation fiction. Recalling the most fervent opponents of women's reading, Jo pronounces her thrillers "trash ... each is more sensational than the last. I've gone blindly on, hurting myself and other people, for the sake of money. I know it's so, for I can't read this stuff in sober earnest without being horribly ashamed of it, and what *should* I do if they were seen at home or Mr. Bhaer got hold of them" (334). "Blinded," this time by the harsh criticism of Professor Bhaer, she "stuffed the whole bundle [of sensation stories] into her stove, nearly setting the chimney afire with the blaze" (334). Alcott's description of Jo burning her stories brimming with every imaginable vice creates an image memorable for its conservatism.

Tomboyish Jo loses her buoyancy in part 2 and becomes a more sedate, nurturing figure in *Little Men* (1871) and *Jo's Boys* (1886), revealing how Alcott prescribed to the more conventional gender expectations of her age, at least in her juvenile fiction. Jo's foray into sensationalism not only advances arguments against women's unsupervised reading but ultimately promotes the socialization argument that women read only improving literature like Bunyan. Marrying Bhaer at the end of *Little Women*, Jo acquiesces: "I may be strong-minded, but no one can say I'm out of my sphere now, for women's special mission is supposed to be drying tears and bearing burdens" (448). To readers today, Jo seems far more persuasive as a tomboy than a married schoolmistress willingly "bearing burdens." Her marriage is disappointing, her conversion into a dutiful "little woman" unconvincing, although Jo's transformation affirms that Marmee and her three married daughters have completed their separate pilgrimages and jointly arrived at the Celestial City. The closing image of Marmee opening her arms "as if to gather children and grandchildren to herself" (459) counters the shadow of Amy's potential loss of her beloved daughter. Society's construction of domestic femininity grows stronger with Marmee's closing words—"Oh, my girls, however long you may live, I never can wish you a greater happiness than this" (459).

Perhaps more interesting to a readership today is the way another nineteenth-century woman author, Emily Brontë, creates a memorable representation of a rebel reader in a book that Gilbert and Gubar provocatively call a radical revision of *Paradise Lost* (1667), a "Bible of Hell" (Gilbert and Gubar 248). Brontë's *Wuthering Heights* counters Alcott's presentation of a religious book as a spiritual and moral guide. Catherine Earnshaw's subversion of the "good book" can be seen as a form of rebellion that Brontë endorses but essentially foils. We do not actually see Catherine Earnshaw as a reader. Rather, we discover her small library when Lockwood is forced to spend the night in Heathcliff's inhospitable home. Brontë first identifies a mildewed book that Lockwood's candle has "injured": "It was a Testament, in lean type, and smelling dreadfully musty: a fly-leaf bore the inscription—'Catherine Earnshaw, her book,' and a date some quarter of a century back."[34] It is not surprising to find a Bible in the room which belonged to Catherine Earnshaw Linton as a child. Well-known is George III's 1805 pronouncement that every child, rich and poor alike, be taught to read the Bible. Especially during the first half of the Victorian period, girls were expected to read the Bible. Of more interest, however, Catherine Earnshaw has written in her Bible. In *Wuthering Heights*, Brontë reveals how a woman expresses her voice in the margins of a book that symbolizes male patriarchal power and stability.

Sabotaging the most sacrosanct of religious books, Catherine transforms the "good book" into a personal "diary" in which to express injustices and woes. While Alcott creates an edifying image of the March sisters dutifully reading Bunyan and becoming stalwart pilgrims or "little women," Emily Brontë fixes an image of Catherine subversively blanketing every inch of blank page with her writing (38). Lockwood describes Catherine's entire library as "select" and "well used, though not altogether for a legitimate purpose; scarcely one chapter had escaped a pen and ink commentary—at least, the appearance of one—covering every morsel of blank that the printer had left. Some were detached sentences; other parts took the form of a regular diary, scrawled in an unformed, childish hand" (38). Catherine is, in fact, making the Bible "her book," as she inscribes it. In the margins of the Bible and other religious tomes (including one by Reverend Jabes Branderham), Lockwood finds disconnected sentences and entire diary entries. One extra page ("quite a treasure probably when first lighted on" [38]) bears a daring caricature of the exacting Joseph, the servant who tyrannically oversees the children's religious education with his staunch Methodism.

Lockwood attempts to decipher Catherine's character through traces of writing, which Brontë describes as "faded hieroglyphics" (38) and Brantlinger calls "palimpsests" (*The Reading Lesson* 118).[35] With Lockwood, we piece together Catherine's personality from the writing in her book. On a rainy Sunday, for example, to Hindley's perverse delight, Joseph preaches a three-hour sermon in the cold garret to the shivering Catherine, Heathcliff, and the plough-boy, ranged in a row on a corn sack. Catherine confides how she and Heathcliff fling Joseph's "good books" into the dog kennel; their slinging of evangelical tracts, *The Helmet of Salvation* and *The Broad Way of Destruction,* marks a rebellion against Joseph's attempts to improve their souls. Hindley swears and mistreats Catherine and Heathcliff. In turn, Catherine reaches for ink and her Bible to write for twenty minutes, a self-conscious reference to her furtive subversive writing, which she herself interrupts to scamper on the moors with Heathcliff. Solitary intellectual activity raised the ire of those who espoused the moral and socialization arguments. Living at a time when women could not educate themselves easily, conduct themselves freely, or inherit property, Catherine daringly acts out in the perimeter of her own Testament: her commentary mocks the very contents of the holy book.

In Catherine's childhood room, Lockwood also discovers Catherine's writing, in large and small characters, spelling out various versions of her name—"*Catherine Earnshaw,* here and there varied to *Catherine Heathcliff,* and then again to *Catherine Linton*" (38).[36] The writing, again, is not prominently positioned. Scratched on the window ledge, it inscribes her social instability as well as her marginal position in society. In reading Catherine's writing on the window ledge, Lockwood falls into a dream wherein the "fire" of Catherine's spirit returns as a spectre. The spirit cries to be let into her window, now the home of one who, as she declares passionately in one of Brontë's most memorable lines, is "more myself than I am" (86). Lockwood finally loosens the grasp of the hand of the wailing child and piles Catherine's own books against the window to block her entry. Lockwood describes the experience as an "intense horror of nightmare" (42) and rationalizes why the experience occurred: "In spelling over the name scratched on the window-ledge. A monotonous occupation, calculated to set me asleep, like counting, or—" (44). From the vantage point of gender and power, the experience speaks to the authority of the written words that the rebellious young Catherine authored.

The authority of her words, however, is limited. Heathcliff has shut up Catherine's childhood room into which Lockwood stumbles for the night (37). Moreover, as J. Hillis Miller notes, Lockwood confronts an accumulation of confusing material that he and we as readers attempt to piece together to make meaning ("*Wuthering*" 372). We look away from Lockwood to Catherine's marginal writings as well as to the commentary the housekeeper, Nelly Dean, provides. Such a process inscribes the marginal place of Lockwood, Catherine Earnshaw, and ultimately the author herself. The narrative instability of the novel speaks to the condition of the woman writer in the early to mid-nineteenth century; likewise, Catherine's own unstable position as "*Catherine Earnshaw*, here and there varied to *Catherine Heathcliff*, and then again to *Catherine Linton*" (38) expresses the restrictions of gender in Victorian society. While *Pilgrim's Progress* in *Little Women* emerges as a guidebook that maintains the status quo, the Bible in *Wuthering Heights*, remade into Catherine Earnshaw's book, preserves the voice of a woman who rebels against the prevailing politics of gender.

As Margaret Homans notes in *Bearing the Word* (1986), the story continues without the first Catherine and linguistically replaces her since Brontë presents the death of Catherine Earnshaw Linton and the birth of her daughter, the new Catherine and Linton's heir, in the same sentence.[37] Homans continues, "Within a text whose symbolic operation mirrors the law of patriliny, it is entirely appropriate to have the mother's death, which includes her death within language (her loss of name), coincide with the perpetuation of the law, for the operation of the symbolic order has all along required the mother's absence. The production of the heir makes the mother not just superfluous but impossible, without identity because unnameable" (81). Catherine's name passes to her daughter, and she becomes the deceased mother. Even if the novel continues without the first Catherine, who struggles for autonomy and loses her adult identity, arguably she returns, as John Sutherland notes, as a child ghost to haunt Heathcliff, successfully distracting him from his plan to disinherit the first Catherine's daughter's and Hareton's descendants from their ancestral lands, Thrushcross Grange and Wuthering Heights, respectively.[38]

In her representation of the second Catherine, Brontë provides a more successful model of reading as empowerment, "showing how society repudiated [the first] Catherine's originality" (299), as Gilbert and Gubar suggest. While Catherine Earnshaw identifies with nature and not paternal law, Catherine's daughter is, to recall Gilbert and Gubar, "culture's child, a born lady" (299). The first Catherine strives to become a lady during her five-week stay at Thrushcross Grange, but her daughter Catherine feels at home in this cultured world ruled by the genteel and learned Edgar Linton. The second Catherine, a dutiful daughter, comes into the novel as "heir" and is thus identified with what Homans calls "the Law of the Father" (82), a symbolic representation of patriliny. Catherine Linton becomes a victim of that law when Heathcliff maneuvers her marriage to the sickly Linton and arranges for her fortune to fall to himself when Linton dies (242–43).[39] As Heathcliff's servant Zillah rightly notes about Catherine's economic status, "what will all her learning and her daintiness do for her, now? She's as poor as you, or I—poorer—I'll be bound, you're saving —and I'm doing my little all, that road" (252). Nonetheless, "culture's child" rises above her own disenfranchisement by civilizing Hareton and Wuthering Heights.

Catherine Linton Heathcliff, an avid reader since childhood, finds herself living at Wuthering Heights without any books. Heathcliff destroys the second Catherine's books, so, unlike her mother, she cannot even use a book subversively as writing material: "I have no materials for writing, not even a book from which I might tear a leaf" (255). Ironically, the illiterate Hareton Earnshaw, Catherine's first cousin whom Heathcliff brutishly molds in his image, has access to books though he cannot even read the name above the door of his ancestral home. Lockwood remarks on entering Wuthering Heights, "a quantity of grotesque carving lavished over the front, and especially about the principal door, above which, among a wilderness of crumbling griffins and shameless little boys, I detected the date '1500,' and the name 'Hareton Earnshaw'" (10). Hareton admits to Catherine, "It's some damnable writing, . . . I cannot read it" (194). Male property means social power, and the Earnshaw line is established three hundred years before the novel begins. Heathcliff—a foster-child with a marginal social status similar to the family housekeeper, Nelly Dean— manages to bring under his power Hindley Earnshaw as well as Hindley's son Hareton and Isabella Linton when he becomes the property owner of Wuthering Heights and Thrushcross Grange.

Described as "sensitive though uncultivated" (257), Hareton remains doggedly devoted to Heathcliff, but he wishes to read to gain Catherine's approval. Reading has no place in the rough and uncultivated world of the Heights. Nonetheless, reading leads Hareton to literacy, culture, and love. The educated, refined, and bright Catherine Linton Heathcliff initially rejects Hareton's attention; she refuses to read to him, mocks his "vile mistakes and mispronunciations" (256) of her favorite works, and rejects his gift of books: "I shall connect them with you, and hate them" (257). Hareton, in turn, "gathered the books and hurled them on the fire" (257). Here, Brontë offers us a memorable image of blazing texts that also recalls the first Catherine and Heathcliff's throwing Joseph's evangelical tracts in the dog kennel. In contrast to Jo March's incineration of her sensation fiction, Brontë offers no moral argument: Hareton acts out of anger and frustration at his unsuccessful attempt at "higher pursuits" (257). He fails to win the approval of Catherine, who signifies the more genteel world of the Grange.

Whether out of boredom or loneliness, Catherine eventually reaches out to Hareton and becomes his reading tutor. Six months after the burning books incident, Lockwood returns to the moors on a whim. Through Lockwood's eyes, we see Catherine and Hareton as readers and young lovers. Catherine insists that Hareton pronounce the word "contrary" correctly before she favors him with a kiss: "The male speaker began to read—he was a young man, respectably dressed, and seated at a table, having a book before him. His handsome features glowed with pleasure, and his eyes kept impatiently wandering from the page to a small white hand over his shoulder, which recalled him by a smart slap on the cheek, whenever its owner detected such signs of inattention" (261). Clearly in command, Catherine teases Hareton when he mispronounces a word, cuffs him when his attention wanders, and bends over him to "superintend his studies" (261). Referred to as the "owner" of the book Hareton learns to read—Catherine, as reader, empowers her life far more than the young Jane Eyre. Along with the ghost child Catherine, Catherine Linton ousts Heathcliff and legitimizes Wuthering Heights, civilizing its rightful heir.

In this reading scene, Brontë weighs the relationship between literacy, social class, property, and genteel culture. Catherine facilitates Hareton's "transformation from peasant 'brutishness' and illiteracy to some approximation, at least, of middle-class culture and respectability," as Brantlinger observes; "Hareton, it seems, is well on his way to becoming another Edgar Linton, if not another Lockwood" (*The Reading Lesson* 119–20). A nod to the gentility argument, reading allows Hareton, born a gentleman, to realize his inborn cultivation and take his place alongside Catherine, born a lady. The rightful dynastic owner now knows that the name above the threshold of the Heights is, in fact, his own name before he comes into possession of it when Heathcliff dies intestate. Moreover, Catherine Linton Heathcliff becomes the rightful heir of the Grange where together she and her now literate and more cultured partner will begin a life together "afraid of nothing" (285), according to Lockwood.

Lockwood again turns to Nelly Dean to understand the transformation he witnesses between Hareton and Catherine. Nelly first confides how Catherine cleverly opens books to tantalizing parts to bait Hareton. Nelly also explains how Heathcliff unintentionally facilitates their reconciliation: growing obsessed with the first Catherine's haunting, Heathcliff banishes Hareton (who uncannily resembles Catherine) from his sight, and Hareton finds himself in Catherine's company in the kitchen. Through Nelly, we learn how Catherine offers Hareton a book to teach him to read, and he grudgingly accepts it. Nelly paints a vivid picture of love blossoming in their newly forged reading alliance, though it is less telling of the dynamics of class, power, property, and gender than the representation Lockwood offers: "I perceived two such radiant countenances bent over the page of the accepted book, that I did not doubt the treaty had been ratified, on both sides, and the enemies were, thenceforth, sworn allies" (267).

Even here we observe Catherine and Hareton from the perspective of an outsider. Akin to Lockwood and Catherine Earnshaw, Emily Brontë was an outsider, in her case of the male literary world. Like her sisters Anne and Charlotte Brontë as well as Alcott, she elected to write under a pseudonym. Critics better received Emily Brontë's work when Ellis Bell was thought to be a man. Critics describe Emily Brontë as a "doubly atypical woman" (Pykett, *Emily Brontë* 13), intensely private, reclusive, elusive, and reserved, while alternately possessing a secret fire, literary power, and mystery. Her biographers have long been confronted with a two-fold problem: lack of material about her life; and filtered material, gleaned through reminisces principally of Charlotte and her friends Ellen Nussey and Elizabeth Gaskell, who wrote *The Life of Charlotte Brontë* (1857). Struck by the ways *Wuthering Heights* both reflects and resists the prevailing fictional practices of its time, Pykett concludes: "In her efforts to write, Emily Brontë 'wanders' between past and present, Romantic and Victorian, realism and romance; she steers a path between the dominant male tradition and the marginalised female tradition, between the largely female tradition of didactic fiction, which invoked duty to God, the family and the community, and the alternative traditions of Gothic and a poetic of the free spirit. Out of the struggle to find her own place and voice comes [her] work" (35). The character of Catherine Earnshaw, likewise, exhibits this same movement between convention and "alternative traditions" as she struggles to find her place and express her voice. She succumbs to gender expectations by marrying Edgar Linton, a man of respectability and property, clearly the socially sanctioned choice. However, in pitting Heathcliff against Linton in a sexual triangle, a common trope in Victorian fiction, Brontë exposes the compromise of a genteel marriage even before Catherine's wedding occurs. Brontë offers a more hopeful if less original picture of a woman reader in the second generation: reading becomes not only a means to acquire an education and culture but to empower both Catherine, a victim of patriarchal law, and Hareton, a victim of Heathcliff's cruelty. Dutiful in a way her mother is decidedly not, Catherine Linton more successfully navigates the law of patriarchy. Becoming heir of the Grange and civilizing the dynastic owner of the Heights, the second Catherine offers enduring testimony for the argument of women's reading as empowerment.

. . .

Collectively, these transatlantic representations of women readers show women who learn lessons from books, adhere to their messages, long for books, appropriate them, burn them, challenge their authority, and use them to improve their lives. Whether a tool for socialization or a means of empowerment, reading plays an undeniable role in the development of these reading women in a form of fiction that Henry James admits, in his 1884 defense of the English novel, "Only a short time ago . . . was not what the French call *discutable*" ("The Art of Fiction" 661). When the Brontës, James, and Alcott created these works, the novel was still not "discutable" in some circles, as these authors—akin to visual artists—aptly envision. From these fictional representations, which explore domestic life from the vantage point of a literate woman's access to books, we begin to see the complex ways women's reading became inscribed and dramatized within a genre hotly contested in the reading debate.

3

Prophetic Reading

Maggie Tulliver of George Eliot's *The Mill on the Floss* (1860)

In *The Mill on the Floss* (1860), George Eliot provides a striking representation of a nineteenth-century woman reader. Akin to Jane Eyre and Isabel Archer, Maggie Tulliver reads independently and without supervision. Maggie is of the impressionable age when commentators feared the biological, medical, addictive, and moral repercussions of girls' reading. As Flint notes, "'Girls read too much and think too little' was a common complaint. Indiscriminate consumption was believed to weaken the mind and turn the necessity for print into a drug-like craving" (*The Woman Reader* 90). While Maggie is not a reading addict, a metaphor I explore in the next chapter, she craves books "with *more* in them."[1] Print culture becomes essential to Maggie's intellectual life, confounding the conservatives of St. Ogg's, who criticize her for not reading discriminatingly enough.[2]

Eliot directs us to the books Maggie reads as well as where she reads and how she reads. Three key texts Maggie reads at important junctures in her life illuminate dominant ideologies governing women's reading—the biological model and the socialization and moral arguments against women's reading habit (which Eliot does not endorse), and arguments for education and empowerment. As in Jane Eyre's reading of Bewick, the texts that Maggie reads lead us to Eliot's life and the literary sources that influenced her and her fictional creation. An examination of Maggie's reading requires us to "change reading from a passive to an active process" (Scholes 164). For example, Keats makes frequent Shakespearian allusions in his letters; to ponder them thoughtfully, Scholes contends, "it is clear, one must know Shakespeare as well" (166). Likewise, I argue that to read Eliot's novel reflectively, we must know Daniel Defoe's *The Political History of the Devil* (1726), Anne Louise Germaine de Staël's *Corinne, or Italy* (1807), and Thomas à Kempis's *The Imitation of Christ* (1426).

In this respect, *The Mill on the Floss* demonstrates what happens to a book when it is introduced into another literary work of art. To recall the concept of "ekphrasis," the storytelling impulse of Eliot's narrative art affects, as well as remakes, the texts introduced in her novel. Moreover, Maggie's reading is prophetic. The books that absorb Maggie Tulliver, some of which she refashions, give us insight into her characterization, develop themes, and foreshadow the plot. We discern her unconventional nature; her conquest of her cousin Lucy's beau; her eventual ostracization from the righteous society of St. Ogg's; her repression, a central theme in Eliot's fiction;[3] and her death by drowning.

Known for her love of books since childhood, Maggie Tulliver reads passionately and far more intelligently than her brother, Tom, who prefers nature to book learning. To her father's dismay, Maggie, in Edward Tulliver's words, is "allays at her book!" (17) As Carla L. Peterson notes in *The Determined Reader*, "similar to Puritan tradition, Mr. Tulliver is deeply suspicious of the printed word: he avoids book reading, he does not write much, and he even finds oral argument puzzling work."[4] Tulliver exhibits an ambivalent pride in Maggie. He boasts about her intelligence: "she can read almost as well as the parson" (13); "It's a pity but what she'd been the lad—she'd ha' been a match for the lawyers, *she* would" (19). However, he simultaneously fears for his daughter, observing: "a woman's no business wi' being so clever; it'll turn to trouble, I doubt" (17). Tulliver also remarks at the beginning of the novel, "when a man's got brains himself, there's no knowing where they'll run to; an' a pleasant sort o' soft woman may go on breeding you stupid lads and 'cute wenches, till it's like as if the world was turned topsy-turvy. It's an uncommon puzzlin' thing" (19–20).

Eliot was keenly aware that a family with a girl more intelligent than her brother was "uncommon puzzlin'" to her fictional St. Ogg's and her contemporaries. Tom's schoolmaster, Mr. Stelling, espouses the biological argument that men's and women's brains are differently constituted. Geddes and Thomson summarize this difference in *The Evolution of Sex* (1889), "Man thinks more, women [sic] feels more."[5] The male mind was rational and capable of deep critical inquiry and insight. In contrast, the female mind was quick, intuitive, emotional (one advice book writer notes, a woman's "emotions are probably a more vital part of her than her reasoning faculties").[6]

Buying into this biological model of intellect, Stelling declares that girls "can pick up a little of everything, I daresay.... They've a great deal of superficial cleverness; but they couldn't go far into anything. They're quick and shallow" (150). Maggie finds herself "oppressed by this dreadful destiny" (151). She longs to inquire deeply and reason critically, qualities that her conservative Victorian community considers inherently masculine. Maggie has the literary appetite and intellect of a man: "Even at school she had often wished for books with *more* in them: everything she learned there seemed like the ends of long threads that snapped immediately" (286). It is not surprising that the passionate girl who drives nails into a fetish to symbolize her earthly misfortunes and craves the affection of her more restrained brother also wants *"more"* from her education (286).

Eliot endorses women's reading for education through Maggie's longing for Byron's poems and all of Scott's historical novels (influential to Eliot, Gaskell, and the Brontës). Maggie confesses in chapter 3 of book 4 that poets and sages interest her more than saints and martyrs. Maggie even imagines "she would go to some great man—Walter Scott, perhaps—and tell him how wretched and how clever she was, and he would surely do something for her" (287). She is quick to display her book learning to family members and visitors. She offers to help Tom with his lessons. When she runs away to the gypsies, she even instructs them about Columbus and geography (109). She hungers for learning and begins "to nibble at this thick-rinded fruit of the tree of knowledge, filling her vacant hours with Latin, geometry, and the forms of the syllogism, and feeling a gleam of triumph now and then that her understanding was quite equal to these peculiarly masculine studies" (287). Here Eliot reveals that Maggie's intellect is deep enough to handle "masculine studies" and a classical education. Later, when Maggie represses her longings, she denies herself the pleasure of books. As she turns her passion for knowledge inward, she spurns Latin, math, philosophy, and literature as vehemently as she once expresses her longing to learn these subjects.

In contrast, in the second chapter of book 1, we find Maggie Tulliver sitting on a stool by the fire, absorbed by the pictures of a book in her lap, which happens to be *The History of the Devil*. Defoe's work (originally titled *The Political History of the Devil*) seems an unusual choice for childhood reading. *The History of the Devil*, as Eliot refers to it, was then one of Defoe's most popular works, although it did not originally appear under his own name.[7] Critics consider Defoe, a writer of the Puritan tradition, the intellectual contemporary of those he assails in this book: Bunyan and John Milton. With an element of irony, Defoe attempts to treat supernatural phenomenon as a matter of logical and historical inquiry. The "history" comprises two parts: ancient history, covering the origin of the devil, his expulsion from Heaven, his influence on mankind (beginning with Eve's fall), and his renewed presence in the world; and modern history, focusing on the devil's influence in the world and means of conversing with mankind. The first part memorably attacks Milton and *Paradise Lost*, which Defoe considers a fine poem but a "devil of a history."[8] The second part, particularly an engraving titled "Ducking a Witch" (fig. 7), sparks Maggie's curiosity and philosophical musings. Four plates originally engraved for an 1814 edition, and dated 1815, appear in early-nineteenth-century editions of *The History of the Devil*, such as Maggie was presumably reading. While Wallis executed the frontispiece (patterning it after Raphael's *Satan Chained*), G. M. Brighty drew the other three engravings, including the one that mesmerizes Maggie.

Unconventional Maggie admits to her father's friend Mr. Riley that "the reading in this book isn't pretty—but I like the pictures, and I make stories to the pictures out of my own head, you know" (19). Akin to Charlotte Brontë and Henry James, Eliot calls our attention to the way Maggie reads. Illustrations often told a story, and Victorian graphics through mid-century likely had a larger audience than any type of literature.[9] While it was not uncommon to "read" telling clues in images accompanying a work, the image, for Maggie, prompts her creative imagining. Here Eliot, like Brontë, nods to the argument of reading as empowerment: Maggie's stories come "out of [her] own head" (19). As Homans comments, "At this point in the story, Maggie feels both free to read independently and to imagine freely" (123). Eliot also assures us, "There were few sounds that roused Maggie when she was dreaming over her book" (16), again suggesting a deep imaginative engagement with the text leading her beyond the book itself into a private realm of her own.

Riley advises Maggie to put aside *The History of the Devil* and get a "prettier" (18) book, one that will morally instruct her rather than lead her to mischief. History and religious books were the safest choices for women, as advice book writer W. C. Waterhouse maintains in *Thoughts on Moral and Spiritual Culture*. Riley approves of *Pilgrim's Progress*, which Marmee gives her daughters in *Little Women*.[10] Embarrassed that he bought *The History of the Devil* at Partridge's sale for the value of its binding, Tulliver claims he was unaware of its contents: "They was all bound alike—it's a good binding, you see—and I thought they'd be all good books" (18). The identical bindings of the volumes—which Tulliver tells us were principally sermons and Jeremy Taylor's *The Rule and Exercises of*

Fig. 7. Illustration by G. M. Brighty, "Ducking a Witch," for Daniel Defoe, *The History of the Devil*, 1819.

Holy Living (1650) and *The Rule and Exercises of Holy Dying* (1651)—lead him, wrongly, to assume that the reading material will all be the same. In his conversation with Riley, Tulliver comes to admit, "it seems one mustn't judge by th' outside" (18). The society of St. Ogg's will not have such a revelation: judged "by th' outside" when journeying down the river with Stephen Guest, innocent Maggie stands condemned, like Defoe's witch in the engraving "Ducking a Witch."

This image accompanies Defoe's section on the ways the devil works through astronomers, interpreters of dreams, and witches, etc. Defoe notes: "if a woman be a witch, throw her into a pond, and if she be a witch, she will swim, and it is not in her own power to prevent it; if she does all she can to sink herself it will not do, she will swim like a cork" (373). The accompanying image offers Maggie far more to "dream over." The setting is ominous: partially covered clouds fail to light up a darkened sky. Five individuals (two men, two women, and a boy) cluster between a barren, grim tree, and a darkened house. The blacksmith dominates the scene: he leers at the witch, who raises her arms dramatically and opens her mouth in fright. The strength in her androgynous figure conveys she is capable of fighting the natural forces, yet the ominous waves suggest the waters will soon close over her head.

Maggie sees the witch as innocent and confides to Mr. Riley about the blacksmith: "He's the devil *really* . . . and not a right blacksmith; for the devil takes the shape of wicked men, and walks about and sets people doing wicked things" (18). Maggie provides an apt overall reading of Defoe. She rightly recognizes that the blacksmith could be a devil in disguise.[11] However, Maggie makes a gendered assertion that misreads Defoe, who argues the opposite: "the walking devils that we have generally among us, are of the female sex; whether it be that the Devil finds less difficulty to manage them, or that he lives quieter with them, or that they are fitter for his business than the men, I shall not now enter into a dispute about that" (Defoe 337).

Concerned for those falsely accused of witchery, Defoe contends: "what will not those savages, called critics, do, whose barbarous nature inclines them to trample on the brightest characters, and to cavil on the clearest expressions?" (374). His critique anticipates Eliot's satire of "those savages" of St. Ogg's, called "the world's wife" (490), who "trample on" Maggie Tulliver by falsely accusing her of being fallen. Even if Maggie misreads Defoe's ideas of gender and deviltry, her sympathetic reading of the witch explains her own position as an untraditional woman in her male-dominated society. As critics have often pointed out, Maggie—the dark-haired, dark complected "gypsy," even by her own admission (300)[12]—is judged a "witch" by St. Ogg's.

The image of Maggie reading a book that Mr. Riley deems "isn't pretty" stamps her character. The "dreadful picture" that Maggie "can't help looking at" (18) foreshadows her fate. Reading the picture, Maggie exclaims: "That old woman in the water's a witch—they've put her in to find out whether she's a witch or no, and if she swims she's a witch, and if she's drowned—and killed, you know—she's innocent, and not a witch, but only a poor silly old woman. But what good would it do her then, you know, when she was drowned? Only, I suppose, she'd go to heaven, and God would make it up to her" (18). Maggie's reading of the witch establishes a fictional pattern to which she falls prey. Condemned as a fallen woman, Maggie faces impossible alternatives in book 7. When the flood waters come, Maggie—like the witch in the drawing—will drown; while this act symbolizes her innocence to St. Ogg's, "what good would it do her then"?

As Carla L. Peterson observes, "It is important to note that, in interpreting this picture, it is Maggie, not Defoe, who comes to the conclusion that the innocent woman must drown and that heaven will be her only reward" (190). While Gilbert and Gubar provocatively connect Maggie's death by drowning to Tom's oppressively rigid moral standards and suggest the punishment is his (493–94), death of the fallen emerges as a convention in Victorian fiction. Nancy Armstrong advances that fiction after midcentury punishes a woman who follows her desires and resists "established forms of political authority" (55), even if her opposition proves hopeless as Maggie's does.

In book 5, after the Tulliver reversal of fortune, Maggie encounters another prophetic book: Madame de Staël's *Corinne*. Now an adolescent, Maggie has secret meetings in the Red Deeps with Philip Wakem (Tom's schoolfellow, son of her father's arch rival). The acutely sensitive Philip urges Maggie to read a work by France's most prominent woman writer of the Napoleonic period to keep her from "starving" her nature (327). *Corinne* foreshadows the Victorian love-triangle plot in *The Mill on the Floss* and the characterization of Maggie, showing how she misses an opportunity of reading for empowerment.

Maggie returns *Corinne* without finishing it because she foresees that the blond-haired Lucile Edgermond will steal the love of Lord Oswald Nelvil from her dark-haired half sister, Corinne. Philip predicts that Maggie will avenge all the raven-haired heroines who lose their lovers to blond-haired rivals. From one vantage point, that is precisely what happens. Dark-haired Maggie tempts Stephen Guest, the lover of her angelic, blond-haired cousin Lucy Deane, who forsakes Lucy for Maggie against Maggie's true will. Even a superficial glance at *Corinne* and *The Mill on the Floss* reveals similarities in the love-triangle plots of, respectively, Lord

Nelvil and Corinne and Lucile Edgermond (half sisters) and Stephen Guest and Maggie Tulliver and Lucy Deane (first cousins).[13] "Sister Maggie," as Eliot contemplated calling her book, resembles de Staël's unconventional raven-haired heroine.[14] Maggie's blond-haired cousin likewise takes after *Corinne*'s Lucile in manner and name. Stephen Guest, like Lord Oswald Nelvil, is torn between his feelings for the dark- and light-haired beauties, though the pampered Guest lacks the valor of Lord Nelvil (who saves an entire village, including its undesirables).[15]

The lives of Corinne and Maggie speak to the limitations restricting women in the nineteenth century, particularly their creators. The novels, respectively, convey de Staël's and Eliot's intimate knowledge of European book culture (German, French, and Italian) as well as a painful awareness of the marginality of a woman who gains "masculine" knowledge or shows "unfeminine" demonstrations of passion.[16] Eliot suffered for pursuing an independent career in her male-dominated London society and then living abroad with her married lover, George Henry Lewes. Madame de Staël withstood similar condemnation because of her commitment to book learning and "masculine studies" as well as her supposed vulgarity. Each author uses her gifted unconventional heroine to comment harshly on a British society that condemns women who veer from its rigid prescriptions or enter a male province, attempting to achieve a classical education.

Renaissance writers and Romantic philosophers (for example, Friedrich and August Wilhelm von Schlegel) fed the aesthetic temperament of de Staël (Carla L. Peterson 43–44). Likewise, Dante, Tasso, Ariosto, and Petrarch captivate Corinne as does Italian Renaissance art and architecture. A renowned artist and poet named after the Greek poet who was Pindar's teacher and muse, Corinne shows off her book learning through her oral addresses and improvisations. She attempts to reconcile the pagan and Christian origins of Western culture whereas Maggie embraces and then rejects Romantic fiction for Christian teachings. Maggie speaks with delight about Scott's romances and Byron's romantic poems, which Eliot also savored. Eliot had keen interest in Romantic authors, including Madame de Staël, and she owned several copies of *Corinne*.[17] Maggie also experiences a pull toward religious readings as Eliot did during two periods of heightened Evangelicalism. Though clever, Maggie does not possess the "genius" of Corinne or de Staël, who was heralded following the publication of *Corinne* and *De l'Allemagne* (1813). Nonetheless, Maggie's intelligence and unconventionality ignite protests from family members and her traditional society.

It is not surprising that each novelist created a heroine with a divided nature. The half-Italian, half-British Corinne identifies with the feminine culture of her Italian mother, but she falls under the influence of the Scottish Oswald, who embodies a patriarchal northern culture. As Carla L. Peterson observes, "Her passion for Oswald creates an irreconcilable conflict between her desire for aesthetic self-expression on the one hand and her desire for approval by patriarchal society on the other; and this conflict leads Corinne, who until this moment had fully enjoyed exercising her artistic talents, to doubt, self-hatred, madness, death" (58–59). Likewise, as John Kucich notes, Maggie's mix of Dodson duty and Tulliver passion "leaves her helplessly self-divided" (137). Stephen Guest and Philip Wakem emerge as inadequate objects of desire.[18] Maggie is one of many of Eliot's characters who "remain endlessly at war with themselves, rather than with society" (Kucich 137). When the tides carry Maggie and Stephen down the river and St. Ogg's condemns her, Maggie becomes an outcast like Corinne, who refuses to follow a conventional path and is ostracized by the Edgermonds.

Living in Italy at the start of the novel, Corinne enchants the reader with her poetry, artistic talent, and beauty, but she also possesses a past she is trying to hide. Her last name is unknown to us, although we eventually learn her father is Lord Edgermond. Following her mother's death, her father adheres to her mother's wishes and leaves Corinne in Florence to be raised by her aunt. Corinne moves to England after her aunt's death, joining her father and Puritanical stepmother, who chastises Corinne for quoting Italian love poetry at the dinner table: "you must try to forget everything that has to do with Italy" (253); "Your talents can help pass the time when you are alone; perhaps you will find a husband who will enjoy them; but in such a small town as ours, whatever attracts attention stirs up envy, and you would never find anyone to marry you if people thought your tastes were foreign to our customs" (253). Here Lady Edgermond vocalizes the socialization argument: a woman should read for the benefit of her husband and to avoid idleness. Uncomfortable with Lady Edgermond's advice and British society in general, Corinne returns to Italy where she meets the man predestined to wed her half sister.

In *The Mill on the Floss* Maggie tells Philip in the Red Deeps, "Take back your *Corinne* . . . You were right in telling me she would do me no good; but you were wrong in thinking I should wish to be like her" (332). Maggie narrates exactly the point where she stops reading the novel: "As soon as I came to the blond-haired young lady reading in the park, I shut it up, and determined to read no further. I foresaw that that light-complexioned girl would win away all the love from Corinne and make her miserable" (332). Philip is the one character who truly understands Maggie's soul, and he predicts *Corinne* will charm her. Living in Italy without a last name or family, Corinne gains fame in a way that Maggie must have envied at this point in the novel aptly titled "Wheat and Tares." Here Eliot suggests that Maggie cannot read beyond society's construction of domestic femininity. Flint concurs in Maggie's reason for not finishing the book: "Maggie, and hence the reader, is made to foresee something of her own inevitable fate according to established patterns of fictionality" (*The Woman Reader* 267–68). Flint also acknowledges, however, that Eliot subverts these conventions that Maggie cannot see beyond.

Maggie views fictional conventions as a predictor for the end of a novel and real life. Maggie's decision "to read no further" than chapter 5, book 16 of de Staël's twenty-book novel is itself troubling. How can Maggie, who always wants "*more*" from books, keep herself from discovering the fate of her dark-haired fictional sister whose destiny she ultimately shares? And how perceptive a reader of *Corinne* is she? Maggie's decision overlooks the complexities of loyalty, duty, and nationalism motivating Oswald's decision to wed Lucile and forsake Corinne, despite his love for her.[19] Equally, Maggie's reasoning does not acknowledge the developments of a plot, which, though predictable, explores the role Corinne plays in her own abandonment (a sisterly act that Maggie echoes in her own love triangle) and the disappointments Nelvil experiences following his marriage to Lucile.[20] Maggie reads de Staël's romance overly simplistically and incompletely. This was a time when woman read mimetically; reading was a way of "introducing the girl vicariously to situations which she might well come across in her own life, or which she would do well to avoid," as Flint contends (*The Woman Reader* 81). Not reading far enough to envision *Corinne* as a paradigm for empowerment, Maggie seemingly overlooks the positive attributes of one who might have stood as an intellectual, artistic role model for her. Had she finished *Corinne*, Maggie would have gleaned information that might well have helped her to revise her destiny.

As intelligent as she is, Maggie interprets conventional romantic plots in terms of her fascination with the dark-haired, unconventional, and unhappy. From childhood, Maggie "had rather a tenderness for deformed things; she preferred the wry-necked lambs, because it seemed to her that the lambs which were quite strong and well made wouldn't mind so much about being petted" (177); when she neglects Tom's rabbits, and they die,

Maggie identifies with the prodigal son (32). She reads Corinne's fate in similar terms. Moreover, Corinne's love for Oswald is doomed much earlier than the point where Maggie stops reading. If the plot of *Corinne* is so predictable, why doesn't she stop reading sooner given her alleged reasoning? Early in the novel, de Staël heavy-handedly foreshadows the destiny of her star-crossed lovers. Corinne reads her lover's expressions as keenly as the architecture of Italy that she describes on their numerous excursions. She recognizes that Oswald will leave her one day. Corinne also gravitates to victimized female protagonists like Shakespeare's Juliet, who suffers a paternal injunction that she and Oswald also face. She convincingly acts the tragic role of Juliet in book 7, which occurs before Maggie stops reading. Corinne watches Mrs. Siddons play Isabella, who goes mad after she marries against her father's wishes, and she eulogizes Roman widows who mourn their husbands—Portia, Agrippina, and Cornelia. These are but some of the clues Madame de Staël provides to foreshadow Oswald's marriage to Lucile Edgermond and Corinne's madness well before the scene where Maggie stops reading and returns her book to Philip.

Buying into the conventions of feminine plotting, Maggie also projects her sympathies for the wayward onto Sir Walter Scott's novels and, in doing so, remakes them. Maggie attests that she will "avenge" her beloved heroines—"Rebecca and Flora MacIvor, and Minna and all the rest of the dark unhappy ones" (332). In *Ivanhoe* (1819), Rebecca, gifted in the arts of healing, nurses wounded Ivanhoe back to health, but suppresses her love for him and ultimately loses him to the fair-haired Lady Rowena. This is Maggie's point of contention, but does Rebecca need vindication? Rebecca's life's work is important to her. When condemned as a witch because of her healing powers, Rebecca proclaims her innocence. Ivanhoe defends her in a trial by combat with her accuser and near-seducer, Sir Brian de Bois-Guilbert, and he saves Rebecca's life. Unlike Rebecca, Flora MacIvor of *Waverley* (1814) is not in a sexual triangle with a blond-haired beauty. The spirited and politically minded Flora (who ultimately retires to a convent) rejects the love of Edward Waverley and encourages him to pursue the fair-haired Rose Bradwardine. Minna Troil of *The Pirate* (1821) also does not have a blond-haired rival. She ultimately separates from Captain Clement Cleveland because he is, as the title declares, a buccaneer. Maggie confides to Philip that she never finishes reading *The Pirate* either, but makes up alternate endings, all unhappy: "I could never make a happy ending out of that beginning" (306). The storytelling impulse in Eliot's narrative recreates Scott's and de Staël's romances. Eliot encourages us to see how Maggie interprets, at times misreads, and even adapts these novels to suit her own needs and dejected state.[21]

Maggie also seems blind to the prophetic truth of Philip's words when he predicts she will steal Lucy's love: "Well perhaps you will avenge the dark women in your own person, and carry away all the love from your cousin Lucy" (332). Maggie angrily retorts: "Philip, that is not pretty of you, to apply my nonsense to anything real, . . . As if I, with my old gowns and want of all accomplishments, could be a rival of dear little Lucy, who knows and does all sorts of charming things, and is ten times prettier than I am—even if I were odious enough to wish to be her rival" (333). The outcome of Eliot's love triangle is not quite as simple as Philip predicts. Maggie steals Stephen's love away from her blond-haired cousin, and, in that respect, she could be seen to "avenge" the dark-haired Corinne. But she refuses Stephen and shares a tragic kinship with Corinne that extends beyond her intelligence, dark hair, and beauty. Corinne and Maggie arguably triumph in becoming vehicles of mourning.[22] Both die without any lover, although in Maggie's case she reunites in a nonsexual bond with her beloved Tom.

Madame de Staël creates a lingering death for Corinne while Eliot invents a natural disaster so that Maggie's prayer for death will be swiftly answered. Both dying heroines are surrounded by natural feminine symbols—Maggie by the waters in which her mother fears she will "tumble in and be drowned some day" (13); Corinne by the heavens containing a moon (Jane Eyre's archetypal mother) partially covered by a cloud (419) (Corinne sadly predicts to Oswald in book 11 that this sign "condemned our love" [196]).[23] The final destinies of the heroines make the novels compellingly alike and demonstrate further how Maggie, in reading of Corinne's destiny, might have found the empowerment to refashion her fate or at least to have foreseen it.

Of importance, when Maggie rejects *Corinne*, she has already taken to heart Thomas à Kempis's fifteenth-century devotional treatise, *The Imitation of Christ*. In "learning to be feminine, her way of reading changes," Homans asserts; "As an adolescent in search of spiritual food and guidance, she becomes an overly literal reader of Thomas à Kempis" (123). Faced with the Tulliver reversal of fortune, her brother's coldness, and the male-dominated, narrow-minded world of St. Ogg's, Maggie becomes Thomas à Kempis's docile pupil. Although she reads two other improving religious books—the Bible and *The Christian Year*[24]—she devours *The Imitation of Christ*, considered second only to the Bible in its influence on Christian thought. Although its mystical tone likely captivates Maggie Tulliver, this improving religious work matches recommendations of conservatives who espoused the socialization argument that reading could mold a woman's character to be modest, dutiful, and self-sacrificing. The devotional treatise preaches simplicity, inner contemplation, and forsaking of earthly pleasure for spiritual fulfillment. Thomas More lauded it as one of three books every Christian should read, and noteworthy Victorians including Thomas Carlyle, Thomas de Quincy, Matthew Arnold, and Eliot praised it for its inspiring message.[25] Like the Bible, *The Imitation of Christ* is made up of various books but is treated as one volume. The passages that Eliot includes in *The Mill on the Floss* are actually compilations of choice lines from the four books.[26] Cumulatively, the lines included in *The Mill on the Floss* reconfirm the message to look inwardly and deny self-love and worldly passion by merging with the divine and emulating the life of Christ. The message of Christ speaks to and through the devout reader, guiding one away from worldly pursuits that bring only dissatisfaction or frustration and granting the reader inner peace and spiritual fulfillment.

Maggie reads Thomas à Kempis's book during her long trial of domestic drudgery, before she begins her secret meetings with Philip. In the Red Deeps, Philip queries: "Have you many books? You were so fond of them when you were a little girl" (305). Maggie's reply signifies the depths of her repression: "No, I have given up books, . . . except a very, very few" (306). We question the completeness and permanence of Maggie's religious transformation. Philip tries to tempt her with novels. Although she reluctantly accepts *Corinne*, her reason for declining *The Pirate* is telling: "No, thank you, . . . It would make me in love with this world again, as I used to be—it would make me long to see and know many things—it would make me long for a full life" (306). With Philip, we bear witness to Maggie's inner conflict: romances will rekindle her insatiable longing for happiness, which now seems impossible to achieve. Moreover, the messages of such romances threaten to disrupt the temporary inner calm she has experienced by following the teachings of Thomas à Kempis.

Eliot, née Mary Ann Evans, thinly veils her Evangelical phase in the characterization of Maggie Tulliver. Eliot began her education in Evangelicalism under the guidance of Maria Lewis, an Irish governess teaching at Mrs. Wallington's school in Nuneaton where Eliot boarded from 1828 to 1832. From Miss Lewis, she learned a Puritanical mistrust of leisure and pleasure. Although the Evans family was not particularly partial to books, Mary Ann was. With Evangelicalism, she came to regard fiction as frivolous at best, at worst a form of lying. Looking back on her childhood, Eliot acknowledges the narrowness and intolerance of her views during this Evangelical phase of her life. By the late 1830s, Eliot began to draw distinctions between types of fiction and to prefer the "standards" of her day, as well as books of character and ideas, over religious works. She read *Robinson Crusoe* (1720), *Don Quixote* (1605, 1615), and Shakespeare, as well as Scott and Byron (Ashton 28).

By 1839, Eliot cast her reading net wider to include classical German, Italian, and English literature. Her letters to Miss Lewis contain quotations from and references to secular literature alongside scriptural allusions. Then, in 1842, Eliot ultimately rejected Evangelicalism. The decision infuriated her beloved father (with whom she seriously sparred regarding her unorthodoxy) and ended her long friendship with Miss Lewis, but the departure freed Eliot. As Eliot's biographer Rosemary Ashton notes, "Having embraced an unforgiving, damnation-conscious form of religion in her youth, she experienced its shedding as a liberation into tolerance" (25). However, during her father's acute illness, Eliot returned to Evangelicalism, beginning what her biographer Rosemary Bodenheimer describes as a "second phase of religious self-discipline" (81).

Eliot again found comfort in *The Imitation of Christ*. In a letter to her friend Sara Hennell dated February 9, 1849, Eliot indicates that she purchased a new copy of *De Imitatione Christi* with "quaint" woodcuts; she describes how "One breathes a cool air as of cloisters in the book—it makes one long to be a saint for a few months. Verily, its piety has its foundations in the depth of the divine-human soul."[27] In book 4 of *The Mill on the Floss*, Eliot writes similarly about it: "It was written down by a hand that waited for the heart's prompting; it is the chronicle of a solitary, hidden anguish, struggle, trust and triumph. . . . And so it remains to all time a lasting record of human needs and human consolations" (291). As Bodenheimer conveys, "With the help of Thomas à Kempis, she had invented a revised form of her former Evangelical ardor, the more effective because of her greater maturity and the more urgent demand of her situation" (81). During a period of a year when Mary Ann assumed the full burden of nursing her dying father, she bore loving service to the man against whom she had rebelled to achieve intellectual freedom. Robert Evans's death released her from a conflict between her pent-up desires and social and religious duties, much as Maggie herself experiences. When *The Mill on the Floss* appeared in print, Eliot's friends and contemporaries noticed the striking parallels between Eliot and Maggie, particularly Sara Hennell (to whom Eliot gave her copy of *De Imitatione Christi*) and Barbara Bodichon (Ashton 239–40).

Eliot twice took to heart the same treatise that Maggie receives in a bundle of books from her childhood friend Bob Jakin. Maggie's religious ardor likewise peaks during a period of loneliness when her embittered father loses ownership of the family mill. Eliot again focuses our attention on how and what Maggie reads: "A strange thrill of awe passed through Maggie while she read, as if she had been wakened in the night by a strain of solemn music, telling of beings whose souls had been astir while hers was in stupor" (289). Reading moves "through Maggie," somehow transporting her beyond her confined existence in St. Ogg's. Renunciation requires going beyond oneself to merge with the divine. Eliot conveys that Maggie—at least momentarily—has such an experience when reading the book; in fact, "she was hardly conscious that she was reading" (290). An enraptured Maggie ponders, "Is it not right to resign ourselves entirely, whatever may be denied us?" (327). The words Maggie clings to tell her to "Forsake thyself, resign thyself, and thou shalt enjoy much inward peace" (290).

True to character, Maggie begins her repression with incredible fervor: "here was a sublime height to be reached without the help of outward things—here was insight, and strength, and conquest, to be won by means entirely within her own soul, where a supreme Teacher was waiting to be heard" (290). While there are degrees of inward turning, Maggie represses her desire for earthly pleasures with an intensity equal to her past longing for them. She believes that all her miseries stem from her yearning for outward things and channels her feelings inward. Maggie—the child who makes "stories to the pictures out of my own head" (19), empathizes with Defoe's innocent "witch," and longs to unburden her woes to Sir Walter Scott—just as ardently imbibes the messages of Thomas à Kempis. We see her "devouring eagerly the dialogues with the invisible Teacher, . . . reading till the sun went down behind the willows" (290), listening to "this voice out of the far-off middle ages" (291), and forming plans for a life of total religious devotion and self-negation. Her new manner, which meets society's approval, guides her to adopt feminine traits of pronounced passivity and self-sacrifice, borne willingly.

Maggie's repression leads her to abandon books and higher cultural pursuits. Thomas à Kempis's teachings coincide with her mother's and society's conservatism and vision of domestic femininity.[28] Ironically, during this phase of religious zeal, Maggie, who takes up plain sewing with vigor, gains beauty and acceptance even by her mother, who delights that her once wayward daughter is "growing up so good" (294). Outwardly, it appears that Maggie's reading of a devotional treatise, which fosters repression, makes her a dutiful daughter and community member, ammunition for the socialization argument. Philip Wakem—who sees into Maggie's soul—recognizes Maggie's repression is really "a narrow self-delusive fanaticism" (327), taking her down a destructive path. Maggie renounces all that is beautiful "Because I should want too much. I must wait—this life will not last long" (307). She attests she finds joy through self-denial. As Kucich notes, "What Maggie does—or comes to feel that she *should* do—to protect herself from the inadequacy of outward responses to her desire is to create a source of impersonal, self-transcending passion inwardly" (154). Maggie dramatically declares: "I must part with everything I cared for when I was a child" (301). In her fervor, she channels her passion without "humility": "And so it came to pass that she often lost the spirit of humility by being excessive in the outward act; she often strove after too high a flight, and came down with her poor little half-fledged wings dabbled in the mud" (292). Caught up in her first phase of Evangelicalism, Maggie even thinks of burning her old books, much as Jo March incinerates her sensational stories, rejecting that idea only because the books are not her own (293).

Philip's acute judgment of Maggie's repression debunks the socialization argument and sets Maggie's discontent in motion. This religious devotion, Philip says to Maggie, "[is] only a way of escaping pain by starving into dulness all the highest powers of your nature. . . . Stupefaction is not resignation: and it is stupefaction to remain in ignorance—to shut up all the avenues by which the life of your fellow-men might become known to you. . . . *You* are not resigned: you are only trying to stupefy yourself" (327–28). Upon hearing Philip's judgment, "Maggie's lips trembled; she felt there was some truth in what Philip said" (328).

Maggie frees herself from her first religious phase but also, like Eliot, enters a "second phase of religious self-discipline" (Bodenheimer 81). Unlike Eliot, Maggie cannot free herself a second time. Maggie is torn between her Dodson duty to submit to the will of others and her Tulliver passion. She feels loyalty to Lucy and Philip, yet yearns for Stephen Guest, whom she loves, but "not with my whole heart and soul" (476). In book 7, when society considers Maggie a fallen woman after she journeys down the river with Stephen Guest, she does not turn to Philip or agree to marry Stephen, an act which might have allowed her fully to "avenge . . . the dark unhappy ones" (332). Rather, she reaches for the "quiet hand" (290), a synecdoche for the life of the pious monk who penned *The Imitation of Christ*.

Maggie is recalling the message of a book that preaches faithfulness, resolve, and self-renunciation as the flood waters come. Thinking "to the calmer past" (515), a clear reference to her first religious phase, Maggie spurns her "real temptation" (514) to go to Stephen and chooses the teachings of Thomas à Kempis. *The Imitation of Christ* is a book, Eliot tells us, for which "you need only pay six-pence at a book-stall" (291), but it "works miracles to this day, turning bitter waters into sweetness" (291). Maggie finds herself speaking the words of Christ in a "low murmur": "I have received the Cross, I have received it from Thy hand; I will bear it, and bear it till death, as Thou hast laid it upon me" (515). These "words . . . rushed even to her lips" (515), again suggesting that Maggie allows the Thomas à Kempis book to work through her. With Christian resolve, Maggie burns Stephen's letter that entreats her to ask him to "Come" to her (514). In true Corinne fashion, she sacrifices her love and silently vows to Stephen, "You will come back to her [Lucy]" (515).

Maggie Tulliver's childhood desire for a classical education, her commitment to override her biological destiny, seems more convincing than her adolescent acquiescence to conventional femininity. Renunciation of her intellectual nature can only lead to a "long suicide" (329), as Philip keenly recognizes midway through the novel. Eliot sacrifices her heroine rather than socialize her. If Maggie's reading of the Defoe engraving foreshadows her death by drowning, her death also allows the blond-haired Lucy to secure the hand of the man whose heart Maggie—proven innocent by drowning—wins, as Philip predicts she will from his reading of de Staël's *Corinne*. But of these three prophetic works that Maggie reads at critical points in her life, *The Imitation of Christ* most forcefully signals Maggie's actual fate—her struggle against her passion that conflicts with her sense of duty, fueled by the teachings "in the little old book she had long ago learned by heart" (515). Considered a contrived ending by many of Eliot's critics, the flood that Eliot devises to take Maggie's life frees her from remaining an overly literal reader of the kind of improving religious doctrines that conservative socialization advocates approved.

4

Romance Consumers

Gustave Flaubert's *Madame Bovary* (1857)
and Mary Elizabeth Braddon's *The Doctor's Wife* (1864)

I begin with three cautionary tales that offer a context for viewing the novel as a controlled substance in Victorian British and American culture. Collectively, these three didactic exemplars illuminate the tropes of consumption and addiction and the moral argument against women's novel-reading habit. They make a fitting prelude to an examination of heroines hooked on romance fiction in Gustave Flaubert's *Madame Bovary* (1857) and Mary Elizabeth Braddon's *The Doctor's Wife* (1864).

In an 1855 article titled "What Is the Harm of Novel-Reading?" published in an evangelical periodical called *The Wesleyan-Methodist Magazine*, an anonymous writer named "S." presents a cautionary tale that brings to bear the worst fears of opponents of women's reading. Maggie Tulliver's death by drowning seems a mild fate in comparison. The story goes as follows. Two brothers from the city of "E—" follow opposite paths in life. The church-going brother, elected "Elder," creates an orderly household with a select library of morally improving works. Not surprisingly, "His children rose up to honour him."[1] The other brother, who associates with immoral companions, eventually marries and has two children. He loses his talented son and wife to an early grave. The heartbroken brother tries to curb his "habit of profane swearing" (933). He introduces Sabbath prayers, but he remains liberal minded, granting his daughter K. complete freedom in her choice of books. His intentions are noble: he wants K. to make her own judgments and escape prejudice and narrow-mindedness.

What is the result of her unsupervised reading? She neglects any book that might improve her mind and becomes addicted to romances: "Writers of fiction absorbed all her hours. Circulating libraries were ransacked, that she might find the most stimulating novels. The influence of this trashy reading was soon apparent in her looks, tempers, language, and manners. Impatient of all restraint, she wandered in the paths of the tempter. The love-tales of her favourite authors inflamed her imagination. She dreamed and spoke of splendid matches, till she became quite unfitted for the matter-of-fact world in which her lot was cast" (933). The story ends predictably. Addicted to "trashy" novels, K. sins in increasing magnitude: "Golden dreams of sinful pleasure—the creation of novel-reading—ended in disgrace, ruin, disease, a broken heart, and an untimely grave! She passed into eternity without hope, in what might have been the very bloom of her days, leaving behind her two unhappy infants, to perpetuate her shame" (933). K. dies damned, and her two surviving illegitimate children become badges of her dishonor.

In its immediacy and dire end, "What Is the Harm of Novel Reading?" and other cautionary tales about romance and sensation fiction[2] resemble Cruikshank's enormously popular temperance series, *The Bottle* (1847) and its sequel *The Drunkard's Children* (1848), each a work of eight plates. In Cruikshank's mid-nineteenth-century moralistic melodramas, one drop of gin leads to the deterioration of a happy middle-class home. In *The Bottle*, the father loses his job due to drunkenness. The family pawns clothing, the household Bible, and eventually all possessions to pay for more alcohol and drinking debts. Tragedy strikes further: the youngest child dies, the drunkard father kills his wife with a liquor bottle, and he goes insane. In *The Drunkard's Children*, the drunkard's son turns to crime and is transported to Australia, dying en route. The drunkard's elder daughter succumbs to prostitution and eventually commits suicide. Death is her fate, like that of the novel-addicted daughter in "What Is the Harm of Novel Reading?"

These verbal and visual cautionary tales eerily anticipate 1930s antidrug propaganda films. *Reefer Madness* (1936) was billed as a "SHOCKING DOPE EXPOSE" depicting the "SEDUCTION OF THE INNOCENT" by "THE MARIJUANA MOB."[3] This campy and downright bad antidrug film about the dangers of the devil's weed illustrates that one "toke" of a marijuana reefer leads swiftly to rape and murder. Dr. Carroll narrates the story of some nice high school students who begin to hang out at the neighborhood drug dealer's house. The fun swiftly turns ugly as one of the teenagers, Mary, is raped and then accidentally shot when her boyfriend rushes in to defend her. Similar to "What Is the Harm of Novel-Reading?" and *The Drunkard's Children*, women pay for their addictions and end up dead.

Reefer Madness is a cinematic failure. Succeeding generations have dismissed cautionary tales as comical. Nonetheless, all three examples of propaganda have sociological and historical importance. They illustrate the singular anxieties and fears that certain types of fiction, alcoholism, and drug use generated, respectively, in Victorian Britain and 1930s America. At the start of the twenty-first century, we esteem the book as an intellectual medium, a vital tool for literacy learning. We acknowledge different types of novels, ranging from classics to popular culture and even trash. The banning of controversial books, still promoted by factions within society today, might be seen as a residue of a view that held far more power a century earlier. Messages similar to those touted by groups urging for responsible and safe drinking (such as, MADD), drug use (DARE), and eating (Weight Watchers) peppered nineteenth-century advice books and periodicals and reached a wide audience. While to some Victorians, reading was a mark of gentility necessary for a woman's education, fervent opponents of women's novel-reading feared the moral and medical ramifications of excessive consumption and addiction.

The trope of reading consumption is so steeped in antifiction criticism that Lady Laura Ridding admits in her 1896 article "What Should Women Read?" that "It is a trite comparison to liken literature to mental food; but the analogy is useful for our present purpose" (29). Drawing on medical and culinary metaphors, Ridding equates well-written works that cheer, enliven, educate, or morally improve to "a wholesome variety of food—well cooked, well digested, nourishing" (29). Romance and sensation fiction are not part of her prescription for a well-balanced reading diet: "The strawberry ices of literature glow on every railway bookstall in the shape of the lighter magazines, the society and comic papers, fashion journals, sensational stories. These are harmless occasional reading, but a mind glutted with them needs medicine as much as a greedy child after a surfeit of sugar-plums" (29). Ridding permits occasional indulgence in "sugar-plums," but will her readers have enough will power to consume them only now and then?

In *Maternal Counsels to a Daughter* (1855), Matilda Pullan similarly likens a craving for light fiction to "that of a child for cakes" and cautions that reading "must be restrained within due bounds, or it will be injurious. No pastry will ever be a proper substitute for a solid joint."[4] Even the intellectual Jane Welsh Carlyle declares in an 1865 letter to her friend Mary Smith: "the appetite for magazine *Tales* and three-volume novels is getting to be a positive lupus—? something! I forget the full medical name of that disease which makes the victim gobble up, with unslaked voracity, pounds on pounds of raw beef and tallow candles! or anything else that comes readiest."[5] To Carlyle, an "appetite" for romance and magazine stories connotes disease. Mary Elizabeth Braddon equates an addiction to thrillers to a craving for tobacco and pudding: Sigismund Smith, her fictional sensation writer in *The Doctor's Wife,* "was the author of about half a dozen highly spiced fictions, which enjoyed an immense popularity amongst the classes who like their literature as they like their tobacco—very strong";[6] he wrote "combination stories"[7] for "a public that bought its literature in the same manner as its pudding—in penny slices" (12).[8] Even Braddon concedes that her romance consumer's reading is "intellectual opium-eating" (29), drawing her character into the arguments that condemned sensation fiction (including her own) for its addictiveness and immorality.

The works of Flaubert and Braddon present the lure of fiction—a major theme of cautionary tales and advice books warning against the novel-reading habit.[9] Critics have long considered *Madame Bovary* to be the novel that best speaks to the immorality and dire results of novel consumption and addiction through its characterization of Emma Bovary, imaginative wife of a dull, provincial country doctor. Pykett is certainly right that "it is undoubtedly the case that many readers of English fiction in the nineteenth century were acquainted with Flaubert's novel through their reading of *The Doctor's Wife.*"[10] In an 1864 letter to Edward Bulwer-Lytton, Braddon confides that *Madame Bovary* also served as a model for *The Doctor's Wife*: "The idea of the Doctor's Wife *is* founded on 'Madame Bovary,' the style of which struck me immensely in spite of its hideous immorality."[11] While *The Doctor's Wife* offers a window into the tropes of consumption and addiction and, relatedly, the moral argument, Braddon equally challenges these arguments and the associations that contemporary readers would bring to bear on novel-reading: she insists that tempting fiction, despite its opiatic addictiveness, need not have permanent effects.

We might not immediately pair these two authors—one French, one British; one male, one female; one ultimately recognized for his artistic genius, the other the queen of sensation fiction. Braddon gained her reputation on the success of *Lady Audley's Secret* (1862); beautiful, angelic-looking Lucy Graham Audley turns out to be a bigamist, child deserter, and murderess with a taint of inherited insanity. In *The Doctor's Wife,* her eighth novel, Braddon felt constrained by codes of British morality; she longed to create a work of art that her public would not dismiss as "sensational."[12] *Madame Bovary*, which caused an immediate scandal in France, is far more sensational than *The Doctor's Wife*. Known always to seek *le mot juste*, Flaubert wrote a book praised for its artistry even though its "immoral" contents shocked many, including Braddon (Wolff 162).

In *Madame Bovary* Flaubert weaves a tale of a woman who projects romantic ideas gleaned during her reading quest onto her life. Dissatisfied with her marriage and extramarital affairs, Emma Rouault Bovary "longed for the ineffable sentiments of love which she had tried to imagine from her books."[13] Unable to match these romantic illusions in real life, Emma pays the ultimate price and dies disenchanted. But as Carla L. Peterson notes in her examination of *Madame Bovary* alongside Stendhal's *Le Rouge et le noir* (1830) and *Lamiel* (1839–42), "the novel is also much more: it is Flaubert's portrayal of the artist in the post-Romantic period, who embodies the failure of earlier Romantic aspirations toward organic synthesis and the reconciliation of opposites" (161). Through Emma, Flaubert expresses his disillusionment with the Romantic ideal. Romance fiction at large fails Emma, who, like James's Isabel Archer, perceives art to be an accurate representation of life.

Akin to Charlotte Brontë, James, and Eliot, Flaubert creates a vivid representation of a woman reader within the early pages of the novel and supremely explores the process of reading fiction. Emma has a "fine education" at a convent boarding school (15), but her real education comes from books. Flaubert requires of his readers only passing knowledge of the types of fiction that Emma consumes, although her choices characterize her as a reader. Like James, Flaubert rarely names an exact title, although he does note that Emma reads *Le Génie du christianisme* (1802), *Paul et Virginie* (1787), and a few authors—Scott, Honoré de Balzac, George Sand, and Eugène Sue—at specific periods in her life.

Emma encounters François René de Chateaubriand's *Le Génie du christianisme* in her convent school. Her attraction to this highly popular work extolling Christianity's positive impact on the modern world likely seems linked to its tone of "romantic melancholy" (31). Flaubert suggests that Emma misreads or refashions this religious text to suit her own romantic needs. Bernardin de Saint-Pierre's *Paul et Virginie* seems a more likely choice for a reader obsessed with romance as do the novels of Eugène Sue, a physician and novelist who wrote exciting sea romances in the dramatic style of Alexandre Dumas *père*. De Saint-Pierre's descriptions of an exotic island paradise and Paul's devotion to Virginie (his childhood friend turned lover) captivates Emma at thirteen (30). Flaubert also tells us that during this period Emma acquires novels from an old woman who came monthly to the convent to mend linen. Emma ransacks lending libraries and "soiled her hands with this dust" (32). Drawn to luxury even in her youth, she delights in her classmates' keepsake albums, which contain contributions by counts and viscounts. We also learn about her love of fine things when she "devoured, without skipping a word, every article about first nights in the theater, horse races and soirées" (50) from two fashion magazines, *La Corbeille* and *Le Sylphe des salons*.

Akin to Maggie Tulliver, Emma, at fifteen, avidly reads Sir Walter Scott's historical romances and becomes obsessed with "things historical" (32). From Scott, she no doubt encountered thwarted passions—such as Rebecca's repressed love in *Ivanhoe* (1819)—and far-off romanticized settings that appealed to her romantic nature: the secluded island of Zetland (Shetland) in *The Pirate* (1821), an Elizabethan castle in *Kenilworth* (1821), and the distant Scottish highlands in *Rob Roy* (1817). An older, married Emma, disappointed in her marriage to Charles Bovary, also reads works by Sand and Balzac, "seeking imaginary gratifications of her desires" (50). Flaubert does not specify which of Balzac's over ninety novels and tales Emma consumes. She likely looks to novels in Balzac's *La Comédie humaine*, such as *Eugénie Grandet* (1833), which blends love and greed in a romantic tragedy that no doubt fuels Emma's fanciful and unfulfilled desires. Again, we are not sure which works by Sand Emma reads, but likely the early and highly romantic novels portraying free love for both women and men—*Lélia* (1833) and *Valentine* (1832)—would have vicariously sated Emma's desires and taught her what she might hope to find in her adulterous liaisons with Rodolphe Boulanger and Léon Dupuis.

The many authors' names that Flaubert mentions pass by quickly, forming a literary smorgasbord that feeds Emma's romantic imagination. Maggie Tulliver reads diverse prophetic texts which define her character and fate, but Emma fixates on romance. Events she never actually experiences become more tangible to her than her real, monotonous life. Flaubert emphasizes Emma's obsessiveness as a reader and her response to romance fiction, filled with "dark forests, palpitating hearts, vows, sobs, tears and kisses, skiffs in the moonlight, nightingales in thickets, and gentlemen brave as lions, gentle as lambs, virtuous as no one really is, and always ready to shed floods of tears" (31–32).

Emma also reads romantic pictures; she palpably "quivered as she blew back the tissue paper from the engravings" (32) of blond-haired, blue-eyed English ladies riding in carriages or dreaming on sofas; naive maidens plucking petals from flowers; sultans and Turkish sabers and fezzes; and fantastic landscapes from foreign and far-off countries. Jane Eyre and Maggie Tulliver make up stories from the pictures that captivate them; they describe the pictures in such detail that we can return to the texts and find the very images that fascinate these fictional women—not so with Emma Bovary. Emma's descriptions are fragmentary. She remains detached from novels and pictures, which whirl into a blend of romantic impressions—vows, stolen kisses, nightingales, and dashing gentlemen.

As Carla L. Peterson concludes, Emma's reading process is passively accepting, distanced, disintegrative, and literal—as opposed to critical, involved, synthetic, and metaphorical: "she is unable to sustain any imaginative activity around her books for very long. So instead of immersing herself in situations portrayed in her novels, Emma draws these situations out of the fictional realm and seeks them in real life" (170). Emma does not actually identify with the fictional realm. Rather, she reads literally and mistakenly projects situations encountered in her reading onto an imagined life against which she measures her boring reality. Her dreams of romantic heroes and settings infect her daily life. Realizing the worst fears of the moral argument, Emma's inability to weave her reading fantasies into the fabric of her provincial existence leads her to take her own life.

Emma ponders how she would respond if she were to encounter romantic heroes and places. She "wished she could have lived in some old manor house, like those chatelaines in low-waisted gowns who spent their days with their elbows on the stone sill of a Gothic window surmounted by a trefoil, chin in hand, watching a white-plumed rider on a black horse galloping toward them from across the far countryside" (32). She worships a number of extraordinary but ill-fated women—Mary Queen of Scots, Joan of Arc, Agnes Sorel, and Héloïse—whose fates could be said to foreshadow her own. While she admires women like Joan of Arc who led daring lives, her dreams inspired by literature seem passive, distant: she waits for the arrival of a chivalric hero to find her hidden away in a Gothic setting. Both the submissive and remarkable images of womanhood, variously inspired by her reading, factor into Emma's romantic imagination. While she constructs a self-image based on these contrasting qualities gleaned from books, Flaubert reveals that Emma is neither passive nor remarkable.[14]

The romantic notions which inform Emma's adolescent identity dominate her reading as an adult married woman and form her expectations of marriage. "Before her marriage," Flaubert tells us, "she had believed herself to be in love; but since the happiness which should have resulted from this love had not come to her, she felt that she must have been mistaken. And she tried to find out exactly what was meant in life by the words 'bliss,' 'passion' and 'rapture,' which had seemed so beautiful to her in books" (29–30). The rhetoric Emma uses to describe her notion of romance reveals her hope to achieve an extreme state of being. Expecting married life to be just like a romance novel, she is destined for disappointment, like Isabel Archer. As James Winchell notes, "This cognitive breakdown—between her readerly expectations and the emotions that fail to materialize for her in marriage—emerges, dramatically enough, only in her experience of postmarital blues. Her intersubjective, public experience of passion fails to resemble the concept of passion she had held within her subjective, premarital, or private desire" (99).

Emma does not readily abandon the concept of passion based upon her "readerly expectations." In fact, in her marriage and subsequent love affairs, she actively seeks situations where she hopes she may finally realize her desires. Flaubert notes that "following theories in which she believed, she made determined efforts to experience love. In the garden, by moonlight, she would recite to him all the passionate verses she knew by heart and sing him mournful adagios accompanied by sighs; but afterward she found herself as calm as before, and Charles did not seem to be any more amorous or stirred up" (37). In these scenes, Flaubert reveals Charles Bovary's lack of imagination. Despite his kindly nature, we sympathize with Emma, who realizes that her love for Charles lacks "'bliss, 'passion' and 'rapture.'" Possessing a sense of superiority linked to her reading, Emma looks down on Charles because he is a nonreader and wonders what might become of her if she were to meet a man more like the heroes of her novels. Emma sighs out of boredom, "Oh, why did I ever get married?" (38).

Emma comes the closest to glimpsing the world of a romance novel when she and Charles stay at La Vaubyessard, the chateau of the Marquis d'Andervilliers. At a ball, we see Emma "eating a maraschino ice from a silver-gilt shell" (44–45), dancing twice with a viscount, and longing "to know all about their lives, to enter into them and become part of them" (46). Even here, Emma remains a voyeur in a real-life situation akin to those she devours in romances and fashion magazines. The viscount becomes a romanticized image in her active imagination long after the event. Projecting the viscount onto her fictional daydreams, "She frequently found similarities between him and the fictitious characters in her books" (50). Following her visit to La Vaubyessard, Emma finds her life mundane and onerous in contrast to the potentialities offered in fiction: "Sighs in the moonlight, long embraces, tears flowing onto yielding hands, all the fevers of the flesh and the languors of love—these things were inseparable from the balcony of a great castle in which life moved at a leisurely pace, from a boudoir with silk curtains, a thick carpet, filled flower stands and a bed mounted on a platform, from the sparkle of precious stones or the aiguillettes of liveried servants" (51).

After the Bovarys move to Yonville-l'Abbaye, Emma—like her Victorian British and American sisters, Jane Eyre, Isabel Archer, and Jo March—gains unlimited access to a man's library, that of the pharmacist Monsieur Homais. It includes works by Voltaire, Rousseau, Scott, and Delille. She also borrows regularly from the lending library in town. Again, Flaubert does not provide titles but suggests Emma reads widely, consuming books that feed her pretensions of superiority as a reader and her desires. Emma continues her passion for reading between her love affairs, which fail to fulfill her romantic anticipations. Flaubert also connects Emma's reading to illicit action in suggesting her reading of romance has awakened her sensuality and taught her to behave in a like manner. Emma reads fiction literally and uncritically. Illuminating the moral argument against women's free access to books, Emma attempts to imitate the actions of adulterous literary heroines she has read about. In her two extramarital affairs, she hopes to find a relationship that resembles that of a romance novel.

When Emma enters into a liaison with the wealthy Boulanger, she feels that she has found, at last, palpitating hearts, deep sighs, moonlit walks, ecstasy, passionate rapture, and stolen kisses, altogether lacking in her drab life with Bovary: "She remembered the heroines of novels she had read, and the lyrical legion of those adulterous women began to sing in her memory with sisterly voices that enchanted her. It was as though she were becoming part of that imaginary world, as though she were making the long dream of her youth come true by placing herself in the category of those amorous women she had envied so much" (140). Just as the heroines of romance novels remain at a distance from her, so do her lovers. She objectifies Boulanger and transforms him into a romantic hero, even though Flaubert reveals he is decidedly not heroic. Emma's aggressiveness in their affair—culminating in her insistence that he run away with her, as might happen in a romance novel—leads her to lose her lover.

Emma repeats these same mistakes in her subsequent affair with Léon Dupuis, the object of her first ardent affection. She perceives Léon as a romantic hero; likewise, he mistakenly projects onto Emma his conception of a romantic heroine. At the beginning of their affair, Emma confides to Léon, "If you only knew all the things I've dreamed of" (201). He returns with "It's the same with me! Oh, I've suffered so much!" (201). Burdened by two sets of romantic expectations and long anticipated yet unconsummated passions, Emma's second affair fails more miserably than the first. Emma finds herself longing for a handsome and passionate man with the soul of a poet—"why was it not possible that she might meet him someday?" (245). "Léon suddenly appeared to her as remote as the others" when she recognizes that "the sweetest kisses only left on one's lips the hopeless longing for a higher ecstasy" (245). The end of each love affair leads Emma back to her romance novels, which provide other passionate models to seek in life.

Flaubert creates an image of an impassioned romance consumer who reads despite the indifference and hostility she encounters. Reading offers a screen to filter Charles, the quintessential nonreader: "She would even bring a book with her at meals and turn the pages while Charles ate and talked to her" (50). Her conservative mother-in-law hurls moral criticisms that come straight from nineteenth-century advice manuals. Emma is filling her head with "silly ideas" (109) and "Reading novels and other bad books that are against religion and make fun of priests with quotations from Voltaire!" (109). Charles's mother determines to cancel Emma's subscription to the lending library, rationalizing that Emma's passion for reading such fiction is deadly: "And wouldn't they have the right to go to the police if he refused to stop spreading his poison?" (109). Here her words anticipate those of Professor Bhaer in *Little Women*—"They haf no right to put poison in the sugarplum" (333)—and Adams's in *Woman's Work and Worth in Girlhood, Maidenhood, and Wifehood* (1884): "The evil influence of a bad book is not to be exaggerated. Its subtle venom slowly but surely spreads through the whole system, like some of the drugs employed by the mediaeval poisoners, which were not less certainly mortal because they did not act immediately, and their presence was unsuspected by the victim" (140). Emma's mother-in-law does not actually cancel her subscription, but Emma recognizes that her novel-reading must remain a secretive act.

We witness Emma's addiction to romance and sensation fiction at its height toward the end of the novel. With the failure of Emma's second extramarital affair, just before she takes her own life, Flaubert describes how Emma banishes Charles to the third floor to keep him away from her at night. Then, "she would stay up all night reading lurid novels full of orgiastic scenes and bloody deeds. Often, seized with terror, she would utter a cry. Charles would come running in, but she would say to him, 'Oh, go away!'" (249–50).[15] The tedious reality of Charles Bovary clashes with the heightened passion of her fictional worlds, again reinforcing Emma's inability to find fantasies of "the most beautiful things she had read" (251) in life.

Madame Bovary has an exquisite style and a compelling heroine. However, in its quick succession of deaths within the final chapters, the novel resembles the cautionary tales that introduce this chapter. Emma's death illuminates the tropes of consumption and addiction and the moral and medical arguments against women's reading. Emma Bovary drifts first into adultery, then into madness when confronted by the seizure of her personal property to cover her excessive debts. Unable to find in life the glamor of romantic fiction, Emma pays the ultimate price, as espoused by the medical model. Taking arsenic obtained illicitly from Homais's pharmacy, she experiences a slow and agonizing death. When Emma Bovary is laid into the ground, "The stones striking the wooden coffin made that awesome sound which seems to us the reverberation of eternity" (293). Loyal to his wife even after her death, Charles discovers Emma's love letters from Dupuis and Boulanger and dies destitute and brokenhearted. Their little daughter, Berthe Bovary, remains under the care of Charles's stern mother, who soon dies; Berthe's maternal grandfather is paralyzed, so an aunt takes Berthe in and puts her to work in a cotton mill to earn her keep. Berthe's life seems uncertain given her delicate health. So ends the life and legacy of an addicted romance reader.

Like Emma Bovary, Mary Elizabeth Braddon's Isabel Sleaford Gilbert is a romanticist, a dreamer, but an equally bored doctor's wife, who does not perceive fiction as an artifice, but an artistic model to emulate in life. Also a work that deals with reading addiction and the failure of Romantic aspirations, *The Doctor's Wife* lacks the luxuriance of the novel that inspired it. The basic plot of *Madame Bovary* reappears in Braddon's *The Doctor's Wife*: fanciful Isabel Gilbert grows disillusioned with her provincial married life since it can never match her romance reading; she then enters into a relationship with an aristocratic "lover."[16]

Braddon constructs the image of Isabel as an obsessive romance reader even more immediately than Flaubert. Like James's more famous Isabel Archer, we first meet Braddon's Isabel alone, reading a book. Braddon's setting also seems like that of a painting. Eighteen-year-old Isabel is in a garden, "lolling in a low basket-chair, with a book on her lap, and her chin resting on the palm of her hand, so absorbed by the interest of the page before her that she did not even lift her eyes when the two young men went close up to her" (23). The outdoor setting, her languishing pose, and her absorption in her book anticipate Homer's depiction of a woman consuming the latest fiction in *The New Novel* (fig. 4). However, Isabel is reading in Camberwell in an overrun garden near Albany Road, an area of London where Braddon also lived when she was approximately the same age as Isabel. Braddon and James seem to equate the "neglected" settings of their readers to their unsupervised educations: we soon learn that "it was in this neglected garden that Isabel Sleaford spent the best part of her idle, useless life" (23). Although Isabel closes her book to greet Sigismund Smith and his companion George Gilbert, "she kept her thumb between the pages, and evidently meant to go on with the volume at the first convenient opportunity" (23–24). As soon as tea is over, Isabel escapes from her male companions to resume reading that same book under her favorite pear tree. She continues this pattern of reading out of doors well into her marriage to George Gilbert and during her affair with Roland Lansdell.

Braddon dwells on Isabel's early education, which she describes as "a smattering of every thing at a day-school in the Albany road" (27). Obsessive novel-reading since the age of sixteen largely forms Isabel's education. Like the wayward daughter in "What Is the Harm of Novel-Reading?" and Emma Bovary, Isabel ransacks the shelves of the circulating library. "She did not feed upon garbage," Braddon assures us, "but settled at once upon the highest blossoms in the flower-garden of fiction, and read her favourite novels over and over again" (28). Works by Scott and Dickens, authors Braddon read before age nine, figure prominently in Isabel Sleaford's imagination (Wolff 36). Isabel knows "enough French to serve for the reading of novels that she might have better left unread" (27). She recites long, sentimental passages from her "pet authors" (28) and even reads during meals when married, like Emma Bovary: "If she [Isabel] had an open book beside her plate, and if her eyes wandered to the page every now and then while he was talking to her, she had often told him [George] that she could listen and read at the same time; and no doubt she could do so" (118).[17] Isabel consumes "just so much of modern history as enabled her to pick out all the sugarplums in the historian's pages,—the Mary Stuarts and Joan of Arcs and Anne Boleyns, . . . the Marie Antoinettes and Charlotte Cordays" (27). Like her literary model, Emma Bovary, Isabel ferrets out the lives of remarkable ill-fated women who die at the stake or the guillotine, although their fates do not augur her own. Her obsessive reading also invites attack from her stepmother, her husband, and even her friend Sigismund Smith, who comments, "she's dreadfully romantic. She reads too many novels" (30). Famous authors and those whose lives exist solely between the pages of a book also seem real to Isabel Gilbert. In fact, Braddon tells us that Isabel finds the death of her beloved Percy Bysshe Shelley "nearer to her than all that common business of breakfast and dinner and supper which made up her daily life" (158–59).

Isabel most poignantly resembles Emma Bovary in the way she reads novels with an uncritical acceptance. Isabel perceives novels as models to imitate in life. Her marriage to a boring country doctor does not match her fictional expectations. Isabel "wanted her life to be like her books; she wanted to be a heroine,—unhappy perhaps, and dying early" (28). Braddon repeats in the very next chapter, "Izzie had sat through the hot hours of drowsy summer days, reading her favourite novels and dreaming of a life that was to be like a plot of a novel" (41). She is not sensual like Emma Bovary, but naive and innocent. When Isabel misunderstands the intentions of her aristocratic lover, unmistakable to a "woman of the world," Braddon concludes, "Isabel Gilbert was not a woman of the world. She had read novels while other people perused the Sunday papers; and of the world out of a three-volume romance she had no more idea than a baby. She believed in a phantasmal universe, created out of the pages of poets and romancers" (253).

On first meeting Isabel, George Gilbert recognizes that she "was fitted to be the heroine of a romance" (30). During her brief stint as governess to the nieces of Mr. Raymond, Isabel longs for just that: "She lived alone with her books and the dreams which were born of them, and waited for the prince, the Ernest Maltravers, the Henry Esmond, the Steerforth—it was Steerforth's proud image, and not simple-hearted David's gentle shadow, which lingered in the girl's mind when she shut the book" (72). The references to her novelistic daydreams go on ad nauseam: "She sighed to sit at the feet of a Byron, grand and gloomy and discontented" (72). Braddon even conjectures that "she would have worshipped an aristocratic Bill Sykes, and would have been content to die under his cruel hand, only in the ruined chamber of some Gothic castle, by moonlight, with the distant Alps shimmering whitely before her glazing eyes, instead of in poor Nancy's unromantic garret" (72–73). She glamorizes dishonorable or lawless characters—not only the robber Sykes of *Oliver Twist* (1838), who brutally clubs the good-hearted Nancy as she prays to her Maker, but proud Steerforth of *David Copperfield* (1850), who ruins and abandons Little Em'ly. A Gothic castle seems a more alluring setting in which to imagine one's death than a garret. Isabel also romanticizes Florence Dombey's being turned out of doors by her father and Jane Eyre's starving on the moors.

We question Maggie Tulliver's insightfulness as a reader of romance when she projects an affinity for the unhappy and downtrodden onto Scott's historical romances and de Staël's *Corinne*. Those familiar with the abundant texts that Isabel cites have graver misgivings about Izzie as a reader of fiction. Isabel approaches her impending marriage like a romance novel: "Were there not three volumes of courtship to be gone through first?" (99). Still, Braddon insists that "Perhaps during all that engagement the girl never once saw her lover really as he was" (102). During her brief courtship (that leads too swiftly to marriage for Isabel's taste), Isabel transforms plain and sensible George into countless fictional characters: "She dressed him up in her own fancies, and deluded herself by imaginary resemblances between him and the heroes in her books" (102). He becomes Charlotte Brontë's Edward Fairfax Rochester of *Jane Eyre* (1847) when he is "abrupt and disagreeable in his manner to her"; Dickens's Mr. Paul Dombey of *Dombey and Son* (1848) when he is "cold"; and Thackeray's Rawdon Crawley of *Vanity Fair* (1848) when he is "clumsy and stupid" (102).[18]

In turn, she casts herself in matching roles and plays submissive Jane to the dominant Rochester, or domineering Becky to the bumbling Rawdon. An informed reader again might question her choices. Rochester bears the guilt of Bluebeard in hiding his mad wife in the attic of Thornfield Hall. Dombey's coldness is so entrenched that his final kindness to Florence after losing his fortune seems unconvincing. Rawdon at least loves the conniving Becky and is a good father to little Rawdy. But none of these protagonists in any way approximates an ideal mate, even if each ultimately reforms. Isabel romanticizes the obvious flaws of these "heroes," recasts George Gilbert in their likenesses, and fails to recognize her incompatibility with the practical George.[19] Braddon even uses book illustration to demonstrate just how unsuited Isabel and George Gilbert are. Isabel longs to look like Florence Dombey as Phiz depicts her in an elegant dress on her wedding day in *Dombey and Son*, but George chooses her a "sombre brown-silk dress" (105) because of its practicality.[20]

Only after the wedding does Isabel realize that she has little in common with the country surgeon. Here Braddon nods to the moral argument:

Isabel's excessive romance reading makes her dissatisfied with domesticity. Even during her dreary winter honeymoon, Isabel "began to think that she had made a mistake" (109) because "No prince would ever come now; no accidental duke would fall in love with her black eyes, and lift her all at once to the bright regions she longed to inhabit" (110). Nonetheless, Braddon, like Flaubert, shows us the failings of the inadequate though kind and loving doctor, poorly matched for his romantic spouse. George Gilbert is devoted to his wife, much as Charles Bovary is to Emma, but Braddon makes him practical to the extreme, devoid of romance, and ostensibly a nonreader (109), a fault he shares with Bovary. Isabel's attempts to delight George with novels and poetry fail, as Emma's do with Charles. For example, when Isabel talks to George about the star-crossed lovers in Scott's *Bride of Lammermoor* (1819) "with her face all lighted up with emotion, the young surgeon could only stare wonderingly at his betrothed" (102). Isabel sadly concludes that, like Esau in the Book of Genesis, "She had sold her birthright for a vulgar mess of pottage" (110).

Braddon's literary references are lavish, lending a self-consciousness to *The Doctor's Wife* that is altogether absent from *Madame Bovary*. Pykett similarly observes, "Although she does not rise to the heights of Flaubertian style in *The Doctor's Wife*, and she does not even attempt the studied impersonality of Flaubert's narrator, Braddon constantly strives for an effect of 'literariness,' not least through her extensive allusions to novels, plays, poems, and paintings" (Introduction ix). Different from Isabel Archer and Emma Bovary, Isabel Gilbert does not possess even a private sense of superiority connected to her reading. Rather, Braddon seems to be using Isabel to show off her own knowledge to a reading public that dismissed her as a sensation fiction writer. By referring to works by her mentor Bulwer-Lytton, as well as Dickens, Scott, Thackeray, Byron, and Shelley, Braddon seemingly projects her desire that *The Doctor's Wife* be grouped along with works by these respected authors. In fact, Braddon interjects "This is *not* a sensation novel" (358) in the third volume of the book. At best, Braddon achieves an "effect" of literariness; much of the literature she quotes actually comes from stage adaptations of works she encountered when she was an actress (Pykett, Introduction ix).

While the frequent allusions are arguably "offered up for the reader's self-congratulatory consumption" (Pykett, Introduction xvi), I also concur with Flint, who contends that Braddon, like Rhoda Broughton, encourages readers "to enter into an active process of interpretation which invites recognition of their own active, rather than passive, role as readers" (Flint,

The Woman Reader 283). As informed readers, we can construct an image of Emma Bovary based on the authors, books, and type of fiction she reads. The process of comparing life to fiction may also be more central to Isabel's reading process than any particular text. In true Emma Bovary fashion, Isabel projects her reading onto her imagined life and encounters a disparity between the artifice of alluring romance fiction and the tiresome reality of provincial life that confronts her in the looking glass. Many of Isabel's references function as disconnected romantic fantasies. However, Braddon—in providing exact titles—seems to invite judgment about Isabel's reading. Like Eliot and Charlotte Brontë, Braddon encourages active readers to use specific texts to assess the ways Isabel reads, misreads, and romanticizes these works which her life does not parallel.[21]

Isabel's novelistic daydreams center on two Dickensian heroines, Edith Dombey and Florence Dombey of *Dombey and Son*. In fact, Braddon refers to *Dombey and Son* nearly two dozen times.[22] Neither Dickensian heroine is a likely role model.[23] Isabel focuses her imagination on the trappings of the unhappy marriage between the beautiful, proud, and bitter Edith Granger Dombey and the cold, proud, wealthy Paul Dombey. Isabel would like to marry a duke and "wear ruby velvet and a diamond coronet ever after, like Edith Dombey in Mr. Hablot Browne's grand picture" (31). Isabel seems to have eyes only for Edith's coronet and velvet, whereas Dickens, in the scenes before Edith's wedding, emphasizes Edith's despair that Dombey, in Edith's own words, "has bought me" (332). Edith Dombey vents embittered rage at a woman's powerless position in her gendered society: "There is no slave in a market: there is no horse in a fair: so shown and offered and examined and paraded, Mother, as I have been, for ten shameful years" (333). This cruel reality seemingly escapes the attention of Isabel Sleaford Gilbert.

Referring to *Dombey and Son* when infatuated with Roland Lansdell, Isabel examines her face in the looking glass and "tried to look like Edith Dombey in the grand Carker scene" (155). But in this dramatic scene, Edith Dombey rebuffs the advances of her husband's manager, Carker, who has enticed her to run off with him to France. Mourning that Isabel will not have the life of the heroines of her favorite novels, Braddon, likewise, comments superficially about this scene: "Are you [Isabel] never to wear ruby velvet, and diamonds in your hair, and to lure some recreant Carker to a foreign hostelry, and there denounce and scorn him?" (78). Both references focus on beauty and artifice—the power of a woman to allure and renounce a man. They overlook the misery that the marriage market brings Edith Dombey as well as the moral overtones of Edith's compromised virtue. Rather, Isabel reads Edith's character in terms of her unsated desire for a grand romance akin to a novel, even an unhappy one.

Isabel also romanticizes and trivializes the dire fate of Florence Dombey. A motherless Dickensian angel, Florence yearns for the love of her father, who denies her very existence and bestows all his love on his dying male heir, little Paul Dombey. Florence's father punishes all who love her and evicts her from her home. Nonetheless, Isabel glamorizes Florence's fate: "if she [Isabel] had only a father to strike her and turn her out of doors, the story of her life might be very tolerable, after all" (88). It is Florence—not Edith—whom Isabel wants to resemble on her wedding day (105) even though Florence marries a humble sailor, Walter Gay. In her frequent references to *Dombey and Son*, Isabel romanticizes, in turn, Edith's grand wealth and Florence's privation. She reads *Dombey and Son* more accurately later in the novel when she realizes that in meeting secretly with Lansdell, she has been falsely suspected of infidelity: she had "become the thing that Mr. Dombey believed his wife [Edith] to be when he struck his daughter [Florence] on the stairs" (280).

Isabel miscasts her aristocratic "lover" as one of two polarized types from romance, hero and villain. Braddon consolidates Emma Bovary's dual temptations—Rodolphe Boulanger and Léon Dupuis—into Roland Lansdell, a mediocre poet who possesses the wealth of the viscount of Emma's daydreams. Braddon makes clear that "Roland Lansdell was not a hero; he was only a very imperfect, vacillating young man, with noble impulses for ever warring against the baser attributes of his mind; a spoiled child of fortune, who had almost always had his own way until just now" (333). Long before they meet, Isabel falls in love with Roland through his poetry, derivative of Alfred Tennyson by his own admission. She carries the slim book of poems he wrote, *An Alien's Dreams*, to the waterfall at Thurston's Crag where she reads alone and constructs a romanticized conception of its author. When Isabel first meets the dashing though world-weary Lansdell, who is "almost as good-looking as Mr. Hablot Browne's portrait of Walter Gay" (88), Braddon tells us, "The dream had come true at last. *This* was romance—*this* was life" (138). In fact, "He was the incarnation of all the dreams of her life" (139). Isabel's resemblance to Emma Bovary stops here.

Isabel initially feels a restless passion when she meets Lansdell—"The slow fever that had been burning so long in her veins was now a rapid and consuming fire" (135)—but their relationship remains entirely platonic. They meet by the waterfall to discuss literature. She reads in the vast library of his grand home, Mordred Priory, when he goes away because he cannot bear to live without her. In fact, Roland's sexual love for Isabel dashes her romantic conceptions. Isabel's often noted avoidance of sensuality in and out of marriage divorces Braddon's novel from the Flaubertian original.[24] Even the short-lived and ultimately disappointing intimacy Emma Bovary experiences in her marriage seems altogether absent in Isabel's marriage in *The Doctor's Wife*. Braddon tells us, "She [Isabel] was fond of him [George] as she would have been fond of a big elder brother, who let her have a good deal of her own way" (118). Critics have speculated about the sexless honeymoon and childless marriage of prudish Isabel and George Gilbert. Nonetheless, that she remains innocent in her affair with Lansdell seems improbable.

Isabel naively perceives Roland's love for her as pure as the love that Dante feels for the married Beatrice Portinari or the self-sacrificing love that Zanoni exhibits for his beloved Viola in Bulwer-Lytton's *Zanoni* (1842). To Isabel, Roland is not a flesh-and-blood man; rather, Isabel "had thought of him as a remotely-grand and star-like creature to be worshipped for ever by kneeling devotees offering perpetual incense, and entirely happy in the radiance of his countenance" (279). After Roland makes clear his passion, Isabel rejects him and concludes that he was not a Dante, and "He was not the true and faithful knight who could sit for ever at the entrance of his hermitage gazing fondly at the distant convent-casement, which might or might not belong to his lost-love's chamber" (277).

Braddon aligns our sympathy with Lansdell, a critical interpreter of Isabel's romantic imagination. Lansdell aptly recognizes: "I have only been the hero of a story-book; and all this folly has been nothing more than a page out of a novel set in action.... I must go away; and she will go back to her three-volume novels, and fall in love with a fair-haired hero, and forget me" (214). True to Lansdell's prediction, Isabel immediately miscasts the disenchanted, lonely, yet ultimately worthy Lansdell into a false knight. He becomes Robert the Devil, a heartless Faust who seduces the trusting Gretchen, and "Steerforth, handsome, heartless, irresistible Steerforth, with no pity for simple Em'ly or noble Peggotty's broken heart" (278). While Isabel reads Steerforth's character more accurately than before, the allusion to *David Copperfield*'s bad angel offers another example of how Isabel miscasts Lansdell. Roland Lansdell wishes to marry Isabel (had she been free) and loves her while Steerforth at best merely fancies Little Em'ly. Proving himself a man capable of rare self-reflection, Roland begs forgiveness for his unconsummated desires in a manner unthinkable of Steerforth, who never shows remorse for sullying Emily's purity, destroying Ham Peggotty's happiness, and disrupting Daniel Peggotty's contented home. On his deathbed, suffering from the fatal blows Isabel's forger father inflicts (he swears to kill Roland for offering evidence that incriminates him), Lansdell conceals the cause of his injury in true martyr fashion to spare his beloved Isabel further pain. He repents in a manner akin to Eugene Wrayburn when Wrayburn believes he is dying in *Our Mutual Friend* (1865).

The dual death scenes of Isabel's husband and lover in the third volume might be seen as Braddon's concession to conventions of sensation fiction. Neither death is sensational, however. Like Flaubert, Braddon delivers the body of the good provincial doctor, but in an undramatic way. George Gilbert dwindles from a fever he contracts from his poor patients whose lives he tries to improve. He never once believes his wife has compromised her love for him, despite the village gossip and his devoted servants' disapproval of Isabel. Lansdell's death calls to mind that of Gaskell's John Barton of *Mary Barton* (1848), who dies in the arms of Mr. Carson (the man whose son Barton murdered) in a sentimental religious conversion scene. In fact, Braddon creates an "imperfect conversion" (389) in Roland's final hours as Lansdell recites interchangeably lines from St. John's gospel and Tennyson's *In Memoriam*.[25] In his quiet pious death, Lansdell becomes a model for Christian mankind as he transforms into "something infinitely better and brighter than you ever knew him here. I never saw such a smile upon a human face as I saw just now on his" (395). Roland leaves Isabel his fortune, urging her toward greater things—"If ever you should find yourself with the means of doing great good, of being very useful to your fellow-creatures, I should like you to remember my wasted life, Isabel" (391). In death, Roland nearly attains the stature of David Copperfield's good angel, Agnes Wickfield, who ever points David "upward."

The drama and tragedy of Emma's fate in *Madame Bovary* seem altogether absent from Isabel's lot in *The Doctor's Wife*. Braddon does not kill off her addicted romance reader even though Isabel enjoys imagining her suicide—"death by poison was only a matter-of-fact business as compared to the still water and the rushes, and would have had a very inferior effect in the newspapers" (226). Braddon further confirms that "the possibility of deliberately leaving her husband to follow the footsteps of this other man [Roland], was as far beyond her power of comprehension as the possibility that she might steal a handful of arsenic out of one of the earthenware jars in the surgery, and mix it with the sugar that sweetened George

Gilbert's matutinal coffee" (276). These two pointed references dismiss Emma's adultery and stealing of arsenic from Monsieur Homais's pharmacy—believable choices that Emma makes when driven by sensuality, a desire for material splendor, and ultimately despair.

Choosing improvement over decline for Isabel, Braddon reforms her character once addicted to "beautiful sweet-meats [books], with opium inside the sugar" (24). She educates her romance reader by adding to her diet biography, philosophy, and history, selections that advocates of the socialization and education arguments endorsed. As Isabel reads improving works in the library of Mordred Priory during Roland's travels, she "expands" her mind and world view: "Her mind expanded amongst all the beautiful things around her, and the graver thoughts engendered out of grave books pushed away many of her most childish fancies, her simple sentimental yearnings. Until now she had lived too entirely amongst the poets and romancers; but now grave volumes of biography opened to her a new picture of life. She read the stories of real men and women, who had lived and suffered real sorrows, prosaic anguish, hard commonplace trial and misery" (235). The repetition of "grave" and "real" in this short passage flaunts Braddon's conviction that Isabel achieves a sober, responsible frame of mind as a reader. Braddon later praises her heroine, "The agricultural labourer, who had known the Doctor's Wife only as a pale-faced girlish creature, sitting under a hedgerow, with a green parasol above her head, and a book in her lap, had good reason to bless the Doctor's Widow" (403).[26] Blessed with Lansdell's fortune, Isabel becomes a "good and noble" (403) widow who performs deeds anticipating those contemplated by Eliot's Dorothea Brooke of *Middlemarch:* Isabel builds model villages with good schools, properly ventilated homes, wonderful ovens, big gardens, and state of the art farming equipment.

Braddon admitted to Bulwer-Lytton that she was not satisfied with the ending of her novel when he criticized her book in progress. Although Bulwer-Lytton liked the first two volumes, he would have preferred that Braddon leave George Gilbert alive; Braddon agreed that was her first intention: "I always meant Sleaford [Isabel's father] to kill Roland, but to the last I was uncertain what to do with George. My original intention was to have left him alive, & Isabel to a commonplace life doing her duty bravely, and suppressing all outward evidence of her deep grief for Roland. Thus the love story would have been an episode in a woman's life, succeeded by an after-existence of quiet work and duty."[27] While Braddon's alternative ending seems more staid than the actual one, Braddon never contemplates killing off her romance consumer. Isabel's transformation may be swift and unconvincing, but, as Flint notes, "Novel-reading remains uncondemned as an activity in itself: what is seen to matter is the cultivation of a self-knowing, responsible attitude towards it" (*The Woman Reader* 291).

While critics such as Leo Bersani conclude that "*Madame Bovary* is obviously a novel about the dangers of reading novels" (xiii), *The Doctor's Wife* decidedly is not.[28] Braddon never sermonizes. At worst, she offers a moderate reprimand against obsessive novel-reading through Sigismund Smith, who excels in writing "combination" stories, yet longs to produce a great novel (31). Smith, who Braddon's biographer Robert Lee Wolff suggests is the voice of Braddon herself (162), declares this view quite early in the book: "Novels are only dangerous for those poor foolish girls who read nothing else, and think that their lives are to be paraphrases of their favourite books" (30).

Isabel's temporary indulgence in the "strawberry ices of literature" does not lead to dire consequences that befall reading addicts, including Emma Bovary. Tempting literature, despite its opiatic addictiveness, need not have dangerous side effects or permanent consequences. Obsessive reading leads not to immorality, decline, and death, but to personal progress and a "fairy tale" fortune in *The Doctor's Wife*. Different from Flaubert, whose novel she bowdlerizes, Braddon allows Isabel to live, prosper, and improve. The ending of *The Doctor's Wife* debunks the pervasive nineteenth-century tropes of consumption and addiction that fuel the moral argument against women's novel-reading habit. In this respect, Braddon makes a daring and calculated move to disarm her opponents in the heated debate over if, what, where, when, and why a woman should read.

5

The Case for Compatibility

Jane Austen's *Mansfield Park* (1814), George Eliot's *Middlemarch* (1872), and Mona Caird's *The Daughters of Danaus* (1894)

Mary Elizabeth Braddon's heroine, Isabel Gilbert, takes after her Flaubertian model, Emma Bovary, in making a disastrous marital match. Of all the compelling reasons for each heroine's failed marriage, it would be of consequence to a nineteenth-century audience that both novel-addicted women marry nonreaders, who decidedly lack a romantic imagination. Numerous Victorian British and American novels contain failed marriages that critics have profitably examined as expressions of unequal gender and power relations at work in a dominant male culture.[1] A critic with a Victorian frame of mind might more readily pin incompatibility in real and fictional couples on other factors, including social class, previous conduct, breeding, temperament, and mismatched reading interests.

The Victorian British and American woman of the middle and upper classes was not limited to housewifely arts, as is often assumed. In the absence of women's meaningful occupation outside the home, wives became confidantes and active helpers in their husbands' lives. Their social graces and cultivation, advanced by lifelong reading, fitted them to be ideal wives. In her study of the Victorian gentlewoman, M. Jeanne Peterson suggests that "Like George Eliot's Dorothea, who married and expected to continue learning, the Victorian women of this circle began habits early that led, for most, to their continuing development as literate and cultured women" (57). Dorothea Brooke's aim to assist her husband in his life's work is the norm for the genteel Victorian lady, not the exception (M. Jeanne Peterson 162). As Annie Swan "insists" in *Courtship and Marriage* (1893), not a woman of inferior intellect, but a "woman of large brain power, provided she has well-balanced judgment, and a heart as expansive as her brain, will more nearly approach the ideal in matrimony than the more frivolous woman, who has no thought beyond her personal aggrandisement and adornment, and who buys her new bonnet with a kiss."[2] A learned and accomplished woman could assume her place as companion to her educated mate, supporting him in his personal and professional life. She was intelligent enough to "merge her individuality in that of another" (20), as Swan recognizes is often necessary in marriage. "After marriage, it would seem, a woman is being tacitly encouraged to seek self-recognition in relation not just to the general structures of patriarchal discourse, but to their individual representative within her life," as Flint likewise concludes (*The Woman Reader* 98).

Reading—a means for gentility, socialization, and education (within moderation)—enabled a woman to forge her identity in terms of her husband's interests. Women should read, advice writer George Bainton recommends in *The Wife as Lover and Friend* (1895), in order to please their mates. Bainton suggests a dutiful wife set aside an hour each day to read subjects "in which her husband is most interested."[3] Reading preferences also predicted marital harmony. As James Mason notes in his two-part 1881 article "How to Form a Small Library," a man can divine his compatibility with a potential mate by looking at her personal library: "a stranger coming in and looking at it might say with confidence either, 'There are many points of contact between that girl's mind and mine;' or, 'I am sure that girl and I will never get on, for she cares for nothing that I like and likes nothing I am keen upon'" (Mason 2: 123).[4] Reciprocally, a young woman can foresee her chances for a happy marriage by contemplating a suitor's attitude toward books: "To all girls I say, never marry a husband who has not a collection of books of more general interest than his cashbook and ledger. The reading young man makes a stay-at-home fireside-loving husband. Like to like" (1: 7). The literature of the period reflects these beliefs and illuminates both sides of the reading debate: the socialization, gentility, education, and empowerment arguments favoring women's reading, as well as the biological, medical, and moral models opposing it.

Jane Austen's *Mansfield Park* (1814) demonstrates that compatibility of a couple stems from the formation of a personal library. Fanny Price's and Edmund Bertram's well-suited literary tastes forecast their blissful union. More examples abound of irreconcilable readers and, in turn, marital incompatibility. The discord between Dorothea Brooke and Edward Casaubon of George Eliot's *Middlemarch* (1872) stems from Casaubon's sterility and superficiality as a scholar, clashing with Dorothea's fervent desire to gain a classical education and assist in meaningful work. We can predict the unhappiness of Hadria Fullerton and Hubert Temperley of Mona Caird's *The Daughters of Danaus* (1894) from their mismatched reading tastes, indicating these couples "will never get on," as Mason predicts. While not negating the dynamics of gender and power that inform a heroine's future happiness, reading in these three novels becomes an index of character and compatibility, offering an alternative perspective to explore the unions in each work and the reading ideologies informing them.

This pairing of novels brings together two authors frequently taught in the classroom with a third whose work still remains in need of recovery. Austen and Eliot need no introduction, although *Mansfield Park* may not be as widely taught as other Austen novels or *Middlemarch*. Caird remains less known than other rediscovered "New Woman" novelists including George Egerton, Olive Schreiner, and Sarah Grand. In 1888, Caird rapidly became the most criticized feminist in England when she published a sixteen-page article titled "Marriage" in the *Westminster Review* (John Chapman's radical quarterly). In response to Caird's indictment of marriage, the *Daily Telegraph* started a letters to the editor column titled "Is Marriage a Failure?"; 27,000 people responded to this provocatively titled column, eventually eclipsed by the Jack the Ripper scandal. In pairing *The Daughters of Danaus* with *Middlemarch* and *Mansfield Park*, I hope to draw more attention to Caird's important yet still underappreciated feminist work, influenced by the work of Ralph Waldo Emerson.[5]

Before Flaubert and Braddon, Austen offers much discussion of women's reading in her novels reflecting concerns bequeathed to the Victorians. Austen creates a heroine addicted to Gothic romance in Catherine Morland of *Northanger Abbey* (1818), a work which, Brantlinger argues, "both presents itself as a serious work of literature and participates in the general depreciation of novels and novel-reading" (*The Reading Lesson* 4).[6] The uncritical reading of romance by Marianne Dashwood of *Sense and Sensibility* (1811) and Catherine Morland of *Northanger Abbey* leads the protagonist of each novel to make embarrassing faux pas. *Pride and Prejudice* (1813) foregrounds the reading of letters in relation to the reading of character. Fanny Price of *Mansfield Park* is a less lively heroine than Elizabeth Bennet or Catherine Morland. Gilbert and Gubar aptly describe Fanny as a "model of domestic virtue" who is "trapped in angelic reserve" (165) and compare her to Snow White in her passivity, purity, immobility, and "invalid deathliness" (165). Nonetheless, I would argue that despite these limitations and her lack of eloquence, Fanny succeeds in *Mansfield Park* because she is a skillful reader of books and character.

As Gary Kelly observes, *Mansfield Park* explores the interrelations of reading aloud, performance art, as well as reading—or actually misreading—the character of another (and in this respect it is akin to *Pride and Prejudice*).[7] The second son of a landed gentleman, Edmund Bertram supervises the education of his first cousin upon her arrival at Mansfield Park. Fanny is the eldest daughter of Lady Bertram's sister Frances, who marries beneath her. The largely uneducated, poor, though willing ten-year-old Fanny comes to Mansfield Park ostensibly to wait on her two aunts, Lady Bertram and Mrs. Norris. Her cousin Edmund, educated at Eton and Oxford, is a prolific reader, destined for the clergy and, accordingly, a career as a public reader and speaker. Of the Bertram family, Edmund alone consistently treats Fanny with respect. The other cousins ignore or condescend to her, Lady Bertram expects Fanny to wait on her, and Sir Thomas Bertram rightly fears that Fanny's installation in his home might lead to "cousins in love."[8] For Fanny and Edmund, as Kelly remarks, "Love begins with reading, with reading together, with literature" (31).

Edmund awakens Fanny's love early in the novel when he takes on the task of supervising her education. He first helps a despondent Fanny write a letter to her beloved brother, William. Fanny has been taught to read and write, nothing more. All but Edmund conclude that she is stupid since she cannot put the map of Europe together or repeat the chronological order of the kings of England. She has no interest in learning music or drawing, typical ladies' accomplishments that might allow for a showy display of her talent. Nonetheless, Edmund's attentions are "of the highest importance in assisting the improvement of her mind, and extending its pleasures" (38). Edmund "continued with her the whole time of her writing, to assist her with his pen-knife or his orthography, as either were wanted; and added to these attentions, which she felt very much, a kindness to her brother, which delighted her beyond all the rest" (34). In his kindness toward his unschooled cousin, Edmund gains Fanny's trust, affection, and love.

Edmund discerns Fanny's intellect: "He knew her to be clever, to have a quick apprehension as well as good sense, and a fondness for reading, which, properly directed, must be an education in itself" (38). Like James and Flaubert, Austen does not offer the exact titles Fanny reads. However, through her presentation of Edmund's guiding of Fanny's reading, Austen illuminates the pro-reading arguments of gentility, education, and socialization. Edmund selects books for Fanny's learning and enjoyment and becomes her reading tutor: "Miss Lee taught her French, and heard her read the daily portion of History; but he [Edmund] recommended the books which charmed her leisure hours, he encouraged her taste, and corrected her judgement; he made reading useful by talking to her of what she read, and heightened its attraction by judicious praise. In return for such services she loved him better than anybody in the world except William; her heart was divided between the two" (38). Edmund chooses right reading for Fanny, recognizing that books are a consideration in a girl's schooling and a Victorian woman's life. Fanny will not only acquire education but codes that augment her genteel nature and ensure her respect and admiration in Edmund's social circle. Moreover, in this passage in volume 1 of her three-volume novel, Austen directs us to how Fanny's love for Edmund grows out of his literary guidance.

Possessing the skill of a Pygmalion, Edmund molds Fanny to his liking. While plain and sensible Fanny Price in no way resembles the ivory statue that Pygmalion fashions after the Greek goddess of love, Edmund acutely sees worth in the clay of Fanny Price: he socializes his untaught cousin, sculpting a woman of thought and opinion, whose views he shares. Austen arguably invites this allusion by suggesting that Edmund "formed her mind": "Having formed her mind and gained her affections, there was a good chance of her thinking like him" (73). Edmund fashions Fanny's thinking through well-thought praise and correction. Acting according to advice books of the day, he instinctively knows he can shape Fanny's mind and character by forming her personal library. Edmund's recommendations for Fanny's reading "charmed her leisure hours." Thus, Edmund's influence extends far beyond their actual moments of reading together; to recall the rhetoric of the period, Edmund provides her with "companions" and "intimate friends" appropriate for a cultivated Victorian lady of the Bertrams' social circle.

Austen's prediction that Fanny will think like Edmund rings true, although fortunately Fanny proves superior to her tutor/sculptor in her reading of character. Austen reveals Fanny's astute judgment when the Bertrams and their friends decide to perform Elizabeth Inchbald's *Lovers' Vows* (1798), a play whose fame stems from its inclusion in this novel. Fanny sees the faults of their attractive neighbors, Mary and Henry Crawford, well before Edmund. Even so, critics have long debated whether Mary or Fanny is the more "likeable" character.[9] Mary's skill in elocution and acting captivates Edmund. Misreading the materialistic and shallow Mary Crawford as charming and witty, Edmund initially falls under her spell. The plot is predictable. Edmund experiences a revelation akin to that of

Elizabeth Bennet of *Pride and Prejudice*, who realizes her misreading of Mr. Darcy and declares, "Till this moment, I never knew myself" (156).

Once Henry and Mary Crawford's various attractions prove fallible to all at Mansfield Park, and Edmund comes to regard his beloved cousin Fanny as a lover—as she sees him all along—Edmund "became as anxious to marry Fanny, as Fanny herself could desire" (406); their marriage swiftly follows. Fanny's apt reading of character raises her in the estimation of the entire Bertram family. Fanny now moves with ease in their social circle. But to the reader, Fanny's suitability as Edmund's mate comes as no revelation at all. In volume 1, Austen, like Edmund, has "judiciously" sown the seeds of marital compatibility in describing Edmund's guidance of Fanny's reading from which their intimacy grows. True to Greek legend, Edmund falls in love with his own creation. The conclusion validates that Edmund has, in fact, successfully "formed her mind and gained her affections" (73). The now genteel Fanny, who appreciates the subjects that "most interest" her husband, achieves marital bliss.

In sharp contrast to Austen, Eliot in *Middlemarch* reveals a fatal incompatibility between her willing female "pupil," Dorothea Brooke, and her middle-aged husband-scholar, Reverend Edward Casaubon, even though her heroine is as willing as Fanny Price to be molded by her mate. Eliot describes Dorothea's learning as "that toy-box history of the world adapted to young ladies which made the chief part of her education."[10] She feels sorely "ignorant" (74) and is overeager to accomplish something "grand" (51) with her life. Dorothea's fervent desire to be initiated into higher learning and gain a classical education sets her up for disappointment.

Dorothea—who knows by heart passages of Pascal's *Pensées* and Jeremy Taylor's work (likely his best known devotionals *Holy Living* and *Holy Dying*)—is known to stay up all night reading theological books. From Pascal's testimonial about Christianity, she may have gleaned some insights into the human condition. Still, as Rosemary Ashton notes, Dorothea is "Puritan, narrowly educated, inclined to self-righteousness, yet generous, spontaneous, intent on doing good, though with little idea of how to set about it. In the absence of careers for women, her only hope is to marry someone whose work she can share" (322–23). If we read Dorothea's character as such, it is not surprising that Dorothea misreads Casaubon in her search for a husband who is "above me in judgment and in all knowledge" (64). She hopes to become his research assistant and devote her life to a "great soul" (43) who will pass on important ideas and values. Acquiring knowledge and confidence as she shares in Casaubon's work, idealistic Dorothea also gains a painful awareness that ultimately empowers her life: Casaubon can neither form her mind nor gain her enduring affections.

As Reynolds and Humble suggest in *Victorian Heroines*, Eliot creates a match similar to the father-daughter marriages in Dickensian fiction (Annie and Doctor Strong of *David Copperfield* is a prime example) (17). Dickens celebrates these nonsexual unions—not so Eliot. Dorothea's friends in her provincial world of Middlemarch balk at Dorothea's attraction to a dried-up scholar with a deadened spirit. Mrs. Cadwallader, who hopes for a match between Dorothea and Sir James Chettam, wishes "her joy of her hair shirt" (85) when she hears of Dorothea's engagement. The rejected suitor, Chettam, similarly states, "Good God! It is horrible! He is no better than a mummy!" (81). Casaubon's cousin and rival, Will Ladislaw, believes "if he chose to grow grey crunching bones in a cavern, he had no business to be luring a girl into his companionship. 'It is the most horrible of virgin sacrifices'" (395). Tantripp, Dorothea's faithful maid, declares to Casaubon's butler after Dorothea's marriage, "I wish every book in that library was built into a catacomb for your master" (522). Even Dorothea's uncle, a friend of Casaubon's, admits, "He is a little buried in books, you know, Casaubon is" (62).

Dorothea's fascination with Casaubon stems from the theological books and classical texts he has literally "buried" himself in during his scholarly career. Visiting Casaubon's home, Dorothea observes with pleasure "the dark book-shelves in the long library, the carpets and curtains with colours subdued by time, the curious old maps and bird's-eye views on the walls of the corridor, with here and there an old vase below" (99). A woman of culture, Dorothea longs to read from a gentleman's library—as Isabel Archer, Jo March, Isabel Sleaford Gilbert, and Jane Eyre do. The scholarly surroundings of Lowick increase Dorothea's attraction to Casaubon. Eliot further associates her suitor with book knowledge by situating him in numerous scholarly libraries: at Lowick, the Grange, and the Vatican. As Elaine Showalter observes, "The classical education was the intellectual dividing line between men and women; intelligent women aspired to study Greek and Latin with a touching faith that such knowledge would open the world of male power and wisdom to them. The feminine novel of the period up to about 1880 reflects women's intense effort to meet the educational standards of the male establishment" (42). Showalter cites Dorothea's grappling with Greek, as well as Maggie Tulliver's studying Latin, to illustrate how nineteenth-century women believed that a classical education would give them access to the realms of male learning and authority. Different from Fanny, who reads to please Edmund, Dorothea, akin to Eliot's Maggie Tulliver, hungers after "masculine knowledge." To the idealistic Dorothea, "These provinces of masculine knowledge seemed to her a standing-ground from which all truth could be seen more truly" (88). Despite her idealism, faith, ambition, and intelligence, Dorothea does not achieve a purpose in her gendered world.

Dorothea's uncle buys into the biological model that men's and women's brains are differently constituted. He believes in "a lightness about the feminine mind—a touch and go" (89). To Mr. Brooke, women should study music and the fine arts; he fears for Dorothea's health, "such deep studies, classics, mathematics, that kind of thing, are too taxing for a woman—too taxing you know" (89). Casaubon argues that Dorothea's studies are not "deep"; she is merely reading what interests him to better serve her mate: "Dorothea is learning the characters simply.... She had the very considerate thought of saving my eyes" (89). Not so to Dorothea: the myopic Dorothea Brooke in book 1 "truly" (though falsely) believes that in learning with Casaubon her mind will elevate to the standards of male education, that she will enter a masculine province of strength and knowledge or at least approach "the intellectual dividing line between men and women" (Showalter 42).

Casaubon's small gift of a manuscript sparks their romance. When Casaubon sends her his pamphlet, she seats herself in the library at the Grange, "taking it in as eagerly as she might have taken in the scent of a fresh bouquet after a dry, hot, dreary walk" (61). Eliot again employs natural metaphors as she notes Dorothea's excitement with Casaubon: "He thinks with me, ... or rather he thinks a whole world of which my thought is but a poor two-penny mirror. And his feelings too, his whole experience—what a lake compared with my little pool!" (47). Dorothea longs to exchange her little "pool" of knowledge for Casaubon's vaster waters. She sees her life as "but a labyrinth of petty courses, a walled-in maze of small paths that led no whither" (51). Wandering aimlessly in the maze of life, she mistakenly believes Casaubon "would deliver her from her girlish subjection to her own ignorance, and give her the freedom of voluntary submission to a guide who would take her along the grandest path" (51). As Ashton acutely observes, "Dorothea aspires, however naively and vaguely, to do good in the world, mistakenly thinking that marriage to Mr. Casaubon will give her the necessary freedom and opportunity. She is under an illusion" (322).

Eliot's Dorothea believes Casaubon will initiate her in higher ideas and enlarge her narrow and limited life (112). Just as Braddon's Isabel Gilbert miscasts her husband and Lansdell as heroes and villains of romance novels, and Flaubert's Emma Bovary hopes to find the excitement of romantic heroes in Rodolphe Boulanger and Léon Dupuis, Dorothea projects the lives of great men onto Edward Casaubon. Recalling a phrase Dr. Johnson borrows from Dryden, Michael Wheeler concludes that Dorothea sees Casaubon through the "spectacles of books."[11] Rejecting marriage to the wealthy, handsome, and amiable Chettam, Dorothea seems caught up in a mood of ecstatic submissiveness. She longs to wed a Hooker, a Milton, "or any of the other great men whose odd habits it would have been glorious piety to endure; . . . The really delightful marriage must be that where your husband was a sort of father, and could teach you even Hebrew, if you wished it" (32). She even naively believes she might have saved a great thinker like Hooker from matrimonial despair or aided Milton at the onset of his blindness. Instead, she meets Casaubon, "noted in the country as a man of profound learning, understood for many years to be engaged on a great work concerning religious history" (33). Eliot's pointed word choice —"noted" and "understood"—implies that Casaubon in no way approximates the great sixteenth- and seventeenth-century thinkers who fascinate Dorothea Brooke. Wheeler suggests an irony in Eliot's naming of her unproductive scholar. Casaubon likely refers to Isaac Casaubon (father of Meric Casaubon), who produced an imposing amount of scholarship at the expense of ill health (Wheeler 86). But to Dorothea, "Here was something beyond the shallows of ladies'-school literature: here was a living Bossuet, whose work would reconcile complete knowledge with devoted piety; here was a modern Augustine who united the glories of doctor and saint" (47).[12] She transforms Casaubon into Pascal, Milton, Hooker, and countless other great thinkers of the past whom she idealizes and idolizes. She hopes that in marrying Casaubon, "There would be nothing trivial about our lives. Everyday-things with us would mean the greatest things. It would be like marrying Pascal. I should learn to see the truth by the same light as great men have seen it by" (51).

Casaubon shares Milton's failing eyesight. He has the bad health of Hooker, Locke, and Pascal (marrying Dorothea, he also has a disastrous marriage like Milton and Hooker). Dorothea innocently declares to her sister, Celia, who deems Casaubon ugly, "He is one of the most distinguished-looking men I ever saw. He is remarkably like the portrait of Locke. He has the same deep eye-sockets" (42). While her ostensibly barren suitor may have eye-sockets as deep as Locke's, he does not possess a "great soul" (43). Cast as a modern Saint Theresa, Dorothea has no hope for her own glory. Rather, Eliot raises the possibility of what an intellectual woman of the upper reaches might achieve at a time when it was far from common to pursue a fulfilling career.

Dorothea lays aside her plans for cottage improvements when she meets Casaubon, who cannot appreciate them. He presents a way for her, vicariously, to achieve a classical education and a meaning and purpose in her life: "But something she yearned for by which her life might be filled with action at once rational and ardent; and since the time was gone by for guiding visions and spiritual directors, since prayer heightened yearning but not instruction, what lamp was there but knowledge? Surely learned men kept the only oil; and who more learned than Mr. Casaubon?" (112–13). Dorothea aspires to be Casaubon's lamp-holder, aiding his life and ennobling her own. She wholeheartedly becomes her husband's research assistant. She insists that she take her place in the library alongside him.[13] She copies endless quotations for him. She reads to him to save his eyes, as Milton's daughters did, even if she does not comprehend what she reads, as they did not. In due course, she rebels like Milton's daughters, as Casaubon predicts she might.

Casaubon has not developed an original paradigm. Ever at work on a tome of historical biblical criticism he never produces, Casaubon "dreams footnotes, and they run away with all his brains" (96). While he has produced small parergon throughout his career, the reception of his secondary manuscripts has been poor, riddling his self-doubt and crippling him further. On his honeymoon, we witness Casaubon working from breakfast till dinner in the Vatican Library. Mired in minutiae, he takes copious notes from the ancient tomes that are not directly useful to his scholarship; "The notes I have here made will want sifting" (232), he admits to Dorothea. Dorothea replies more critically, "you have often said that they wanted digesting" (233). With this one word, Eliot unmasks the passive and highly unoriginal mind of a sterile pseudo-scholar who feeds off the ideas of others and never begins "A Key to All Mythology," his intended magnum opus.

Akin to Eliot's barren scholar Bardo, who represents Renaissance book culture in *Romola* (1863), Casaubon seems blind to the spirit of the classical works he has studied for over thirty years. He perceives the pagan myths as corruptions of the original myth, as recorded in the Bible. Carla L. Peterson also suggests that Casaubon's fruitless efforts to write "A Key to All Mythology" can arguably be viewed as an ironic recasting of Louis Lambert's romantic quest for origins in Balzac's *Louis Lambert* (1835) (204). While Louis Lambert and Edward Casaubon aim to trace the origins of culture, only Casaubon attempts to posit the original myth of Christianity as the key to all pagan mythologies. Eliot again uses irony in titling Casaubon's problem-ridden work a "Key."

Ethnocentrism and ignorance of German hinder Casaubon. He ignores the work of German scholars who—as Eliot knew from her own experience in translating David Friedrich Strauss's *Das Leben Jesu* (1835)—were then producing cutting-edge historical biblical criticism. Ladislaw, Casaubon's cousin and rival, becomes a critical interpreter of his research methods. He tells Dorothea, "the Germans have taken the lead in historical inquiries, and they laugh at results which are got by groping about in the woods with a pocket-compass while they have made good roads. When I was with Mr. Casaubon I saw that he deafened himself in that direction: it was almost against his will that he read a Latin treatise written by a German" (240). Dorothea feels a "pang" (240) when she realizes her "guide" has ignored the gateways of modern scholarship and lost his way.[14] Casaubon emerges as an outdated pedant; "in his own age he is a scholastic anachronism," as W. J. Harvey observes.[15] By his own admission, he is a man who "lives[s] too much with the dead. My mind is something like the ghost of an ancient, wandering about the world and trying mentally to construct it as it used to be, in spite of ruin and confusing changes" (40). Desk-bound and barren, Casaubon remains untouched by change and progress, influential neither through his writings nor his life.

Dorothea's marriage does not fail because she relies on books to judge her future husband's character. Rather, what she perceives as Casaubon's vast "lake" of knowledge is revealed to be a mirage. She learns enough Latin and Greek to realize "that the large vistas and wide fresh air which she had dreamed of finding in her husband's mind were replaced by anterooms and winding passages which seemed to lead nowhither" (227–28). His world suddenly seems "an enclosed basin" (228),[16] a "virtual tomb" (516). Propelled back to her own self, Dorothea doubts Casaubon's labors and the worth of his unfinished "Key" (519). She shrinks from the thought of sifting through "shattered mummies, and fragments of a tradition which was itself a mosaic wrought from crushed ruins—sorting them as food for a theory which was already withered in the birth like an elfin child" (519). Eliot confides to her readers that "in spite of [Dorothea's] small instruction, her judgment in this matter was truer than his: for she looked with unbiassed comparison and healthy sense at probabilities on which he had risked all his egoism" (519). Casaubon's failed legacy comes to resemble "the volumes of polite literature" in the bookcase in Dorothea's room at Lowick, which "looked more like immovable imitations of books" (306). Eliot mocks Casaubon's pretensions of culture by having his wife-cum-pupil discover the limitations of his learnedness. Dorothea cannot achieve "self-recognition in relation not just to the general structures of patriarchal discourse, but to their individual representative within her life" (Flint, *The Woman Reader* 98).

Casaubon's egotism, insecurity, outdatedness, and burning jealousy irreparably shatter Dorothea's short-lived idealism and their union. Still, Eliot presents him sympathetically, perhaps owing to a personal connection she felt with her character. George Henry Lewes likened Eliot to Dorothea, himself to Casaubon, and his multivolume *Problems of Life and Mind* (1873–79)—an early, ambitious psychology treatise—to Casaubon's unfinished "Key." But Eliot told Harriet Beecher Stowe: "Impossible to conceive any creature less like Mr. Casaubon than my warm, enthusiastic husband . . . I fear that the Casaubon-tints are not quite foreign to my own mental complexion" (Ashton 325). Even if Eliot claims a likeness to Casaubon, we cannot ignore the Lewes-Casaubon connection: Eliot completed the final volume of *Problems of Life and Mind* after Lewes's death, much as Casaubon imagines Dorothea will continue on with his "Key."

Despite her affinity for her unproductive scholar, Eliot pities Dorothea more than she commiserates with Casaubon. As one nineteenth-century critic aptly puts it, "She [Dorothea] held the lamp, but it contained no oil" (Adams 149). Eliot reveals a fatal incompatibility between her young female pupil, who fervently wants her husband to form her mind, and her middle-aged, unproductive scholar, who cannot even light his own way. "Books were of no use" (516) to a Dorothea drained by her marriage. She has grown restless even with the companionship of her favorite book friends: "from Herodotus, which she was learning to read with Mr. Casaubon, to her old companion Pascal, and Keble's *Christian Year*" (515), a popular nineteenth-century book of religious poetry that Maggie Tulliver turns to during a period of repression.

Fortunately, Casaubon dies before he can exact a promise that Dorothea continue his vain efforts. He pushes her into the arms of his rival through a codicil in his will that Dorothea forfeit her fortune if she marry Ladislaw. Fittingly, in Casaubon's own library, the widowed Dorothea accepts Ladislaw and begins a new life with a man with artistic sensibilities, who considers Dorothea to be "a poem—and that is to be the best part of a poet—what makes up the poet's consciousness in his best moods" (256). As wife of Ladislaw, a public man, Dorothea does not triumph: "the effect of her being on those around her was incalculably diffusive: for the growing good of the world is partly dependent on unhistoric acts; and that things are not so ill with you and me as they might have been, is half owing to the number who lived faithfully a hidden life, and rested in unvisited tombs" (896). Dorothea is restricted by pervasive social conditions that Eliot and a few of her intellectual contemporaries (for example, Octavia Hill and Florence Nightingale) managed to overcome in Victorian times (Ashton 327). But we take comfort that Dorothea is no longer "buried in books."

Hadria Fullerton in *The Daughters of Danaus* marries Hubert Temperley and escapes the restrictions of her parents' home, Dunaghee. Unlike Dorothea Brooke, she is not eager to forge her identity in terms of her husband's interests. While Edmund Bertram selects books for Fanny Price and molds her reading tastes, Hubert Temperley courts a woman whose mind is formed long before he meets her. Hadria Fullerton has marked reading preferences, including a penchant for feminist fiction, which contrast sharply to the interests of the conservative, classically schooled Temperley. In contrast to Austen whose fiction advances the ideology of reading for socialization and gentility, Caird makes a strong argument for women's reading for personal interest, education, and empowerment, real and imagined. *The Daughters of Danaus*—which earned gratitude from countless Victorian women readers—lambastes the sacred Victorian institutions of marriage and motherhood and evoked criticism for its revolutionary message about women's rights.

Rather than expose her suitor after marriage like Eliot, Caird presents a developed portrait of an intellectually curious "modern" reader to forecast her disastrous marriage to a man with traditional literary taste and temperament. Caird introduces us to the works of two nineteenth-century authors—one fictional (Valeria Du Prel), one real (Ralph Waldo Emerson)—to construct Hadria Fullerton as a reader.

Before her marriage, Hadria, an avid composer and reader, defies her conservative mother, who sacrifices her own intellectual pursuits for marriage and motherhood. The most spirited of the five Fullerton siblings, Hadria complies to Mrs. Fullerton's directions by day, but stays up late to read and compose (110). An angry Mrs. Fullerton espouses the moral and medical arguments against women's education: she considers Hadria's intellectual work a "selfish" (109) preoccupation that will "ruin her health for life" (110). Hadria consumes provocative novels by the feminist Valeria Du Prel, whose radical fiction her mainstream Victorian society scorns.

When Du Prel vacations in Scotland near Hadria's home, Hadria develops a fast friendship with the author. Ironically, Du Prel emerges as a disappointingly conventional character, who readily admits: "I believe in the normal, . . . having devoted my existence to an experiment of the abnormal" (423).[17] Not her life, but her novels, *Parthenia* and *Caterina*, inspire Hadria. In *Parthenia,* Du Prel lauds women's liberation. In *Caterina,* Du Prel's unconventional heroine questions traditional ideals, leaves her husband and home, and lives independently to remain true to her conscience. Hadria claims that *Parthenia* "has given me faith in all that is worth living for" (51). A testimony to the argument of reading for empowerment, *Caterina* ultimately proves instrumental to Hadria's self-fashioning of her identity. In part 2 of *The Daughters of Danaus,* a despondent Hadria Fullerton Temperley communes with the dead in the village churchyard, a frequent haunting. Her once animated face exhibits sadness and suffering. Her fate worsens as Hadria shrinks from the responsibilities of mothering two sons. However, like Caterina, Hadria bravely leaves husband and home in part 2 of the novel. She pursues her dream to compose music in Paris, although duty eventually summons her home.[18]

Hadria also seems to fashion her identity in response to Emerson's philosophy. *The Daughters of Danaus* opens with Hadria and her siblings debating Emerson in the garret of their ancestral home, Dunaghee. The Fullertons hold a meeting of their secret circle, the Preposterous Society, at which Hadria presides. In the opening chapter, Hadria—undeniably Caird's mouthpiece—emerges as an intelligent reader and an advocate for women's rights, including education. Caird wrote fiction and nonfiction to advance the women's movement; in all her novels and essays, the rights of women appear foremost. Although Caird never received a formal university education, in the 1860s and 1870s, she read widely in a range of disciplines including sociology, economics, history, feminist thought, science, and philosophy (McKinney 625–26), at which point she presumably encountered the works of Emerson.[19]

The topic of Hadria's lecture is Emerson's "Fate," which becomes a central theme of the novel. Hadria opposes arguments that Emerson advances in his essays "Fate" and "Character": she claims that for women in nineteenth-century society, circumstance is more powerful than will.[20] In "Character," which comes from the second series of *Essays* (1844),[21]

Emerson defines character as an irresistible power essential to self-reliance; with character, one can resist or conquer circumstance by exerting will. The individual determines events—not vice versa. Critics read "Fate," the lead essay in *The Conduct of Life* (1860, rev. 1876), as one of Emerson's more pessimistic works in its omission of an external absolute against which to measure our actions and its suggestion that fate limits man's power.[22] Still, in "Fate," Emerson advances optimistically, one's irresistible will, in turn, opposes fate.[23]

Hadria begins her discourse quoting nearly verbatim a passage from the body of "Fate": "But the soul contains the event that shall befall it, for the event is only the actualization of its thoughts; and what we pray to ourselves for is always granted. The event is the print of your form. It fits you like your skin. What each does is proper to him. Events are the children of his mind and body."[24] Hadria sees clearly that women in her patriarchal society do not often achieve their desires. To Hadria, the world is comprised of "organizers," endowed with Emersonian character, and "destroyers," who remain idle or undo what organizers have achieved. Making this distinction, Hadria claims:

> But is not circumstance, to a large extent, created by these destroyers, as I have called them? Has not the strongest soul to count with these, who weave the web of adverse conditions, whose dead weight has to be carried, whose work of destruction has to be incessantly repaired? Who can dare to say "I am master of my fate," when he does not know how large may be the share of the general burden that will fall to him to drag through life, how great may be the parasites who are living on the moral capital of their generation? Surely circumstance consists largely in the inertia, the impenetrability of the destroyers. (10)

Hadria argues in direct opposition to Emerson: defeat is not always a simple case of character failing to conquer circumstance.

In her discourse on "Fate," Hadria returns to "Character," paraphrasing part of a line that actually reads, "the soul of goodness escapes from any set of circumstances, whilst prosperity belongs to a certain mind, and will introduce that power and victory which is its natural fruit, into any order of events."[25] One is not always master of one's fate: a stifling circumstance might prove too powerful for even the most forceful person to overcome it with will alone.[26] In fact, the greatness of a woman's talent often leads to the greatness of the obstacle, if her talent runs against the grain of tradition.²⁷ Hadria concludes that Emerson is "ridiculous" (11) and spiritedly retorts: "Emerson never was a girl!" (14); "If he had been a girl, he would have known that conditions *do* count hideously in one's life" (14).²⁸

Worse, prejudices are "twined in with the very heart-strings of those one loves! Ah! *that* particular obstacle has held many a woman helpless and suffering, like some wretched insect pinned alive to a board throughout a miserable lifetime! What would Emerson say to those cases? That 'Nature magically suits the man to his fortunes by making these the fruit of his character'? Pooh! I think Nature more often makes a man's fortunes a veritable shirt of Nessus which burns and clings, and finally kills him with anguish!" (15).²⁹ Hadria's knowledge of Greek mythology deflates Emersonian optimism. She projects onto "Nature" the Greek myth of Nessus, the centaur ultimately responsible for Heracles's death.³⁰ "Nature" turns man's fortunes into the supreme agony that Heracles endures when he dons Nessus's tunic (which Deianira sends her unfaithful husband): the tunic is smeared with the blood of the centaur (whom Heracles shoots) as well as the poison of his own arrow; it burns his flesh, leading him to take his own life.³¹ Hadria's fate is not so dramatic, though it comes to match her chillingly graphic description of "some wretched insect pinned alive to a board" of tradition.³²

Although Hadria seems accurate in her presentation of Emerson and very persuasive in her dialogue, her reading of Emerson's essays transforms his philosophy. Akin to the concept of ekphrasis, Hadria, in debating Emerson, condenses his views into a simple schema. She reads both essays through the spectacles of late-nineteenth-century feminism, finding Emerson too optimistic, absolute, and idealistic.³³ Nonetheless, like Maggie Tulliver and Dorothea Brooke, Hadria reveals a keen and inquiring mind as she establishes her reading interests.³⁴

Hadria is far more developed as a reader than Hubert Temperley, but Caird offers enough indication to forecast his unsuitableness as Hadria's mate. He has a deep reverence for things dating from antiquity: "He spoke with eloquence of literature, and praised enthusiastically most great names dating securely from the hallowed past. Of modern literature he was a stern critic" (73). Caird implies that Temperley, son of a judge, had the kind of classical education that leads Dorothea Brooke to marry Casaubon.

Temperley bristles with Du Prel and sternly criticizes the works of modern literature that engage Hadria's imagination. Temperley's "opinions were of an immovable order, with very defined edges. In some indescribable fashion, those opinions partook of the general elegance of his being" (76). His nature is rigid and unchanging: "What he had thought at twenty, at thirty-five had acquired sanctity and certainty, from having been the opinion of Hubert Temperley for all those favoured years" (161). His conservatism seems extreme.[35] Ironically, Hadria and Hubert begin their courtship playing music together, but in music, as in literature, he venerates the past. He dislikes Hadria's avant-garde compositions because of their dissonance.

A character passionately engaged in modern literature and avant-garde music and another fixed in his admiration of classical literature and music prove decidedly discordant companions. Hubert's traditional sister, Henriette, mistakenly tells him that Hadria will settle down contentedly in marriage as soon as she weds him: "There is really nothing to be alarmed at in her ideas, regrettable as they are. She is young. That sort of thing will soon wear off after she is married" (134). More perceptively, Henriette admits that Hadria's ideals may "have to be rooted out" (134), but advises Hubert to humor Hadria before the wedding day. Hubert might well have liked to "root out" Hadria's beliefs in women's equality, but he does not marry a Fanny Price or even a Dorothea Brooke, who will "merge her individuality in that of another," to recall Swan's advice. Professor Fortescue, Caird's "New Man" in the novel, concludes before their marriage: "I know that a marriage between those two would end in misery" (94). Although Valeria Du Prel approves the match, she admits, "If he shatters *her* illusions, she will certainly shatter *his*" (92).[36]

Caird uses Hadria's reading as more than a means to dash illusions and showcase a feminist ideology. Hadria's opposition to Emerson's ideas in part 1 ultimately demonstrates her divided character as well as why, in part 3, her musical aspirations fail, despite her great talent. As Caird confides, "In spite of the view that Hadria had expounded in her capacity of lecturer, she had an inner sense that somehow, after all, the will *can* perform astonishing feats in Fate's despite. Her intellect, rather than her heart, had opposed the philosophy of Emerson" (17). In Paris, Hadria tries to "perform astonishing feats in Fate's despite." She composes music of excellent quality which her Parisian mentor, Monsieur Jouffroy, admits is far ahead of its time. The response Hadria receives from her Parisian audience ultimately concurs with Hubert's severe judgment of her music: "It was rebel music, offensive to the orthodox. Hubert had always said that 'it was out of the question,' and he appeared to have been right" (321). Of small consolation, Hadria's life story fuels her opening argument that for women "the greatness of the power may serve to make the greatness of the obstacles" (14).

Obstacles and duties overpower Hadria. Caird whisks her away from

Paris to tend her sick mother[37] and leaves her wedded to a mate with whom she "will never get on," as forecasted by an examination of their personal libraries and appetites for fiction. Had Hubert seen Hadria's personal library containing works by Emerson and Du Prel, he might have exclaimed, in the words of advice writer Mason, "I am sure that girl and I will never get on, for she cares for nothing that I like and likes nothing I am keen upon" (2: 123) Likewise, Hadria, glancing at Hubert's classical books, might well have foreseen she had no interest in her husband's life's work. Hadria finds marriage to Hubert unpleasant, occasionally tolerable. Of note, Caird does not villainize Hubert. As Margaret Morganroth Gullette suggests, "Caird makes Hadria's marriage a simple case of incompatibility, itself an ingenious invention anticipating no-fault divorce" (502).

Austen marries her contented Fanny Price to Edmund Bertram, who has formed her personal library and her mind. Eliot allows Dorothea to see what is behind a mirage of books and escape from Casaubon's imprisoning library. Caird does not emancipate Hadria, who narrowly avoids an affair with the chauvinistic Professor Theobald, revealed as the father of the illegitimate Martha, whom Hadria "adopts."[38] Hadria loses her beloved mentor, Professor Fortescue, at the inconclusive end of the novel. Enduring "a miserable lifetime," Hadria longs to die, though she appears slightly heartened by Fortescue's final words of praise.

If Hadria's fate is unhappy subsistence, Gullette praises Caird for avoiding "the deepest trap in the culture, the (male-invented, realist) stereotype of female decline, which led other novelists like Schreiner and Chopin to slaughter their brave women rebels at the end of the story" (503). Equally daring are Caird's endorsement of reading to empower women's lives and praise of women who pursue their own interests, not those of their mates. Although Hadria does not achieve marital bliss by refusing to tailor her life and reading tastes to her husband's—as Fanny Price does willingly—at least, to recall Gilbert and Gubar's criticism of Fanny Price, Hadria is no Snow White. Caird envisions a spirited heroine who reads avidly and widely even if, like Dorothea Brooke, she must lead a "hidden life."

• • •

Fiction represents and, at times, reacts to the cultural regard for the woman reader. Beginning with *Jane Eyre* and concluding with *The Daughters of Danaus*, part 2 raises conflicting ideologies about women's reading coexisting in Victorian Britain and America. Some ideological representations seem fleeting: Mr. Stelling briefly espouses the biological model when he squelches Maggie Tulliver's desire to learn Latin; Professor Bhaer voices the moral argument when he censures sensation novels, embarrassing Jo March; Dorothea's uncle, Mr. Brooke, fears for her health if she continues her avid reading; and Charles Bovary's mother offers a snapshot of the medical and moral arguments when complaining about the potential harm and selfishness of Emma's romance reading habit. Other more sustained representations—the March sisters' modeling their pilgrimages after *Pilgrim's Progress;* Edmund Bertram forming Fanny Price's select library; Isabel Archer's clouding her expectations of life from fiction; Hadria Fullerton's spirited disagreement with Emerson's ideas; Emma Bovary's reading romances by candlelight; and Catherine Linton's empowering her life and Hareton's by teaching him to read—function as picture windows into dominant ideologies on both sides of a heated debate, requiring us to read nineteenth-century texts with "bifocal lenses," as the Victorians once did.

Some literary representations of the woman reader may be more ideal than real. *Little Women,* for example, heralds domesticity, no doubt to assuage the hearts of Americans weary from the Civil War; nonetheless, Alcott resisted the conventional path she prescribes to the March sisters. Other representations, in their refusal to condemn sensation fiction (*The Doctor's Wife*) or in their promotion of a woman's independent education, apart from the woman's mate (*The Daughters of Danaus*), challenge the status quo and invite social change. Literature transforms when a novelist re-creates it through the eyes of a character who lives between the pages of a book. From the memorable image of Jane Eyre reading Bewick's illustrations in a window seat at Gateshead, pictures accompanying a text spark the creative imagining of Victorian British and American readers—Isabel Archer, Jo March, Maggie Tulliver, Emma Bovary, Isabel Gilbert, and Jane Eyre. In fact, the reading of pictures, a leitmotif throughout part 2, offers a fitting prelude to part 3, which examines illustrations of the woman reader accompanying popular fiction of the period.

III

Illustrations of the Woman Reader

6

An Illustrative Gallery of Victorian British and American Women Readers

The Illustrated Fiction of Charles Dickens, Louisa May Alcott, Henry Wadsworth Longfellow, Mark Twain, Frances Hodgson Burnett, and Anthony Trollope

What record of the woman reader does illustrated literature of the Victorian period offer us? Why do illustrators make reading part of their imagery, and how does the inclusion of a book in an illustration complement a narrative? In what ways does a telling, occasionally overlooked, illustrative detail—principally a book but also a letter—reinforce or challenge prevailing cultural views about gender? Artists and illustrators used the visual arts as a medium to observe, comment on, and shape the role of an emerging woman reader. The meaning of reading changes, for example, if a woman reads alone or in the company of others; outdoors or in the private home. Is the book partially closed, and thus under the artist's, not the subject's, control? If the book is open, does the reader direct her eyes to the printed page to absorb its contents, or does her gaze extend beyond the book, suggesting she is day dreaming or her reading is interrupted? Does the book function as a prop of gentility rather than learnedness?

In "Women as Readers: Visual Interpretations" (1998), Linda J. Docherty uses the iconographic practice of typing (organizing images by type or kind) to explore the rise of the woman reader in American portraiture, genre painting, and impressionism from the colonial period through the onset of World War I. Typing attempts to distinguish one group from another; thus, a pictorial type combines common physical and/or behavioral characteristics. Docherty offers eight chronologically arranged pictorial types, each a "visual formula" (339) that many artists applied during a particular period in history. Any pictorial type, when imposed on a model, may reinforce and reflect the beliefs of the artist and prevailing cultural assumptions, denying the individuality of the subject. As in literary representation, types may, at times, present an ideal vision, rather than a real image, and can lead to exaggeration and stereotyping, as Docherty cautions. Nonetheless, paintings "possess historical value not as documents of fact but as windows on ideology" (Docherty 339). These pictorial types—namely, conjugal, venerable, material, cerebral, interrupted, isolated, cultivated, and worldly—offer a framework for understanding the rise of the woman reader and give insight into commonly held views.

Typing in portraiture and genre painting translates readily to book illustration, likewise produced by and for an ostensibly white, middle- to upper-class audience.[1] The Victorian illustrated book tells a story through and with illustrations that convey a moral or augment theme, plot, and characterization. In Victorian Britain and America, illustrators and author-illustrators[2] treated the book as a potent objective signifier and used several prevailing visual formulas to align reading with domesticity and the social construction of femininity. We find examples of interrupted and isolated readers, prevalent in mid-nineteenth-century genre painting, as well as what I call the social reader and the antiquated reader, a satirical reworking of the honorific venerable type.[3] Docherty's observation about interrupted and isolated types in midcentury genre painting seems relevant to book illustration: "While the interrupted reader's character was expressed by what she does for others, the isolated reader—who would reappear in the next century—was characterized by what she reads" (370). We define the interrupted and social reader by her actions for others and the isolated reader by what and where she reads. The reading preferences and stereotypical appearance of the venerable reader from portraiture remain dominant in the antiquated type in book illustration. All four pictorial types are reliable indicators of ideologies that govern women's reading practices. As visual formulas, they inscribe cultural attitudes and, in some cases, manage our perception of women's reading as a socially sanctioned or subversive act.

It is not my aim to align books or illustrators with one given visual formula or to suggest a chronological arrangement of types. In book illustration, much as in the history and theory of women's reading and literary representation, we find a multiplicity of ideologies surrounding women and books. My research underscores that as notions of the woman reader evolved, numerous types appear simultaneously in British and American book illustration and reflect the conflicting ideologies running concurrently throughout Victorian Britain and America. Some books include illustrations of women readers cast as various pictorial types (such as in *David Copperfield*). Certain characters appear as different types of women readers within a given book (*Little Women*) or among versions of a book illustrated by divers artists (*Evangeline*). I rely on original illustrations from British and American texts to establish these four categories of representation. For works that first appeared unillustrated (or without professional illustration, as in the case of *Little Women*), I have selected accessible editions illustrated by important nineteenth- and early-twentieth-century artists to portray types, which, in turn, illuminate the dominant ideologies of the age.

THE INTERRUPTED READER

The interrupted reader in book illustration might best be seen as a visual response to increasing options available for women who possessed the power and opportunity to read and educate themselves. In the nineteenth century, domesticity reigned supreme in conventional ideology on both sides of the Atlantic. As the socialization and gentility arguments advocate, reading brings cultivation to a woman's circle and supports domesticity. To recall Trollope, a "course of novel-reading . . . has become necessary for a British lady" (*Orley Farm* 1: 262). From right reading, a lady learns decorum, sensibility, morality, and taste. A book functions as a suitable prop of gentility for the Victorian angel in the house: even Mrs. Coventry Patmore, wife of the author of the sequence of poems *The Angel in the House* (1854–63), appears in a *carte de visite* in a standing pose, reading a book, while covered with a feminine lace mantilla.[4] The interrupted reader, who puts aside her book to attend to her child or visitor, chooses social responsibility over personal pleasure and represents an ideal vision.

Arguably the best literary model to illuminate this pictorial type in book illustration appears in Elizabeth Stuart Phelps's "The Angel Over the Right Shoulder" (1852). The protagonist, Mrs. James, begins the story sighing, "There! a woman's work is never done."[5] Since she longs for time to herself, her husband proposes an experiment: for a month, Mrs. James will have two hours a day to herself, without interruption. She intends to launch a course of study, but the plan fails miserably. Her husband, children, and callers constantly interrupt a disappointed Mrs. James. Then, in a prophetic dream, she sees two angels writing up good and evil deeds of a traveler, whom she later discovers is herself. Through her dream, she realizes that even what she perceives as insignificant tasks performed routinely—finding her child's mittens, bathing her children, or mending her husband's clothes—are deeds important enough for "the angel over the *right shoulder*" to record in a golden book. Awaking, she understands that what she once considered daily intrusions are truly her life's work "on which the comfort and virtue of her family depended" (25). Phelps's interrupted reader gains contentment when she lays aside her plans for self-education and personal growth; she chooses domesticity willingly.

The interrupted reader locates her power in her separate domestic sphere, primarily the home and its analogue, the school. Eastman Johnson's *Bo-Peep* (fig. 2) and Homer's *The Country School* (1871) offer prime examples of interrupted readers. While the former depicts a mother interrupting her reading to amuse her young child, the latter features a Yankee schoolmistress looking away from the *McGuffey's Reader* in her hands, leaving off her reading lesson with one male pupil to address the other males in the classroom.[6] Both examples of interrupted readers promote a woman's social responsibility to educate the rising generation, a concept aligned with Republican motherhood.[7] As Catharine Beecher and Harriet Beecher Stowe promote in their landmark *The American Woman's Home* (1869), teaching is a natural outgrowth of domesticity. Through schooling, missionary work, and other benevolent activities, a woman promotes learning and morality in her community and private home. An affirmation of the socialization argument, the interrupted reader, in school or home, crystallizes societal concerns that education should not distract from—but affirm—a woman's primary duty to family and community.

The interrupted reader in book illustration confirms this vision. This type features a woman in a social setting, primarily a home, holding an open book but not engaging its contents. Not surprisingly, illustrators typically cast the Victorian angel in the house as an interrupted reader. The most socially sanctioned nineteenth-century fictional type appears as the most approved illustrative type.

The angel is pervasive in nineteenth-century illustrated fiction. In fact, the Dickensian angel well demonstrates this idealized model of womanhood, exceedingly popular in the 1840s and 1850s in Britain and America. The selfless angel approaches the divine on earth by functioning as a holy refuge for her brother, father, and husband, who often do not deserve her. Still, the angelic heroine offers unconditional love and support to her male counterpart even if he repeatedly spurns her, as Florence Dombey's father does in *Dombey and Son* (1848); burdens her until he dies, like Lizzie Hexam's father in *Our Mutual Friend* (1865); or improves only late in the novel, as is the case of Agnes Wickfield's father in *David Copperfield* (1850).[8] In Dickens's bildungsroman chronicling David's development into a successful writer, Hablot Knight Browne (Phiz), Dickens's illustrator, twice pictures the quintessential Victorian angel, Agnes Wickfield, as an interrupted reader. Her characterization illumines the reading arguments of gentility and, particularly, socialization.

Agnes Wickfield acts as surrogate wife to her rapidly deteriorating father and as sister to David. She embodies qualities immortalized in *The Angel in the House:* patience, unselfishness, earnestness, faithfulness, and devotion. As a Victorian angel in the house, Agnes likewise possesses the traits Barbara Welter describes as essential to the cult of true womanhood in antebellum America: purity, submissiveness, piety, and domesticity (152). Agnes epitomizes Dickens's ideal woman, a rich reward for every man, as well as for David, Dickens's fictionalized self and most beloved character. Agnes also crystallizes the notion Martha Banta asserts in *Imaging American Women* (1987): a book keeps a woman under bourgeois control within the private home. Dickens ties the morality of ideal womanhood to hearth and home. Equally, he associates David's "good angel" with the stained glass windows of a church. Agnes is ever pointing David to higher things, and Dickens rewards David's "good angel" richly: the final lines offer a tribute to Agnes, ever pointing him "upward!" until his own death, which he imagines in the final paragraph of the novel (737).

Browne identifies with Dickens's project and intensifies the image of the Victorian angel in the house that Dickens promotes. He pictures patient Agnes looking contented as she stands among the guests at David's marriage to Dora Spenlow in "I Am Married"; late in the novel, Agnes finally admits to David: "I have loved you all my life!" (725). In "Uriah Persists in Hovering Near Us, at the Dinner Party" (fig. 8), Agnes smiles sweetly even though a slimy Uriah Heep hovers behind her at a party given in the London home of her hosts, Mr. and Mrs. Waterbrooks. Agnes sits apart from the other female partygoers and holds an open unidentified book in her lap. The book here is a sign of gentility. Well-known is Browne's willingness to subordinate himself to Dickens's will, as Jane Cohen documents (61–62). Dickens makes no mention of Agnes's reading in the text; nonetheless, we can assume that Browne's additions of an open, unread book (a second closed book rests beside her on the table) and an angel figurine (positioned above Agnes) pleased Dickens, who exerted great control over his illustrators, approving and rejecting plates even under tight deadlines.

Browne captures Agnes at the very moment of interruption: David has come to introduce Agnes to Thomas Traddles, an old schoolfellow. Agnes's graceful hands cover the pages of the book she amiably sets aside.

Fig. 8. Illustration by Hablot Knight Browne, "Uriah Persists in Hovering Near Us, at the Dinner Party," for Charles Dickens, *The Personal History of David Copperfield*, 1850.

While the interrupted type can conceivably express some tension, no conflict emerges between Agnes's social duties and her reading for enjoyment or self-betterment. An objective signifier, the book conveys Agnes's intelligence and cultivation. It magnifies her already elevated stature in Dickens's eyes, even if not in the eyes of readers today who do not like Dickensian angels and find her character unsatisfactory. As Nina Auerbach contends in *Woman and the Demon* (1982), "We no longer adore angels; we do not even like them, dismissing them impatiently as soggy dilutions of human complexity" (64). I would argue that Agnes is more saccharine than "soggy." While the open book attests to the increased education of women, the cheery grace with which Agnes greets interruption confirms that her primary obligation is to her domestic sphere. She carries the keys of the household and reigns as her father's "housekeeper," by her own admission (199).[9] Even if she were interested in reading for pleasure or to gain the liberating power of learnedness, genteel Agnes accepts her social role and subordinates her learning to the domestic realm.

The prop of an open unread book, again not mentioned in the text, reappears in Agnes's lap in "A Stranger Calls to See Me" (fig. 9), her second

Gallery of Victorian British and American Women Readers ~ 145

Fig. 9. Illustration by Hablot Knight Browne, "A Stranger Calls to See Me,"
for Charles Dickens, *The Personal History of David Copperfield*, 1850.

depiction as an interrupted reader. Browne's inclusion of a book supports the ideology of the middle-class home in this final illustration of *David Copperfield*. Here Browne shows Agnes sitting contentedly by the hearth in the family parlor, surrounded by her beloved David and their well-mannered, rosy children. The open book suggests Agnes's role as teacher of her children as well as her beloved David. A second book lies open on the floor beside Agnes, indicating that reading aloud is an integral part of her family circle. On the left side of the image, an open book propped on a stand and several other books on a parlor table (likely including a dictionary and a Bible) intensify the atmosphere of learning and morality in their happy home. Akin to the notion of Republican motherhood (an American ideal which grew out of the division of home and production accompanying industrialization), the Victorian British home became a haven for wife and mother to raise a model family, bringing up a new generation.

Much as in her appearance in "Uriah Persists in Hovering Near Us, at the Dinner Party," Agnes gazes beyond her book and her child (whose curly head is buried in her lap) to greet her visitor. Recalling the imagery of the previous illustration, the mantel, with a portrait of David's deceased first wife Dora above it, also fittingly contains a symmetrically placed pair of angel figurines. Complementing Dickens's narrative by including such details, Browne again emphasizes Agnes's awareness of her duty to extend a warm welcome to her guest, just as she includes Dora's memory within her family circle. The book in both illustrations confirms that the quintessential Victorian angel recognizes the importance of learning in moderation and her influential role as teacher in the private home.

In *David Copperfield*, Dickens and Browne also use a book as a potent signifier to elevate one type of womanhood over another.[10] Agnes recognizes the value of books and learning, becomes a schoolteacher, and runs her own school before marrying David at the end of the novel. Precisely because she is learned, Agnes appears well suited to be David's wife in a way that Dora, "the first mistaken impulse of [his] undisciplined heart" (558), seems decidedly deficient. Why does Agnes succeed as a wife? She fits the model that advice writer Swan promotes in *Courtship and Marriage* (1893): a "woman of large brain power, provided she has well-balanced judgment, and a heart as expansive as her brain, will more nearly approach the ideal in matrimony than the more frivolous woman, who has no thought beyond her personal aggrandisement and adornment, and who buys her new bonnet with a kiss" (22). In the absence of careers for women, Dickens makes clear Agnes will become David's lifelong confidante as well as an active participant in his intellectual life. She possesses an "expansive" heart and brain and "well-balanced judgment," while sweet Dora is a "frivolous" woman, par excellence.

David comes to see Dora as a "plaything" (511)—a fragile "Little Blossom," as Aunt Betsey calls her—once he takes Annie Strong's wisdom to heart and realizes "There can be no disparity in marriage like unsuitability of mind and purpose" (558).[11] In an attempt to "form my little wife's mind" (585), David reads Shakespeare to Dora, but he "fatigued her to the last degree" (585). The cookbook David gives Dora to improve her housekeeping "made Dora's head ache" (510). Thus, "the principal use to which the cookery-book was devoted, was being put down in the corner for Jip to stand upon. But Dora was so pleased when she had trained him to stand upon it . . . that I was very glad I had bought it" (511).

In "Our Housekeeping" (fig. 10), David's "child-wife," as Dora prefers him to call her, has stored a pickle jar on the bookshelves amongst volumes fallen into disarray. Browne scatters books on the shelves, table, and floor. The pickle jar, in fact, is the only upright object on the bookshelf. The general bewilderment of the image distinguishes Dora from angelic Agnes,

Fig. 10. Illustration by Hablot Knight Browne, "Our Housekeeping," for Charles Dickens, *The Personal History of David Copperfield*, 1850.

described and depicted as a model housekeeper. Most likely the cookbook, which Dora neglects for its actual worth, is one of the volumes Phiz places in the far-left corner, wedged under Jip's Chinese pagoda doghouse. The forgotten cookbook symbolizes Dora's woeful ignorance and incompatibility as David's partner once he becomes a famous writer. Dora never attempts to enter into David's literary world like Agnes, who recognizes that a woman must be her husband's intellectual companion. David might well have judged the suitability of his mate by her attitude toward books. However, David stops trying to form his child-wife when Aunt Betsey warns him against repeating the mistakes of the murderous Mr. Murdstone, who destroys David's own mother (the same type of woman Dora is). Dora pleads to sit beside David as he writes books that begin to make him famous: "Please let me hold the pens, . . . I want to have something to do with all those many hours you are so industrious. May I hold the pens?" (546). As "Little Blossom" withers away, even she recognizes, "I was too young and foolish. It is much better as it is" (647). Browne's "Our Housekeeping" joins with Dora's prophetic words to confirm the superiority of the interrupted reading angel and the ideology of the middle-class home.[12]

Many Dickensian angels appear as interrupted readers, providing further testimony to the potency of the gentility and socialization arguments. Illustrators also cast Florence Dombey of *Dombey and Son*, Rose Maylie of *Oliver Twist* (1838), and Lucie Manette of *A Tale of Two Cities* (1859) in this role. An angelic heroine, young Florence loses her mother and beloved brother Paul and experiences cruel rejection from her father. In this gloomy setting, "Florence bloomed there, like the king's daughter in the story. Her books, her music, and her daily teachers, were her only real companions" (267).[13] Dickens repeatedly calls attention to how books are Florence's "only real" friends as she endures a lonely childhood: "Always: at her books, her music, and her work: in her morning walks, and in her nightly prayers: she had her engrossing aim in view. Strange study for a child, to learn the road to a hard parent's heart" (269). Befriended mainly by household servants and lower-class characters, Florence emerges as a sweet, pure, intelligent, submissive, and innocent young woman, who continues to love the father who spurns his "angel" (238), as Dickens calls her.

Browne's "The Shadow in the Little Parlour" (fig. 11) depicts Florence in the home of her kindly friend Captain Cuttle, who gives her refuge after Mr. Dombey throws her out of the house. Florence is just about to be reunited with her childhood sweetheart, Walter Gay (whom she eventually marries). Here she, like Agnes, holds an open, unread book in her lap. In this scene, Dickens makes no mention of his heroine reading, although he notes Florence is occupied with another genteel art: "being busy with her needle in the little parlour" (575). Browne's inclusion of a book promotes Dickens's intent to show that Florence's genteel nature, dutifulness, and native intelligence flourish even within her working-class setting. However, Florence looks away from the open unidentified book to listen to Captain Cuttle recount the amazing tale of Walter's shipwreck, near death by drowning, and miraculous survival. Cuttle eventually directs Florence's attention to the looming shadow on the wall, the figure of Walter Gay, her lover come home. As in the case of Agnes, we focus on Florence's actions, not what she reads. In fact, the interrupted reader's very suitability as a model Victorian wife depends upon the sweet manner in which she interrupts her reading to attend to others.

The Dickensian angel as interrupted reader is not exclusive to Browne's illustrations. Cruikshank—who sparred with Dickens over sovereignty, as Patten skillfully narrates in *George Cruikshank's Life, Times, and Art*—

Fig. 11. Illustration by Hablot Knight Browne, "The Shadow in the Little Parlour," for Charles Dickens, *Dealings with the Firm of Dombey and Son Wholesale, Retail, and for Exportation*, 1848.

represents the angelic Rose as an interrupted reader in the first version of "Rose Maylie and Oliver," also known as "The Fireside Plate" (fig. 12). Dickens rejected this initial attempt at the final illustration for *Oliver Twist* because Oliver and Rose look too old.[14] In this first rejected version, however, Cruikshank, like Browne, identifies the book as a potent objective signifier of gentility. Now returned to his rightful social station, Oliver sits in a warm and respectable parlor. Rose curls her right arm around Oliver, who positions the open book he holds in her lap. Their intimacy, carried

Fig. 12. Illustration by George Cruikshank, "Rose Maylie and Oliver," for *Oliver Twist; or, The Parish Boy's Progress by 'Boz' Charles Dickens,* vol. 3 (1838). (Courtesy of Bodleian Library, University of Oxford, Reference [shelfmark] Don. e. 556–558.)

through their body posture, suggests that Oliver may have, in fact, been reading to Rose as well as vice versa. Rose gladly looks away from the book she is either listening to or reading aloud to focus wholeheartedly on social responsibilities, including her maternal role toward Oliver.

The angel as interrupted reader also persists in Dickens's oeuvre as evident in Browne's depiction of Lucie Manette in "Under the Plane Tree" (fig. 13). *A Tale of Two Cities* introduces Lucie as a lady with blue eyes and "a quantity of golden hair,"[15] accentuating her angelic nature at a time

Fig. 13. Illustration by Hablot Knight Browne, "Under the Plane Tree," for Charles Dickens, *A Tale of Two Cities*, 1859.

when Victorians linked external beauty to inner goodness. Lucie remains devoted to Dr. Manette, freed from imprisonment in the Bastille. Before she marries Charles Evrémonde, called Darnay, Lucie professes to her father: "I am deeply happy in the love that Heaven has so blessed—my love for Charles, and Charles's love for me. But, if my life were not to be still consecrated to you, or if my marriage were so arranged as that it would part us, even by the length of a few of these streets, I should be more unhappy and self-reproachful now than I can tell you" (188). Ever an angel, Lucie suffers the loss of a beloved son and remains loyal to her husband as he faces sure death by the Parisian guillotine for the sins of his Evrémonde forefathers. Nor is she without intellectual virtue. In "Under the Plane Tree," Lucie, like her angelic sisters, looks away from the open book in her lap to engage in conversation with Charles Darnay, seated beside her.[16] In casting Lucie as an interrupted reader, Browne associates her with Agnes Wickfield, Rose Maylie, and Florence Dombey. Since Dickens mentions that Lucie reads to her father (although not specifically in this scene), it is not surprising that Browne places a book in her lap.

Despite his quiet presence as an illustrator and his tendency to mirror Dickens's intentions through illustration, Browne, over time, establishes the book as a prop of gentility and aligns the Dickensian angel with the interrupted type. Browne's depictions of Victorian angels as interrupted readers promote domesticity, implicit in the socialization argument. Even Thackeray, as author-illustrator, casts his somewhat deficient angel, Amelia Sedley, once in this pose rather late in *Vanity Fair* (1848). He introduces Amelia as a "dear little creature,"[17] "so guileless and goodnatured a person" (7). Clearly not an Agnes Wickfield, Amelia loosely conforms to type, though some critics consider Thackeray's characterization to be a satirization of the angel in the house. For example, Amelia's schoolmistress, Miss Barbara Pinkerton, confides that Amelia is deficient in geography and deportment, but she is skilled in the genteel arts of needlework, music, and dancing, she can spell aptly, and she is industrious and obedient. She marries the vain, unworthy George Osborne, who dies an unheroic death; then she idolizes her son and dead husband.[18]

In chapter 60, "We Return to the Genteel World," we find a widowed Amelia living with her father in reduced circumstances. Returning from India to discover Mrs. Sedley is dead and Amelia living without her son Georgy (she has given him to her father-in-law to raise since she cannot afford to keep him), Jos Sedley installs Amelia as head of his own table. In his circle, she "was voted, . . . rather a pleasing young person—not much in her, but pleasing, and that sort of thing" (766). She gets a visiting book and drives about in a carriage making calls. "The lady's maid and the chariot, the visiting-book and the buttony page, became soon as familiar to Amelia as the humble routine of Brompton" (766), or so Thackeray confides. Thackeray's accompanying illustration complements his text: Amelia holds the visiting book in her hand with a thumb-in gesture. The book functions here as a prop of gentility. Though the book is open, it faces downward; her eyes politely engage a visitor while honest William Dobbin looks on in the background, repressing his passion for the woman he has always loved. While the visiting book suggests Amelia's rise in the world, she knows not to glance at it when company calls. Rather, Thackeray focuses our attention on Amelia's sense of duty: "She accommodated herself.

... If Fate had ordained that she should be a duchess, she would even have done that duty too" (766).

Interrupted readers in book illustration are not only angelic women or young women, for that matter. The type includes women who are single and married, beautiful and unattractive, young and old. For example, in *The Adventures of Tom Sawyer* (1876), Mark Twain's spinster Aunt Polly, who visually conforms to the antiquated type, appears in the pose of an interrupted reader in True Williams's "What Tom Saw." This illustration depicts Aunt Polly, Mrs. Harper, Sid, and Mary commiserating over Tom Sawyer and Joe Harper, whom they believe are drowned (along with Huck Finn). It is not a somber moment in the text since Tom, who is very much alive, sneaks back home from playing pirates and witnesses this very scene. Williams places the prop of an open book in Aunt Polly's lap—likely a Bible she has opened for comfort—although there is no explicit mention of her reading in the text. Like Dickens's Agnes and Thackeray's Amelia, Aunt Polly knows to turn her attention away from her book to her guests, especially the grieving Mrs. Harper, dramatically covering her face with a handkerchief.[19]

We cannot as readily assume that Williams identifies with Twain's project as Phiz with Dickens. As Beverly David and Ray Sapirstein note, Twain was a scrupulous editor of his work and in close contact with Williams, but he may have given Williams some leeway since Twain, then overwhelmed with personal and publishing matters, did not want to provoke Williams, given his tendency to turn to drink. David and Sapirstein describe Williams's illustrations as "accurate but flat":[20] "in many cases he gave no more and no less than Twain described" ("Reading the Illustrations in *Tom Sawyer*" 26). The open but unread Bible in this illustration functions, nonetheless, as a telling detail intensifying Aunt Polly's values and the ideology of the middle-class home.

Illustrators of Marietta Holley's exceedingly popular nineteenth-century *Samantha* series often cast Samantha Allen in an interrupted pose. Holley was considered a female Twain, or so the nineteenth-century popular press liked to call her. Holley's 204-pound Samantha Allen physically and intellectually dominates her frail, bearded, bald, and foolish 100-pound husband. Illustrators typically show Mrs. Josiah Allen, as she calls herself, with the visual appearance of the antiquated type: a portly physique, bun, and glasses. Her character is complex, however. Holley's biographer Kate Winter notes that Samantha's "hardy self-confidence, independence, and intellectual vigor belied the prevailing notion that women were weak, passive, mindless, and powerless" (51). Samantha emerges as an intelligent and

Fig. 14. Illustration by E. A., "'But Fit with Their Tongues, Fearful,'" for Marietta Holley, *Samantha Among the Brethren*, 1892.

fairminded woman who champions the rights of both sexes, but she in no way endorses radical feminism and shares many traditional qualities with married women of her day. While Holley emphasizes her humor, illustrators highlight her conventional traits and depict her with props of gentility, such as the Bible, accouterments of sewing, and books. *Samantha Among the Brethren* (1890), for example, features Samantha in an interrupted pose in an illustration by E. A. (possibly Edward Austin Abbey) titled "But Fit with Their Tongues, Fearful" (fig. 14).[21] Books are on the table, Josiah holds a newspaper in his hands, and Samantha has an open book on her lap. Here, true to interrupted type, Samantha looks away from the open book, to her companions—her troublesome guest, Lodema Trumble (shown sewing), and her husband (also in an interrupted reading pose)—to solve the problem brewing in her household.[22]

An enduring type, the interrupted reader even extends into the early twentieth century. A prime example appears in *Verses for Jock and Joan* (1905), a book of nursery rhymes by Helen Hay Whitney, illustrated by

Gallery of Victorian British and American Women Readers ~ 155

Fig. 15. Illustration by Charlotte Harding, "Algy," for Helen Hay Whitney, *Verses for Jock and Joan*, 1905. (Courtesy of the Hyde Collection, Glens Falls, New York.)

Charlotte Harding. The image of a mother and son (fig. 15) accompanies "Algy," a poem about a young boy who prefers his mother's kisses to those of his father's little black dog. The interrupted type thus evolves to indicate a change in domesticity. As Ruth Copans observes, "No longer engaged in domestic tasks of home, the mother, instead, indulges in the leisure activity of reading."[23] Harding's illustration, more endearing than the poem, complements Whitney's verse and captures a loving bond between mother and son. The dog, described as having "*such* an angry face,"[24] looks intently at the little boy, who gazes directly at the reader and seems to speak the lines of the poem: "And if some one must kiss me, why/I'd rather have mamma" (lines 11–12). The setting is a prosperous home. Light reflects upon the doting mother, who sits in a wicker chair, framed by lush foliage. The arms of mother and son encircle each other. The mother, who kisses her son's cheek, seems content to put her leisure reading aside. The open book on her lap is an objective signifier of her gentility while her caress speaks to her maternal nature.

Like the archetype of the angel in the house, the interrupted reader has historical value: throughout the nineteenth century, even as social change made reading for women a mark of bourgeois leisure, responsibility reigns supreme. In promoting this type, Harding, Browne, and other illustrators on both sides of the Atlantic illuminate the notions of grace and domesticity essential to the arguments of gentility and socialization. Illustrators in close collaboration with authors champion widespread cultural assumptions that the needs of family, home, and community must supplant personal gratification, despite the many choices available to educated women.

THE SOCIAL READER

As Victorian British and American life became increasingly industrialized and factories supplanted home workshops, the division between private and public spheres widened. The concept of home as a safe haven for an ideal mother to raise a model child grew out of the division of home and production that accompanied industrialization, the home's counterpoint. Not all women served their families or society by setting their books aside. The home fostered education, as well as love and cooperation. While the prevailing cult of domesticity kept women in the private sphere, reading had social merits. As Sicherman notes, "At times reading aloud was a duty as well as a pleasure: parents might read to children, older siblings to younger ones, adult daughters to their mothers, women to invalids. Above all, reading aloud was social" ("Sense and Sensibility" 206).

I have coined the term "social reader" as a pictorial type for one who accedes willingly to social norms; in this respect, she is akin to the interrupted reader. Social reading is more than entertainment: it is a responsibility a parent or older sibling assumes for child raising. Social reading occurs in collaboration with others. It can promote family unity, as Thomas Webster captures in *A Letter from Abroad* (n.d.): in this painting, family members with mixed emotions gather around to gaze at an overseas letter that the postman has delivered, possibly from the son whose silhouette is on the wall.[25] Affirming the notions Beecher and Beecher Stowe promote in *The American Woman's Home*, the social reader in book illustration also performs missionary or benevolent work (such as bringing the Holy Book to the poor, elderly, or less fortunate). Like the angel in the house, she promotes learning and morality in her community and private home. The social reader does not have a stereotypical appearance, though she is frequently a mother reading to her children. Like the interrupted reader, this type illuminates the socialization and gentility arguments: the social reader moves with grace and acts in socially sanctioned ways within her larger domestic sphere.

Little Women (1868, 1869) quintessentially demonstrates the social, dutiful, and pleasurable aspects of reading aloud in the family circle.[26] Although the first edition of *Little Women* has four illustrations by Louisa's sister, May Alcott (an amateur artist fictionalized as Jo's youngest sister, Amy March), the edition was withdrawn since May's illustrations were judged "pretty awful" and criticized for "a want of anatomical knowledge."[27] Illustration became an important component of *Little Women*, and the book attracted many leading late-nineteenth- and early-twentieth-century illustrators. Considered the first to portray the novel with inspiration, Frank T. Merrill includes over 200 images in his 1880 quarto edition (which prints part 1 ["Little Woman"] and part 2 ["Good Wives"] as one novel). Jessie Willcox Smith, an accomplished woman artist of the American golden age of illustration (1890–1920), memorably illustrated the novel in 1915. Both artists depict an unforgettable scene of social reading from the first chapter, "Playing Pilgrims."

Responding to Alcott's vision, Merrill constructs the woman reader's identity in a social context. Reading together is a sign of familial intimacy and gentility. When Marmee arrives home with a letter from father March, a chaplain in the Civil War, her daughters exuberantly pronounce: "A letter! a letter! Three cheers for Father!" (9). The March sisters cluster around Marmee's "big chair" (9) as she reads what Alcott describes as a "cheerful, hopeful letter, full of lively descriptions of camp life, marches, and military news, and only at the end did the writer's heart overflow with fatherly love and longing for the little girls at home" (10), whom he calls his "little women" (10). Prominently positioned as the frontispiece, Merrill's black-and-white illustration "They all drew to the fire, mother in the big chair, with Beth to her feet" (fig. 16) depicts social reading poignantly. Reading father March's letter to his "little women," Marmee passes on patriarchal ideals to a receptive female audience; we assume her daughters will become social readers themselves. The glow of the fireplace, which Merrill does not picture, shines upon the faces of Meg, Jo, Beth, and Amy as they gather around Marmee. With a hushed smile on her face, Marmee reads the cherished letter aloud. Meg and Amy perch on Marmee's chair, nestling close to her. Jo leans over the back of the chair, and Beth, seated on the floor before Marmee, places her arms on Marmee's knees and gazes

Fig. 16. Illustration by Frank T. Merrill, "They All Drew to the Fire, Mother in the Big Chair, with Beth to Her Feet," for Louisa May Alcott, *Little Women or Meg, Jo, Beth and Amy*, 1880.

lovingly upon her. In Merrill's depiction, Marmee and her four daughters literally form a reading circle. Their close positioning gives concrete form to the intimacy they share. On the table alongside Marmee rest two volumes. Although Merrill does not include the titles, we presume they are the Bible and *Pilgrim's Progress*, a framing device for the entire novel.[28] Such books complement Alcott's description of the March home, richly endowed with goodness, morality, and respect for parents, who reign supreme in the domestic circle that Alcott envisions.

Willcox Smith, who earned fame and fortune for her illustrations of American domesticity, creates a more feminine color plate of this same

Gallery of Victorian British and American Women Readers ~ 159

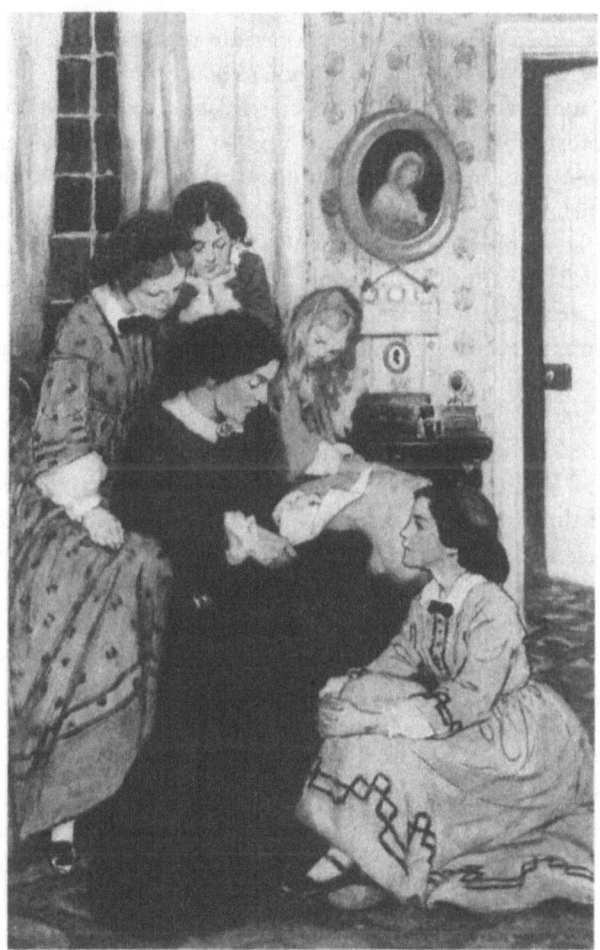

Fig. 17. Illustration by Jessie Willcox Smith, "They All Drew to the Fire," for Louisa May Alcott, *Little Women or Meg, Jo, Beth and Amy*, 1915.

scene.[29] In "They all drew to the fire" (fig. 17), the March sisters clearly look like "little women." Marmee reads father March's letter, as in Merrill's depiction. The positioning of the March sisters around Marmee also seems identical although the orientation of the image is reversed. Dressed in a black sateen gown with a cameo-style pin on her white lace collar, a maternal Marmee holds the Civil War letter in her hands. The girls have bows in their hair and pastel or earth tone dresses and sport proper white collars and cuffs. Meg, Jo, and Beth look particularly womanly, their hair pulled back in nets. Only Amy has flowing locks, designating her the youngest.

Alcott claimed the hearts of her American readers with *Little Women* and transformed her own nurturing and philanthropic mother, Abba, into the ideal "mother-woman" of the Victorian age (Saxton 13). The highest paid and most sought after American woman illustrator of her era, Smith captures the tenderness and tranquility that we associate with Alcott's domestic fiction. The glow of the fire, again not pictured, illuminates their faces and the act of reading aloud by the hearth, the metaphorical heart of their home. The warmth of this scene also comes from their love and affection that radiates in this literal and figurative reading circle. The closeness of the figures and the warm and soft hues of their dresses make the reading circle appear natural and idyllic.

As in Merrill's version, Smith's includes books, again likely the Bible and *Pilgrim's Progress,* prominently positioned on a table below an oval portrait and a miniature (presumably of family members) to establish the virtues of this Victorian American home. Marmee embraces her role as moral guide and educator of her daughters. We soon learn that she manages to scrape together enough money to buy each daughter her own copy of *Pilgrim's Progress* for Christmas. We can readily imagine Marmee reading stories to her children, much as we see Agnes Wickfield reading to her children in a similar Victorian parlor where she poses as an interrupted reader, picture book on her lap.

Both Merrill's and Smith's renditions of social reading respond to what Sarah Stickney Ellis praises in *The Mothers of England* (1843). Ellis prescribes the socialization and gentility arguments endorsing women's reading: "A novel read in secret is a dangerous thing; but there are many works of taste and fancy which, when accompanied by the remarks of a feeling and judicious mother, may be rendered improving to the mind, and beneficial to the character altogether; nor is it possible to imagine a scene of much greater enjoyment, than is presented by a thoroughly united and intelligent family, the female members of which are busily at work, while a brother or father reads aloud to them some interesting book approved by the mother, and delighted in by her daughters."[30] Warm, maternal, fun-living, yet responsible—Marmee possesses all the qualifications of Ellis's ideal mother: she inculcates values that will enable her daughters to move gracefully in their social circle. The girls' attentive expressions in Smith's and Merrill's depictions indicate that Marmee's daughters are uniformly absorbed by her reading and wholly united in their closeness. Of course, Marmee reads aloud to them—not a brother or father as Ellis ideally imagines. Thus, gender dynamics in Alcott's family circle have captured the attention of critics like Auerbach, who remarks that "The glowing sanity of

Gallery of Victorian British and American Women Readers ~ 161

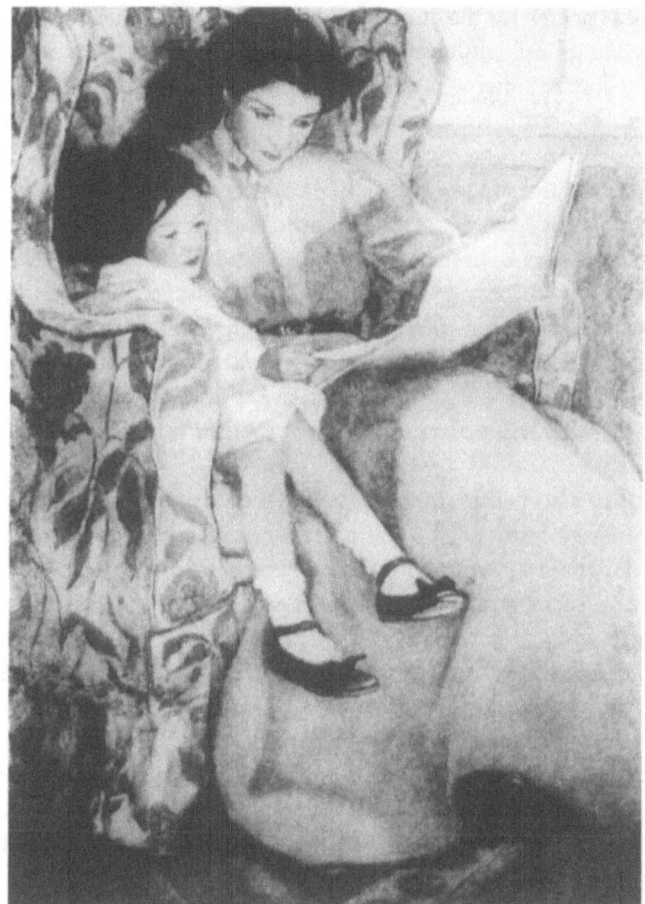

Fig. 18. Illustration by Jessie Willcox Smith, "A Rainy Day," for Aileen Cleveland Higgins, *Dream Blocks*, 1908. (Courtesy of the Hyde Collection, Glens Falls, New York.)

an independent female family allows revolt at the same time that it cherishes home" (Afterword to *Little Women* 470). Nonetheless, conservative ideology prevails in these illustrations. In listening intently to their father's letter, positioned prominently in both renditions, the sisters draw father March into their family circle. Even while he is away at war, he exerts influence on his "little women" in this ideal, socially sanctioned reading circle.

Smith sustains such an ideal characterization of mother as social reader into the early twentieth century in "A Rainy Day" (fig. 18), an illustration for Aileen Cleveland Higgins's *Dream Blocks* (1908). The color plates in this book of poems for the young depict mothers with children, children in nature settings, and children simply imagining.[31] The poems are unremarkable, but the pictures make the book memorable and preserve, as Copans notes, "our definition of the prosperity and domestic tranquility in the United States in the early decades of the twentieth century" (267). "A Rainy Day" captures the closeness of a mother and daughter spending a day of inclement weather reading indoors. Akin to the Alcott illustrations, reading seems central to the creation of this cultivated woman's identity as a mother. As advocates of the socialization argument endorsed, reading becomes a means to pass down traditions and values through generations of women. "A Rainy Day," like Marmee's reading circle, ties reading receptivity to gender: the willing listener in scenes of social reading is typically a daughter, who will embrace ideals her mother transmits, as Ellis envisions.

Gentility also dominates this image of domestic tranquility: Smith's mother wears a fashionable dress of light orange with a collar and knotted tie; her daughter, too young to read by herself, sports a bright white dress, white ankle socks, and black Mary Jane–style shoes with bows. Although the hearth again is not pictured, firelight reflects on the faces of mother and daughter as they settle into a big, cozy chair to read together. Bringing the outdoors inside, large red flowers, presumably roses, bloom on the patterned fabric of the chair in this prosperous home. The size of the volume suggests it is a picture book resting in both of their hands: once again, mother, daughter, and book create a literal reading circle.[32]

The poem gives voice to the happy thoughts of the little girl in the poem, despite the dreary start to the day:

> Before I go to bed, I think
> I've never had a day so *pink*.
> Without the sun to make the shine,
> This whole day long has been just mine
> And Mother's, in the fireplace glow.—
> Because it rained, it made it so.[33]

The whole illustration appears dreamy, soft, and feminine. To Smith, social reading becomes a moment of intimacy, warmth, pleasure, and connection.

Not all social readers are mothers, nor do all examples of social reading appear intimate or pleasurable. Merrill's depiction of "Reading That Everlasting Belsham" (fig. 19) contrasts with his most memorable image of social reading (fig. 16) in *Little Women*. Jo takes the job as companion to her rich, crotchety Aunt March after father March loses his property by

Gallery of Victorian British and American Women Readers 163

Fig. 19. Illustration by Frank T. Merrill, "Reading That Everlasting Belsham," for Louisa May Alcott, *Little Women or Meg, Jo, Beth and Amy*, 1880.

aiding an unfortunate friend (likewise, Meg becomes a nursery governess to help the family). As part of her duties, Jo reads aloud improving literature to her aunt. In this picture, Aunt March dozes as "Josy-phine" (or so Aunt March calls her) reads essays by Thomas Belsham, a Unitarian divine of the eighteenth century whose *Memories of Theophilus Lindsey* (1812) was frequently reprinted.[34] This image reveals tension, which may stem from Jo's being a paid companion or her distaste for the reading material and/or Aunt March. Merrill empathizes with Alcott's personal understanding that an educated middle-class woman often experiences conflict between pleasure and social responsibility, which wins out here. In terms of human interaction (though not of physical characteristics), this plate anticipates reading practices in images of the elderly antiquated reader assuming a posture of morality in bringing reading to her community (as will be seen in fig. 22).

Jo earnestly reads Belsham's essays to Aunt March, who nods her head to the right, pushes up her glasses, drops her knitting, and falls asleep. Still, in this chapter appropriately titled "Burdens," Jo keeps on reading. However, Alcott tells us that as soon as Aunt March dozes, Jo switches to Oliver Goldsmith's *The Vicar of Wakefield* (1766), one of Alcott's own favorite books which includes subplots of bankruptcy, seduction, incarceration, and desertion along with villainy and humor. Aunt March wakes up in a better mood, but reminds Jo of her "sins" (39) in preferring "frivolous work" (40) over the "worthy and instructive Belsham" (40). While Goldsmith may be more engaging than Belsham, how "frivolous" can *The Vicar of Wakefield* be since advice writer James Mason includes it in "How to Form a Small Library" (1881) as one of five fictional works for a girl to include in her select library of fifty volumes, along with the Bible, *Pilgrim's Progress*, and a dictionary?

Akin to the interrupted reader, the social reader reveals her nature by what she does for others as "chief minister" of the home. In the words of Beecher and Beecher Stowe, her "great mission is self-denial, in training its members to self-sacrificing labors for the ignorant and weak: if not her own children, then the neglected children of her Father in heaven" (19). Frances Hodgson Burnett's "Little Saint Elizabeth" (1890) offers a prime example of the social reader, acting in a manner approved by Victorian standards. Although Burnett is best known for *The Secret Garden* (1911) and *Little Lord Fauntleroy* (1886), this principal story in Burnett's collection titled *Little Saint Elizabeth and Other Stories* (1890) tells about an orphan who lives in Normandy with her reserved, deeply religious Aunt Chlotilde. Renouncing the world owing to a disappointment in love, Chlotilde devotes herself to the religious education of "sweet and gentle"[35] Elizabeth, "vowed to the Virgin in her babyhood, and . . . always dressed in white and blue" (19). Reginald B. Birch's "The Villagers Did Not Stand in Awe of Her" (fig. 20) features seven-year-old Elizabeth and her Aunt Chlotilde bringing the word of God to the less fortunate in their Normandy community. Elizabeth and Chlotilde wear crucifixes and hold Bibles in their hands. Dressed in a nunlike gown with a white yolk, Chlotilde (whom the villagers call Saint Mademoiselle de Rochemont) looks like "a marble female saint who had descended from her pedestal to walk upon the earth" (18). Aunt Chlotilde appears more severe than benevolent, and in this respect Birch emphasizes her hardness, evident in the text; in fact, Chlotilde's face, positioned in profile, resembles that of Cinderella's stern stepmother. Though firm, Chlotilde acts charitably, and—like Marmee and the mother in "A Rainy Day"—she has a receptive female companion to follow in her footsteps and become a social reader herself. Birch's rendition of Elizabeth closely matches Burnett's text. With her sweet face and docile manner, Elizabeth approximates a "child saint" (20), whom the poor instinctively "began to adore . . . almost to worship" (20). Bringing the good book to those in need becomes but an outward manifestation of Elizabeth's angelic character.[36]

An 1869 edition of Henry Wadsworth Longfellow's *Evangeline* (1847) likewise depicts Evangeline Bellefontaine as a social reader undertaking charitable deeds as an essential part of her pious identity. An instant popu-

Gallery of Victorian British and American Women Readers ~ 165

Fig. 20. Illustration by Reginald B. Birch, "The Villagers Did Not Stand in Awe of Her," for Frances Hodgson Burnett, *Little Saint Elizabeth and Other Stories*, 1890.

lar success, *Evangeline* relates the bittersweet tale of young lovers, separated in the confusion during the British expulsion of the 6,000 inhabitants of the former French colony of Acadie, an area in Nova Scotia. Gabriel Lajeunesse boards a ship to Louisiana while Evangeline sails to New England. After many years of fruitless searching, Evangeline arrives in Philadelphia where she becomes a Sister of Mercy, tending the poor and the sick. There she encounters her beloved Gabriel, dying in an almshouse for the homeless during an epidemic that plagues the city. Evangeline dies soon after, and the two join in death, buried side by side in a Catholic cemetery. Although originally published without illustration, numerous illustrated editions followed in the wake of *Evangeline*'s success (it was even adapted

Fig. 21. Illustration by F. O. C. Darley, "But Evangeline Knelt by His Bedside," for Henry Wadsworth Longfellow, *Evangeline, A Tale of Acadie*, 1869.

for the screen and the stage).³⁷ In "But Evangeline Knelt by His Bedside" (fig. 21), F. O. C. Darley, the most popular midcentury American illustrator, depicts Evangeline with the bloom of youth long gone, ministering the word of God to her beloved Gabriel on his deathbed.

Assessing Darley's contribution to American illustration, Sue W. Reed comments that "He made literary and historical characters and events graphically visible to his contemporaries and helped to codify our image of America's past" (113). In this illustration, which matches Longfellow's vision in a work rich in historical significance, Evangeline wears a plain, black-hooded cloak and simple dress as she kneels on the floor and "Kissed his dying lips, and laid his head on her bosom./Sweet was the light of his eyes; but it suddenly sank into darkness."³⁸ A bowl of food and a medicine bottle are close by. An open book—presumably the Bible—rests on a small table at the foot of Gabriel's bed. The book, again not mentioned, suggests that Evangeline—who has spent years with no "wish in life, but to follow / Meekly, with reverent steps, the sacred feet of her Saviour" (144)—has been easing her beloved Gabriel's final moments on earth. She is justly rewarded. Darley enhances the textual image by including a spiritual light shining on Evangeline's face as she holds her lover in her arms and murmurs "Father, I thank thee!" (154).

Foremost an affirmation of the socialization argument, the social reader illuminates how in ideal Victorian society, social responsibility reigns supreme. Social reading in *Evangeline* and *Saint Elizabeth*, as well as in *Little Women*, reinforces the goodness and piousness of the ideal Victorian woman. As these cases reveal, the social reader is "chief minister" of her home and community. But this pictorial type is more complex than that. A mother reading to a daughter in *Dream Blocks* and *Little Women* showcases the gentility of social reading and the pleasures of motherhood. The illustration of Jo March reading improving literature in *Little Women*, however, reveals how tension can surface in this pictorial type.

THE ANTIQUATED READER

In Victorian British and American book illustration, we find examples of elderly antiquated readers that recall the physical characteristics and reading preferences of the venerable type from portraiture. While mid-eighteenth-century portraiture emphasizes beauty and fertility over learning for youthful subjects, piety emerges as the esteemed attribute of women past child-bearing age.[39] As the portraits of John Singleton Copley and Joseph Badger convey, the venerable type in portraiture honors the religious origins of Puritan America. Wearing old-fashioned, plain dress and holding a book in her hand (often a hymnal or a Bible), the venerable type serves as a model of righteousness. She also exudes an austerity and a grave spirituality associated with the Puritan age. As Docherty notes, "The book also honored advanced age, yet venerability was achieved at the cost of femininity. The use of male portrait models for representations of elderly women as readers demonstrates the ideological incompatibility of intellectuality and female sexuality" (348).

The type I call the antiquated reader appears in book illustration on both sides of the Atlantic as an elderly woman performing socially sanctioned roles, such as disseminating religious teachings and educating children other than her own.[40] She is a secondary or minor character, though not exclusively so. More than any other type of woman reader in book illustration, the antiquated reader has a stereotypical appearance: a bun (often covered by a lace cap), glasses, a gaunt or portly physique, old-fashioned dress, austere manner, and a masculine or shriveled appearance. Moreover, the same "ideological incompatibility of intellectuality and female sexuality" from portraiture occurs in antiquated readers in nineteenth-century book illustration, but with a twist. We do not revere the antiquated type, who assumes a position of moral authority or self-proclaimed learnedness at the cost of traditional notions of femininity and sexual desirability. Esteem—essential to venerable portraiture—gives way to ridicule, curiosity, and amusement in the antiquated type. Even though nineteenth-century antiquated readers assume respectable postures akin to interrupted and social readers, they illuminate derisive gender stereotypes associated with intellectual women. Those cast as antiquated readers fall into undesirable categories: spinsters, also called redundant women, and eccentrics. In terms of ideology, this type supports the pervasive biological and medical arguments that intellect comes at the cost of femininity and fertility.[41]

Prime examples of antiquated readers connected satirically to notions of piety live between the pages of Twain's illustrated fiction. *The Adventures of Tom Sawyer* and its sequel *Adventures of Huckleberry Finn* (1885) immortalize Victorian American boyhood and provide a window into the religious, racist, post–Civil War southern society that the novels reflect and influenced. Illustrations in books and weeklies (exceedingly popular in the Victorian American age) helped to define America's perceptions about remote peoples, historic places, and events, as well as race and gender. When Twain published his books by subscription, illustration was integral to the marketing of the first editions of *Tom Sawyer* and *Huckleberry Finn*.[42]

Although best known for Tom and Huck, now celebrated as cultural icons, Twain's works contain depictions of three antiquated readers: Widow Douglas, Miss Watson, and Aunt Polly. The antiquated reader as "moral" teacher becomes the object of ridicule most forcefully in E. W. Kemble's rendition of Widow Douglas for *Huck Finn*. Kemble was a well-established cartoonist and illustrator before he collaborated with Twain, and his rendition of Widow Douglas reveals his training in caricature. Childless and past child-bearing age, Widow Douglas, through Kemble's eyes, visually conforms to type. She has a bun, lace cap, Puritanical dress, thin physique, and unflattering appearance in "Learning about Moses and the 'Bulrushers'" (fig. 22). Positioned in profile to accentuate her long thin nose and wrinkled cheeks, Widow Douglas gazes directly at a Bible. In venerable portraiture, the Bible is a potent objective signifier to esteem advanced age

Gallery of Victorian British and American Women Readers   169

Fig. 22. Illustration by E. W. Kemble, "Learning about Moses and the 'Bulrushers,'" for Mark Twain, *Adventures of Huckleberry Finn*, 1885.

and social position. To Beecher and Beecher Stowe, Widow Douglas is here following their guidance in educating a child other than her own. But in Twain's fiction, the Bible that Widow Douglas holds is an ironic symbol: it pays tribute to the religious origins of Puritan America that neither Twain nor Huck Finn endorses. Her bony right index finger points severely at the revered words she attempts to instill into an unwilling Huck, whom we can imagine saying, "The Widow Douglas, she took me for her son, and allowed she would sivilize me."[43] Her steady gaze on the open text and her firm grasp on the book convey an air of assumed self-righteousness and moral authority: religious teachings are an integral part of her civilized life if not of Huck's.

Homeless, uneducated, and motherless, Huck has an absent, abusive father. Twain allows Huck to overcome his questionable background and gain complexity as a character. He is candid, intelligent, admirable, and courageous. Not only is he brave enough to risk his life for others (for example, he plays a key role in saving Widow Douglas and Jim) but also he is bold enough to defy mainstream religious teaching and resist repeated attempts to make him conform to the rigid rules of Victorian American society. Kemble shows Huck, just back from a spree, wearing a stiff-looking suit as he confides that Widow Douglas cries over him and "called me a poor lost lamb, and she called me a lot of other names, too, but she meant no harm by it. She put me in them new clothes again, and I couldn't do nothing but sweat and sweat, and feel all cramped up" (18). Huck's excuse for her, "she meant no harm by it," actually goads our curiosity to know what other names Widow Douglas calls him. Widow Douglas expects Huck to follow her unyielding rules for dress, table etiquette, and decorum to make him more respectable. She reads him Bible stories like Moses and the "Bulrushers" (18), as Huck prefers to call her religious teaching. In part, Twain's rendition of a satirical reworking of an honorific type may bespeak the perspective of young boys about religion and reading. Unlike Marmee, the mother in "A Rainy Day," and Aunt Chlotilde—Widow Douglas does not have a receptive listener in Huck.

Critics have reproached Kemble for stereotyping African-Americans and relying on one white model for all the boy characters in *Huck Finn*. However, David and Sapirstein suggest that Kemble improves on Twain's description of Huck, making him "animated" and emphasizing his "idiosyncratic charm and good-natured rascality."[44] Kemble's depiction of Huck —with tattered straw hat, patched pants held by one suspender, and a face brimming with good-natured mischievousness—endures as the definitive portrait, "helping endear him to generations of readers" (33), despite Twain's lukewarm response to the cover design: "All right and good, and will answer, although the boy's mouth is a trifle more Irishy than necessary" (David and Sapirstein, "Reading the Illustrations in *Huckleberry Finn*" 33).

In "Learning about Moses and the 'Bulrushers,'" a captivating Huck cocks his head to the side, leans against his hand, and gazes sympathetically at the reader-viewer. Huck admits that at first, "I was in a sweat to find out all about him [Moses]; but by-and-by she let it out that Moses had been dead a considerable long time; so then I didn't care no more about him; because I don't take no stock in dead people" (18). When Widow Douglas refuses Huck the right to smoke ("it was a mean practice and wasn't clean" [18]), Huck concludes, "Here she was a bothering about Moses, which was no kin to her, and no use to anybody, being gone, you see, yet finding a power of fault with me for doing a thing that had some good in it" (19). Twain again lets us see the hypocrisy of the righteous Widow

Fig. 23. Illustration by Worth Brehm, "Then She Told Me about the Bad Place, and I Said I Wished I Was There," for Mark Twain, *Adventures of Huckleberry Finn*, 1923.

Douglas when Huck complains that she criticizes his smoking, but indulges in snuff: "of course that was all right, because she done it herself" (19). Huck wants to smoke—not listen to a story about dead Moses or adhere to conventions of polite society. Our sympathy lies with Huck. We long to light out to the territories with him.

In the opening chapter of a 1923 illustrated edition of *Huck Finn*, Worth Brehm depicts Widow Douglas's spinster sister, Miss Watson, instilling Huck's moral education in "Then She Told Me about the Bad Place, and I Said I Wished I Was There" (fig. 23). In terms of human interaction, this and the previous image of Widow Douglas as an antiquated reader recall the illustration of Jo March as a social reader (fig. 19): each reader has an unreceptive audience—an uninterested boy or a dozing aunt—creating tension, which cuts across pictorial types. However, we can assume that

Fig. 24. Illustration by True Williams, "Aunt Polly Seeks Information," for Mark Twain, *The Adventures of Tom Sawyer*, 1876. (Courtesy of Schaffer Library, Union College.)

Aunt Josephine March, unlike Huck Finn, wants to read in collaboration with others since she pays Jo to be her reading companion.

Twain describes Miss Watson as "a tolerable slim old maid, with goggles on" (19). Likewise, Brehm casts her as an antiquated type. A thin and unattractive Miss Watson wears glasses, a bun, and Puritanical attire (dark dress with a prim white collar). Brehm distinguishes the illustration in creating an equally proper and respectable parlor; all the items on the mantel, the framed oval picture, and the tablecloth belong in a proper Victorian American home. Brehm places an opened spelling primer in Miss Watson's hands. Her bony thumbs hold the open book rigidly upright. Her unforgiving eyes penetrate Huck, who squirms in his dress clothes as he sits on an embroidered chair with delicately carved woodwork. Although Miss Watson drills Huck about spelling, his behavior leads her to the topic of moral education, the real subject of this illustration. A proper education is essential to her rigid conception of a polite, respectable life. Pictured in profile, Miss Watson has a stiffness and sternness that emanate from her "goggled" eyes as she delivers her view about the "bad place" and the "good place." True to type, Brehm's childless Miss Watson has seemingly traded her femininity for self-proclaimed "morality" and "learnedness." Twain tells us that Miss Watson keeps "pecking" at Huck, with whom we sympathize, until it is time for her to assume other pious duties (conducting evening prayers for their servants).

In *The Adventures of Tom Sawyer,* True Williams casts Aunt Polly as an interrupted reader but more memorably depicts her as an antiquated type.[45] Williams earned praise for his dramatic night scenes crucial to the plot of *Tom Sawyer,* but critics complained about his haphazard and inconsistent portrayals of characters (particularly Tom and Huck), his failure to realize Twain's text with inspiration, and his habit of carrying over graphics from earlier works (a trait not uncommon among book illustrators). For instance, the grandmother who clutches a switch in "History Repeats Itself" in Twain's *Sketches, New and Old* (1875) reappears one year later in the headpiece to chapter 19 as Tom's devout, strict, proper, though goodhearted Aunt Polly, a woman quick to discipline and to forgive.[46] Williams's "Aunt Polly Seeks Information" (fig. 24) illustrates Twain's satire of the Bible, Aunt Polly's air of assumed authority, and the "ideological incompatibility of intellectuality and female sexuality" of the antiquated type (Docherty 348), associated with the medical argument against women's reading.

Wearing dark glasses and a severe black dress, cloak, bonnet, and gloves, Aunt Polly looks particularly austere and manly as she assumes the position of divine healer on a mission of service. Never sick herself, Aunt Polly reads numerous quack medical journals to which she subscribes to cure her loved ones. Aunt Polly "was one of those people who are infatuated with patent medicines and all new-fangled methods of producing health or mending it. . . . and she never observed that her health-journals of the current month customarily upset everything they had recommended the month before."[47] In this illustration, patent medicines in bottles of all shapes and sizes and stacks of health pamphlets surround Aunt Polly (the words "THE CEPHALIC PILL" and "CURE" are visible on the covers). Not only literate, Aunt Polly is an avid consumer, a trait common to the material reader, another pictorial type that Docherty discusses; early-nineteenth-century portraits show the material reader arrayed with worldly goods, including a book (Docherty 349–51). However, Aunt Polly reads to treat Tom's ailing spirits. The text informs us that Aunt Polly learns about a water cure: a morning deluge of cold water in the woodshed, followed by a scrub and a rest, and a wrap in wet sheets under blankets. "Infatuated" with the idea of promoting health, Aunt Polly, "simple-hearted and honest as the day was long ... was an easy victim" (108).

Good-hearted "victim" or not, Aunt Polly—with her mistaken notions of healing—becomes the butt of Twain's satire, as he continues: "She gathered together her quack periodicals and her quack medicines, and thus armed with death, went about on her pale horse, metaphorically speaking, with 'hell following after.' But she never suspected that she was not an angel of healing and the balm of Gilead in disguise, to the suffering neighbors" (108). Loading allusions to the Books of Revelation, Jeremiah, and Malachi into one sentence, and repeating the word "quack," Twain satirizes Aunt Polly's self-proclaimed calling. Paraphrasing John's prophecy ("hell following after"), Twain transforms Aunt Polly into Death—the rider on the pale horse, one of the Four Horseman of the Apocalypse from the Book of Revelation. Reading her phony journal, which she holds tightly between her dark gloved hands, Williams's Polly is not sprouting the healing wings of an angel, the reward promised to the righteous in the Book of Malachi. She is "armed with death," not with the balm of Gilead, noted for its healing properties and praised in the Book of Jeremiah.[48] In fact, in cloaking her all in black, Williams makes her look like Death on the pale horse. Aunt Polly considers herself an "angel of healing," but we pity "Tom [who] had become indifferent to persecution by this time" (109) as well as Polly's afflicted neighbors, who have suffered at the hands of a quack.

Aunt Polly, Miss Watson, and Widow Douglas look the part of dried-up and sexually undesirable spinsters. All three are satirically connected with notions of piety. However, in nineteenth-century book illustration, the visual appearance of the antiquated type becomes separated from even an ironic notion of moral authority and loses all connection to the honorific venerable type. All pictorial types become more oppositional and variable once people begin to form strong opinions about them. The antiquated type in book illustration well demonstrates this point. A purely visual representation of the antiquated reader evolves in book illustration, as witnessed in countless Victorian British and American novels.

Gallery of Victorian British and American Women Readers   175

Fig. 25. Illustration by Hablot Knight Browne, "Traddles and I, in Conference with the Misses Spenlow," for Charles Dickens, *The Personal History of David Copperfield*, 1850.

Among the cast of Dickens's *David Copperfield* are several eccentric women, minor and major, whom Browne poses with books or newspapers and grants the visual appearance of the antiquated type. In "Mr. Dick Fulfills My Aunt's Prediction," a spectacled and portly Mrs. Markleham (Annie Strong's widowed mother, whom David's school friends jestingly call "Old Soldier") tucks her hair into a lace cap and holds a newspaper as wide as her girth. Corpulent to the point of being unattractive, the Old Soldier, complete with a masculine name, appears as a sexless, strong, shrewd character who secures her daughter's hand in marriage to a man old enough to be her grandfather. "Traddles and I, in Conference with the Misses Spenlow" (fig. 25) features Dora Spenlow's spinster aunts, also vi-

Fig. 26. Illustration by Hablot Knight Browne, "The Momentous Interview," for Charles Dickens, *The Personal History of David Copperfield*, 1850.

sually cast as antiquated types. Browne depicts them just as Dickens describes them: "They both had little bright round twinkling eyes, by the way, which were like birds' eyes. They were not unlike birds, altogether; having a sharp, brisk, sudden manner, and a little short, spruce way of adjusting themselves, like canaries" (503).[49] Browne intensifies the sexual undesirability and eccentricity of Dora's maiden aunts. Sporting curls and a flirtatiousness more appropriate for a girl than a maiden aunt, Aunt Clarissa coyly holds David's letter asking for Dora's hand in marriage. Despite her lace cap, Aunt Lavinia looks more masculine than her sister and particularly unattractive; positioned in profile, she has a pointed nose that resembles a bird's beak. Beautiful Dora will not follow in the footsteps of Aunt Lavinia, left hoping for a Mr. Pidger to declare his intentions "if he had not been cut short in his youth (at about sixty)" (501).

A more complex character than Aunts Lavinia and Clarissa, Aunt Betsey Trotwood in "The Momentous Interview" (fig. 26) sits rigidly upright in her chair beside an open book, likely a Bible, and a crumpled letter, perhaps from the Murdstones announcing their "momentous" visit. Her posture and facial features make her look as Dickens describes her, "unbending and austere" (170). While Dora's birdlike aunts may be comparable to canaries, Aunt Betsey, who has tirades against donkeys and blatantly prefers girls to boys, resembles a hawk. Once again, Browne accentuates her sharp nose by positioning her in profile. While Aunt Betsey's firmness reflects a strength of character necessary to confront David's would-be murderers and contrasts strongly with the kindly and humorous expression on Mr. Dick's face, only the painting of the good Samaritan adorning Betsey's drawing room wall speaks to the kinder nature of one who becomes David's true protectress.

Browne pictures Aunt Betsey here with the stereotypical appearance of an antiquated reader: angular frame, Puritanical dress, bun, and bonnet with frills that seemingly mock her unattractive, manly appearance. As the novel progresses, Aunt Betsey transforms before our eyes into a loyal and likeable character because of her nonconformity, as witnessed by her commitment to the crazed Mr. Dick and David, whom she raises, protects, and guides. She sees the folly of David's first marriage, calling him "blind, blind, blind!" (425). Betsey also keeps David from "forming" Dora, leading critics such as Merryn Williams to claim, "It is possible to argue that Betsey Trotwood is the real heroine of this novel" (83). But here and throughout the novel, Browne depicts Aunt Betsey's eccentricities and the hardness in her features, making her visually conform to the antiquated type.

These eccentric Dickensian women posed with books and newspapers visually resemble Twain's spinsterly women who assume postures of moral authority or learnedness: all have seemingly traded away or lost their conventional femininity and fertility, affirming the risks rooted in the nineteenth-century medical model opposing women's reading. Different from the interrupted and social readers who uphold the sacrosanct sphere of the Victorian home, the antiquated type in book illustration is not presented as a model to emulate. Nor does she disturb the conventions of patriarchy. Even Aunt Betsey—who earns our esteem, not for her piety but for her good sense—is burdened by a visual stereotype, which holds firm as the antiquated type evolves in book illustration.

THE ISOLATED READER

We characterize the isolated reader in Victorian British and American book illustration by what, where, and how she reads, not by what she does for others. Typically pictured alone, the isolated reader often appears as a threat, destabilizing prevailing notions of gender. The isolated reader, immersed in a book, is often oblivious to her surroundings and free to imagine. As Homer's *The New Novel* demonstrates (fig. 4), the type was, to some, even a figure of disgrace or ruination. As women of the upper reaches gained increasing opportunities for education and social betterment, anxieties arose that reading would lead to domestic disaster, as Cruikshank humorously conveys in "My Wife Is a Woman of Mind" (fig. 1). The isolated reader in book illustration also taps into the tropes of consumption and addiction and the moral argument that fiction is a controlled substance, akin to drink and drugs, leading to immorality. Concomitantly, to those who espoused the ideology of reading for empowerment, the isolated reader conceivably gained "space—physical, temporal, and psychological" (Sicherman, "Sense and Sensibility" 202) and "a room of her own" (Woolf 52). Moreover, by the 1890s, when fears of a woman's downfall from reading books dwindled, artists and illustrators reflected upon and weighed choices available to women who read in the private home, in nature, or on holiday. The isolated reader increasingly came to represent bourgeois leisure and idleness, as Childe Hassam depicts in *Summer Sunlight* (1892), and Lewis Carroll shows in *Alice's Adventures under Ground* (fig. 31).[50]

Again a range exists within this pictorial type. In a 1905 edition of Longfellow's *Evangeline*, Howard Chandler Christy casts Evangeline Bellefontaine as an isolated reader singularly absorbed in her prayer book to emphasize her beauty and piousness (fig. 27). Christy shows a lovely, youthful Evangeline in Puritan dress and cap, kneeling in a church pew, fully engrossed in her reading. Behind Evangeline sits her beloved Gabriel Lajeunesse, as engrossed in Evangeline as she is in the words of God. Evangeline does not seem to notice him. Her eyes are closed, suggesting that prayer has inspired her—not to imagine a world apart from social reality (common in the case of the isolated reader), but to take her religious teachings to heart. Christy visually fixes the characterization of a worthy woman who can endure the pain of separation, years of vain searching, and a life of devotion to God as a Sister of Mercy.

Carroll's opening depiction of Alice's sister reading by the riverbank in his self-illustrated *Alice's Adventures under Ground* (1864) also seems

Fig. 27. Illustration by Howard Chandler Christy, "She Was a Woman Now," for Henry Wadsworth Longfellow, *Evangeline*, 1905.

worth mentioning here since it conveys how the isolated reader, pictured on holiday or in nature, increasingly came to represent leisure in nineteenth-century culture (see fig. 31 in chapter 7). Alice's sister, who reads outdoors, is not actually alone. Alice sits alongside her older sister and gazes away from the pictureless book, which prompts Alice's imaginative journey. Although rarely the object of a critic's gaze, Alice's sister appears engrossed in her book, oblivious of Alice and her surroundings, free to think and perhaps imagine. At the end of *Alice's Adventures under Ground,* Alice's sister does, in fact, dream "after a fashion"[51] and experiences what Carroll calls "a dream within the dream, as it were" (90): "and

Fig. 28. Illustration by Henry Sandham, "She Spent Most of Her Time in the Library Reading Her Papa's Big Books," for Frances Hodgson Burnett, *Editha's Burglar*, 1888.

she listened for the words of the tale, and lo! it was the dream of her own little sister" (89–90).

Illustrators also cast girls in the role of the isolated reader. In Burnett's *Editha's Burglar* (1888), illustrator Henry Sandham twice depicts Editha as an isolated, addicted reader. Burnett describes Editha as "always rather a queer little girl, and not much like other children."[52] Like Burnett's Sara Crewe and Mary Lenox, Editha is ignored: her father (an author and a newspaper editor) is too busy to educate her; her pretty young mother is primarily interested in going out; and her governess comes only in the mornings. Seven-year-old Editha is an only child who "had always been very fond of books, and had learned to read when she was such a tiny child, that I should almost be afraid to say how tiny she was when she read her first volume through" (11). Responding to fears of reading addiction surrounding girls' unsupervised reading, Burnett cautions, "Editha perhaps read more than was quite good for her" (11).

Intensifying these fears associated with the isolated type, Sandham features Editha alone in the library of a prosperous home in "She Spent Most of Her Time in the Library Reading Her Papa's Big Books" (fig. 28). The oversized volume on her lap captivates Editha, seated in a big stuffed chair in a gentleman's library. Other books ripe for consumption surround her, including an open book propped on the library table. Behind her is a backdrop of impressive volumes, some no doubt written by her author father. Worse, Editha is often left alone for many hours a day to read her father's books "and even his newspapers" (12). Her golden locks and lace collar give her the look of a genteel young lady, but her singular absorption in the text and her intense expression serve as early signs of reading addiction.

Sandham's next illustration titled "Through the Newspapers She Found There Were Men Who Lived by Breaking into People's Houses" shows Editha sitting alone on the floor, enveloped by newsprint. "Newspapers are scarcely supposed to be read by women at all," notes the forward thinking Emily Davies in her critique of Victorian girls' education; "When the *Times* is offered to a lady, the sheet containing the advertisements, and the Births, Deaths, and Marriages, is considerately selected."[53] But Editha selects sheets that contain current events, including burglaries in London, which trouble her young mind (12). Editha's reading puts her on the lookout for the burglar who enters her home. She bravely confronts him, asks him not to disturb her mama, and convinces him to take her own things instead of her parents' treasures. In the end, the burglar is caught, Editha's possessions are returned, and her mother promises to become "a better mother to her, after this, and take care of her more" (59). The implicit message is that Editha will no longer have free reign of her father's library: Editha's mother will now supervise her daughter's education.

Illustrations of isolated readers in Anthony Trollope's *Orley Farm* (1862) and Alcott's *Little Women* offer quintessential examples of the isolated reader as a figure risking ruination or societal disapproval in her search for empowerment. "The Angel of Light" (fig. 29), called "Mary's Letter" in some editions, is one of forty black-and-white illustrations that Sir John Everett Millais provided for *Orley Farm*. A Royal Academy painter and founding member of the Pre-Raphaelite brotherhood, Millais offers carefully rendered illustrations of contemporary life for a number

Fig. 29. Illustration by Sir John Everett Millais, "The Angel of Light," for Anthony Trollope, *Orley Farm. A Novel*, 1862.

of novels by Trollope, who became his close friend. In this compelling image, Millais depicts Mary Snow reading a love letter by candlelight. The letter is from Mary's lover, not her betrothed. The image captures the isolated reader transgressing the norms of social decorum.

Orley Farm tells the story of a criminal case surrounding the possible guilt and long-held secret of the lead character, Lady Mason. The law suspects that Lady Mason has forged her late husband's will to ensure that her son, Lucius, and not her husband's oldest son from his first marriage, will inherit Orley Farm. Mary Snow is bride-elect of rising barrister Felix Graham, involved in the legal proceedings against Lady Mason. This courtroom drama weighs actions motivated by the heart against English law and custom; it is also a love story where suitors in their prime (young Peregrine Orme and Felix Graham) and golden years (Sir Peregrine Orme) try their hand at lovemaking to varying degrees of success.

Trollope initially tells us Graham "was one of those few wise men who have determined not to have a partner in life at hazard, but to mould a young mind and character to those pursuits and modes of thought which may best fit a woman for the duties she will have to perform" (*Orley Farm*, 1: 178). Like Edmund Bertram, who molds Fanny Price to his liking in *Mansfield Park*, Graham attempts to form Mary "so that she might be made fit to suit his taste" (*Orley Farm*, 1: 139). The circumstances of Mary Snow's class and parentage resemble Fanny's. Mary is a pretty though half-starved child of an impoverished and drunken widower. Playing the part of the good Samaritan that the Bertrams more grudgingly play for Fanny, Graham educates Mary, clothes and feeds her, and becomes her legal guardian with the intention of marrying her "if her conduct up to that age had been becoming" (258). Left in the care of a teacher, Mrs. Thomas, Mary meets a young aspiring medical man, Albert Fitzallen, who induces her to meet him in secret under a lamppost. She accepts Fitzallen's love letter, which she reads in private in "The Angel of Light."

Millais intensifies the illicitness of the act by creating a melodramatic atmosphere. A single candle forms the only light source in the room. Mary leans toward the candle and holds the letter close to her face as she sits alone, rereading her forbidden love note late at night. Her eyes consume its contents. Reading, Mary relishes "stolen pleasures": "Poor Mary thought it was very nice and very sweet, and though she was so much afraid of it that she almost wished it away, yet she read it a score of times. Stolen pleasures are always sweet. She had not cared to read those two lines from her own betrothed lord above once, or at the most twice; and yet they had been written by a good man,—a man superlatively good to her" (1: 264). In the dark, Mary feels free to imagine a life different from that intended for her as wife of her "own betrothed lord" and patron. Unsure of her lover's intentions, she trembles as she daringly imagines a future other than an unpleasant though respectable social reality. Fortunately, Felix Graham does not follow in the footsteps of Austen's Edmund Bertram, but seizes upon Mary's infidelity to release himself from the marriage bond. By then, Graham has fallen in love with a woman of a higher social standing, Madeline Staveley, whom he eventually marries. The illicit letter becomes an excuse to release him from his prior commitment. Nonetheless, the illustration of Mary as an isolated reader preserves her indiscretion and hope for a different life.[54]

Fig. 30. Illustration by Frank T. Merrill, "Curling Herself Up in the Big Chair," for Louisa May Alcott, *Little Women or Meg, Jo, Beth and Amy*, 1880.

Illustrators also cast Alcott's Jo March in daring roles. In fact, Merrill depicts Jo as an isolated reader within the same chapter that she appears dutifully reading aloud to dozing Aunt March.[55] The bookishness of spirited Jo, a budding writer, no doubt led Merrill to cast her as the isolated type. Alcott tells us that Jo likely takes the position as Aunt March's companion because of her uncle's "large library of fine books, which was left to dust and spiders since Uncle March died" (36). Merrill places Jo in a gentleman's library of towering bookshelves crammed with tempting volumes (fig. 30): "The dim, dusty room, with the busts staring down from the tall bookcases, the cozy chairs, the globes, and, best of all, the wilderness of books in which she could wander where she liked, made the library a region of bliss to her. The moment Aunt March took her nap, or was busy with company, Jo hurried to this quiet place, and, curling herself up in the easy chair, devoured poetry, romance, history, travels, and pictures, like a regular bookworm" (36). In this illustration, Jo nestles comfortably in a large, decorative armchair to devour the contents of the oversized volume she holds on her lap. Wearing a prim dress, with her hair pulled up in a net, she looks the part of a respectable lady. However, her eyes fix on the page with an intensity altogether absent in an earlier depiction of her more conventional sister Meg, eating apples and crying over Yonge's *The Heir of Redclyffe* (1853).[56]

On the one hand, Alcott makes clear that Jo's independent reading is secretive and escapist, a nod to the moral argument. Nonetheless, this well-lit library contrasts to Mary Snow's clandestine setting. Whereas Millais' image of Mary Snow highlights the fears of immorality surrounding reading in secret, Merrill's image of Jo reading alone emphasizes the empowerment of independent reading. Jo, for the moment, seems free to read what she wishes and to dream. The book exposes Jo to worlds beyond the restrictions of Victorian gentility. Like her nineteenth-century sisters—Jane Eyre, Maggie Tulliver, Isabel Archer, Emma Bovary, and Isabel Gilbert—Jo avidly absorbs pictures and texts, and both spark her artistic side and creative imagining (Merrill places a portfolio alongside Jo's chair). A backdrop of books of romance, poetry, history, and travel create a literary world through which Jo, the isolated reader, travels and experiences "bliss." "But, like all happiness, it did not last long," Alcott tells us, "for as sure as she had just reached the heart of the story, the sweetest verse of the song, or the most perilous adventure of her traveler, a shrill voice called, 'Josy-phine! Josy-phine!' and she had to leave her paradise to wind yarn, wash the poodle, or read Belsham's *Essays* by the hour together" (36). Abruptly, Jo must leave her reading "paradise" for domestic duties.

Although akin to the mind traveler introduced in the next chapter, Jo is closely tied to her social reality. Even though she heeds duty, Merrill's depiction of Jo, nonetheless, becomes a vehicle introducing complex gender issues of the age: an isolated woman reader can temporarily free herself from the control of her bourgeois world, even though, as Banta notes, the act of reading indoors ties her to the private home. For brief moments, Jo finds the liberty to roam, to choose pleasure over responsibility, until duty rears its head in the form of a shrill call to service or a gentle tug of concern for her ailing sister.

. . .

The interrupted, social, antiquated, and isolated types in book illustration preserve popular cultural notions and stereotypes of gender as well as dominant Victorian ideologies governing women's reading practices on both sides of the Atlantic—for example, gentility, socialization, empowerment, addiction, the medical model, and morality. A question remains: why do illustrators choose reading to characterize a woman? At a time when women were reading widely, sparking an ideological debate, illustration—like genre painting—became a means to comment on choices increasingly available to women. Casting women as various pictorial types, illustrators, in collaboration with authors, connect the illustrated book to a larger historical debate surrounding, at times influencing, and even repressing women's reading practice in Victorian Britain and America.

The success of a collaboration between text and illustration seemingly stems from a compatible vision between author and illustrator, as these examples show. Artists did not re-create a text; in fact, reviewers have criticized Williams for doing just that in *Tom Sawyer*. However, including a book not mentioned explicitly in the text, as Browne exhibits in *David Copperfield*, responds to textual cues and complements a narrative.

Gender issues and stereotypes also surface in book illustration. The receptive listener in scenes of social reading is typically a female, often a daughter, who will continue in her mother's path. We find a rampant privileging of domesticity and service through depictions of the interrupted and social reader as well as an inclination to mock a woman who trades her femininity for alleged learnedness or morality, as the antiquated type conveys. Of these four pictorial types in British and American book illustration, those who transgress social norms or seek empowerment by reading in isolation prove most interesting to readers today. Sandham's Editha, Millais' Mary Snow, and Merrill's Jo March usher in liberating images of the woman reader explored in the next two chapters—woman as mind traveler and the revolutionary woman reader.

7

The Book as Portal

Depictions of the Mind Traveler
in Lewis Carroll's *Alice's Adventures under Ground* (1864)
and Charlotte Perkins Gilman's "The Yellow Wall-Paper" (1892)

In nineteenth-century book illustration, women read in secret and within the socially sanctioned family circle. They read indoors and outdoors, by firelight and candlelight, in the library and the parlor. They interrupt their reading to engage in conversation, greet guests, and comfort their children. They minister to their community and, at times, assume an air of moral authority to instill their values in unreceptive listeners. But the book also emerges as a portal, leading a character into a voyage of the mind.

John Keats's sonnet "On First Looking into Chapman's Homer" (1816) describes reading as journeying into another world. The opening quatrain narrates: "Much have I travell'd in the realms of gold,/And many goodly states and kingdoms seen;/Round many western islands have I been/Which bards in fealty to Apollo hold" (lines 1–4). The riches of literature take concrete form in the imagination. An inspiring book or poem becomes a portal to a "goodly state," a fantastic kingdom, an exotic island vivid within the reader's mind. Keats humbly admits in the second quatrain that his ignorance of Greek limited his understanding of Homer, a work he discovered through Chapman's translation. In the sestet, Keats extends the image of reading as mind traveling. The enlightened reader (for example, Keats after reading Chapman's translation of Homer) shares the glory of an astronomer locating a new planet on the horizon and the exultation of an explorer discovering a new continent.[1]

As examined in part 2, authors such as Charlotte Brontë and George Eliot direct our attention to a reader's deep imaginative engagement with a text. They offer examples of active—as opposed to passive or frivolous—

reading and celebrate the effect that literature has, respectively, upon Jane Eyre and Maggie Tulliver. Enshrined like a Turk in the window seat at Gateshead, Jane makes up tales from the Bewick pictures that absorb her, speak to her isolation, and, in some cases, terrify her. "Each picture told a story"—Jane tells us (6). Quick to show off her book learning, Maggie also reads pictures and invents stories "out of my own head" (19). "There were few sounds that roused Maggie when she was dreaming over her book" (16), Eliot assures us. Reading transports Maggie—and Jane—into "goodly states and kingdoms seen."

How might we observe the effect of literature on a woman reader in book illustration? We judge the interrupted reader and the social reader by her actions within the domestic circle, the antiquated reader by her unfeminine appearance, and the isolated reader by the type of material she reads when alone, often in secret. For example, Browne twice depicts Agnes Wickfield, the quintessential interrupted reader, putting aside her books, rather than showing the effect reading may have on her character. Only in illustrations of the isolated reader do we begin to imagine how a reader responds to texts that engross her as fully as Jane Eyre and Maggie Tulliver. We glimpse Mary Snow's secret thrill of reading an illicit love letter by candlelight and the region of "bliss" that Jo March enters while poring over travel books, romance, and poetry in Uncle March's library. Although neither Anthony Trollope nor Louisa May Alcott, respectively, sustains solitary reading and imagining, the isolated reader paves the way for another type of reader—the mind traveler.

Reader-response theory directs our attention to different types of hypothetical and real readers. Equally, it can illuminate the reading process of fictional woman in books filled with scenes of reading. Reader-response theory explores how readers rely on knowledge of literary conventions to make sense of the texts they read. Readers also modify their preconceptions as they continue reading. Most relevant is the work of Jane Tompkins and Janice Radway. These critics approach reader-response theory from the context of gender to study the effects of reading on women and, in Radway's case, to explore how women and men read differently.[2]

Depictions of the mind traveler in Victorian British and American fiction offer a visual dimension to feminist reader-response criticism: we gain a vivid impression of the effect literature has on a reader. Lewis Carroll's opening image in his self-illustrated *Alice's Adventures under Ground* (1864) (the first version of *Alice's Adventures in Wonderland* [1865]) illustrates the influence of a book on a resisting reader: Alice launches her dream-journey by critically rejecting her sister's pictureless, conversation-less book, traveling into the rich world of her imagination. For Charlotte Perkins Gilman's "The Yellow Wall-Paper" (1892), illustrator Joseph Henry Hatfield captures the narrator's determination to write despite doctor's orders; the narrator eventually becomes an active and persistent reader of a nontraditional text—the wallpaper lining the walls of her nursery prison. Both examples foreground the reading practice of an imaginative, independent female, which antifiction critics opposed on the grounds of biology, morality, addictiveness, and the medical model. Equally, Alice's and the narrator's mind travels illuminate the "transformative potential" (Kelley 404) of a text and the argument of reading for empowerment.

The *Alice* books, next to the Bible and the works of Shakespeare, are the most widely translated and quoted today. Critics have called *Alice* an allegory of Darwinian evolution, a parable of birth trauma, a series of mathematical puzzles, and a story about toilet training. While Carroll's biographer Morton N. Cohen reads the *Alice* books as a rite of passage for the author, Nina Auerbach considers it a "loving parody of Genesis and of contemporary fallen women" ("Falling Alice" 51). *Alice*—which Harvey Darton credits for sparking a "revolution" in Victorian children's books[3]—features a heroine whose adventures rival those in nineteenth-century boys' books, which followed in the wake of *Robinson Crusoe* (1719). Only at the end of the tale do we learn that the magical land to which Alice travels is really the world of her dreams.[4]

If Carroll "made himself," as Cohen notes, "into a man worth writing about" (533), the same holds true of the opening lines of *Alice's Adventures under Ground* that inform us why Alice is critical of her sister's book: "Alice was beginning to get very tired of sitting by her sister on the bank, and of having nothing to do: once or twice she had peeped into the book her sister was reading, but it had no pictures or conversations in it, and where is the use of a book, thought Alice, without pictures or conversations?" (1). In *Alice's Adventures under Ground* (hereafter cited as *under Ground*), Carroll draws, as his first illustration, a bored Alice scorning the open book on her older sister's lap (fig. 31).[5] Carroll prominently positions it as a headpiece to the left of the decorative vines encircling "Chapter 1."[6] Alice's sister looks absorbed in the text she is reading—her eyes directly engage the page—but we wonder why: the pages, as Carroll depicts them, appear blank. Alice props her head with her right hand while her right elbow rests on her sister's knee. Her face has a slight pout, and her slightly down-turned eyes suggest her boredom with this book.

Unlike Marmee in *Little Women*, Alice's older sister does not gain a willing listener or reader in Alice. The hot day, Carroll tells us, "made her

Fig. 31. Illustration by Lewis Carroll, chapter 1 headpiece, for Lewis Carroll, *Alice's Adventures under Ground*, 1864.

feel very sleepy and stupid" (*under Ground* 1). However, the sight of a white rabbit wearing a waistcoat rouses Alice, who is curious enough to follow him down a rabbit hole into an enchanting "wonderland." In this wondrous place, animals talk intelligently, dance wildly, and, at times, act madly. The Queen threatens decapitation at the merest whim, gardeners paint roses to change their color, and in the Wonderland court of law, the sentence comes before the verdict. Inquisitive and imaginative, Alice changes size every time she drinks or nibbles, only to find herself elongated and shrunk. She grows larger than the White Rabbit's house and nearly drowns in a pool of her own tears.

Carroll illustrates these transformations as well as his remarkable characters, some of whom he doesn't describe at all. In fact, Carroll advises the reader: "(if you don't know what a Gryphon is, look at the picture)" (*under Ground* 78).[7] Carroll's *Alice* stories diverge from the richly descriptive fiction of their day. Pictures and conversations define Carroll's characters. We are dependent upon Carroll's illustrations to travel along with Alice into "realms of gold." Moreover, in rejecting a boring book in favor of imagination, Alice empowers herself. During her underground adventure, Alice alters her size by eating and drinking, protects three cards from beheading by slipping them into her pocket, and defies an outrageous Queen by asserting, "you're nothing but a pack of cards!" (88).

Carroll never again depicts Alice in a reading scene in *under Ground*, nor does Tenniel show her with a book in *Alice's Adventures in Wonderland* (hereafter cited as *The Annotated Alice*).[8] However, Alice's conversations suggest that more than a dislike of her sister's boring book sparks her entry into a fantastical realm. Carroll is clearly using the book that Alice rejects to lambaste Victorian education. Throughout *under Ground* and *Wonderland*, Carroll parodies popular didactic poetry that lined Victorian bookshelves, transforming them into pure nonsense. For example, in Alice's recounting of Sir Isaac Watts's "Against Idleness and Mischief" (1715), a didactic poem about an industrious bee becomes a satire about a hungry crocodile. Alice confirms her knowledge of the real poem when she despairs, "I'm sure those are not the right words" (*under Ground* 15). The caterpillar also scolds Alice for her ridiculous recitation of Robert Southey's, "The Old Man's Comforts, and How He Gained Them" (1799).[9] In Carroll's parody, Southey's reverent soul who remembers his God transforms into a fat old chap who stands on his head, somersaults in the air, and then balances an eel on his nose. Alice once clearly mastered this long-forgotten moralizing verse; when the caterpillar chides, "That is not said right," Alice replies, "Not *quite* right, I'm afraid" (*under Ground* 60). Alice's perplexed response to her own burlesquing of didactic strongholds reveals the solidity of her Victorian book knowledge and the readerly expectations she brings to her underground world. The very book that Alice rejects symbolizes her traditional Victorian education. Even if moralizing verses come out wrong in wonderland, Alice knows by heart what was once staple fare in Sunday schools and regularly presented as prize books.

Alice is also well versed in "awful example" stories, common in the Georgian and Victorian periods and written to root out children's inherently sinful natures. When contemplating whether to imbibe the bottle marked "DRINK ME" (a tonic which makes her stretch out like a telescope), Alice recalls reading "several nice little stories about children that got burnt, and eaten up by wild beasts, and other unpleasant things, because they *would* not remember the simple rules their friends had given them" (*under Ground* 7)—like checking to see whether a bottle is labeled "poison" before you drink from it. The terrifying outcomes of disobedience in these stories—for example, being burned and dying—were intended to frighten young children into perfect obedience. For example, Mary Martha Sherwood's *The History of the Fairchild Family* (1818, 1842,

1847), a staple British prize book throughout the nineteenth century, includes the "Sad Story of a Disobedient Child." Not raised in fear of God, Augusta Noble, whose besetting sin is vanity, pauses to look at her reflection in a mirror while walking down the stairs.[10] She catches on fire from the candle she holds to light her way and dies in agony from burns (84–86). This is conceivably one of the "nice little stories" that Alice recalls.

While Alice has such a head full of book facts—making her not unlike Sissy Jupe and the other "pitchers" that Thomas Gradgrind attempts to fill in *Hard Times* (1854)—she seems to have confused them in her underground world. On her dream journey, Alice tries in vain to remember "all the things I used to know" (*under Ground* 14). She knows some French, a typical girls' school accomplishment; in fact, she foolishly recites "où est ma chatte?" (where is my cat?) (20), the very first sentence out of her lesson book, to a mouse, who grows angry at her for talking about his arch rival, the cat. She mixes up multiplication tables and capitals: "four times five is twelve, and four times six is thirteen, . . . London is the capital of France, and Rome is the capital of Yorkshire" (14). Then, she criticizes herself and exclaims, "oh dear, dear! *that's* all wrong, I'm certain!" (14).

Carroll extends his spoof on Victorian education in *Wonderland*, nearly twice the length of *under Ground*. The Mad Hatter parodies Jane Taylor's well-known poem "The Star" (1806) in *Wonderland* (*The Annotated Alice* 98). Carroll includes an extended pun on Victorian education through the Mock Turtle's discourse on what the "Tortoise" "taught us" (*The Annotated Alice* 127). Standard reading, writing, and arithmetic sportively transform into reeling, writhing, and four branches of arithmetic: ambition, distraction, uglification, and derision (129–30). Only after Alice outgrows a house, plays croquet with an ostrich, and spoofs didactic rhymes does she awaken from a dream world that she entered presumably to resist the kind of literature her sister is reading and she has been spoon-fed. Interestingly, *under Ground* and *Wonderland* end with Alice's sister reliving Alice's fantasy and mind traveling herself. Even if Carroll includes Alice's sister's "dream within the dream, as it were" (*under Ground* 90) to immortalize the loving simplicity of childhood, Alice's "curious dream" (89) is potent enough to induce her sister to enter it.

Alice cannot consciously exit from her reverie; still, she leaves the dream state by waking up. In this respect, her fate diverges from that of Gilman's solitary mind traveler. The nameless narrator of "The Yellow Wall-Paper" struggles to read the wallpaper in her bedroom that at first repels her and comes to preoccupy her entirely. Resistance to reading becomes a portal into Alice's imagination, which turns the rigid rules of her

Victorian world topsy-turvy. The very act of deciphering the wallpaper leads Gilman's narrator to journey into an imaginative realm where she, more obviously than Alice, confronts the limitations of her Victorian American world.

Widely interpreted in literary criticism, "The Yellow Wall-Paper" unfolds as a diary written by a woman undergoing a three-month rest cure for postpartum depression. She is suffering from a nervous condition called neurasthenia. Forbidden to write, the nameless narrator gives way to hallucinations, dramatically tears the wallpaper from the walls, creeps on the floor, and arguably succumbs to a type of madness. Not all critics see her as "destroyed," as Elaine R. Hedges concludes in her afterword to "The Yellow Wall-Paper."[11] Opinions of the narrator's fate range along a spectrum marked by extremes: liberation versus entrapment, triumph versus defeat.

While little in the text has escaped the critic's gaze, the original illustrations accompanying the story in its first publication in the January 1892 issue of *New England Magazine* have not received much attention. Different from Dickens's and Twain's collaborations, Gilman makes no mention of Hatfield's illustrations in her diary, autobiography, or letters. Such an omission seems puzzling since Gilman herself was an artist. Several of her stories published around the time of "The Yellow Wall-Paper," such as "The Giant Wistaria" (1891) and "The Lake of Mrs. Johnsmith" (1898), also appear with illustrations.[12]

A staff illustrator for *New England Magazine*, Jo. H. Hatfield was a noted Boston area artist. Akin to his genre and landscape paintings, his magazine illustrations, executed in a realistic style typical of the late nineteenth century, demonstrate his talents as an artist.[13] They also lend insight into the nameless narrator's struggle to "read" the pattern of the wallpaper lining her room, a former nursery that her physician-husband chooses for her rest cure.

Hatfield's first illustration (fig. 32) depicts the narrator as a respectable Victorian woman engaged in writing the story we are presumably reading. She wears a demure, high-necked dress. Her hair sweeps neatly into a bun. She has a contented expression as she sits in a rocking chair by the window and writes. Light shines on her face and the diary she holds in her hands, and her eyes make contact with the text she is writing. In this tranquil image, Hatfield makes visible what the narrator admits in her opening diary entry—writing is "a great relief to my mind" (39)—even if she must hide her diary and write in secret. Hatfield thus captures the narrator in an act that directly confronts the opinions of those who prescribe the rest

Fig. 32. Illustration by Jo. H. Hatfield, "I Am Sitting by the Window in this Atrocious Nursery," for Charlotte Perkins Gilman, "The Yellow Wall-Paper," *New England Magazine*, January 1892. (Courtesy of Schaffer Library, Union College.)

cure: her physician-husband, who "hates to have me write a word";[14] Dr. S. Weir Mitchell, foremost Victorian specialist for neurasthenia, whom John threatens to consult in the fall if the narrator does not improve; and her sister-in-law Jenny, a "perfect—, an enthusiastic—, housekeeper" who "hopes for no better profession" and believes "it is the writing which made me sick!" (43).

As the story progresses, the narrator writes less, as critics often comment. Two weeks pass between her writing of the first two entries (41), and the entries grow shorter, with the exception of the twelfth and final one (46–51). Conceivably, the narrator writes less because she reads more. The second illustration (fig. 33) seems most pertinent to this discussion of active reading as a portal to the imagination. The narrator still looks sane: her dress and hairstyle appear identical to the first illustration although

Fig. 33. Illustration by Jo. H. Hatfield, "She Didn't Know I Was in the Room," for Charlotte Perkins Gilman,"The Yellow Wall-Paper," *New England Magazine*, January 1892. (Courtesy of Schaffer Library, Union College.)

her expression seems tenser, unsettled. Hatfield's second illustration complements Gilman's insight that John and Jennie appear puzzled by the narrator's growing fascination with the wallpaper. John, who calls his wife "little girl" (46) and a "blessed little goose" (42), "scoffs openly at any talk of things not to be felt and seen and put down in figures" (39). The narrator admits that "John is practical in the extreme" (39). In contrast, the narrator, like Carroll's Alice, is imaginative and gives way to "fancies" (41), much to John's chagrin.[15] In a "height of romantic felicity" (39), the narrator even imagines that the ancestral hall must be a "haunted house" (39). She feels something strange about the house and the captivating wallpaper.

The wallpaper is arguably a palimpsest, a parchment written upon, erased, and then written upon again over faded remnants of original writing.[16] Hatfield's second illustration depicts the narrator as a perceptive reader of people and palimpsestual texts. The wallpaper as depicted has a dominant and a muted pattern. The narrator successfully "reads" the expression of her sister-in-law, who cannot discern the muted pattern of the wallpaper. In fact, Hatfield magnifies this point by including a flamboyant design in the portion of wallpaper framing Jennie, seemingly invisible to Jennie's eyes, but plainly visible to the narrator and the reader-viewer.

Gilman reveals that the narrator is a reader, although her references to books are not as developed as Carroll's. The narrator not only calls the ancestral hall a "haunted house" (39) but comments, "It makes me think of English places that you read about" (40). If we look to Gilman's diaries (rather than her autobiography in which Gilman fashions her identity as a reader of nonfiction eager to make a more "human world"), Gilman emerges as an avid reader of British fiction. For example, in her diaries she records that she particularly enjoyed works by Charles Dickens, Eliot, and Carroll.[17] Like Gilman herself, the narrator may have been reading Gothic or Victorian fiction before coming to this ancestral hall that she and John let for the summer. The narrator does not specify what English places she may have encountered through fiction, but we can easily imagine the Tilneys' Gothic abbey of *Northanger Abbey* (1818), filled with clandestine apartments; Edward Fairfax Rochester's grand, mysterious Thornfield Hall of *Jane Eyre* (1847); or Casaubon's Lowick of *Middlemarch* (1872), a somber estate in the old English style.

During the rest cure, John forbids his wife from writing or even reading her own writing. That John becomes more optimistic about the narrator's condition as she gives way to a form of madness leads Wai Chee Dimock to conclude: "the husband is not just a doctor but an emphatically bad one. This means, of course, that he is a bad reader, who, when confronted with a set of symptoms, repeatedly fails to come up with the right interpretation."[18] The narrator, in contrast, is not only a persistent reader but a perceptive one. Her creative response to an untraditional text, the ubiquitous wallpaper, even resembles the way her fictional Victorian sisters—Jane Eyre and Maggie Tulliver—pore over book illustrations to derive meaning from them. Arguably, the narrator chooses wall*paper* for reading material since she is denied other forms of paper. Gilman changes her spelling and referents for wallpaper within and between versions of the story, a point which has captured numerous critics' attention.[19] Several of the variations—wall paper, wall-paper, and, in particular, paper—give emphasis to the second part of what we now consider a compound word and establish the wallpaper as reading material.

Noting the narrator's increasing obsession with the wallpaper in her psychological reading of "The Yellow Wall-Paper," Beate Schöpp-Schilling comments that "The story's heroine, after having been forbidden by her husband to exercise her creative powers in writing, defies him by turning to a different kind of paper, the hideous wallpaper with which he forces her to live" (143). Schöpp-Schilling concludes that the narrator's obsession with wallpaper leads to madness, a state Hatfield depicts in the third and final illustration of the narrator crawling over her husband in a dead faint.[20] Judith Fetterley takes this point further: "Blocked from expressing herself *on* paper, she seeks to express herself *through* paper. Literally, she converts the wall*paper* into her text."[21] Though Fetterley observes that initially the narrator "reads the text as enemy" (257), the narrator becomes fascinated by what Fetterley calls its subtext (and what I call its muted pattern): a woman trapped behind the bars, symbolizing her patriarchal world. In her mind travels, the narrator seemingly sees the trapped woman as a reflection of her position in her patriarchal society. If "in going mad she [the narrator] fulfills his [John's] script and becomes a character in his text" (259), as Fetterley resolves, then Gilman has exposed "how men drive women mad through the control of textuality" (259). Thus, Fetterley shifts her argument away from the narrator's reading as empowerment to make her a "character" in John's prescriptive text. From this vantage point, the end of the story validates John's fiction and the narrator's defeat in madness.

Aligned with the argument of defeat, Gilman's story of a woman who reads in isolation has itself been read as a cautionary tale of reading addiction akin to the exemplars discussed in parts 1 and 2. For example, in "The Reading Habit and 'The Yellow Wallpaper,'" Barbara Hochman advocates, "From a nineteenth-century point of view, the narrator becomes what Nancy Glazener has recently called an 'addictive' reader: one who reads incessantly and who, while doing so, loses her last remaining hold on reality.... To perceive the narrator as a kind of fiction reader is to see that Gilman's story projects a brilliant nightmare version of what many nineteenth-century commentators represented as a common reading practice—and a dangerous one."[22] The narrator confesses that "John has cautioned me not to give way to fancy in the least. He says that with my imaginative power and habit of story making, a nervous weakness like mine is sure to lead to all manner of excited fancies, and that I ought to use my will and good sense to check the tendency" (42). An antifiction critic of the day could easily argue that the narrator's reading practice becomes "dangerous" because she falls prey to her own "imaginative power" and cannot "check the tendency." Hatfield's third image also shows the narrator with a frizzled mane of hair eerily creeping on the floor over her fainted husband.

Whereas didactic exemplars in the trope of addiction (such as those presented in chapter 4) present a clear-cut, nightmarish fate for an addicted reader, the ending of Gilman's landmark tale remains fruitfully ambiguous, sparking a range of interpretations. The narrator temporarily gains control over John as she crawls over him. Gilman does not reveal what will happen to the narrator when John wakes up from his dead faint. Does the narrator lose touch with her reality? Is she "destroyed" by choosing to read the wallpaper? Through her active engagement in reading a nontraditional text and in choosing to identify with a fictional realm, might the narrator come to face her uncomfortable reality as graphically reflected in the wallpaper?

Identification, as Kelley and Sicherman note, was a way that nineteenth-century women readers used fiction for self-fashioning. Kelley and Sicherman, for example, focus on the liberating effect of literature on a nineteenth-century woman reader and perceive stimulation of the imagination as creative and empowering (Kelley 404–5, 414–15; Sicherman, "Sense and Sensibility" 202). Their historical viewpoint foregrounds the narrator's determination and success as she actively reads the elusive pattern of the wallpaper, a reading practice promoted in numerous advice books of the period. Likewise, from the vantage point of contemporary feminist reader-response criticism, we can profitably examine the wallpaper as a portal into the narrator's imagination and consider the empowering effect reading the wallpaper has on the narrator. Over time, the narrator deciphers the meaning of a text that comes to symbolize the gendered reality of her Victorian American world.

The wallpaper that the narrator reads changes in form, odor, and color as the story progresses through twelve diary-like entries. Like a Rorschach test, the wallpaper invites a multiplicity of readings from critics and the narrator herself.[23] The narrator confides about the wallpaper, "it changes as the light changes" (47), and "There are things in that paper that nobody knows but me, or ever will" (46). In the third entry, the narrator perceives "bloated curves and flourishes" that "go waddling up and down" (44); here she reads images of pregnancy in the paper as she undergoes postpartum depression.[24] In the sixth entry, the pattern "slaps you in the face" (47) and so recalls her patriarchal husband, who "scoffs" and "laughs" at his wife (39). Only a few lines later, the flamboyant design of the wallpaper reveals a dominant text of bars.[25] Behind the bars, the muted text seems at first "a strange provoking formless sort of figure" (43), and then "like a woman stooping down, and creeping about behind that [dominant] pattern" (46). Again in the sixth entry, the narrator "reads" the pattern as a woman plainly trapped behind the bars of the paper itself: "now I am quite sure it is a woman" (47). Her earlier metaphoric qualification, "like," gives way to certainty when she discovers a woman shaking the bars in an effort to be free. Identification becomes part of her active reading process: as numerous critics have previously noted, the image of a woman caged by the bars of the wallpaper symbolically parallels the narrator's own desire to escape from the room John chooses for her, a former nursery with barred windows (40), a microcosm of her male-dominated world.

A testimony to the argument of reading for empowerment, the narrator succeeds as a reader by figuring out the palimpsestual pattern of the wallpaper that she claims she, alone, will do: "I am determined that nobody should find it [the pattern] out but myself!" (48). The narrator believes she is getting better not "in spite of my wall paper" (48), as Dimock's "bad reader" concludes, but "*because* of the wall-paper!" (48). In a dramatic moment of linguistic fusion, the narrator and the woman trapped behind the bars of the wallpaper fuse into "we" as the narrator pulls down the paper that she has read skillfully, critically, and sensitively: "I pulled and she shook, I shook and she pulled, and before morning we had peeled off yards of that paper" (51). She frees the trapped woman and arguably herself as she reads the politics of gender (not clearly visible to her before). The narrator's actions undeniably grow more mad as she identifies and seemingly joins with the figure trapped within the paper she reads. Even if her experience of reading the paper is born of an hallucination, the narrator finds a purpose through her reading and gains a stronger voice. For example, the narrator defers to John in the opening entries and alludes to herself as "one" ("But what is one to do?" [39])—a pronoun linguist Otto Jespersen aptly calls "a kind of disguised *I*" (Jespersen 150); as the story continues, she increasingly authors sentences with "I" (for example, "I don't know why I should write this" [45]) and, in the final entry, calls John "him" and "that man" (Gilman, "The Yellow Wall-Paper" 53).[26]

The narrator does not read in moderation, as conservative supporters of women's reading advised, or even wake up by the riverbank in time for tea. As Hedges argues, the narrator as reader "directly confronts the sexual politics of the male-female, husband-wife relationship.... It is a feminist document, dealing with sexual politics at a time when few writers felt free to do so, at least so candidly" (124). What the narrator is reading becomes synonymous with a painful reality. However, her determination as a reader, tearing down the "bars" and "astonishing" (52) John, and her declaration—"you can't put me back!" (53)—can be interpreted as empowerment, liberation, or at least a dubious victory.[27] In fact, to Sandra Gilbert and Susan Gubar, the madwoman's imaginings are her triumph (89–92).

To recall the ideas of Radway, the responses of fictional female mind travelers might, in part, reflect how men and women read differently. Particularly applicable to the narrator's case is what Radway describes as the identificatory process of reading romantic fiction. Associating oneself with fictional characters "allows," as Flint argues, "the woman to feel, imaginatively, at the powerful centre of her own life" (*The Woman Reader* 32). In reading and responding to the wallpaper—identifying with and freeing the trapped woman within it—the narrator finds herself at the powerful center of her own life, at a cost.

The perceived dangers of reading in isolation held force in the nineteenth century. Gilman and Carroll envision women imagining in response or reaction to reading material during a time when physiology and psychology were considered indelibly linked. George Henry Lewes, editor of *The Fortnightly Review*, argues that certain "feminine natures" (where brain and heart are directly linked) made a woman prone to effects of literature.[28] In Victorian Britain and America, hypotheses about women's physiology and psychology permeated nineteenth-century medical journals and publications geared for a wider nonspecialist audience. The many theories regarding the physiological differences between men and women fueled the biological and medical arguments against much of women's reading practices, particularly of romance and sensation fiction. It was commonly believed that women had bigger organs of sensory perception contained in the frontal part of the brain. Women had larger foreheads than men and less room for the faculties of reasoning lodged in the back of the brain. As Alexander Walker conveys in *Woman Physiologically Considered* (1840): "the *sensibility* of woman is excessive; she is strongly affected by many sensations, which in men are so feeble as scarcely to attract attention"; he adds accordingly, "the IMAGINATION, a peculiarly and strongly marked function in woman, is highly susceptible of excitement, and yields easily to every excess."[29]

In *Sex in Education* (1873), Dr. Edward H. Clarke dwells on the results of such excess. He reports how mental strain from overtaxing education results in a host of physical and mental ailments: "our modern methods of education do not give the female organism a fair chance, but that they check development, and invite weakness" (104). He also refers to his colleague Dr. T. W. Fisher's case studies of bright women who become victims of hysteria and depression following a course of rigorous study and positively concludes: "Every physician could, no doubt, furnish many similar ones [cases]" (105). Gilman's nemesis, S. Weir Mitchell, the real-life physician whom Gilman indicts in the story, claims in *Doctor and Patient* (1887) that "the man who does not know sick women does not know women" (10).

To a nineteenth-century audience, Lewes's, Walker's, Clarke's, and Mitchell's concerns were palpably real. A woman's excessive imagination and propensity to hysteria fueled anxiety about if, what, when, where, and to what extent a woman should read. As one Inspector Bryce narrates in Dorothea Beale's *Reports Issued by the Schools' Inquiry Commission on the Education of Girls* (1869), girls "are affected far more than young men are by the books they read. It is, therefore, a matter of the first importance to form their taste, to show them the books that are best worth reading, to give them some notions of the canons whereby literary productions should be tried, and in fine to make it their habit and their pleasure to exercise their minds upon what they read, whether it be a history, a poem, or a novel."[30] As this nineteenth-century educator argues, a young woman must "exercise" her mind to ensure she will not overstimulate her imagination. In fact, as Flint notes, "to study literature was ... conceived of as a means of training the imagination and developing sympathy" (135).

Not all in the nineteenth century, however, believed imagination should be "formed" or "trained." The narrator's discovery of the palimpsestual nature of the wallpaper, a key component in what I believe to be her success as a reader, arguably is linked to her imaginative nature, which remains unfettered and untrained. The *Alice* stories also feature a highly inventive heroine. In dismissing a boring book, Alice slips into a fascinating dream world that mirrors and mocks her Victorian reality, including Victorian education. In depicting women as empowered mind travelers who confront their Victorian reality through their imaginations, Carroll and Gilman, along with Hatfield, challenge a deeply ingrained view held by nineteenth-century antifiction critics who feared the reading habit. *Alice's Adventures under Ground* and "The Yellow Wall-Paper" reveal the power of a female protagonist to deliver herself from boredom or oppression by reading critically and exercising her own imagination.

8

"What Is the Use of a Book?"

Becky Sharp as Revolutionary Reader
in William Makepeace Thackeray's *Vanity Fair* (1848)

At the opening of *Alice's Adventures in Wonderland* (1865), Alice poses a now famous question—"'and what is the use of a book,' thought Alice, 'without pictures or conversations?'" (*The Annotated Alice* 25)[1] Although not partial to books with either pictures or conversations, Thackeray's rebellious Becky Sharp recognizes the "use" of a book even more instinctively than Carroll's Alice. As author-illustrator of *Vanity Fair* (1848), Thackeray aptly casts Becky as a Napoleon figure whose discernment and ultimate success as a reader affect how we perceive her character and the arguments of reading for education and empowerment. In the pictorial capital to chapter 64 (fig. 34), Becky even looks the part of the Little Corporal, wearing Napoleon's distinctive hat and uniform over her petticoats. Through Thackeray's illustrations, Becky emerges as a revolutionary who commands not lands and peoples, as Napoleon did, but a number of forms of textuality.[2]

Nineteenth-century novelists, illustrators, and author-illustrators often used books to comment upon character or to advance the plot. Cruikshank's abundant illustrations exemplify this point. Cruikshank includes the most commonly read book in the Victorian period, the Bible, in the first three plates of his Temperance series *The Bottle* (1847) to pronounce the moral decline of a once prosperous middle-class household. The family immediately falls prey to the evils of alcohol; in the third plate of this eight-plate series, creditors seize the once prominently displayed family Bible to pay for debts incurred by drinking.

A book forms the centerpiece of Angus B. Reach's novel *Clement Lorimer; Or, The Book with the Iron Clasps* (1849), set in Antwerp in April,

A VAGABOND CHAPTER

WE must pass over a part of Mrs. Rebecca Crawley's biography with that lightness and delicacy which the world demands—the moral world, that has, perhaps, no particular objection to vice, but an insuperable repugnance to hearing vice called by its proper name. There are things we do and know perfectly well in Vanity Fair, though we never speak of them: as the Ahrimanians worship the devil, but don't mention him:

Fig. 34. Illustration by William Makepeace Thackeray, pictorial capital for chapter 64, for William Makepeace Thackeray, *Vanity Fair: A Novel without a Hero*, 1848.

1610, and illustrated by Cruikshank. A theatrical plate, "The Book with the Iron Clasps" displays an open trunk that houses in its center compartment a thick iron-clasped book, which bears two words on the back cover, "La Vendetta." In the opening chapter which Cruikshank memorably illustrates, a dying Raphael Benosa instructs his son Michael to revenge him by destroying the family of Stephen Vanderstein and recording each successive act of vengeance in this very book to which he points dramatically in the frontispiece.[3]

In *Oliver Twist* (1838), Dickens and Cruikshank use the book as a plot device, weaving together the lives of lower- and middle-class characters. In "Oliver Amazed at the Dodger's Mode of 'Going to Work,'" Oliver encounters Mr. Brownlow at a bookstall where Mr. Brownlow accuses Oliver of a crime he never commits. Considered the Rembrandt of book illustration, Cruikshank skillfully uses light and shadow to create suspense: only the viewer sees in shadows the bookstall keeper who, in the following chapter, arrives in court just in time to proclaim Oliver's innocence. Living with Mr. Brownlow in Pentonville, Oliver is abducted by Sikes and Nancy when returning books to that very same bookstall.

In these examples, a book condemns a middle-class family's fall into disgrace, dictates the actions of the Benosa clan, and brings Oliver to his first middle-class home, only to rend him from it. None of the characters command a book or wield its power. This is also the norm in fictional and illustrative examples of women readers transgressing gender boundaries in parts 2 and 3, including depictions of the isolated reader and the mind traveler. In *Wuthering Heights*, Catherine Earnshaw secretively writes in the periphery of her testament, inscribing her marginal position in her patriarchal society. Young Jane experiences a stolen moment of reading pleasure in a window seat in *Jane Eyre*. Mary Snow of *Orley Farm* reads in secret by candlelight for fear of detection. The call of duty cuts short Jo March's literary reverie in *Little Women* while Gilman's narrator of "The Yellow Wall-Paper" finds a degree of freedom at a price. Though ultimately successful as a reader, Catherine Linton requires the cooperation of her cousin Hareton—and his access to books—to initiate him as a reader and improve her own life. Of his British and American contemporaries, Thackeray offers the most striking alternative interpretation of an empowered, intelligent woman reader. Commanding texts from her first depiction, Becky Sharp stands apart from her fictional Victorian British and American sisters.

Vanity Fair brought Thackeray distinction as a major novelist, but it also enabled him to fulfill his original ambition: to become a book illustrator. Different from authors collaborating with outside artists, Victorian author-illustrators, including Lewis Carroll, Dante Gabriel Rossetti, George Du Maurier, Beatrix Potter, and Thackeray, tell a story through and with pictures, using two art forms to present one creative vision. Between 1833 and 1837, Thackeray studied at the École des Beaux Arts, various Parisian ateliers, and London studios. Although Cruikshank claimed him as his pupil, often noted is Charles Dickens's rejection of Thackeray as illustrator for *The Posthumous Papers of the Pickwick Club* (1837).[4] Critics today and Thackeray's contemporaries have criticized and praised his caricature-style illustrations for *Vanity Fair*; Charlotte Brontë even calls him "a wizard of a draughtsman."[5] More important than the question of technical merit is how Thackeray's illustrations advance the characterization and plot of *Vanity Fair*. The images consistently show a cunning, clever Becky Sharp handling texts in active ways.[6]

Perhaps uncomfortable with his plan to reveal a pretentious Victorian society through *Vanity Fair*, Thackeray, a self-conscious narrator, dons a harlequin suit in several of his illustrations, casting himself in a comical, humble role.[7] In his "Before the Curtain" preface, he calls himself the "Manager of the Performance" (1–2), who will bring forth his puppets to entertain in "VANITY FAIR; not a moral place certainly; nor a merry one, though very noisy" (1). On the cover for the monthly installments, Thackeray draws himself as a jester, mounted aloft a barrel. The jester presides over his characters, including Becky Sharp, who manipulates a small harlequin puppet, presumably an extension of Thackeray himself. Moreover, by intertwining his characters with history, Thackeray de-emphasizes their significance in their own fictive drama and attempts, through them, to inspire a remodeling of a more moral society.[8]

Becky appropriates the book in Thackeray's novel that is itself a "looking-glass," giving back to "every man," including the narrator, a cracked reflection of his own face, as Thackeray depicts the jester/narrator in his title page illustration (15). The cracks accentuate the many imperfections of the novel. "Just as the society *Vanity Fair* depicts is a charade, so is the novel," notes Brantlinger in *The Reading Lesson;* "in a society in which both written and spoken language are ordinarily shallow, hypocritical, or deceitful, the novel written from within that society, whether it provides a truthful representation or not, will perforce also be shallow, hypocritical, and so on" (128).[9] A highly imperfect character whose own "cracks" seem readily apparent, Becky ends up with her own stall in the shallow, hypocritical world of Vanity Fair because she rejects society's construction of domestic femininity and promotes her own self-interest. Although Kate Flint concludes her essay titled "Women, Men and Reading in *Vanity Fair*" (1996) by advancing that "to read well, for Thackeray, was to read as a man" (262), Thackeray's most successful reader is a woman who (despite her penchant for French novels) reads like a man. An active reader, Becky adopts a masculine style of reading to promote her own self-interest. While Brantlinger argues that "Becky's main reading interest has to do with the bottom line, the text of money" (*The Reading Lesson* 129), Thackeray visually piques our interest in Becky's savvy handling of texts of romance and adultery, as well as money. In fact, from her very first depiction titled "Rebecca's Farewell," Becky emerges as a revolutionary reader who knows how to help herself.

Thackeray repeatedly associates Becky Sharp with a range of forms of literacy: dictionaries, letters, French novels, and bank notes. Thackeray fills his novel with references to telling plays and novels (such as *The Rape of the Lock*); IOUs and bills; letters written pseudonymously (for example, Becky writes Rawdon under the pseudonym of Eliza Styles); letters requesting money; billets-doux, including adulterous ones; eviction notices; and wills. Thackeray questions the validity of written documents in making letters ineffectual, leaving bills and IOUs unpaid, and opening wills up to suspicion.[10] I place Becky in the center of this flurry of textuality, both real and counterfeit. Moreover, Becky's lack of sentimentality as a reader underscores another of her "male" virtues and contrasts with the nature of her maudlin novel-reading counterpart, Amelia Sedley, who lovingly buys her son Georgy classic Victorian childhood books: Thomas Day's *Sandford and Merton* (3 vols. 1783–89) and Maria Edgeworth's *The Parent's Assistant* (1796). In fact, Becky shocks dear Amelia at the opening of the novel by purposefully discarding a dictionary, a parting gift from Miss Pinkertons' Academy.

In "Rebecca's Farewell," the first full-page engraving at the close of chapter 1, Thackeray captures Becky "flinging" Johnson's *Dictionary* through her carriage window as she departs Chiswick Mall (fig. 35). The book that Becky jettisons is intended as a keepsake. Miss Barbara Pinkerton presents each of her dear graduates a copy of "Johnson's Dixonary," as she pompously pronounces it (Dr. Johnson once paid a visit to Miss Pinkerton, and so the fame of her establishment grew). She only intends for Amelia to receive the *Dictionary* since Becky is not a paying pupil. When the more sentimental sister, Miss Jemima Pinkerton, retrieves two copies of the dictionary, the elder Pinkerton chastises her: "'MISS JEMIMA!' exclaimed Miss Pinkerton, in the largest capitals. 'Are you in your senses? Replace the Dixonary in the closet, and never venture to take such a liberty in future'" (6). Jemima protests, "poor Becky will be miserable if she don't get one" (6). Jemima defies her imperious older sister and slips Becky a copy of the dictionary, along with some sandwiches for her journey. Despite her good intention, the sentimental Jemima clumsily discloses Miss Barbara Pinkerton's dislike for Becky in her farewell address: "and Becky, Becky Sharp, here's a book for you that my sister—that is, I—Johnson's Dixonary, you know; you mustn't leave us without that. Good-bye. Drive on, coachman. God bless you!" (10).

To recall the words of Carroll's Alice, Becky Sharp finds a "use" for this book. "But, lo!" Thackeray tells us, "and just as the coach drove off, Miss Sharp put her pale face out of the window, and actually flung the book back into the garden" (10). Thackeray makes Becky's features and the angle of her book-flinging arm look as sharp as her name and temper. The discarded dictionary appears in midair, flying toward Miss Jemima, its decorated pages fluttering wantonly in the wind. Using caricature technique, Thackeray depicts an astonished Jemima with raised arms and open mouth. Jemima's pose and expression recall those of an astonished Oliver when he discovers his new friends are really pickpockets in "Oliver Amazed at the Dodger's Mode of 'Going to Work.'" Thackeray also exaggerates the de-

Fig. 35. Illustration by William Makepeace Thackeray, "Rebecca's Farewell," for William Makepeace Thackeray, *Vanity Fair: A Novel without a Hero*, 1848.

meanor of another Pinkerton pupil, little Laura Martin, who melodramatically covers her face to hide her sadness at sweet Amelia's departure. Still, our gaze rests firmly upon Becky and the object of her wrath.

Similar to the verbs "to cast" and "to throw" (when used with the adverbs "away" and "aside"), "fling" conveys the act of discarding an object. Thackeray's choice of the verb "fling" grants Becky more power than if she were simply to "cast" or even "throw" the book out of the window. Though used "as a variant" of throw and cast in both idiomatic expressions and phrases, "fling," according to the *OED*, is "more emphatic and expressive of greater violence."[11] In connoting intensity and forcefulness, as well as quickness and impulsiveness, the verb "fling" grants force to the illustration and anticipates Jemima's dramatic reaction: she nearly faints, or so Thackeray tells us, recovering herself to conclude of Becky, "'Well, I never,' —said she—'what an audacious—' Emotion prevented her from completing either sentence" (10–13).

It is interesting to note that Thackeray uses this same action verb in chapter 18 in describing the movements of Napoleon Bonaparte: "Napoleon is flinging his last stake, and poor little Emmy Sedley's happiness forms, somehow, part of it" (212). As in Becky's "flinging" of a Johnson's *Dictionary*, Napoleon's actual escape from Elba and resurgence in France was quick, calculated, and forceful. In *Vanity Fair*, Napoleon lands in Cannes, and Thackeray's "surprised story," as he calls it, "now finds itself for a moment among very famous events and personages and hanging on to the skirts of history" (211). Thackeray continues, "So imprisoned and tortured was this gentle little heart [Amelia], when in the month of March, Anno Domini 1815, Napoleon landed at Cannes, and Louis XVIII fled, and all Europe was in alarm, and the funds fell, and old John Sedley was ruined" (214). In "flinging his last stake," Napoleon upsets the business ventures of numerous merchants, including Amelia Sedley's father, who goes bankrupt because he does not anticipate the Hundred Days of Napoleon's return and brief but triumphant glory. In using the same verb to describe the actions of Napoleon Bonaparte and Becky Sharp, and later casting Becky as a Napoleon in petticoats (chapter 64), Thackeray creates an implicit association between the powers of the "Corsican upstart" (211) and his own British upstart, so proud of her French ancestry.

Becky's flinging of the dictionary also recalls the dramatic scene in chapter 1 of *Jane Eyre* when John Reed discovers Jane reading Bewick's *History of British Birds* in the window seat at Gateshead. Using the passive voice with the verb "to fling," Brontë gives more attention to the object than the actor, as she notes: "the volume was flung, it hit me [Jane], and I fell" (8). John Reed throws the Bewick volume at his orphan cousin, and Jane, the victim of John's fury, receives further punishment—she is locked in the Red Room. In *Vanity Fair*, the Pinkertons do not even temporarily come out victorious. Becky knowingly rejects a reluctantly given gift that would have ticketed her a charity student. She rides off in a carriage, and Miss Barbara Pinkerton's prized "Dixonary" lands on the ground.

Thackeray dwells on the outcome of this incident at the opening of the second chapter: "When Miss Sharp had performed the heroical act mentioned in the last chapter, and had seen the Dixonary flying over the pavement of the little garden, fall at length at the feet of the astonished Miss Jemima, the young lady's countenance, which had before worn an almost livid look of hatred, assumed a smile that perhaps was scarcely more agreeable, and she sank back in the carriage in an easy frame of mind, saying, 'So much for the Dixonary; and, thank God, I'm out of Chiswick'" (13). From a Saussurean perspective, the signifier—the word dictionary/"Dixonary"—has become separated from the signified—the dictionary itself. The book Becky rejects stands symbolically for the pretensions of a girls' finishing school and the imperious Miss Barbara Pinkerton who presides over it. Becky has acquired enough education to know that instruction at a finishing school is not an end in itself. She sees no point in possessing a book that will not help her on her chosen path. She sneers in satisfaction in defying a snooty establishment that suffocated and exploited her skill in French as an articled pupil-cum-teacher. She is thumbing her nose, flaunting her disdain, at the injustices she has received at this snobby girls' school where she could neither forget nor rise above her class origins—her father, who gave drawing lessons at the school, was a drunkard; her French mother was an opera-girl (although Becky was known to inflate the importance and rank of her French ancestors). Hurling the book at Miss Jemima, Becky, presently on route to being a governess, is rebelling against a literate society that has not helped her advance on the social scale—at least not yet.[12] In calling this a "heroical act," Thackeray recognizes that to Becky, the flinging of the dictionary launches her quest for social advancement: "At all events, if Rebecca was not beginning the world, she was beginning it over again" (21).

Self-interest next leads Becky to attempt to catch Amelia Sedley's brother, who might save her from the fate of becoming a governess. At the end of chapter 2, Becky ponders, "If Mr. Joseph Sedley is rich and unmarried, why should I not marry him?" (23). Two chapters later, in the pictorial capital for chapter 4, Thackeray humorously draws Becky attempting to hook Jos, who anthropomorphically assumes the shape of a fat fish. The piscatorial capital design makes light of Becky's pursuit of Jos, shown here ogling but not taking the bait. That same chapter contains a full-page engraving titled "Mr. Joseph Entangled," showing Becky winding Jos's pudgy hands in a web of her own making. In the narrative as well, Thackeray presents Becky as a husband hunter; in fact, the pictorial capital for chapter 4 gives concrete form to a conversation between Mr. and Mrs. Sedley in which the former says: "Here is Emmy's little friend making love to him as hard as she can; that's quite clear; and if she does not catch him some other will. That man is destined to be a prey to woman, . . . But, mark my words, the first woman who fishes for him, hooks him" (36). Presumably the first woman to "fish" for Jos Sedley in earnest, Becky feels keenly the loss of

Fig. 36. Illustration by William Makepeace Thackeray, "It Was the Death-Warrant," for William Makepeace Thackeray, *Vanity Fair: A Novel without a Hero*, 1848.

her first beau (George Osborne dissuades Jos since he does not want a poor governess for a sister-in-law). Becky is candid about this topic and admits to George Osborne: "Well, 'entre nous,' I didn't break my heart about him [Jos]; yet if he had asked me to do what you mean by your looks (and very expressive and kind they are, too), I wouldn't have said no. . . . for could a poor penniless girl do better? Now you know the whole secret. *I'm* frank and open" (173–74).

In the illustration accompanying Jos's epistolary rejection (fig. 36), we witness Becky's painful awareness of the power of words. Becky fears to look upon the "death-warrant" (74), which Jos sends to his sister, announcing his departure for several months. Becky dramatically weeps by Amelia's side: "Amelia did not dare to look at Rebecca's pale face and burning eyes" (74). The look on Rebecca's face reveals the contents of Jos's letter before Amelia "dropped" it in Becky's lap, and Thackeray concludes, "All was over" (74).[13] Subsequent representations of Becky as a siren and the murderess Clytemnestra[14] suggest that "All was [not] over" and that

Jos does fall "prey to woman" as Mr. Sedley predicts, taking the very bait he ogles in the pictorial capital to chapter 4.

Letters also form part of Becky's many schemes for personal advancement. Sometimes under the guise of other names, Becky cleverly writes and receives numerous letters and saves her most valuable papers, letters, memoranda, and bank notes in a little desk that Amelia gave her in their early days of friendship in Russell Square. Moreover, Thackeray tells us, "she kept [it] in a secret place" (676). Becky's actions of locking the desk and hiding it convey her keen awareness of the potency of words inscribed on love letters, death notices, and bank notes.

Much as Thackeray demonstrates in the "death-warrant" illustration, Becky averts forms of textuality that thwart her attempt to rise in the world. As governess to the Crawley family, Becky ignores the education of her young charges, whom she calls "thin insignificant little chits" (91). In the full-page engraving titled "Miss Sharp in Her Schoolroom" (fig. 37), Thackeray features Becky seated in a big chair in front of a table with a writing desk upon it. In the foreground, her pupils squabble over an open book; in fact, the younger, more boisterous Miss Violet yanks at a page. Whereas Hablot Knight Browne depicts Dickens's quintessential angel in the house with an open book on her lap to guide her children in "A Stranger Calls to See Me" (fig. 9), Thackeray does the opposite. Thackeray's Becky, who boasts "I'm no angel" (15), takes no interest in the education of her young charges. To make this point palpably apparent, Thackeray turns Becky's head away from her bickering pupils; in a theatrical aside, she sneers for the benefit of the reader-viewer.

With characteristic sarcasm, Thackeray tells us that Becky "did not pester their young brains with too much learning, but, on the contrary, let them have their own way in regard to educating themselves: for what instruction is more effectual than self-instruction?" (106). Like Henry James, Thackeray does not dwell on particular titles that Becky reads, although we know she understands intimately Alexander Pope's *The Rape of the Lock* (1712), rejects Samuel Johnson's *Dictionary* (1755), and reads Tobias Smollett's *The Expedition of Humphrey Clinker* (1771). Becky discerns that her elder charge, Miss Rose, shares her fondness for reading French and English books. Becky pulls from the much neglected bookshelves of Queen's Crawley eighteenth-century "light literature" (106) by Henry Fielding, Smollett, and Voltaire. Becky's selections are unsuitable reading for young girls—some are even dangerous according to contemporary advice book writers—but they interest her. Becky's education serves her well: she instructs Miss Rose for her own reading pleasure. In

Fig. 37. Illustration by William Makepeace Thackeray, "Miss Sharp in Her Schoolroom," for William Makepeace Thackeray, *Vanity Fair: A Novel without a Hero*, 1848.

fact, the artful Becky tells the religious, righteous Sir Pitt Crawley, her charges' half brother, that she and Miss Rose are reading Smollett. She allows Sir Pitt Crawley to infer that they are reading *Complete History of England* (1758), not Smollett's comic epistolary novel, *The Expedition of Humphrey Clinker*: "'It is history you are reading?' 'Yes,' said Miss Rose; without, however, adding that it was the history of Mr. Humphrey Clinker" (106). Pitt Crawley also discovers Rose reading an unnamed book of

French plays, but withdraws his objection when Becky insists it is to acquire conversational idioms and craftily compliments Pitt's proficiency in French.

A cunning character, Becky is bright and book worldly. Throughout the novel, she writes clever letters, conveying her intellect. She announces her elopement to Rawdon through a letter to Miss Briggs, the wealthy Miss Crawley's servant and confidante. Thackeray privileges Becky's note through his full-page engraving called "The Note on the Pincushion." Betty, the upstairs maid, finds this very note in the governess's empty bedchamber. A grinning Betty astutely observes that "The little white dimity bed was as smooth and trim as on the day previous, when Betty's own hands had helped to make it" (195). Piquing our curiosity further, Thackeray directs our attention to Becky's note: "on the table before the window—on the pincushion—the great fat pincushion lined with pink inside, and twilled like a lady's nightcap—lay a letter. It had been reposing there probably all night" (195). Despite his qualification, Thackeray's prominent placement of the letter, with its wax seal facing upwards, makes palpable Becky's absence from her bedchamber and piques our interest in her letter.

Thackeray employs the rhetoric of reading as consumption when he tells us Briggs "devoured the contents" (195) of Becky's letter, which Thackeray allows us to read for ourselves. Briggs runs to Miss Crawley, who immediately snubs her beloved nephew Rawdon and her heretofore favored Rebecca, calling out "Rawdon married—Rebecca—governess—nobod'" (198). An undefeated Becky assures Rawdon, "'I'll make your fortune,' she said; and Delilah patted Samson's cheek" (199).[15] Samson derives his power from his hair, and Delilah from her beauty. Becky—whose attractive eyes "shot dead" (16) the young Reverend Mr. Crisp of Chiswick, Jos Sedley, Sir Pitt Crawley the elder and younger, Rawdon Crawley, George Osborne, and Lord Steyne, among others—wields her power through her charm and her pen. In fact, Becky composes all of Rawdon's letters to his aunt, a point Miss Crawley (on whose fortunes Becky's hopes are pinned) all too quickly discerns. Nonetheless, Becky, whom Thackeray casts as Delilah and Napoleon, as well as Clytemnestra, perseveres and triumphs as a perceptive reader. She recognizes a text as a means of empowerment.

Midway through the novel, we encounter a jubilant Becky in an epistolary scene (fig. 38) that contrasts sharply with the "death-warrant" illustration in Russell Square. Thackeray draws the episode when Becky "took

Fig. 38. Illustration by William Makepeace Thackeray, "She Took Up the Black-Edged Missive," for William Makepeace Thackeray, *Vanity Fair: A Novel without a Hero*, 1848.

up the black-edged missive, and having read it, she jumped from the chair, crying 'Hurray!' and waving the note round her head" (517). A befuddled and despondent Rawdon carries this missive to her, "as he did all difficulties, to Becky" (517). In true Napoleonic fashion, Becky takes supreme command. Here pictured as a conquering hero, Becky holds high above her head a real death warrant announcing the demise of Rawdon's father, Sir Pitt the elder.

Akin to representations of the isolated woman reader, we focus in both epistolary scenes on what Becky reads or refrains from reading as well as the way she instinctively responds to textual material. In the Russell Square illustration, a defeated Becky averts a text that she perceives as a roadblock to self-advancement (fig. 36). In the second example, an empowered Becky waves a letter that she considers a gateway to power and wealth (fig. 38). Images of Becky weeping or triumphantly wielding a text at a sleepy, puzzled Rawdon (and the reader) convey that Becky knows all too well the power of words. Although Rawdon has already squandered the fortune he receives when he comes of age, Becky views the death notice as an opportunity to gain materially from Rawdon's brother, who inherits the family fortune, and thus realize her personal ambition via marriage: "your brother shall give you a seat in Parliament, you stupid old creature. I mean that Lord Steyne shall have your vote and his, my dear, old, silly man; and that you shall be an Irish Secretary, or a West Indian Governor: or a Treasurer, or a Consul, or some such thing" (518).

Rawdon does eventually become governor of Coventry Island (a promotion that might aptly be called his personal "death-warrant"), but at what cost to Becky? Well noted for being an ambiguous novelist, Thackeray refuses to convict Becky of adultery and murder. She declares "I am innocent . . . before God, I am innocent" (675) when Rawdon unexpectedly returns from the debtor's prison (into which he has seemingly been tricked for the night) and discovers Becky entertaining Lord Steyne in his and Becky's home on Curzon Street. Earlier that day, Becky sends a note to her "MON PAUVRE CHER PETIT," feigning "such a headache and such a heartache!" (672), telling Rawdon she cannot free him till the following morning. But in this instance, words fail Becky. Rawdon writes to his brother and sister-in-law, and Lady Jane Crawley secures his release. Aroused by jealousy, the good-natured Rawdon goes to Becky's "secret place" (676) and forces Becky to open her private desk. In fact, Rawdon's ransacking of Becky's treasure trove of letters and bank notes distracts the reader from the previous romantic scene, which may be Thackeray's intention.

The interlude between Becky and Lord Steyne is worth lingering over. Becky has sent the servants away. A table is set for a romantic dinner. Steyne holds her hand in his, and she dazzles in diamonds: "The wretched woman was in a brilliant full toilette, her arms and all her fingers sparkling with bracelets and rings; and the brilliants on her breast which Steyne had given her" (675). These are the very brilliants that Becky wears when she is presented at Court and Lord Steyne quotes *The Rape of the Lock* to her.

Thackeray resists compromising a character whom he at times refers to as "heroine" in his "Novel without a Hero."[16] Our notoriously ambiguous narrator fills *Vanity Fair* with disclaimers of not knowing all about his central characters, a point critics including Kate Flint, Juliet McMaster, and

Martin Meisel explore in greater detail.[17] In regard to Becky's possible adultery, Thackeray refrains from answering definitively the incriminating questions that he raises: "What *had* happened? Was she guilty or not? She said not; but who could tell what was truth which came from those lips; or if that corrupt heart was in this case pure?" (677). Thackeray also shies away from the Battle of Waterloo ("Our place is with the non-combatants" [361]) as well as Becky's presentation at Court. He relies on second-hand information, rumor, supposition, and newspaper reports. Becky tells Rawdon and Sir Pitt Crawley (who gave her a few of the brilliants) that she hires the jewels from Polonious in Coventry Street, and presumably they believe her. However, Lord Steyne, who arranges for her presentation at Court, "knew whence the jewels came, and who paid for them" (604). Thackeray also tells us, "As he [Steyne] bowed over her [Becky] he smiled, and quoted the hackneyed and beautiful lines, from the *Rape of the Lock*, about Belinda's diamonds, 'which Jews might kiss and infidels adore'" (604). Here Thackeray is closely paraphrasing Pope's lines that read: "On her white Breast a sparkling *Cross* she wore,/Which *Jews* might kiss and Infidels adore" (Canto 2, lines 7–8). Becky knows her Pope and fittingly replies, "'But I hope your lordship is orthodox,' . . . with a toss of her head" (604).[18]

In this literary allusion, Becky, who has "brains" (533) by her own admission, is "flinging" at Lord Steyne her perceptive reading of Pope's mock-epic as well as her sandy locks. The consummate actress, Becky here plays not Delilah or Napoleon, but Pope's Belinda, revealing her keen awareness of the lecherous nobleman's desire to kiss the jewels he has bestowed upon her white breast, eliciting the attention of the high society of Vanity Fair as well as Rawdon. In fact, when Rawdon finds Becky alone with Steyne, "He tore the diamond ornament" that Steyne has given her "out of her breast" (676). Whether or not Becky—the shrewd "adventuress" (604), as Thackeray calls her in this scene—is innocent of adultery, the allusion to *The Rape of the Lock* intensifies male sexual desire. Had Thackeray illustrated Becky playing the part of Belinda to the notoriously lascivious Steyne, he might have compounded the weight of his potentially damning illustrations of Becky as a siren and the murderess Clytemnestra, a role she plays "killingly" (646) in a theatrical at Steyne's Gaunt House.[19]

Thackeray offers a network of visual and verbal allusions to insinuate that the sandy-haired Becky, enormously attractive to men, is a siren and in no way "orthodox" herself. From the opening of the novel, Thackeray credits Becky with musical arts. She nearly brings Jos to tears and matrimony by singing a *"byoo-ootiful* song" to him (44). She entices and entraps Rawdon Crawley by playing the piano and singing to him (even the equally mercenary Mrs. Bute Crawley cannot stop Becky's scheme to hook Rawdon through song). Following Becky's marriage to Rawdon, she continues to practice the arts of a siren by singing to audiences from whom she can profit: her brother-in-law, Sir Pitt Crawley; wealthy Lord Steyne, who showers Becky with money and jewels. It is not for her husband's or son's affection that this siren sings. She boxes little Rawdon's ears when he listens to her singing an enchanting tune to "that bald-headed man with the large teeth" (561) and forbids him to come near her when she entertains Lord Steyne. Twice Thackeray pictures Becky as a siren: first, in the pictorial capital to chapter 44 as an enchanting siren, strumming a lute (sharp rocks are visible below the water line); second, in the pictorial capital to chapter 63 as a diabolical siren, surrounded by rocks and skulls.[20] Readers cannot help but wonder if Becky gives sexual favors to Lord Steyne in return for the jewels and bank notes he bestows upon his Belinda.[21]

Jos Sedley and Lord Steyne frequently supply Becky with bank notes, a form of textuality that enables her to rise in society. Honest William Dobbin even suspects Becky of murdering Jos for profit: "It was found that all his [Jos's] property had been muddled away in speculations" (874). Jos leaves his only remaining asset, a two-thousand pound insurance policy on his life, to Becky and Amelia equally. Dobbin returns Amelia's share of the tainted legacy that the insurance company at first refuses to pay (of course, the company would profit in doing so). The solicitor of the insurance company calls this the "blackest case that ever had come before him" (877).[22] Nonetheless, Becky holds onto her share of the policy and "triumphed finally. The money was paid, and her character established" (877).

Earlier in the novel, Thackeray draws a smiling, cunning Becky handing a cashier a note bearing Lord Steyne's signature following her presentation at Court. This image titled "Becky in Lombard Street" (fig. 39) shows an attractive and confident Becky holding out a request for payment that we learn is sizeable. Dismissing her thought to pay back those she owes (such as, Briggs and Raggles), she takes one hundred and fifty pounds in small notes and the remainder in one grand sum. We later learn that Becky visits "the before-mentioned desk, which Amelia Sedley had given her years and years ago, and which contained a number of useful and valuable little things: in which private museum she placed the one note which

Fig. 39. Illustration by William Makepeace Thackeray, "Becky in Lombard Street," for William Makepeace Thackeray, *Vanity Fair: A Novel without a Hero*, 1848.

Messrs. Jones and Robinson's cashier had given her" (611). This is the very "private museum" that Rawdon unlocks when he discovers Becky in a compromising position with Lord Steyne: "Rawdon flung open boxes and wardrobes, throwing the multifarious trumpery of their contents here and there, and at last he found the desk. The woman was forced to open it. It contained papers, love-letters many years old—all sorts of small trinkets and woman's memoranda. And it contained a pocket-book with banknotes. Some of these were dated ten years back, too, and one was quite a fresh one—a note for a thousand pounds which Lord Steyne had given her" (676).

Thackeray does not reserve the verb "to fling" solely for Becky's actions. However, the power of this action verb, closely associated with Becky, seems situational in Rawdon's case since he is rarely angry or jealous. Momentarily in command, Rawdon "flings" open Becky's possessions and vows to dispense of her hoard to pay off their debts. If "Becky's main reading interest has to do with the bottom line, the text of money" (Brantlinger, *The Reading Lesson* 128), this scene signals a setback for Becky, though not her defeat. I would argue, rather, that Becky exhibits the most savvy as a reader in saving not monetary texts, but one incriminating love letter. It proves to be the most priceless of her "useful and valuable little things" (611).

As both a siren figure and a military strategist in petticoats, Becky implicitly understands the significance of an adulterous billet-doux. The letter Amelia's husband George Osborne plants in Becky's bouquet at the Duke of Richmond's ball (just before his death in the Battle of Waterloo) serves as a major plot device in *Vanity Fair*. In chapter 29 titled "Brussels," Thackeray does not illustrate the scene but tells us: "George went away then with the bouquet; but when he gave it to the owner, there lay a note, coiled like a snake among the flowers. Rebecca's eye caught it at once" (357–58). Becky resists the serpent George, who begs her to run away with him. She wisely keeps in her locked writing desk George's note, "coiled like a snake," along with a picture of Jos Sedley riding an elephant (purchased at the auction of the Sedley home), and the bank notes from Lord Steyne. Becky's possessions in her "private museum" all serve a purpose. The picture of Jos riding an elephant completes her conquest of her first fat beau when she meets him late in the novel, by chance, in the ducal town of Pumpernickel. Thackeray concludes, "She had cast such a strong anchor in Jos now as would require a strong storm to shake. That incident of the picture had finished him" (864). The bank notes that Becky stockpiles lay a nest egg that Rawdon discovers. Instead, the adulterous love note ultimately enables Becky to achieve the financially secure future she imagines for herself: it confirms Osborne's unworthiness and fully awakens Amelia from her sick idolization of her dead husband, leaving Jos prey to Becky.

Ever a discerning and astute reader, Becky ultimately finds a "use" for George's love note in the final chapter: "she opened it and flung it into Emmy's lap" (866), much as she "flung" the Johnson's *Dictionary* out the carriage window in the opening chapter. The action verb "flung" in both instances advances Becky's portrayal as a revolutionary reader, who well calculates the best moment to hurl a text to empower her life. Not Napoleon here, but Becky is now "flinging [her] last stake"; once again, "poor little Emmy Sedley's happiness forms, somehow, part of it" (212).

Amelia at first shouts "It's false! It's false!" when Becky tries to warn Emmy of George's true adulterous nature (866). Thackeray pictures this note, fully "uncoiled." It forms a telling detail in "The Letter before Waterloo" (fig. 40), a full-page engraving in the last chapter titled "Which Contains Births, Marriages, and Deaths." Featured in the hand of a weeping Amelia, with a triumphant Becky by her side, the love letter offers undeniable proof of George's baseness. Becky—in what could be construed as an uncharacteristically kind action—may be "flinging" this letter to free her weak counterpart from her self-imposed cage of devotion to an undeserving idol. Becky recognizes too well that Amelia needs a man like Dobbin who can protect her. Her words to Amelia are particularly sharp: "You are no more fit to live in the world than a baby in arms. You must marry, or you and your precious boy will go to ruin. You must have a husband, you fool; and one of the best gentlemen I ever saw has offered you a hundred times, and you have rejected him, you silly, heartless, ungrateful little creature!" (866). Becky continues caustically about George: "He never cared for you. He used to sneer about you to me, time after time; and made love to me the week after he married you. . . . He wrote that to me—wanted me to run away with him—gave it me under your nose, the day before he was shot—and served him right!" (866). The depiction of tearful Amelia (covering her face to hide her crying) alongside a composed though cynical Becky reverses their positions in the "death-warrant" scene (fig. 36) and speaks to the force of words whose truth even Amelia cannot deny. Becky's savvy in saving this adulterous letter underscores her shrewd understanding that words, when written down, have the power to move an individual to tears, much as she herself responded to Jos's "death-warrant" so many years ago in Russell Square.[23]

Following Becky's presentation of convincing evidence of George's adultery, Thackeray ponders whether for Amelia "the barrier was removed which modesty had placed between her and a new, a real affection" (869) for the devoted Dobbin. "'There is nothing to forbid me now,' she thought. 'I may love him [Dobbin] with all my heart now,'" Amelia confesses (869). But one short paragraph later, Thackeray complicates the scene by divulging that Amelia has written to Dobbin that very morning, prior to receiving the damning love note that Becky "flings" to free her from her false idolization of George.[24] Thackeray's inclusion of this point may lead us to question Becky's intention in helping Amelia, who has seemingly (and

Fig. 40. Illustration by William Makepeace Thackeray, "The Letter before Waterloo," for William Makepeace Thackeray, *Vanity Fair: A Novel without a Hero*, 1848.

incredulously) helped herself for once. Perhaps Becky's real intention in "flinging" the note is to get Amelia out of the way. In this same scene, Becky tells Amelia, "Jos can't protect you, he is too weak, and wants a protector himself" (866). In fact, Becky becomes Jos's dubious "protector." We later learn from a dying Jos that "All my money is placed out most advantageously. Mrs. Crawley—that is—I mean,—it is laid out to the best interest" (874). Becky is now free to "hook" her fat fish Jos, who once only eyed the bait.

Perhaps, too, Becky longs to tumble Amelia's callous idol whose portrait still graces Amelia Sedley Osborne's home. Early in the novel, Thackeray divulges Rebecca's true feelings for George: "'It was George Osborne who prevented my marriage.'—And she loved George Osborne accordingly" (75). Carrying her grudge against George long after his death, Becky even admits to Amelia in this final chapter that his unheroic death "served him right!" (866). Moreover, Becky's savvy in saving love notes emerges even more brilliantly in comparison to the way George Osborne undervalues their worth. Of all the male characters in Thackeray's "Novel without a Hero," George Osborne emerges as the most deficient. Thackeray visually and verbally chides the cad who uses Amelia's love letters to light his cigars. Thackeray admits that "Such a number of notes followed Lieutenant Osborne about the country, that he became almost ashamed of the jokes of his mess-room companions regarding them" (140).[25] Nonetheless, how would sweet, simple Amelia—who is "exceedingly alarmed" (14) when Becky flings the Johnson's "Dixonary" out the carriage window—respond if she knew that George "was seen lighting his cigar with one [of her love letters], to the horror of Captain Dobbin, who, it is my belief, would have given a bank-note for the document" (140)?

In a full-page engraving titled "Lieutenant Osborne and His Ardent Love-Letters" (fig. 41), one of Amelia's love letters appears in full flame as George uses it to light his cigar. Behind Osborne rests a box brimming with more notes from Amelia, likely to meet the same fate. Thackeray makes graphic that to George, a love letter from Amelia is not a message to be read and cherished or worth far more than a bank note, as Dobbin recognizes. It is a match; once used, it no longer possesses any value. The burning letter becomes a synecdoche for Amelia herself, whose heart George burns through his insincerity and infidelity. Some critics including John Sutherland even suspect that George may have compromised Amelia prior to their marriage. Thackeray tells us the young bride, after just nine days of marriage, is in a "most interesting situation" (319), a Victorian expression that suggests she is pregnant.[26] It takes the pleading of honest Dobbin to rouse George to disobey his father and honor his commitment to marry the girl pledged to him from childhood. Once married, George, now cut off from his fortune, squanders his little money, not considering how to provide for Amelia. "Placing Amelia on a bench" (356) at the Duke of Richmond's ball, he promptly ignores her and flirts with her rival, Becky.

Unlike Becky's "heroic" act of flinging a book upon an establishment that mistreats her, George's burning of Amelia's love notes flatly disqualifies George from hero status even before he dies on the battlefield, face in the mud. As readers, we are by Amelia's side when we learn that "Darkness

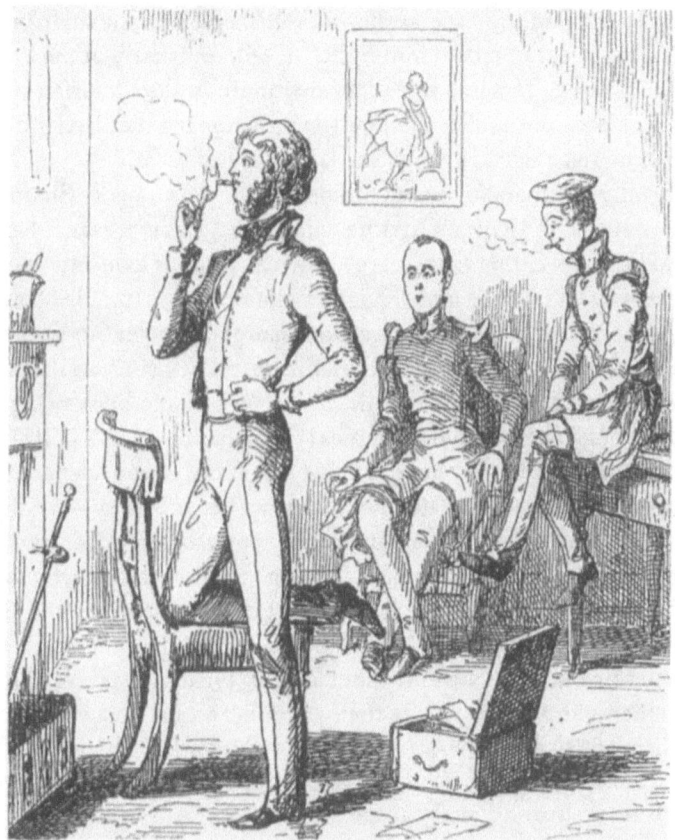

Fig. 41. Illustration by William Makepeace Thackeray, "Lieutenant Osborne and His Ardent Love-Letters," for William Makepeace Thackeray, *Vanity Fair: A Novel without a Hero*, 1848.

came down on the field and city: and Amelia was praying for George, who was lying on his face, dead, with a bullet through his heart" (406). The man who pierces Amelia's heart fittingly dies "with a bullet through his heart."[27] Linguistically de-emphasizing George's importance, Thackeray makes George an object of the preposition "for," a nonessential sentence part. He presents George's death in a secondary relative clause that is nonrestrictive. George's death can even be dropped from the sentence itself, and it would stand grammatically complete. Further, Thackeray closes the September 1847 issue with this unflattering image of George Osborne's derrière. We do not learn of the particulars of George's death until the third chapter of the subsequent, October 1847, installment. Becky is seemingly speaking for the author as well herself when she concludes that George's death "served him right!" (866). A casualty of the Battle of Waterloo, George remains fixed for one month in the Victorian readers' minds in a pose not unlike the Johnson's *Dictionary* that Becky discards from her carriage window when she launches her quest.

Shrewdly commanding texts throughout the novel, Becky Sharp flings her last "stake" at George Osborne, who strategically prevents her marriage to Jos. How fitting that George's own adulterous love letter becomes the means by which "the idol of her [Amelia's] life was tumbled down and shivered at her feet" (866). Once again, George "tumbles" to the ground. In contrast, Becky, the Little Corporal in petticoats, rises and returns to England from her continental exile. Becky "appears to be very wealthy" (877), although she does have enemies ("Who has not?" [877]). If she uses her education to empower her life in ways that not all consider admirable, Becky—who knows how to use her brains and her authority—triumphs in her quest for self-advancement and gets her own booth in Vanity Fair.[28]

From her opening deed when she "flung" the Johnson's *Dictionary* out the carriage window to her closing dramatic action in which she "flung" George Osborne's adulterous love note at her maudlin counterpart, Thackeray's heroine in this "Novel without a Hero" wields the power of literacy at just the right moment. More than any other woman reader depicted in Victorian British and American fiction and illustration, Thackeray's Becky Sharp transgresses gender boundaries, empowers her life, and paves the way for future revolutionary readers.

Conclusion

George Cruikshank's "My Wife Is a Woman of Mind" (fig. 1) introduces my examination of the Victorian woman reader. This 1847 caricature crystallizes fears surrounding the rise of the intellectual woman. I close with an engraving titled "In the Library" (fig. 42) by Franz Robert Richard Brend'amour from *Art Gems for the Home and Fireside* (1888), a little-known book edited by Charlotte Perkins Gilman.[1] The setting for learning is not a chaotic room filled with screaming children, as Cruikshank depicts. Brend'amour portrays the sanctity of a library in a prosperous home, akin to Casaubon's library at Lowick where Dorothea Brooke undertakes her classical studies in *Middlemarch*. Brend'amour's woman in the library looks startling dissimilar to Cruikshank's "woman of mind," whose hair is severely pulled back to show the phrenological bumps on her forehead, declaring her intellect. Brend'amour's woman reader is soft, feminine, and attractive. Her beauty captivates us as much as the book on the handsome and elaborately carved library table fascinates her.

Akin to Henry James, Brend'amour does not divulge the title of the volume that absorbs his figure of the woman reader. Nonetheless, we can infer that the tome is not light literature since many visual clues—the dark colors of the room, massive volumes lining the bookshelves, newspapers spread over the library table, and a bust of Homer at the far right side of the engraving—indicate the setting is a gentleman's library. In her accompanying commentary for this book of fifty eclectic images ranging from landscapes and domestic portrayals to biblical scenes, Gilman uses some of these same indicators to read the province as a masculine domain and conclude: "A man makes this his den . . . And presumably he loves Greek."[2] Gilman determines that the owner is not an "ascetic bookworm," owing to luxuries including Persian style rugs, ornamental ink stands, elaborate sconces, and books with vellum bindings.

I concur that the decor of this library marks its owner a gentleman of

Fig. 42. Illustration by Franz Robert Richard Brend'amour, "In the Library," for Charlotte Perkins Gilman, *Art Gems for the Home and Fireside*, 1888.

breeding and taste; he is an Edmund Bertram or a Hubert Temperley who loves classical literature and English politics, indicated by the *Times* prominently displayed on the table. Gilman and I, however, part company in our reading of the figure of the woman reader in this engraving. I offer my interpretation first.

Placing an attractive woman reader in a library setting suggests that a "woman of mind" has made visible gains as the nineteenth century progressed. The bows and lace of her gown speak to her femininity that she has not sacrificed to enlarge her mind, as Cruikshank burlesques. Although the reader's standing pose with a book could signify aesthetic cultivation, Brend'amour's depiction differs from turn-of-the century representations of what Linda Docherty calls the cultivated woman reader (see, for example, William McGregor Paxton's *The Yellow Jacket* [1907]): the figure is not in a sun-lit room, but in a library; she reads a text, not an art book; her hands do not linger lightly on the pages to imply only a passing curiosity.[3] Brend'amour offers an active image of a woman reader alone with a book. No one interrupts her. No social responsibilities demand her attention. The figure's direct gaze at fine rows of print and, in particular, her hand gestures suggest the book is not merely a prop of gentility. Brend'amour positions both of her hands on the book: the thumb of her left hand holds a page down seemingly to read it better; her right hand gracefully holds the opposite page between her fingers to suggest she is reading intently. Perhaps she reads Ralph Waldo Emerson's essays, like Hadria Fullerton, or a book of Latin to garner the kind of "masculine studies" that fascinate Maggie Tulliver and Dorothea Brooke. Her self-education in a man's library may lead her to a book of German thought, like Isabel Archer. Equally, she could be reading history to broaden her world view, like Isabel Gilbert, who reads in Roland Lansdell's library at Mordred Priory.

Even if this library is the province of a husband or father, the figure clearly appears comfortable in a masculine domain. The lighting highlights her interest in reading while her relaxed pose and slight smile indicate her self-confidence as a reader. Moreover, the placement of this engraving within an oversized art volume—equivalent to a coffee table book today—suggests that *Art Gems* likely found its way into a Victorian American parlor, a testimony to the distance the woman reader traveled by the later Victorian age. We can imagine the pleasure a Victorian woman must have experienced when she opened *Art Gems for the Home and Fireside* to discover this picture of an attractive woman reading in a handsome library.

Gilman may be projecting her frustrations with society's construction of domestic femininity onto the Brend'amour image when she argues that this charming woman is a decorative ornament to set off a decidedly male ambiance of learning: "It may be surmised that the young lady so pleasingly represented is scarcely a literary person; there is surely a strong suggestion that she is here solely because her complexion seems clearest against the old vellum and calf-skin bindings, and her brocade dress more dainty and fresh beside the old oak furniture. And as for really caring for the book she is looking at, no one would believe it. It may be that she came to see 'papa' a moment, and papa having left, she idly turned the leaves to see what his books were like. At any rate she is not the habitué of this library" (96). While it is a late-nineteenth-century convention to depict a woman as a decorative object (for example, the cultivated type), this practice does not place the woman reader in a library. Nonetheless, Gilman concludes, "As for the young lady who lingers here over a triolet or some 'vers de société,' politics do not trouble her; and for books she affects, instead of old folios, the dainty white and gold 'garlands of verse,' or the least serious of French novels" (96). "Scarcely a literary person," as Gilman surmises, the woman in the library is but an adornment to contrast with the old vellum bindings and oak furniture. Through Gilman's eyes, this beautiful page turner becomes a nineteenth-century counterpart to *Wheel of Fortune*'s Vanna White.

The lack of visual clues to substantiate Gilman's story of this woman reader suggests her characterization of the figure is a projection, especially because she shows, rather than tells, her interpretation of the masculine domain. Why might a writer now celebrated for her enduring feminist contributions—meaningful work for women, child care, professional housekeeping, and the creation of a more "human world"—portray the figure as she does? Attitudes toward women readers had not changed radically by the end of the nineteenth century, regardless of what was happening in art. Perhaps the most revealing line in Gilman's interpretation is, "And as for really caring for the book she is looking at, no one would believe it." An avid reader since childhood, Gilman knew firsthand what it meant for a woman to be passionately interested in reading fiction and nonfiction.[4] Her phrasing suggests that she is imposing on this image her personal disappointment with a pervasive view that "no one would believe" an attractive woman can care deeply about books. In fact, this same sarcastic tone emerges in other of her commentaries on images of women included in *Art Gems*.[5]

Gilman saw no point in writing without a social purpose. As I have previously argued, she used any and every literary vehicle to drive her socialist and feminist ideologies.[6] Emphasizing the didactic intent in her first book of poems, *In This Our World* (1893), Gilman told an interviewer in 1896: "I don't call it a book of poems. I call it a tool box. It was written to drive nails with."[7] Her frank utilitarian metaphor characterizes Gilman's hard-hitting rhetorical stance in all of her writing. Through her art commentary in *Art Gems for the Home and Fireside*, Gilman is likely "driving nails" against a widespread and persisting nineteenth-century ideology that stereotypes a Victorian woman as attractive and domestic, thus not intellectual. Gilman interprets this handsome nineteenth-century engraving in terms of an oppressive doctrine of domesticity that kept women trapped in the private home—the source for woman's oppression that she lambastes in *Women and Economics*, published a decade after *Art Gems*. Brend'amour's engraving becomes a variation on the same false dichotomy that Cruikshank presents in his caricature published in *The Comic Almanack* four decades earlier. While Cruikshank's "woman of mind" has traded away her femininity to develop her intellect, "no one would believe" that Brend'amour's reading woman could possibly be interested in politics or old tomes, Gilman argues, because she is so feminine. If Gilman does not acknowledge the progress of women in terms of education or self-confidence, it suits her ideological purpose to criticize a dominant belief that fed the biological argument against a woman's unsupervised reading in a gentleman's library.

We cannot ignore the social purpose and sarcasm behind Gilman's interpretation or the significance of her frustration with the social construction of domestic femininity: ideological characterizations of the woman reader were fluid yet persistent. We tend to think of the Victorian era as a time of progress and change. Although all ages are periods of transition, the Victorians were self-consciously aware that theirs was an age undergoing rapid change in industry, science, religion, education, economy, and gender roles. In an era marked by progress, one might not suspect that Victorians on both sides of the Atlantic held fast to certain ideals as they embraced social change.

Conflicting notions coexist in many arenas undergoing change and reorganization, particularly Victorian visions of childhood, which, in turn, affected the juvenile literary market and women's education. The concept of child of innocence, which Wordsworth and Dickens championed, gradually gained force over the nineteenth century, but it did not simply replace the persisting doctrine of sin, which Lewis Carroll ridicules in *Alice*. Likewise, even as women made gains in education, social change for women in Victorian Britain and America did not override the importance of home, matrimony, and motherhood that Louisa May Alcott celebrates; overturn persisting fears about women's novel-reading, advanced by those espousing the arguments of consumption, addiction, and morality; or replace outdated reading practices.

Part 1 of this book summarizes the range of coexisting and conflicting ideologies supporting both sides of a heated transatlantic debate in which commentators concomitantly challenged and endorsed the domestic ideal and the status quo in gender relations. As parts 2 and 3 also illustrate, throughout the Victorian era, literary and visual representations of a woman enlarging her narrow and limited life or acquiring the kind of classical education that George Eliot herself did obtain abide alongside visual and verbal characterizations promoting the pervasive notion of domesticity that Gilman battled her entire life. Fictional women within the pages of these Victorian British and American novels, and others standing behind them, communicate that women read for education and empowerment, as well as for gentility and socialization, all the while that critics feared fiction for its biological, medical, and moral repercussions and criticized it widely.

Of import, the rise of literacy and women's education and the women's movement came together within the construct of the woman reader during the Victorian era. The family circle sheltered Victorians from the anxieties of modern life and provided them a place in which to instill values of high moral purpose and religious devotion. Reading within the context of domesticity could be seen to support traditional values. The intellectual woman reader might equally have grown disenchanted with the notion of separate spheres, particularly at a time when the suffragette movement gained force in Britain and America. As the century progressed, women eventually gained the right to hold property; they urged for the right to vote; they attended universities and reproduced, debunking fears of infertility; they read widely in a range of subjects. Thus, the figure of the woman reader has historical value not only as a window into dominant ideologies about women's readings but as a portal into the larger political and educational climate of the Victorian era.

Other interesting ideas emerge as an outgrowth of my examination of the woman reader. One might profitably explore the figure of the reader in relation to social class as presented in history, text, and illustration. Books, drawings, and letters play key roles in representations of the working class and the upper reaches. Earlier I raise Martha Banta's insight on reading as a mark of culture in *Imaging American Women*. Elizabeth Gaskell's *Mary Barton* (1848) offers a prime example for intensive study of social class, text, and image as object: Harry Carson's caricature of a laborer incites the working classes to rise against the masters of the mill; Jem's valentine to Mary becomes wadding in the gun that kills the young dandy Harry Carson; and the Bible becomes key to the elder Carson's conversion. As just this one Victorian text illustrates, the construction of a reader's identity across the new class society in text and image deserves investigation. The privileging of visual culture in texts without illustration, as well as those illustrated by outside artists and author-illustrators, emerges as another prime area for research. Numerous fictional women—principally Jane Eyre and Maggie Tulliver, but also Isabel Archer, Emma Bovary, Isabel Gilbert, and Jo March—avidly "read" book illustrations. James, for example, divulges that Isabel Archer often chooses her selections according to a frontispiece of a volume. Charlotte Brontë and Eliot describe how an illustration sparks their readers' creative imaginings. The actions of Jane Eyre reading Bewick's images of popular culture and Maggie Tulliver poring over an image in *The History of the Devil* reflect the reading preferences of numerous Victorians who read pictures "with passionate interest," as author-illustrator George Du Maurier expresses in "The Illustrating of Books" (350). This is a period when adults read pictures for plot, theme, and characterization. Examples from Victorian life, art, and fiction suggest the growing influence of pictures within the illustrated book and reinforce the argument underlying the third part of this book—that illustration, a key aspect of visual culture studies, deserves more investigation.

If we accept the premise of this book—that literature and book illustration are of historical importance as indicators of, simultaneously, the desire and anxiety surrounding female reading practice in the nineteenth century—then future studies might explore book illustration as an indicator of culture, illuminating social class, art, architecture, dress, and gender roles, as well as reading practices of Victorian women. Just as incorporating a written work into a book necessarily transforms it "ekphrasiastically," as *The Mill on the Floss* reveals, for example, with *Corinne*, I would argue that excluding illustrations from a text designed with pictures alters the vision of an illustrated book as an author and outside illustrator or author-illustrator conceived it. As this examination reveals, illustrations of Becky Sharp memorably flinging Johnson's "Dixonary" out her carriage window and Marmee reading to her daughters in the March family circle combine with literary representations and history to bring the world of the Victorian woman reader vividly to life.

The debate over women's access to books has quieted, not ended. Concerns that arose in the Victorian era precede the nineteenth century and continue beyond it. History, text, and illustration envision women readers' journeys and preserve stereotypes that authors and illustrators challenged but did not defeat. The idea of an unattractive intellectual woman that Cruikshank burlesques and Gilman finds offensive still exerts force in popular culture. The difficulty Victorian women readers faced in not being allowed to select their own reading material also recalls the banning of books still operating in many traditional communities. The obstacles our Victorian sisters confronted stand in sharp contrast to the privileges twenty-first-century women readers take for granted. Equally, fictional representations of the woman reader pioneer the greater education and empowerment reading women experience today.

Notes

INTRODUCTION

1. For a contrasting depiction of a "man of mind," see a small wood engraving originally designed for the June 1842 issue of *Ainsworth's Magazine* titled "Our Library Table" (1842); it appears in Vogler, *Graphic Works*, 33, with an extended note on 137.

2. "My Wife Is a Woman of Mind" is plate 181 in Vogler, *Graphic Works*, 78, with a helpful explanatory note on 154.

3. The novel, however, was not without its supporters. For example, Henry James's 1884 essay "The Art of Fiction" defends the novel and elevates its importance as a literary genre.

4. The now forgotten but once influential Scottish biologist Geddes, along with Thomson, advances in *The Evolution of Sex* (1889) that the female has to conserve energy for survival and reproduction. Likewise, Dr. Clarke, from the Harvard Medical School, raises concerns over the rise of women in American higher education by attempting to use scientific reasoning to curtail women's intellectual progress. In *Sex in Education* (1873), an influential and widely read book, Clarke argues that excessive study would deplete a woman's limited energy and lead to infertility, uterine disease, neuralgia, and hysteria. In *What a Young Woman Ought to Know* (1899), Dr. Wood-Allen cites novel-reading as a cause for early menstruation, painful menses, and nervousness. I discuss these sources in more detail in part 1. See also Flint's chapter on "Medical, Physiological, and Psychoanalytic Theory" in *The Woman Reader*, 53–70.

5. The book in Victorian Britain and America gains complexity when studied from the vantage point of gender. The gender focus within these studies particularly informs my own examination.

6. Flint, *The Woman Reader*, 11.

7. David D. Hall, "Readers and Reading," 339.

8. Davidson, *Revolution and the Word*, 49.

9. Baym, *Novels, Readers, and Reviewers*, 13.

10. Reynolds and Humble, *Victorian Heroines*, 27.

11. Docherty, "Women as Readers," 339. She offers an important understanding of the role of books as pictorial signifiers in painting from the colonial period through World War I.

12. Also see Sicherman, "Sense and Sensibility," 202.
13. Mailloux, "Interpretation," 127.
14. Sally Mitchell, *The New Girl*, 144.
15. Heffernan, *Museum of Words*, 3, 192 n.6. Heffernan acknowledges, for example, the work of Linda Hutcheon, who applies the term "ekphrasis" to postmodern literature when examining how John Fowles and Julio Cortazar introduce newspaper articles into their novels in her paper on "Postmodern Ekphrasis" (paper presented at the Tenth International Colloquium on Poetics, Columbia University, 1986). Heffernan also mentions Mack L. Smith's dissertation, "Figures in the Carpet: The Ekphrastic Tradition in the Realistic Novel" (Rice University, 1981) in which Smith explores examples of writing about texts (for example, Joyce's use of *Hamlet* in *Ulysses*) alongside writing about pictures (for example, Tolstoy's descriptions of portraits in *Anna Karenina*).
16. From mid-century until century's end, depictions of the Queen commanded attention; artists captured Victoria as a youthful bride, loving wife and mother, grieving widow, and powerful matriarch. Artists also depict women as monumental goddesses, working women, rejected and expectant lovers, fallen women, and New Women at the close of the century. Many representations are distorting mirrors of ideal Victorian British and American life.
17. Some Victorians would no doubt bemoan the decline of adult illustrated fiction. As John Robert Harvey aptly states in *Some Victorian Novelists and Their Illustrators*, "In respect of illustration the modern novel has a withered limb, and while with many novelists it may just as well be withered, since they have no need of it, one cannot say who might have used it with the strength, suppleness, and sensitivity of a hand" (181). Lewis Carroll preferred to draw out his wondrous characters in *Alice's Adventures under Ground* (1864) rather than describe them. Carroll's credo also responds to a priority dating back to the *ut pictura poesis* tradition, often associated with Plato and Horace, which became central to the Victorian age.
18. Henry James, *A Small Boy and Others*, 44. James's preference for Cruikshank's over Dickens's art is widely quoted.
19. Du Maurier, "The Illustrating of Books," 350.
20. Modern Language Association, "Statement on the Significance of Primary Records," 28.
21. Many paperback editions retain illustrations erratically. For instance, *Vanity Fair* (New York: Signet, 1962) retains some of the pictorial capitals and an occasional woodcut. Following Dickens's own later selection of illustrations, *Oliver Twist* (Oxford and New York: Oxford University Press, 1982) retains eight of Cruikshank's original illustrations, which editor Kathleen Tillotson numbers as twenty-five to include "The Fireside Plate" Dickens rejected. "Fagin in the Condemned Cell" and "Oliver Asking for More" appear, but less memorable illustrations, such as "Sikes and His Dog," are included rather than, for instance, "The Last Chance" or "Mr. Bumble and Mrs. Corney Taking Tea."
22. See, for example, Jane R. Cohen, *Charles Dickens and His Original Illustrators*; Steig, *Dickens and Phiz*; Patten, "Boz, Phiz, and Pickwick in the Pound"; Harvey, *Some Victorian Novelists and Their Illustrators*.

CHAPTER 1. WOMEN READERS AND READING IN VICTORIAN BRITAIN AND AMERICA

1. I recommend Flint, *The Woman Reader*, which devotes a chapter to the notions that the Victorians inherited; see chapter 2, "Theory and Women's Reading." Flint's book provides a rich historical analysis.

2. For information on the book as symbol, I recommend James Hall, *Dictionary of Subjects and Symbols in Art*, 50–51.

3. In addition to Salmon's "What Girls Read" (1886), Yates's "Do Our Girls Take an Interest in Literature?" (1906), and Clarke's "The Novel-Reading Habit" (1898), the topic of girls' reading appears frequently in *Godey's Lady's Book* and numerous advice books of the period.

4. Beginning in the 1970s, scholars have given attention to the woman reader and writer. Earlier historical work on readership, nonetheless, presents important information on literacy and the rising availability of print among the lower-middle and working classes, which has relevance to this examination. See Altick, *The English Common Reader*, and Louis James, *Fiction for the Working Man*. Both James and Altick offer important material on the rise of literacy and the dissemination of print matter in the lower-middle and working classes. For example, James raises the idea of domestic fiction and parenthetically hints that its readership is predominantly female, even if he does not consider how female readers might have read it differently than male readers. Altick's still influential work offers a social history of the English reading public. In the 1830s, books were what Altick calls a "minor luxury" (276) for the middle class. A combination of factors drove prices down and made books more accessible for the middle class in the new class society. As literacy rates rose, book prices fell. Technological advances (principally the steam operated printing press), machine-made paper (as opposed to hand-made), innovations in binding (for example, paper board and cloth covers instead of leather covers), and serial publication increased the speed and efficiency of print production and also lowered cost. Serial novels were published separately in part issues or monthly or weekly periodicals. The Victorian periodicals market continued to grow rapidly due to legislation, particularly the abolition of the newspaper stamp tax (1855) and the duty on paper (1861). The lending library—with numerous libraries springing up around mid-century—also made books more available to the growing reading public.

5. A seminal historian of the book, Engelsing uses "intensive" versus "extensive" to explain how by the end of the eighteenth century in Germany the nature of reading changed. For a summary of Engelsing's main arguments, I recommend "Die Perioden der Lesergeschichte." Scholars have criticized Engelsing's work on several levels.

6. In *Revolution and the Word*, 72–73, Davidson questions the claim that reading became less intensive when it grew more extensive. Sicherman, in "Sense and Sensibility," refutes the notion that reading became more isolating for women by exploring the concept of reading aloud in the domestic family circle (206). In contrast, Bledstein emphasizes that the Victorian reading experience was isolating (*The Culture of Professionalism*, 77–78).

7. Anne Brontë's *Agnes Grey* offers a more developed and realistic portrait of a governess than her sister Charlotte's *Jane Eyre*. Elizabeth Missing Sewell, author of over forty literary and devotional works, wrote *Amy Herbert*.

8. Brontë, *Jane Eyre*, 2nd ed. (New York: W. W. Norton, 1987), 109. Subsequent references are to this edition.

9. Emily Davies in an essay by J. G. Fitch, "The Education of Women" (1864), quoted in Flint, *The Woman Reader*, 120.

10. See Emily Davies, "On Secondary Instruction as Relating to Girls," quoted in Flint, *The Woman Reader*, 120.

11. M. Jeanne Peterson, *Family, Love, and Work*, 41, 43.

12. Sally Mitchell, "Sentiment and Suffering," 45. Mitchell is interested in the popularity of sensation fiction as well as periodical fiction. Also see her book *The Fallen Angel*.

13. In *The Bonds of Womanhood*, Cott suggests that in Revolutionary times, only approximately half of New England women could sign their names, whereas by 1840 literacy was nearly universal among women and men (101).

14. Kelley, "Reading Women/Women Reading," 406.

15. Kelley cites the case of Martha Hauser, writing in 1853 to her friend Julia Conrad Jones.

16. Arnold does not advocate novels as the main reading to educate the masses.

17. Trollope, *Orley Farm* (New York: Dover, 1981) 1: 262. This reference is to the education of Mary Snow, whom Felix Graham attempts to mold into a perfect wife. Subsequent references are to this edition, which binds the two volumes as one.

18. Banta, *Imaging American Women*, 358.

19. In "How to Form a Small Library," for example, Mason likens books to companions and hopes that the books in one's library should "all rank with your best friends," 2:123.

20. Heller, "Frankenstein," 327.

21. Trollope, "Higher Education of Women," 85–86.

22. Adams, *Woman's Work and Worth*, 136.

23. Some arguments for reading had ready objections. Reading was considered a socially acceptable way for a female traveler to shield herself from unwelcome intrusion—something women still recognize today. That idea of shielding raised opposition; John Ruskin in *Sesame and Lilies* (1865, 1871) argued that the traveler absorbed by the book in her hand could not appreciate the wonders of the world through which she was traveling.

24. Eastman Johnson (1824–1906) earned a reputation for domestic subjects. He completed many genre paintings in the 1860s and 1870s, including *Christmas Time (The Blodgett Family)* (c. 1864), *A Woman in a White Dress* (c. 1873), and *Husking Bee, Island of Nantucket* (c. 1876).

25. Ellis, *The Mothers of England*, 196–97.

26. See Gilman, *In This Our World*, 160–61. The final couplet reads, "She died, as all her mothers died before./Her daughter died in turn, and made one more."

27. *Godey's Lady's Book* 1 (1828), quoted in Welter, "The Cult of True Woman-

hood," 166. Welter notes that this type of comment was frequent in *Godey's* editorials.

28. *The Annual Catalogue of the Officers and Pupils of the Young Ladies' Seminary and Collegiate Institute* (1855), quoted in Welter, "The Cult of True Womanhood," 168.

29. Salmon, "What Girls Read," 526.

30. Cruse, *The Victorians and Their Reading*, 338.

31. Cobbe's "What Shall We Do with Our Old Maids?" first appeared in *Fraser's Magazine* in November 1862. This quote comes from its reprinting in Broomfield and Mitchell, *Prose by Victorian Women*, 254. Cobbe notes that since 30 percent of women never marry, the "old assumption that marriage was the sole destiny of woman" should be revised. Education for women obviously offers one alternative model (236–37).

32. Cobbe quoted in "The Higher Education of Women," 155.

33. Woolf, *A Room of One's Own*, 52.

34. Showalter, *A Literature of Their Own*, 152.

35. "Novel-reading" quoted in Flint, *The Woman Reader*, 81.

36. In this article, Sicherman directs the reader to accounts by Florence Kelley, Charlotte Perkins Gilman, and Mary Richmond, among others.

37. Sicherman, "Reading *Little Women*," 252.

38. See Helen Irving, "Literary Women," quoted in Welter, "The Cult of True Womanhood," 166.

39. Conway, "From 'Stereotypes of Femininity,'" 76.

40. S. Weir Mitchell, *Doctor and Patient*, 138.

41. To his credit, however, in his chapter on "Nervousness and Its Influence," S. Weir Mitchell suggests that if girls have more exercise in early life, they will be more fit to pursue higher education during the "critical years" (144) and become strong and vigorous rather than nervous (*Doctor and Patient*).

42. See George Henry Lewes, "The Heart and the Brain," quoted in Flint, *The Woman Reader*, 55. Lewes wrote it under the title of editor.

43. Sally Mitchell, *The New Girl*, 164.

44. Wood-Allen, *What a Young Woman Ought to Know*, 124. Wood-Allen treats sensation fiction, love stories, romance, and novel-reading interchangeably. In a chapter on "Solitary Vice," she notes how novel-reading can stimulate the organs and lead the girl to experiment in masturbation, which causes loss of memory, strength, and intelligence; poor complexion; weakened eyesight; and possibly insanity.

45. Charlotte Mason, *Home Education: A Course of Lectures to Ladies* (1886), quoted in Flint, *The Woman Reader*, 84.

46. Clarke, *Sex in Education*, 18. Clarke's book, an outgrowth of a lecture to the New England Women's Club of Boston, went into a second edition in little more than a week after the first edition was published. See also Solomon, *In the Company of Educated Women*, 56; Smith-Rosenberg and Rosenberg, "The Female Animal."

47. Trained as a neurologist, Freud approved the rest cure popularized by S. Weir Mitchell, whom Clarke cites in his influential study. The rest cure—administered to

well-known British and American figures of the period including Gilman, Alice James, and Virginia Woolf—aimed to treat symptoms of strain and depression by healing the body. Men could experience neurasthenia, but they usually were prescribed vigorous activity, typically ranching in the west. For women, in contrast, all activity, including reading, sewing, feeding oneself, and sitting up, was limited for a six- to eight-week period, although in some cases women were read to for a short period of time each day. There were five components to the rest cure: rest (typically for 6 to 8 weeks), seclusion (from familiar surroundings and family members), diet (excessive feeding), massage, and electricity (to guard against muscular atrophy). For more information, see Golden, *The Captive Imagination*, 46.

48. Howe, *Sex and Education*, 14, 9.

49. Sidgwick, *Health Statistics*, 66.

50. Ridding, "What Should Women Read?" 29.

51. Kellogg, *The Ladies' Guide in Health and Disease*, 160.

52. Florence Nightingale, *Cassandra*, quoted in Flint, *The Woman Reader*, 32.

53. Clarke, "The Novel-Reading Habit," 674.

54. Though best known for his paintings of the Maine coastline and pastoral scenes of rural America, Homer, an illustrator turned painter, offers numerous depictions of a woman reader. See, for example, *Fiction* (1875) and *Reading by the Brook* (1879).

55. Homer seemingly manipulates the language of art to comment on the perils of novel-reading. The sun is setting, but Homer's reader is too entranced in popular culture to lay her book down and go inside. She seems unaware of any possible danger or breach of decorum. The lighting magnifies the power of fiction to mesmerize.

56. R. C. Waterston, *Thoughts on Moral and Spiritual Culture*, quoted in Welter, "The Cult of True Womanhood," 165–66.

57. "The Fatalist," *Godey's Lady's Book* 4 (January 1834), quoted in Welter, "The Cult of True Womanhood," 166.

58. "What Is the Harm of Novel-Reading?" 933.

59. See Beecher and Beecher Stowe, *The American Woman's Home*, 257–58.

60. In *Imaging American Women* (360), Banta includes Coles Phillips's June 8, 1911, cover of *Life* titled "The Lure of Books." It shows a gentlewoman of the house relaxing over a stack of books. In contrast, in *The House Maid*, the unmistakable maid's uniform and duster (tucked under her arm) mark this woman as maid in a painting whose title also declares her status. Additionally, I cite Frederick Friesecke's *In the Library* (1919) as an early-twentieth-century example showcasing women's reading as a leisure pastime.

61. Sherwood wrote *The History of the Fairchild Family* (1818, 1842, 1847), a standard Sunday School prize book, for both sexes, but some Victorians questioned if such moral domestic tales would pacify boys. Girls' fiction developed in the nineteenth century after boys' fiction. A relatively new juvenile market for girls' fiction in America led publishers to commission Alcott to write *Little Women* in the 1860s. Girls in the mid- to late nineteenth century were coming of age at a time when

society allotted leisure time to girls of the middle and upper classes for literary pursuits. By the early twentieth century, as Sally Mitchell notes, girls' books became a usual category on British publishers' lists. However, commentators defined adolescence variously as ranging from eight to eighteen or fourteen to twenty.

For the rise of gender-specific fiction, see, for example, Darton, *Children's Books in England*; Avery, *Nineteenth Century Children*; Bratton, *The Impact of Victorian Children's Fiction*; Cadogan and Craig, *You're a Brick Angela!*; Sally Mitchell, *The New Girl*.

62. As Cadogan and Craig also point out in *You're a Brick Angela!*, boys' tales became more manly. Boys' books from mid-century onward typically have no girls in them. Girls typically read tales with protagonists of both sexes, and the girls' stories modeled after boys' adventure tales were decidedly less energetic and less appealing to girls.

63. Charlotte Mary Yonge quoted in Avery, *Nineteenth Century Children*, 138.

64. *The Girl's Own Paper* came into existence one year after *The Boy's Own Paper* and twenty-five years after *The Boy's Own Magazine* (a forerunner of *The Boy's Own Paper*).

65. There were journals more feminist in leaning, such as *Atalanta* (1887–98), which L. T. Meade founded for a slightly older audience of upper- and middle-class girls aged fourteen to twenty-five. It contained articles on women writers, philanthropists, artists, and girls' schools; and a "Scholarship and Reading Union" with commentary on British writers from leading authorities, including Anne Thackeray on Jane Austen and Thomas Hughes on Charles Kingsley, as well as essay questions which, if responded to, would be critiqued for a fee and included in a prize competition. Other periodicals such as *Girl's Realm* also offered a "Reading Union" as a regular feature until home education became less common. By the turn of the century, schoolwork left girls little time to write the essays required by unions. Meade was a popular novelist who wrote school stories and other fiction following the careers of nurses, teachers, art students, journalists, and settlement workers.

66. Helen Corke quoted in Sally Mitchell, *The New Girl*, 139–40.

67. From the 1887 diary of Agnes Hamilton quoted in Sicherman, "Sense and Sensibility," 207.

68. *North American* quoted in Baym, *Novels, Readers, and Reviewers*, 49. Susan Warner's *Queechy* (1852) was also a popular hit.

69. Roosevelt, *An Autobiography*, 16. Of the girls' stories he liked, Roosevelt includes Alcott's *Little Women* and *Little Men*.

70. "Colonial" would apply to the British girl living in British colonies, such as India and the West Indies, governed by the Colonial Office.

71. See Low, "The Reading of the Modern Girl," and Barnicoat, "The Reading of the Colonial Girl," quoted in Flint, *The Woman Reader*, 159–61.

72. For example, Carroll parodies Isaac Watts's didactic "Against Idleness and Mischief" (1715), turning an industrious bee into a lazy crocodile.

73. In aligning himself with Carroll's fiction, Grahame is making a strong state-

ment about the evolution in literature for children, itself a reflection of the gradual shift in notions of childhood—the traditional view of sin versus the emerging concept of child of innocence—which slowly developed over the nineteenth century.

74. Nineteenth-century authors incorporated literature into their works in a range of ways. They included quotations (as an epigram to a chapter or within it), referred to reading practices (for example, frequency of reading) and reading selections (such as romance or poetry), and, of course, mentioned specific texts characters read. The use of quotations as well as references to reading, the subjects of previous examinations, are worthy of separate and further study.

CHAPTER 2. TRANSATLANTIC REPRESENTATIONS
OF THE WOMAN READER

1. Henry James, "The Art of Fiction," 665. "The Art of Fiction" first appeared in *Longman's Magazine* in 1884 and was included in *Partial Portraits* in 1888. The text here is the 1888 version.

2. Previous critics have discussed Jane Eyre's reading as well as Brontë's method of loosely adapting Bunyan's narrative model in *Jane Eyre*. See, for example, Qualls's "The Terrible Beauty of Charlotte Brontë's 'Natural Supernaturalism,'" in *The Secular Pilgrims*, 43–84; Wheeler's "The Heroine as Reader: *Jane Eyre*" in *The Art of Allusion*, 27–43.

3. Henry James, *The Portrait of a Lady*, 25. Subsequent references are to this edition.

4. Fritz Eichenberg, for example, illustrates this scene for the 1945 Random House edition of Brontë's *Jane Eyre*. In a marginal let-in illustration, he shows Jane sitting in the window seat with legs tucked in and totally absorbed in her Bewick book. All textual references to *Jane Eyre* are taken from the Norton 2nd edition.

5. See Gilbert and Gubar, *The Madwoman in the Attic*, 342, 339.

6. See Brantlinger, *The Reading Lesson*, 116.

7. Scholes, *The Rise and Fall of English*, 164.

8. See Gérin, *Anne Brontë*, 55, and Barker, *The Brontës*, 103. A copy of Bewick's *History of British Birds* was sold at the parsonage sale following Rev. Brontë's death.

9. The poem to Bewick appears in Barker, *The Brontës*, 3–6. The note to the poem offers more discussion of the influence of Bewick on the entire Brontë family (103). Charlotte also recommended Nussey read Audubon; on this point, see Stedman, "Charlotte Brontë and Bewick's 'British Birds,'" 36.

10. See Anne Brontë, *The Tenant of Wildfell Hall*, 469, to explore this scene.

11. Stedman, "Charlotte Brontë and Bewick's 'British Birds,'" 36. Stedman refers to the bird imagery in the novel and the importance of Bewick to Charlotte Brontë. Stedman also suggests that Charlotte read the 1804 edition, published in 1805, but was likely familiar with later editions, such as the 1826 (the last in Bewick's lifetime) and the 1832, published by Bewick's son. Charlotte presumably enjoyed both volumes of Bewick's book although Jane refers only to volume 2. Whereas Audubon published his volumes on birds when Charlotte was an adoles-

cent, his works would have been too costly for a clergyman's family; Bewick was more affordable.

12. Bewick earned a reputation for ornithological illustrations conveying scientific information and beauty. Although Bewick diverges from the Romantic William Wordsworth in stressing the alienation of mind from nature as well as the affinity between them, Bewick resembles the Romantic born a generation after him in his love of the natural world, nurtured from childhood.

13. Richard J. Dunn also identifies and includes this image and excerpts from Stedman's article on Bewick in Charlotte Brontë, *Jane Eyre*, 3rd ed. Ed. Richard J. Dunn. (New York: W. W. Norton, 2001). He also suggests a possible vignette corresponding to Jane's fascination with "the rock standing up alone in a sea of billow and spray" (6). Dunn does not make mention or include a copy of the graveyard image (427–28). Stedman, however, does mention the graveyard image in her article, 38.

14. While the graveyard image is a tailpiece to the "Razor-Bill" (vol. 2) in the 1804 Newcastle edition, it appears as a tailpiece to "The Dun Diver" (vol. 2) in an 1826 edition Newcastle published under the title *A History of British Birds*. Likewise, the image of the fiend is a tailpiece to "Of the Finch" in volume 2 of the 1826 edition whereas it is a tailpiece to "Black-Throated Diver" in volume 2 of the 1804 edition.

15. See Morawski, *Inquiries*, 341.

16. Jane realizes "all was eerie and dreary; the giants were gaunt goblins, the pygmies malevolent and fearful imps, Gulliver a most desolate wanderer in most dread and dangerous regions" (17).

17. Jane finds she "could make no sense of the subject; my own thoughts swam always between me and the page I had usually found fascinating" (32).

18. Dorothy Van Ghent, "From *The English Novel: Form and Function*," in *Perspectives on James's "The Portrait of a Lady*," ed. William T. Stafford, 118.

19. Isabel appears with books in other scenes throughout the novel, as discussed by Tintner in "The Books in the Books," 69–96.

20. In a novel that values color and creates a verbal portraiture, it is not surprising that Isabel selects her books "chiefly" by their pictorial frontispieces. In *The Mill on the Floss* (1860), Eliot's Maggie is also captivated by pictures, as explored in the next chapter.

21. Edel and Tintner, *The Library of Henry James*, 31. In the inventory, there are nine works by Eliot.

22. Long, *Henry James*, 110.

23. Interestingly, Lord Warburton, who we learn "cares for literature, for art, for science, for charming young ladies" (74), is also destined for dissatisfaction in love. He admits to Isabel, when offering a marriage proposal that she promptly rejects: "Of course I've seen you very little, but my impression dates from the very first hour we met. I lost no time, I fell in love with you then. It was at first sight, as the novels say; I know now that's not a fancy-phrase, and I shall think better of novels for evermore" (104). James does not encourage the reader, however, to think better of novels. Rejected by Isabel, Warburton becomes—in the reader's eyes—one whose vision of love is also ruined by romantic literature.

24. Austen, Flaubert, and Braddon explore this very point in their respective novels of voracious female readers, *Northanger Abbey* (1818), *Madame Bovary* (1857), and *The Doctor's Wife* (1864). Chapter 4 explores the works by Flaubert and Braddon in detail.

25. Alcott wrote *Little Women* in response to pressure from her publisher. Alcott's sensation fiction, published pseudonymously, reveals an author working against the grain of tradition in gender roles while her book of girls' fiction, by which she is best known, purports traditional values. Alcott modeled the March family after her own family of four sisters, excluding the dominating force of her much-loved though exacting father, Bronson Alcott—revered nineteenth-century sage, Transcendentalist, and educator.

26. See Auerbach, afterword to *Little Women*, 470.

27. Alcott focuses on doing good for others and self-discipline and thus recasts the decidedly Calvinistic preoccupation with sin and obedience in Bunyan's Christian allegory. Like *Pilgrim's Progress*, *Little Women* is a book in two parts; critics including Auerbach praise Alcott's celebration of the independent female family in part 1 over "Good Wives."

28. Born to a family of humble means, Bunyan was a tinker and traveling preacher who pored over the Bible, which became an inextricable part of the landscape and language of his work and genius. *Pilgrim's Progress* also sits on the bookshelves of countless fictional households in British and American literature, such as the Tullivers in *The Mill on the Floss*.

29. Alcott, *Little Women* (Bantam Books, 1983), 10. Subsequent references are to this edition.

30. Saxton's feminist biography, *Louisa May*, appeared after Stern's republication of the "lost" thrillers. The masked sides of Alcott's life have captured the attention of other feminist critics including Nina Auerbach, Madelon Bedell, Ann Douglas, Judith Fetterley, Elizabeth Keyser, and Patricia Meyer Spacks. Their work is included in Stern's *Critical Essays on Louisa May Alcott*.

31. For more discussion of sensation fiction, I recommend Sutherland, introduction to *The Woman in White*, and Brantlinger, "What Is 'Sensational' about the 'Sensation Novel'?"

32. Sutherland, introduction to *The Woman in White*, xiii.

33. I consciously make this allusion given Alcott's admiration of *The Scarlet Letter* (1850), written by her Concord friend and neighbor.

34. Emily Brontë, *Wuthering Heights*, 38. Subsequent references are to this edition.

35. Brantlinger's argument about Catherine's remaking of the Bible as an act of self-expression and rebellion is similar to my own.

36. All three names are ones which Catherine's daughter actually assumes. One might argue Catherine Heathcliff names Catherine's true identity, a possibility realized when her spirit joins with Heathcliff's on the moors. Pykett elaborates this point in *Emily Brontë*, 87.

37. See "The Name of the Mother in *Wuthering Heights*" in Homans's *Bearing the Word*, 80–81.

38. Sutherland elaborates this point in "Who Gets What in Heathcliff's Will?" in *Can Jane Eyre Be Happy?*, 66–67.

39. Heathcliff buys the lawyer's compliance by forbidding Mr. Green to visit the dying Edgar Linton, who wants to safeguard Catherine's fortune by putting it in trustees' hands for her use in life, to pass on to her children if she has any.

CHAPTER 3. PROPHETIC READING

1. Eliot, *The Mill on the Floss*, 286. Subsequent references are to this edition.

2. The conservatives of St. Ogg's, however, do approve her reading of Thomas à Kempis and other Christian teachings when she enters a phase of Evangelicalism.

3. See Kucich, *Repression in Victorian Fiction*, 114–200. Kucich examines repression in the fiction of Charlotte Brontë, Dickens, and Eliot.

4. Carla L. Peterson, *The Determined Reader*, 185.

5. Geddes and Thomson, *The Evolution of Sex*, 271. They elaborate this point: "The feminine passivity is expressed in greater patience, more open-mindedness, greater appreciation of subtle details and consequently what we call more rapid intuition. The masculine activity lends a greater power of maximum effort, of scientific insight, or cerebral experiment with impressions" (271).

6. Lucy Soulsby, *Happiness* (1899), quoted in Flint, *The Woman Reader*, 64.

7. Most of Defoe's works did not originally appear under his name.

8. Defoe, *The History of the Devil*, 20. Subsequent references are to this edition. Defoe criticizes Milton's Arianism in the treatment of Christ and his description of hell as well as other matters.

9. See Jane R. Cohen, *Charles Dickens and His Original Illustrators*, 4.

10. Even in *Pilgrim's Progress*, Maggie ferrets out the devil. She shows Riley a picture that Tom colored of the devil in his true form while fighting Bunyan's protagonist Christian. The devil, now with red glowing eyes and a black body, seems full of fire. These images catch Maggie's imagination, much to the chagrin of Mr. Riley. In *The Determined Reader*, Carla L. Peterson sees this image as illustrative of the arm-to-arm fight between Tulliver and the devilish Mr. Wakem and the verbal fight between Tom and Philip (185).

11. Defoe assures his readers that as the devil goes about the world incognito and assumes various disguises, the devil often walks among us without the telltale mark of the cloven hoof, just as all those with the cloven hoof are not necessarily the devil.

12. Maggie tells Philip, "I really *was* like a gypsy. I daresay I am now" (300).

13. In *The Determined Reader*, Carla L. Peterson examines Corinne and Maggie in separate chapters. Although Peterson's work informs this chapter, her focus is decidedly different. She pairs each heroine with a male protagonist (Corinne with Balzac's Louis of *Louis Lambert* and Maggie with Hardy's Jude of *Jude the Obscure*) to compare the male and female reading experience. Parallels between Maggie and Corinne emerge forcefully when we examine Maggie alongside the central character of the book she is reading.

14. Eliot typically called her novel "Sister Maggie" or just "Maggie" when she was writing it. See the introduction to *The Mill on the Floss*, vi.

15. In this scene in book 1, chapter 4 of *Corinne*, the blatant anti-Semitism and cruel treatment of lunatics is disturbing. Villagers blame Jews for the fire that ravages the Italian town of Ancona. They "begged Oswald to let the Jews burn. They were in no way evil; rather their superstitious imaginations had been sharply struck by a great misfortune. Yet Oswald barely managed to control his indignation when he heard their strange entreaties" (14). Madame de Staël excuses the behavior of the villagers due to their "great misfortune." Worse, the Jews, when released from a locked and burning ghetto, rush directly to their burning shops "with that appetite for wealth so disquieting when it leads to risking death" (14). Here de Staël intensifies the stereotype of Jews as money grubbing. The people of Ancona beg Oswald to let the lunatics burn as well: "everyone thought it nonsense to risk death for men who were incurably mad one and all: *It's a blessing from heaven, both for them and their families, if they die and it's nobody's fault*" (15). Oswald saves them all.

16. These works could be seen as fictional re-creations of the authors' own lives since Corinne and Maggie read as avidly as their creators. For more discussion of the autobiographical elements of de Staël's *Corinne*, I recommend Gutworth, *Madame de Staël, Novelist*, and Gennari, *Le Premier Voyage de Madame de Staël en Italie et la Genese de Corinne*. Of the many biographies of Eliot, I recommend Ashton, *George Eliot: A Life*, and Bodenheimer, *The Real Life of Mary Ann Evans*, as well as the earlier work of Haight, *George Eliot: A Biography*.

17. See Baker, *The Libraries of George Eliot and George Henry Lewes*, 110. Baker refers to a two-volume and a one-volume edition of *Corinne*.

18. Maggie's love for Stephen admittedly pales in comparison to Corinne's passion for Oswald. Maggie cannot break her earlier bond to Philip and tells Stephen she loves him "not with my whole heart and soul, Stephen, ... I have never consented to it with my whole mind" (476). Family ties burden Maggie and Stephen's love, like Corinne and Oswald's, and keep them from joining. In Corinne's case, "the whole of paternal authority condemned her love" (357). Lord Nelvil cannot overcome his duty to his dead father's wishes and ultimately forsakes Corinne, whom his father (unbeknownst to him) rejected as a possible partner in favor of her pure and reserved English half sister.

19. Duty to family members (alive and dead) permeate both novels. A tortured Lord Nelvil cannot overcome his duty to his deceased Scottish father who favored English reserve. Similarly, loyal Maggie cannot break her earlier ties to Philip Wakem.

20. Within the dynamics of each Victorian sexual triangle, Corinne and Maggie make a supreme sacrifice motivated by sisterly love. Corinne secretly follows Oswald to England, visits the home of her half sister, and comes upon Lucile weeping on their father's grave and praying that her father and Corinne, whom she believes dead, might intercede to secure the love of Oswald, intended as her husband. Corinne's response to this scene foretells the depth of her love for her half sister and her own wish to die: "grant her wish, father, and to your other daughter, a gentle, quiet death" (357). Corinne's sacrifice to ensure Lucile's happiness anticipates Maggie's decision to forsake Stephen because of his previous ties to Lucy and hers to Philip Wakem. Just

before the flood waters come, Maggie receives a letter from Stephen imploring her to return to him and feels "her real temptation had only just begun" (514). Maggie battles her passion and burns his letter. In both sexual triangles, the love between women seals the fate of the dark-haired heroine.

Corinne continues to love her half sister, and in the final days of Corinne's life, Lucile Edgermond and Corinne rekindle the bond they shared when Corinne helped to raise her half sister while living in England. When Lucile learns of Oswald's attachment to her half sister, she is more dismayed by Oswald's leaving Corinne than she is jealous. Corinne instructs Lucile how to please her husband, and they form an alliance anticipating the bond between Lucy Deane and Maggie Tulliver. Lucy—though ill from the news of Maggie's flight with Stephen—finds the strength to slip away and visit Maggie and forgive her. It is these and other actions that might be seen as a celebration of sisterhood even within a romantic genre that, as Adrienne Rich notes in her reading of *Jane Eyre*, typically places women in situations of rivalry as points of a triangle, with the hero triumphing always. See Rich's "Jane Eyre: The Temptations of a Motherless Woman."

21. Maggie's reading here illustrates Tompkins's claim in "Masterpiece Theater" that "literary texts are man-made, historically produced objects, whose value has been created and recreated by men and women out of their particular needs" (127).

22. The dark-haired heroine is not fully avenged in *The Mill on the Floss,* nor does the blond-haired woman completely triumph, points that can also be said of *Corinne*. Philip, Stephen, and Lucy grieve for Maggie Tulliver while Oswald, Lucile, and their child Juliette—who resembles Corinne and to whom Corinne passes on her talents—mourn Corinne. Dead, Corinne and Maggie exert power over their lovers and sister-women.

23. Following a five-year decline in which she loses her artistic genius, Corinne dies of complications of a broken heart. Corinne predicts her eventual fate as soon as Oswald marries: "I sense that I do not have long to live, and the thought brings peace to my soul. It is sweet to grow weak in my present state, the feeling of pain is blunted" (372). Likewise, Maggie, alienated from her brother, ostracized by St. Ogg's, and tempted by Stephen, cries out before the flood waters come: "I will bear it, and bear it till death. . . . . But how long will it take before death comes! I am so young, so healthy. How shall I have patience and strength?" (515).

24. Although she calls it a hymn book, Eliot refers to John Keble's extremely popular nineteenth-century collection of religious verse, *The Christian Year,* published in 1827. Dorothea Brooke in *Middlemarch* also reads it.

25. Interestingly, however, the Thomas à Kempis book irked Thackeray. See his correspondence with Mrs. William Brookfield on Christmas Day, 1849 in Ray, *The Letters* 2:616. Thackeray says, "The scheme of that book carried out would make the world the most wretched useless dreary doting place of sojourn."

26. Eliot used the Challoner translation. In the places where Eliot quotes from *The Imitation of Christ,* she has put in ellipses to indicate she has pulled from various sections. I have identified a number of the passages which come from, for example, book 3, chapter 37 and book 3, chapter 53.

27. See Haight, *The George Eliot Letters*, 1:278. In *The Libraries of George Eliot and George Henry Lewes*, Baker notes that George Eliot's presentation copies to S. S. Hennell and John Walter Cross are now in the Coventry Public Library and the Yale University Library. Baker also lists "*De Imitatione Christi I*" in this inventory of the books of Eliot and Lewes, 83.

28. See Homans, *Bearing the Word*, 123, for more on this point.

CHAPTER 4. ROMANCE CONSUMERS

1. "What Is the Harm of Novel-Reading?" 933–34.

2. See, for example, Reverend Francis Paget's *Lucretia* (1865), a now forgotten novel that sermonizes against sensation fiction.

3. For more information, I recommend "Classic Movie Reviews," <http://www.geocities.com/Hollywood/5555/reefer.html>. These lines are taken from the movie poster.

4. Matilda Pullan, *Maternal Counsels to Daughters*, quoted in Flint, *The Woman Reader*, 51. Flint offers other choice lines from advice books.

5. Jane Welsh Carlyle quoted in Flint, *The Woman Reader*, 51.

6. Braddon, *The Doctor's Wife*, 11. Subsequent references are to this edition.

7. The term "combination stories" refers to stories which borrow, exaggerate, and combine plots from several existing works.

8. "What Is the Harm of Novel-Reading?" likewise concludes with the same metaphors of reading as consumption and regards the novel as a controlled substance: "The press teems with fiction, set forth in the most fascinating style, the tendency of which is to allure into forbidden paths. Ought we not to be as careful about the food of the mind, as we are about the food of the body? In either case poison, however sweet, will destroy life. The difference is, that in the one case the body is killed, in the other the soul!" (934).

9. Fruitful similarities resound in the lives of these authors as well as their novels. Both lived outside mainstream society. Alienated from his materialistic, bourgeois society, Flaubert—an artist in a family of scientists, son of a distinguished surgeon—studied briefly as a law student, a course which ended when he was struck with an epileptic attack. He turned his full attention to writing, and his first novel earned him instant success as well as a lawsuit for immorality, a charge of which he was later acquitted. Braddon's father was a failure as a solicitor, so she took up the stage to support her mother, whom she adored. She then began to write sensation fiction and was attacked for corrupting young minds, although she never actually faced a lawsuit for immorality. However, Braddon braved British morality by living out of wedlock for fourteen years with publisher John Maxwell. She raised his five children and had six of her own with him. The death of his insane wife freed Maxwell to marry Braddon. While Flaubert is still acclaimed as a writer and Braddon relegated to popular culture, both authors won notable admirers during their respective lifetimes. Flaubert formed friendships with Turgenov, Sand, and the Goncourt brothers and earned the praise of James and Guy de Maupassant among others. Braddon had

a long literary friendship with Bulwer-Lytton and also won Hardy, Dickens, Stevenson, and Thackeray as admirers.

10. Pykett, introduction to *The Doctor's Wife*, xxv. Pykett goes on to conclude: "It is in this respect that Braddon's novel can be said to have played an important part in mediating Flaubert's text into English culture" (xxv). Flaubert also directly or indirectly influenced Hardy and Eliot. Noting the centrality of Braddon's now relatively unknown work, Heywood argues that Eliot in *Middlemarch* (1872) and Hardy in *Return of the Native* (1878) indirectly borrowed from the Flaubert classic in borrowing from *The Doctor's Wife*. See two articles by Heywood: "Miss Braddon's *The Doctor's Wife*," and "A Source for *Middlemarch*." His arguments are not uniformly convincing.

11. Braddon quoted in Wolff, *Sensational Victorian*, 162.

12. Critics praised Braddon for her wholesomeness, but criticized the novel's artistic faults, despite her contention, "I have done my best with *this* book." Braddon quoted in Wolff, *Sensational Victorian*, 161.

13. Flaubert, *Madame Bovary*, 245. Subsequent references are taken from this edition.

14. Emma Bovary's dancing with the viscount is not distinguished, nor are her artistic talents. She is aggressive in her love affairs. Carla L. Peterson argues in *The Determined Reader* that Emma's "simultaneous application of contradictory models of imitation to herself serves further to complicate her quest for identity" (170). Peterson's discussion informs my own.

15. Flaubert stages a scene akin to Robert Martineau's Victorian narrative painting *The Last Chapter* (1863) included in Flint, *The Woman Reader*, 6.

16. Chaste in a way that Emma is decidedly sensual, Isabel never sees her aristocratic/poet "lover" as a real man, but as the incarnation of her romantic ideals. She rejects his "illicit" offer to go away with him. While romance reading absorbs the naive and innocent Isabel Sleaford Gilbert as much if not more so than Emma Rouault Bovary, it in no way awakens her sexuality.

17. Also see 189, where Braddon refers again to Isabel reading at meals.

18. Unlike the characters she compares him to, George has "sober common-sense" (102).

19. *The Doctor's Wife* also fits the paradigm in the following chapter on reading interests as a predictor of marital compatibility.

20. As a reader of book illustrations, Isabel joins with her fictional Victorian British and American sisters—Emma Bovary, Jane Eyre, Isabel Archer, and Maggie Tulliver.

21. Chapter titles include references to John Dryden, Alfred Tennyson, and William Shakespeare.

22. Little wonder that Dickens preferred *The Doctor's Wife* above Braddon's others. Wolff, in *Sensational Victorian*, 9, explains that Dickens's daughter Kate Perugini recalls her father favoring *The Doctor's Wife* while Thackeray, according to his daughter Anne Thackeray Ritchie, particularly liked *Lady Audley's Secret*.

23. As Pykett rightly notes, "only the most resistant readers of Dickens would be

likely to regard Edith Dombey (one of Isabel's frequently invoked heroines) as a happy role model for the young wife of a provincial doctor" (Introduction xvi).

24. At the same time that Braddon scorns Isabel's attachment to her "lover" Roland Lansdell, she exposes Gilbert's failings—his lack of imagination; his refusal to improve his home to please his wife. Braddon's decision to keep the affair platonic (in sharp contrast to Emma Bovary's affairs), satisfied the moral sensibilities of her English critics. See Heywood, "Miss Braddon's *The Doctor's Wife*," 259.

25. The final lines Roland speaks are from Tennyson's *In Memoriam*, canto iv: "an infant crying in the night; an infant crying for the light; and with no language but a cry" (392).

26. Braddon concludes that Isabel "is altogether different from the foolish wife who neglected all of a wife's duties while she sat by the mill-stream at Thurston's Crag reading the 'Revolt of Islam'" (402).

27. Undated 1864 letter from Braddon to Bulwer-Lytton, quoted in Wolff, *Sensational Victorian*, 165.

28. Bersani in the introduction to *Madame Bovary* goes on to qualify that "Now Flaubert's work is *not* a very serious attack on romantic fiction, and this fact should help us to see both the exact relation of *Madame Bovary* to a period of literary history, and the radical, 'non-historical' nature of its critique of literature" (xiii).

CHAPTER 5. THE CASE FOR COMPATIBILITY

1. See, for example, Gullette's afterword to *The Daughters of Danaus*, 493–534. Gullette includes a humorous 1899 response Caird wrote in reply to an essay topic set by the *Ladies Realm* titled "Does Marriage Hinder a Woman's Self-development?" Rosemary Ashton explores Dorothea's failure in terms of her restricted social conditions and gender in *George Eliot: A Life*, 326–28. I also recommend to the interested reader Showalter, *A Literature of Their Own* and Gilbert and Gubar, *The Madwoman in the Attic*.

2. Swan, *Courtship and Marriage*, 22.

3. George Bainton, *The Wife as Lover and Friend* (1895), 99, quoted in Flint, *The Woman Reader*, 98.

4. Mason also offers advice on how many books make up a young woman's respectable library as well as what titles to include. He advises fifty books for a small library. The Bible, *Pilgrim's Progress*, and a dictionary are among his top ten choices.

5. Limited biographical and critical material is available on Caird, who wrote to advance the woman's movement. Caird offers a brutally frank critique of marriage, home, and motherhood. A. R. Cunningham and Vicinus among others refer to Caird in their discussions of "New Woman" fiction, but Gullette, in her afterword, offers the only full-length discussion of *The Daughters of Danaus*, Caird's only novel currently in print. See the following studies: A. R. Cunningham, "The 'New Woman Fiction' of the 1890's"; Gail Cunningham, *The New Woman and the Victorian Novel*; and Vicinus, "Rediscovering the 'New Woman' of the 1890s." Caird's essays appear in recent nonfiction anthologies: Broomfield and Mitchell, *Prose by Victorian Women,*

625–53; Hamilton, "*Criminals, Idiots, Women, and Minors,*" 271–307. Caird's use of Emerson in *The Daughters of Danaus* also supports how women's reading can profitably be examined as a transatlantic phenomenon.

6. Brantlinger goes on to say, "In doing so, it offers a striking instance of the way many novels between 1700 and 1900 express ambivalence about—sometimes, outright contempt for—novels and novel-reading" (*The Reading Lesson* 4).

7. Kelly, "Reading Aloud in *Mansfield Park.*"

8. Austen, *Mansfield Park*, 25. Subsequent references are to this edition.

9. For the origins of the discussion, see, for example, Mudrick, *Jane Austen*, 161–67, or Trilling, "Jane Austen and *Mansfield Park,*" 116–18. Kelly also refers to this controversy in "Reading Aloud in *Mansfield Park,*" 32.

10. Eliot, *Middlemarch*, 112. Subsequent references are to this edition.

11. Wheeler, *The Art of Allusion*, takes the phrase which Dr. Johnson borrowed from John Dryden in his *Life of Milton* (from *The Lives of the English Poets* [1779–81]): "He saw Nature, as Dryden expresses it, *through the spectacles of books;* and on most occasions calls learning to his assistance" (Wheeler 78). This phrase becomes a central lens that Wheeler uses to read Dorothea and Casaubon's ill-fated relationship.

12. In his discussion of *Middlemarch* in *Woman's Work and Worth*, advice book writer Adams recognizes that Dorothea "dressed him up in the colours of her own imagination" (146).

13. Eliot indicates at one point that "But for her visitors Dorothea too might have been shut up in the library" (360).

14. In a later discussion, Ladislaw states, "The subject Mr. Casaubon has chosen is as changing as chemistry: new discoveries are constantly making new points of view. Who wants a system on the basis of the four elements, or a book to refute Paracelsus? Do you not see that it is no use now to be crawling a little way after men of the last century—men like Bryant—and correcting their mistakes?" (254).

15. See 903, chapter 21, note 1, of *Middlemarch* for W. J. Harvey's commentary to page 240.

16. Eliot notes, "Having once embarked on your marital voyage, it is impossible not to be aware that you make no way and that the sea is not within sight—that, in fact, you are exploring an enclosed basin" (228).

17. Ironically, Valeria Du Prel "gave no encouragement to certain of her companion's most vehement sentiments. She seemed to yearn for exactly that side of life from which the younger shrank with so much horror" (67). Having revolted against tradition, the middle-aged Du Prel finds herself uncomfortably alone in the world. She urges Hadria to marry.

18. Interestingly, Hadria does take along Martha, an illegitimate child whom she "adopts."

19. To date, no record exists of Caird's personal library. Although we associate Emerson with Henry David Thoreau, Bronson Alcott, Margaret Fuller, and the Transcendentalist movement, Thomas Carlyle first introduced Emerson to British readers in 1841; although Emerson's ideas did not take hold immediately in England, they steadily gained influence as the century advanced. Emerson met Carlyle in the early

1830s while traveling abroad to improve his health, and their ensuing friendship led to reciprocal benefit. Emerson brought Carlyle's works to the attention of American readers. Carlyle introduced Emerson's essays to the British reading public. Carlyle wrote in his 1841 introduction to "Essays, First Series," "No editor or Reprinter can expect such a Book ever to become popular here." Carlyle quoted in Goddard, introduction to *Essays*, xv.

20. Hadria's brother Ernest, an ardent Emerson admirer, presumably presents on "Character" before the novel begins.

21. Emerson's first series of *Essays* (1841) contains his most famous and optimistic "Self-Reliance."

22. "Fate" emerged relatively late in Emerson's career, yet it exhibits an intellectual intensity evident in his earlier prose.

23. For a general introduction to Emerson's works, see Yannella, *Ralph Waldo Emerson;* Yannella provides commentary on "Character" and "Fate."

24. Caird, *The Daughters of Danaus,* 8. Subsequent references are to this edition. The final sentence in Emerson actually reads, "Events are the children of his body and mind."

25. See Emerson, *Essays,* 273. Hadria paraphrases Emerson, rather, as "*If the soul is strong enough, it can overcome circumstance*" (11).

26. Hadria even wonders "whether her father also had been born with certain instincts, which the accidents of life had stifled or failed to develop" (36). Likewise, "A few volumes of poetry, and other works of imagination, bore testimony to the lost sides of her [mother's] nature" (33), submerged because of circumstance.

27. Here Caird anticipates a line of argument that Virginia Woolf develops in *A Room of One's Own* regarding what might have happened if Shakespeare had had a talented sister named Judith.

28. In chapter 4, Hadria similarly concludes, "Terrible was the tyranny of circumstance! What had Emerson been dreaming of?" (36).

29. This line reads exactly the same in Emerson's "Fate," though a comma is inserted between "fortunes" and "by."

30. This reference, like the title of the book, reveals Caird's intimacy with Greek mythology. The book title alludes to the fifty daughters of Danaus, married en masse, condemned to draw water in sieves from a fathomless well for murdering their husbands on their wedding night.

31. The robe is stained with the blood of the Centaur Nessus, whom Hercules killed, and the agony Hercules bears ultimately leads him to lay his body down to die on a pyre.

32. Even if a woman could use "the power of the human will to break the back of circumstance" (62), the effort extended, Caird concludes, "leaves one prone, with a victory that arrives ironically too late" (62). Late in the novel, Hadria's sister validates her view that fate does not always conform to our natures: "I can't believe, for instance, that among all those millions in the East End, not *one* man or woman, for all these ages, was born with great capacities, which better conditions might have allowed to come to fruition. I think you were right after all. It is a matter of relation" (462).

33. Although Emerson spoke in support of women's equality and ardently opposed slavery, Caird criticizes him for failing to consider class and gender issues in his discourse on circumstance and will. On class, see, for example, Caird's "The Duel of the Sexes," 112; she advances, "Why do we never hear of a genius arising among the slum-populations of our great cities . . . ?" To Caird, the Victorian home imprisons intellectually curious women, whom she likens to chained dogs and caged prisoners, trapped in a marital system which amounts to lawful injustice.

34. In addition, not all of her quotations from Emerson are exact.

35. For example, when Du Prel suggests that Columbus might not have sailed had he listened to his relatives, we glimpse Caird's humor through Hubert's retort: "And how do you know they were not right?" (162).

36. Hadria at first refuses Temperley. At the end of part 1, Hadria gives way to pressure, likely to escape her repressive home. The night she accepts Hubert, she is also dazzled by the moonlight. Her beloved sister, Algitha, pronounces news of her marriage the "worst" and suggests that Hadria, against her better judgment, "has been led into accepting Hubert Temperley" (144).

37. Hadria tends her ailing mother, who has fallen dangerously ill because of financial misfortune and her daughters' waywardness. Mrs. Fullerton blames her illness on the willful actions of her daughters, particularly Hadria. Algitha also acts against the grain of tradition when she decides to go to London to do settlement work, rather than stay at home until marriage.

38. Hadria cares for Martha when her mother, a fallen woman, dies. Theobald finally comes forward as Martha's rightful parent to spite Hadria for spurning him.

CHAPTER 6. AN ILLUSTRATIVE GALLERY OF VICTORIAN BRITISH AND AMERICAN WOMEN READERS

1. This practice is also used in early photography; see, for example, Sekula, "The Body and the Archive."

2. Leading British painters such as Sir John Everett Millais, Dante Gabriel Rossetti, and Arthur Hughes, among others, dabbled in the lucrative field of book illustration. The American painter N. C. Wyeth also turned to book illustration. Moreover, author-illustrators, such as Thackeray and Carroll, used two art forms to convey one cohesive vision.

3. I have consulted with Linda Docherty about my application of these pictorial types to book illustration. She concurs that what I have called the "social reader" is a logical extension of the interrupted type and suggests it can be found in painting of this period as well. She also suggests the term "antiquated" to describe a satirical reworking of the honorific venerable type from portraiture.

4. Flint in *The Woman Reader* includes and discusses this *carte de visite* on 319–21. She suggests this is Patmore's second wife, Marianne Caroline Byles, who married Patmore in 1864, following the death of Emilia Augusta Andrew, his first wife.

5. Phelps, "The Angel Over the Right Shoulder," 17. Subsequent references are to this edition.

6. Both portraits appear in Docherty's "Women as Readers," 362, 365. In *The Country School*, Homer illustrates patriarchal values—the girls in the classroom are left to tutor each other.

7. While this movement did result in improvements in schooling for women, domestic feminists endorsed separate spheres for men and women. See Docherty, "Women as Readers," 361–62.

8. Dickens, *David Copperfield*, 708. This edition includes all of the original illustrations. Agnes creates a haven for Mr. Wickfield despite the fact that his love for his child, by his own admission, becomes "diseased" (708). Rarely does Agnes venture from the home despite the taint imbued by the growing incompetence of her father. Subsequent references are to this edition.

9. On first meeting David, Agnes confides: "Papa couldn't spare me to go anywhere else, . . . His housekeeper must be in his house, you know" (199). Dickens takes pains to describe how Agnes "set glasses for her father, and a decanter of port wine" and how "Agnes made the tea, and presided over it" (195).

10. The unopened book in a later dramatic image, "I Am the Bearer of Evil Tidings," signifies the finality of life for Steerforth and two of Dickens's eccentric women: the proud Mrs. Steerforth, obsessed with love for her arrogant son, and the scarred enraged Rosa Dartle, equally consumed by her love for James Steerforth, who destroys her beauty. As David comes to tell them of Steerforth's death, he glances at a closed book on the floor positioned midway among them. The closed book symbolizes the death of David's "bad angel" and the spiritual deaths of these two women consumed by a diseased love for a young man who lived a life of shame and fancy.

11. Interestingly, Dora calls herself "such a little goose" (536), a once endearing but now seemingly condescending term that the patriarchal Doctor John uses to refer to his wife in Charlotte Perkins Gilman's "The Yellow Wall-Paper."

12. David's schoolmaster, Doctor Strong, engaged in writing a dictionary, is repeatedly shown reading. In "I Return to the Doctor's after the Party," Annie Strong sits at the feet of her husband in a room brimming with books. He is too absorbed in his paper to appreciate the arresting beauty of his young wife, here wearing a low-cut dress, accentuating her sensuality. Although Annie Strong ultimately emerges as the character whose words prompt David to realize the folly of his first marriage, this image uses the act of reading to enshrine a nonsexual form of love that Dickens reveres but readers today find peculiar and unsatisfying. David enters the scene just as Doctor Strong is "patting her [Annie's] head, in his fatherly way, and saying he was a merciless drone to let her tempt him into reading on; and he would have her go to bed" (214). In "Mr. Dick Fulfils my Aunt's Prediction," Annie again kneels at her husband's feet in a library. The Old Soldier holds a paper but does not gaze upon it—her eyes fix upon Doctor Strong, who turns from his reading here to look paternally at Annie.

13. The Oxford edition of *Dombey and Son* includes some of Browne's original illustrations.

14. Rose Maylie helps return Oliver to his rightful home and family and is richly

rewarded at the end of the text when Oliver exclaims: "'Not aunt,' cried Oliver... 'I'll never call her aunt—sister, my own dear sister, that something taught my heart to love so dearly from the first'" (337). Her visual characterization suffers, in part, because of Cruikshank's limitations in drawing an attractive woman. Ironically, Rose seems fresher and younger in this original composition, which Dickens rejected. For more information on the rejected "Fireside Plate," see Patten, *George Cruikshank's Life, Times, and Art*, vol. 2, 87.

15. Dickens, *A Tale of Two Cities* (New York: Penguin Books, 1997), 29. Subsequent references are to this edition.

16. At a distance stands Lucie's other ardent admirer, Sydney Carton, who gazes at her with longing.

17. Thackeray, *Vanity Fair* (Oxford: Oxford University Press, 1983), 7. This edition includes 193 illustrations by the author. Subsequent references are to this edition.

18. See also Sutherland, introduction to *Vanity Fair*, xxii. Thackeray contrasts Amelia to her "sharp"-tongued, dangerous, though more ingenious friend, Becky Sharp, the decided heroine of the novel. Becky rises until a crisis in the novel, and Amelia falls in fortune until a happy turn of events. Thackeray even calls Amelia a clinging "parasite" when she finally joins with Dobbin (871).

19. Browne also once casts the eccentric Aunt Betsey Trotwood in the pose of an interrupted reader in "Traddles Makes a Figure in Parliament, and I Report Him" in *David Copperfield*. The open book faces down on her lap as she and Mr. Dick enact a Parliamentary scene that David, practicing his reporting skills, attempts to write up.

20. David and Sapirstein, "Reading the Illustrations in *Tom Sawyer*," 26.

21. The illustrator could possibly be Edward Austin Abbey; the illustrator's initials match those Austin used for part of his signature as identified in Castagno's *American Artists*, 1.

22. In her series, Holley presents conservative feminism: family and farm life must come first, but women should have the rights of education, equal pay, and the vote. From Holley's first novel titled *My Opinions and Betsey Bobbet's* (1873), she tells her story in twenty-one novels and countless short stories. Holley tackles the chauvinism of the church, race problems, intemperance, and marriage without genuine affection, and she became a spokeswoman for various causes in which she exudes her wisdom. Samantha became a heroine to countless women readers for espousing women's rights of citizenship and humanity as well as her intellectual savvy.

Two of Twain's illustrators, Williams and Kemble, provided illustrations for Holley's books along with a range of other talented artists. Williams, who illustrated several volumes in the series, fixed an image of Samantha, which recurs across the series with some variations (See David and Sapirstein, "Reading the Illustrations in *Tom Sawyer*," 29). For example, Williams's robust Samantha with glasses and hair pulled back in a bun has more masculine features in illustrations by Frederick Opper and Baron C. de Grimm, who enlarge Samantha's nose and also make her thinner. Likewise, akin to Twain's Widow Douglas, Holley's Samantha, at times, assumes moral and intellectual authority, seemly acquired at the cost of beauty and conventional femininity. And she becomes a source of amusement.

23. Copans describes this image in "Dream Blocks," 254, and reprints the image on 255.

24. Whitney, *Verses for Jock and Joan*, 18, line 2.

25. See Lister, *Victorian Narrative Paintings*, plate 8, opposite page 46.

26. Although Alcott did not wish to write this book, it established her place as a writer in the growing market of juvenile literature. Writers as diverse as Jane Addams in the nineteenth century and Cynthia Ozick in the twentieth reread it countless times, and its popularity has never waned. See Sicherman, "Reading *Little Women*," 246–47. Although designed as a girl's story for the expanding market of gender-specific fiction, the text, read by those of both sexes and all ages, is instrumental in our understanding of reading and the creation of female identity in a nineteenth-century context.

27. May Alcott was a more serious artist than Amy in the novel, but the images were not well received. See, for example, a review by David A. Randall and John T. Winterich titled "One Hundred Good Novels," 87, in Stern's *Critical Essays on Louisa May Alcott* and an anonymous "Review of *Little Women*, part 1, 1868," also in Stern, 81. May Alcott was aware of her shortcomings, and the pictures were first replaced with illustrations by a professional though unidentified artist. Having seen the four original illustrations, I concur that they are poorly executed.

28. Along with *Little Women*, these staples in the Victorian home remained top choices well into the twentieth century, as indicated in a 1927 *New York Times* reading survey. High school students ranked *Little Women* first, before the Bible and *Pilgrim's Progress*. It is still considered among the best American books for preadolescent and adolescent girls. See "*Little Women* Leads Poll," *New York Times*, March 22, 1927, reprinted in Stern, *Critical Essays on Louisa May Alcott*, 84. Alcott uses *Pilgrim's Progress* to frame the pilgrimages of Meg, Jo, Beth, and Amy in *Little Women*; however, in focusing on good deeds and self-discipline, Alcott secularly recasts the Calvinistic preoccupation with sin and obedience in Bunyan's Christian allegory.

29. Harvé Stein also virtually recreates this domestic reading circle in a 1932 illustrated edition. However, Stein downplays Marmee's importance in excluding her from the reading circle and placing father March's letter in Meg's hands.

30. See Ellis, *The Mothers of England*, 196.

31. For example, a small boy builds a fanciful castle in the air, a little girl observes a spider's web, a child dresses up to go to the zoo, and a mother reads aloud a favorite book to her daughter.

32. The mother holds the left edge of the book in her left hand, but her right arm curls around her daughter, nestled close to her; her daughter holds open the right side of the book with her right hand.

33. Higgins, *Dream Blocks*, 14, lines 9–14.

34. For more information on Belsham and other books Alcott includes in *Little Women*, I recommend Crisler's "Alcott's Reading in *Little Women*."

35. Burnett, *Little Saint Elizabeth and Other Stories*, 19. Subsequent references are to this edition.

36. With the untimely death of Aunt Chlotilde, Elizabeth returns to New York City to live with her uncle, but she remains true to her religious teachings and longs to give alms to the poor of Normandy and New York. Risking her life to sell her family jewels for money for the poor, Elizabeth, along with a kindly doctor, succeeds in reforming her rich, uncharitable uncle while she learns "to live a more natural and child-like life" (55).

37. Although Episcopal clergyman Horace Lorenzo Connolly originally urged Nathanial Hawthorne to use this story as the basis for a novel, Hawthorne declined. Longfellow asked Hawthorne's permission to write it in verse form as *Evangeline*.

38. Longfellow, *Evangeline*, (Boston: Fields, Osgood, and Co., 1869), 153. Subsequent references are to this edition.

39. See, for example, John Singleton Copley's *Mrs. Sylvanus Bourne* (1766) or Joseph Badger's *Mrs. John Edwards* (c. 1750–60); both are included in Docherty's "Women as Readers," 346–47.

40. In this respect, the antiquated type responds to the wisdom of Beecher and Beecher Stowe in *The American Woman's Home:* "The blessed privileges of the family state are not confined to those who rear children of their own. Any woman who can earn a livelihood, as every woman should be trained to do, can take a properly qualified female associate, and institute a family of their own, receiving to its heavenly influences the orphan, the sick, the homeless, and the sinful, and by motherly devotion train them to follow the self-denying example of Christ, in educating his earthly children for true happiness in this life and for his eternal home" (20).

41. Antiquated readers' lack of femininity, suggesting they have traded it for knowledge, recalls an argument against higher education for women, which Cruikshank captures in his 1847 caricature "My Wife Is a Woman of Mind" (fig. 1): a wife will neglect home and family if she develops her intellect.

42. Twain's works were sold by subscription, and illustration became an influential sales tool. Agents carefully examined full-, half-, or three-quarter-page illustrations, as well as the large chapter-title illustrations (or headpieces) to glean plot, theme, and characterization and determine if potential readers could easily be lured into a story. Works sold by subscription were generously illustrated with hundreds of pictures per volume in a range of sizes, as the Twain volumes and Merrill's 1880 edition of *Little Women* reveal.

Akin to Dickens, Twain considered the role of illustration in the creation and editing of his text, and in some instances the image influenced his decision on how much description to include in the text. For more information, I recommend David and Sapirstein's essays "Reading the Illustrations in *Huckleberry Finn*" and "Reading the Illustrations in *Tom Sawyer*."

43. Twain, *Adventures of Huckleberry Finn* (New York and Oxford: Oxford University Press, 1996), 17. Subsequent references are to this edition.

44. See David and Sapirstein, "Reading the Illustrations in *Huckleberry Finn*," 33.

45. Williams shows her with props of gentility or acting in stereotypical ways:

knitting in the final illustration (274), sobbing over Tom's mischief (100), holding an open book (presumably the Bible) in her lap (130), or rejoicing that Tom really wrote a note on a piece of bark to explain that he has gone pirating (160).

46. To Twain and his publisher, Elisha Bliss, Williams seemed the natural choice to illustrate *Tom Sawyer*. Williams had successfully illustrated other Twain works for the American Publishing Company. For more information, see David and Sapirstein, "Reading the Illustrations in *Tom Sawyer*," 24–31.

47. Twain, *The Adventures of Tom Sawyer* (New York and Oxford: Oxford University Press, 1996), 108. Subsequent references are to this edition.

48. The Ishmaelites were carrying the balm of Gilead when they bought Joseph from his brothers. For further examination of the biblical references in this passage, see Rev. 6:8, Mal. 4:2, and Jer. 8:22; 46:11.

49. Two of the titles of the books on their mantelpiece—"Paradise Regained" and "Loves of the Angels"—announce David's "great expectations" in making this visit to Dora Spenlow's aunts. However, the pair of lovebirds in the cage, the two goldfish in their bowl, and the paintings on the wall (titled *The Momentous Question*, *Arcadia*, and *The Last Appeal*) also make clear the reason for David's visit to Dora's maiden aunts.

50. Docherty includes Hassam's *Summer Sunlight* in "Women as Readers," 369.

51. Carroll, *Alice's Adventures under Ground*, 89. Subsequent references are to this edition.

52. Burnett, *Editha's Burglar*, 11. Subsequent references are to this edition.

53. Emily Davies, "On Secondary Instruction as Relating to Girls" (1864), quoted in Flint, *The Woman Reader*, 121.

54. Graham saves Mary's respectability by arranging for her lover Fitzallen to marry her.

55. Merrill casts Jo as a social reader, an interrupted reader (for example, tending to her dying sister), and an isolated reader. A full-page illustration titled "With her head in Jo's lap, while the wind blew healthfully over her" shows a solicitous Jo laying down her book to search for faint signs of color in her dying sister Beth's faded, thin cheeks.

56. The image of Meg is a chapter headpiece to chapter 3 titled "The Laurence Boy." Merrill places apples beside Meg, suggesting the eating of apples is as important, if not more so, than reading *The Heir of Redclyffe*.

CHAPTER 7. THE BOOK AS PORTAL

1. Keats credits Cortez with discovering South America, rather than Balboa, as we now commonly recognize. The sestet reads, "Then felt I like some watcher of the skies / When a new planet swims into his ken; / Or like stout Cortez when with eagle eyes / He star'd at the Pacific—and all his men / Look'd at each other with a wild surmise— / Silent, upon a peak in Darien."

2. See, for example, Radway, *Reading the Romance*, and Tompkins, "Masterpiece

Theater." This Tompkins piece included in *Falling into Theory* comes from her book *Sensational Designs* (1985).

3. See Darton, *Children's Books in England,* 263–69, particularly 268.

4. Nonetheless, Alice's pose in the opening illustration and Carroll's remarks that a "very sleepy" Alice is "considering in her own mind" subtly introduce the dream motif (1).

5. See Carroll, *Alice's Adventures under Ground,* 1, and *Alice's Adventures in Wonderland* in *The Annotated Alice,* 26. Subsequent references are to these editions.

6. Sir John Tenniel elected not to illustrate this scene for *Alice's Adventures in Wonderland,* choosing the white rabbit as his first image. Tenniel also did not illustrate another memorable scene: Alice as "all head" when she shrinks suddenly after nibbling a mushroom stalk, and "she felt a violent blow on her chin: it had struck her foot" (*under Ground* 61).

7. Alice, the Red Queen, and the Mock Turtle echo Carroll's advice to "look at the picture" and underscore his authorial intention. The dialogue commonly uses verbs relating to sight. For example, "to see" in nominative and verb forms appears thirty-eight times in the ninety-page manuscript. For more discussion of Carroll's life, I recommend Morton N. Cohen's *Lewis Carroll: A Biography.*

8. Tenniel pictures Alice near a text in one image in *Through the Looking Glass* (1871). On a train, she sits opposite to a gentleman (presumably a caricature of Benjamin Disraeli), dressed in white paper and reading a newspaper.

9. Southey's work first appeared on January 17, 1799 in *The Morning Post.*

10. "Besetting sin" is a Victorian expression meaning the sin to which one is most prone.

11. See Hedges, "Afterword to 'The Yellow Wallpaper,'" 132. Gilman's story invites a range of critical perspectives: psychological, linguistic, feminist, new historicist, biographical, sociological, and a combination of the above. Golden, *The Captive Imagination,* offers a good compilation of criticism by leading scholars. It also includes the illustrations printed with Gilman's story in its first publication in *New England Magazine* (January 1892).

12. Some of the signatures of the illustrators are difficult to decipher. For example, "The Giant Wistaria" appeared in *New England Magazine* NS 4 (June 1891): 480–85 with two illustrations by two different artists, G. Satig(?) and Stacy Tolman. "The Lake of Mrs. Johnsmith" appeared in *The Criterion* 18 (October 22, 1898): 3–4 with three illustrations by G. H. Underwood. And "Mrs. Beazley's Deeds" first appeared in *Woman's World* 27 (March 1911): 12–13, 58, with three illustrations by Pobein(?).

13. For more information on Hatfield, see Golden, "The Pictures on the Paper."

14. Both the 1892 and 1899 editions are widely reprinted. The quotes are taken from Gilman's original manuscript reprinted in *"The Yellow Wall-Paper" and Selected Stories of Charlotte Perkins Gilman,* 41. Subsequent references are to this edition.

15. John urges the narrator to exert "proper self-control" (40).

16. See Golden, "The Writing of 'The Yellow Wallpaper.'"

17. See Knight, *The Diaries of Charlotte Perkins Gilman*. For example, Gilman records receiving *Through the Looking Glass* for Christmas of 1882, when she was 22 years old (Mon. December 25, 1882, 1: 165).

18. See Dimock's essay on "Feminism, New Historicism, and the Reader," 89; in this essay, Dimock includes a discussion of "The Yellow Wall-Paper" and suggests that in the absence of any "competent" reader within the story, we look outside the story to an "implied reader" (90), a model of reading that Wolfgang Iser proposes. That this reader—an authoritative, educated, professional woman—did not exist in the 1890s is the charge of the story, that is, to usher in such a reader.

19. Gilman scholars interpret the numerous spellings and referents for wallpaper in the manuscript, the 1892 version, and the 1899 version variously as a means to present the wallpaper as an ever changing untraditional text; as an intentional tool to create ambiguity about a referent resisting easy analysis; or, more mundanely, as a reflection of Gilman's notoriously inconsistent spelling. See, in particular, Feldstein's essay "Reader, Text, and Ambiguous Referentiality."

20. The third and final illustration of the narrator as a wild-haired madwoman recalls Brontë's description of Bertha Mason locked away in Thornfield Hall and supports the view that the narrator is destroyed. Bits of the paper she has ripped from the walls lay strewn on the floor. Rather than look merely at the final outcome of the narrator creeping over her husband, we might more positively focus on the success Gilman's narrator achieves as Fetterley notes in "Reading About Reading" and Gilbert and Gubar suggest in *The Madwoman in the Attic*.

21. Fetterley, "Reading about Reading," 257. She compares "The Yellow Wall-Paper" to Susan Glaspell's "A Jury of Her Peers" and Edgar Allen Poe's "The Murders in the Rue Morgue."

22. See Hochman, "The Reading Habit," 90–91. Hochman further argues that "Gilman designed her tale to discourage her readers from identifying with the narrator as the narrator identifies with the woman in the wall-paper's subpattern" (99), and she equates Gilman's landmark tale with the type of addictive reading lambasted by antifiction critics of the period (102). Hochman thoroughly grounds her article in nineteenth-century views about the novel-reading habit. While provocative, her argument that we read "The Yellow Wall-Paper" as a cautionary tale that Gilman intended as a model of how *not* to read, of consequence, sidesteps the ambiguity of the ending (which stands in stark contrast to cautionary tales of addictive readers). Hochman lends an intentionality to Gilman that she does not substantiate and, of lesser concern, bases claims on Gilman's autobiography, generally recognized in Gilman circles as an unreliable source given Gilman's propensity to consciously fashion her identity. I shared some of this critique with Hochman when I heard a shorter version of the paper also titled "The Reading Habit and 'The Yellow Wall-Paper,'" presented at the Third International Charlotte Perkins Gilman Conference, Columbia, S.C., March 30–April 1, 2001.

23. I am indebted to Carol Farley Kessler's comment made at The Third International Charlotte Perkins Gilman Conference, Columbia, S.C., March 30–April 1, 2001.

24. I thank my colleague Charlotte Goodman for calling this insight to my attention at the Third International Charlotte Perkins Gilman Conference, Columbia, S.C., March 30–April 1, 2001.

25. The narrator confides in the sixth entry, "At night, in any kind of light, in twilight, candlelight, lamplight, and worst of all by moonlight—it becomes *bars!* The outside pattern, I mean" (47).

26. For a fuller linguistic reading, see Golden, "The Writing of 'The Yellow Wallpaper.'" This reading perceives the narrator as reader and writer, a point often disputed if the narrator's madness leads simply to defeat (for example, who finishes the story?). For more discussion of this seminal point, see Golden, *The Captive Imagination*, particularly essays by Feldstein and Golden.

27. See Golden, "The Writing of 'The Yellow Wallpaper,'" 304.

28. See George Henry Lewes, "The Heart and the Brain," quoted in Flint, *The Woman Reader*, 55.

29. The complete title for the book is *Woman Physiologically Considered as to Mind, Morals, Matrimonial Slavery, Infidelity and Divorce* (1840), 12, 28. It is quoted in Flint, *The Woman Reader*, 54–55.

30. Dorothea Beale, 81, quoted in Flint, *The Woman Reader*, 122.

CHAPTER 8. "WHAT IS THE USE OF A BOOK?"

1. A similar line occurs in *Alice's Adventures under Ground*, which reads, "where is the use of a book, thought Alice, without pictures or conversations?" (1). I refer to that version in chapter 7.

2. The pictorial capital alludes to Benjamin Robert Haydon's series of paintings titled *Napoleon Musing at St. Helena*. B. R. Haydon (1786–1846) began painting Napoleon, whom he much admired, in 1829 and from then on produced over thirty paintings of the Emperor, many called *Napoleon Musing at St. Helena*. Hatted like Napoleon, Becky wears a uniform over her petticoats as she gazes at the sea from a high cliff and holds a spy glass in her hand. Becky, like Napoleon, is in exile, barred from her homeland. In "A Vagabond Chapter," Thackeray writes, "She felt she was alone, quite alone: and the far-off shining cliffs of England were impassable to her" (816).

3. The elderly Raphael Benosa, an Italian moneychanger, declares a vendetta between his family and that of Stephen Vanderstein. In a book with iron clasps, Benosa notes the cause of the feud, not to be disclosed until the vengeance is consummated. Before dying, Raphael Benosa has the satisfaction of knowing he has brought about the death of Stephen Vanderstein in his prime.

4. Along with Browne (Phiz), John Leech, and Alfred Crowquill, Thackeray applied for the post of illustrator of *The Posthumous Papers of the Pickwick Club* to replace Robert Seymour following his unfortunate suicide. Dickens was not satisfied with the work of Robert Buss, who followed Seymour. For more discussion, see Jane R. Cohen, *Charles Dickens and His Original Illustrators*, 51–58.

Melville's *William Makepeace Thackeray* (1: 103–4) includes Thackeray's own speech made following Dickens's at the Royal Academy dinner on May 29, 1859; Thackeray claims that his initial "disappointment" by Dickens instigated his career shift. He never would have tried to be a writer had Dickens hired him, in his words, to be a "designer of pictures," the "object of my early ambition" (1: 103). For additional information on Thackeray's artistic training, see Ray, *The Uses of Adversity,* 170–72. Ray also notes Thackeray's attempts to be an illustrator for Dickens and William Harrison Ainsworth (189). Popular romance writer Ainsworth (whose work Cruikshank frequently illustrated) contracted Thackeray as illustrator for his serial *Crichton* (1837). Thackeray's marriage plans interfered with the completion of the *Crichton* drawings, and his later sketches did not please Ainsworth. *Crichton* appeared without illustration.

5. See a letter to W. S. Williams from C. Bell dated March 11, 1848, in Shorter, *The Brontës,* 1: 402; therein Charlotte Brontë calls Thackeray "a wizard of a draughtsman; touched with his pencil, paper lives." Trollope in *Thackeray* admits that "unlike Hogarth, he had never learned to draw" (30), but concludes that "had he persisted [in his drawing] he would have been a second Hogarth" (30). Scholarship focusing on Thackeray's inadequacy as an artist is exhaustive. See, for instance, Hannah, "The Author's Own Candles," 119–27, particularly 120–22. In his chapter titled "A Voice Concurrent or Prophetical" in *Victorian Novelists and Their Illustrators,* Harvey is critical (79–82) but praises Thackeray for realizing "the possibilities of the illuminated letter" (84).

6. Thackeray also depicts males as readers. In the opening chapter of *Vanity Fair,* Thackeray writes, "All which details, I have no doubt, Jones, who reads this book at his Club, will pronounce to be excessively foolish, trivial, twaddling, and ultra-sentimental" (8), and also draws Jones reading. He draws William Dobbin (51) reading the *Arabian Nights,* and he features Captain Rawdon Crawley reading the letters Becky writes him under the alias of Miss Eliza Styles (188). Thackeray also depicts house servants reading. Mr. Bowls, servant to wealthy Miss Crawley, is shown reading aloud the religious tract "the *Fire and the Frying-Pan* to his aide de camp in a loud and ghostly voice" (431). For more on this topic, I recommend Kate Flint, "Women, Men and the Reading of *Vanity Fair.*"

7. The harlequin as buffoon dates to the Commedia Dell'arte, an early form of low Italian comedy that influenced the English stage through pantomine, a theatrical form which, in turn, inspired Thackeray in his creation of *Vanity Fair.* While the notion of the Shakespearian fool might suggest there is meaning to Thackeray's seeming buffoonery, Thackeray consciously casts himself in the role of humble harlequin, asking to be excused for unveiling actions presumably objectionable to his readers. For more information on Commedia Dell'arte, see Holman, *A Handbook to Literature,* 112–13.

8. In fact, in the pictorial capital to chapter 18, Thackeray shows himself as a jester bowing low to the figure of Napoleon to illustrate the lines, "Our surprised story now finds itself for a moment among very famous personages, and hanging on to the skirts of history" (211).

9. Brantlinger also calls Becky a representative of "bourgeois businessmen" (*The Reading Lesson*, 129): "Becky is an extraordinary example of that key, usually male, bourgeois virtue, self-help" (130). Brantlinger aligns Becky with Defoe's heroines Moll Flanders and Roxana as well as Thackeray's Jones (129).

10. In *The Reading Lesson*, Brantlinger makes a similar point, 130–31, and quotes from *Vanity Fair*.

11. *The Compact Edition of the Oxford English Dictionary*, 1st ed., s.v. "fling."

12. In *The Reading Lesson*, Brantlinger makes a similar observation: "And Becky's initial act of rebellion—throwing Dr. Johnson's *Dictionary* out of the coach window as she and Amelia leave the Miss Pinkertons' academy—is hardly one of illiteracy or even of miseducation, but can instead be construed as a rejection of all forms of literate culture that do not serve her immediate self-interest of getting ahead in the world" (129).

13. Interestingly, Thackeray positions Becky slightly to the left of the portrait of a massive Joseph riding atop an elephant during his Indian exploits; the portrait (which surfaces later as a plot device) emphasizes that Jos, at this point in the novel, has not been hooked.

14. Thackeray has planted visual and verbal evidence to lead us to suspect Becky is the literal murderer of Jos—just as he implies her adultery through the siren motif—but he offers no physical evidence to convict her of a legal crime aside from the images which impact upon the suspended nature of the narrative. That Becky's fictive role as Clytemnestra and her character become one through "Becky's Second Appearance in the Character of Clytemnestra" helps to explain why one contemporary, Elizabeth Rigby (later Lady Eastlake), wrote a letter to the *Quarterly Review*, December 1848, to "advise our readers to cut out that picture of our heroine's 'Second Appearance as Clytemnestra,' which casts so uncomfortable a glare over the latter part of the volume." See Elizabeth Rigby in the *Quarterly Review* (Dec. 1848), quoted in Meisel, *Realizations*, 338. The case of Clytemnestra demonstrates how Thackeray's representational "realizations," rather than his highly allegorical pictorial capitals, create difficulties for his ambiguous narrative and compromise the unity of text and illustration as one art form. Although Thackeray leaves the crime unresolved, Becky's solicitors—Messrs. Burke, Thurtell, and Hayes—bear the names of contemporary murderers. Making a word play on "thieves," Thackeray installs their office in "Thavies" Inn. Jos's insurance company only reluctantly pays Jos's life insurance annuity to Becky. The company, presumably, suspects Becky's guilt of a legal crime. However, the insurance company stands to profit by this action.

15. Thackeray later states in chapter 44 that "Delilah had imprisoned him and cut his hair off, too" (578) in describing Becky with a now tamed Rawdon when they are visiting Lady Jane and Sir Pitt Crawley following the elder Sir Pitt's death.

16. In addition to calling Becky's flinging of the Johnson's *Dictionary* an "heroical act" (13), Thackeray states, for example, in chapter 30, "If this is a novel without a hero, at least let us lay claim to a heroine" (369).

17. For more on Thackeray as ambiguous novelist, see, for example, McMaster's

chapters on "Narrative Technique: *Vanity Fair,*" 1–49, and "Ambivalent Relationships," 177–224, in *Thackeray: The Major Novels;* Meisel's chapter on "The Paradox of the Comedian: Thackeray and Goethe," 322–50, in *Realizations;* and Flint, "Women, Men and the Reading of *Vanity Fair,*" 246–48.

18. Steyne is "stained" by his intentions, whether or not they are consummated. Thackeray gives us no real reason to believe Steyne is "orthodox." Discovering Becky alone with Steyne, Rawdon, in fury, "tore the diamond ornament out of her breast, and flung it at Lord Steyne. It cut him on his bald forehead. Steyne wore the scar to his dying day" (676). Evidence mounts against Becky's sexual innocence; for example, good Lady Jane Crawley refuses to let Becky in her house. But Thackeray simultaneously offers counter evidence. Rawdon challenges Lord Steyne to a duel to protect his wife's honor.

Critics of the day never cite Becky as an honorable character. Adams in *Woman's Work and Worth* raises Eliot's Dinah Morris of *Adam Bede* and Charlotte Brontë's Shirley of *Shirley* as worthy characters to emulate (135). Swan, author of *Courtship and Marriage, and the Gentle Art of Home-Making* (1893), criticizes Becky's maudlin angelic counterpart, Amelia Sedley, for being overly sentimental and spineless, but she does not suggest readers emulate Becky in her stead (25).

19. The image of Becky as murderess gives lasting shape to what Thackeray refrains most from speaking about: Becky's legal crime. In the nineteenth century, the power of assuming a role other than oneself functions as a compromising literary symbol of moral peril for a woman. Acting raises important questions concerning the conflation of performance with life. Performing can be but an imitation of a feeling which the actress need not possess, but for Becky to act the role of a bloody murderess equally suggests she knows how to act this way. For more discussion on this point, see Meisel, "The Paradox of the Comedian: Thackeray and Goethe," in *Realizations,* 333.

20. Thackeray offers counter assertions to soften her moral culpability. When Becky maintains, "I am innocent" (677), Rawdon entertains this possibility—"It may be so" (688), and Sir Pitt defends Becky to the outraged Lady Jane—"Upon my word, my love, I think you do Mrs. Crawley injustice" (696). The pictorial capitals of Becky as a comely creature of the sea (chapter 44) and as a diabolical, writhing siren (chapter 63) compromise this ambiguity. Only quite late in the novel, in chapter 64, when Thackeray pictures her as Napoleon in the pictorial capitol, does he name Becky a "siren" and urge us not to look below the water line where we might see "the monster's hideous tail" (812). Becky looks "writhing and twirling, diabolically hideous and slimy, flapping amongst bones" in the pictorial capital for chapter 63, which compromises the narrative by making clear "the less that is said about her doings is in fact the better" (813) as well as how Becky is often employed when she is "out of the way" (813). This later capital design, more than the seductive mermaid capital for chapter 44, gives shape to the "things we do and know perfectly well in Vanity Fair, though we never speak them" (812).

21. In his note to page 693, Sutherland queries how long the "fearlessly lecher-

ous" Steyne would wait before attempting to compromise Becky's virtue (Thackerary, *Vanity Fair* [Oxford: Oxford University Press, 1983], 941).

22. In *The Reading Lesson,* Brantlinger calls this "the final counterfeit text in the text of *Vanity Fair*" (137).

23. Thackeray's word choice is interesting: whereas Amelia "dropped" (74) the "death-warrant" in Becky's lap, Becky "flung" (866) George's love letter in Amelia's, underscoring Becky's power.

24. Becky responds with a line from Rossini's *The Barber of Seville,* which refers to a scene in which Rosina, prompted by Figaro, shows him a letter that she has already written.

25. Although Thackeray criticizes Amelia's love letters for their repetition, doubtful grammar, and inclusion of whole pages of common verse, he ultimately defends them: "But oh, mesdames, if you are not allowed to touch the heart sometimes in spite of syntax, and are not to be loved until you all know the difference between trimeter and tetrameter, may all Poetry go to the deuce, and every schoolmaster perish miserably!" (140).

26. In his introduction to *Vanity Fair,* Sutherland cites that the phrase "interesting situation" appears in Dickens's correspondence to signal his wife's pregnancy (xxiii–xxiv). With Amelia being married for just nine days, Thackeray hints at premarital pregnancy. It also would explain Dobbin's urging George to marry her, "George, she's dying" (223).

27. George pays for his unheroic actions and his poor treatment of Amelia, whom Thackeray continually supports even though he admits, at the end, that she is a "tender little parasite" (871).

28. Becky "busies herself in works of piety" (877) and gives to charities for "The Destitute Orange-girl," the "neglected Washerwoman," and the "Distressed Muffinman" (877) and the like. In fact, "She is always having stalls at Fancy Fairs for the benefit of these hapless beings" (877). Although Thackeray admits "She has her enemies," he defends Becky to the last by retaliating, "Who has not?" (877).

CONCLUSION

1. Little information exists on Brend'amour, although Gilman, writing in the 1880s, calls him "noted." He was a German artist, born October 16, 1831, dying January 22, 1915. He is best known for *Der Kaffee nach Tisch* (1890), modeled after the style of Charles Hermans. I have not yet been able to date the engraving "In the Library" included in Gilman's 1888 book, and she does not date it. However, its inclusion and Gilman's commentary make it relevant to this study of the woman reader in Victorian British and American fiction.

2. See Gilman, *Art Gems for the Home and Fireside,* 96. This title appears on the cover, whereas *Gems of Art for the Home and Fireside* is on the title page. I follow Knight, who refers to the book as *Art Gems for the Home and Fireside* in "Charlotte Perkins Gilman's Lost Book," an article which presents Knight's discovery of Gil-

man's authorship of this book. Since it was published under the name of Mrs. Charles Stetson, critics long attributed it to Gilman's close friend and Charles Walter Stetson's second wife, Grace Ellery Channing. It is interesting that Gilman wrote this book during her breakdown and makes no mention of it in her autobiography, allowing her contemporaries to assume that its author was her artist husband's second wife, not herself. The selections seem arbitrary and wide ranging, including artists, for example, from Germany, Belgium, Finland, Denmark, and Italy. Images of birds and children join with domestic scenes, a still life, architecture, and scenes from mythology and the Bible. In many cases, Gilman does not identify the artist, nor does she date the images. For more information, see Knight, "Charlotte Perkins Gilman's Lost Book."

3. See Docherty, "Women as Readers," 373–76; she includes Paxton's *The Yellow Jacket*, along with one by Edmund C. Tarbell titled *Girl Reading* (1909) to illustrate the cultivated type.

4. See, for example, Gilman's *The Diaries*, where she refers to fiction by Dickens, Poe, and Carroll, for example. She also discusses her reading in her autobiography, *The Living*.

5. See, for example, Gilman's commentary on E. Seeldrayers's "The First-Born," 78.

6. See Golden, "'Written to Drive Nails With.'"

7. Gilman, *Topeka State Journal*, June 15, 1896, vol. 7, quoted in Scharnhorst, *Charlotte Perkins Gilman*, 40.

Bibliography

Adams, W. H. Davenport. *Woman's Work and Worth in Girlhood, Maidenhood, and Wifehood.* Chicago: Rand, McNally and Company, 1884.

Alcott, Louisa May. *Little Women.* 1868, 1869. Reprint. With an afterword by Nina Auerbach. New York: Bantam Books, 1983.

———. *Little Women or Meg, Jo, Beth, and Amy.* 1868, 1869. Reprint. With illustrations by Frank T. Merrill. Boston: Little, Brown, and Company, 1880.

———. *Little Women or Meg, Jo, Beth, and Amy.* 1868, 1869. Reprint. With illustrations by Jessie Willcox Smith. Boston: Little, Brown, and Company, 1922.

Altick, Richard D. *The English Common Reader.* Chicago: University of Chicago Press, 1957.

Armstrong, Nancy. *Desire and Domestic Fiction: A Political History of the Novel.* Oxford: Oxford University Press, 1987.

Arnold, Matthew. *Culture and Anarchy.* 1869. Reprint. New York: Macmillan, 1913.

Ashton, Rosemary. *George Eliot: A Life.* London: Allen Lane, Penguin Press, 1996.

Auerbach, Nina. Afterword to *Little Women,* by Louisa May Alcott. New York: Bantam Books, 1983.

———. "Falling Alice, Fallen Women, and Victorian Dream Children." In *Soaring with the Dodo,* ed. Edward Guliano and James R. Kincaid. Charlottesville: University of Virginia Press, 1982.

———. *Woman and the Demon: The Life of a Victorian Myth.* Cambridge: Harvard University Press, 1982.

Austen, Jane. *Mansfield Park.* 1814. Reprint. With an introduction by Margaret Drabble. New York: Penguin Books, 1989.

———. *Northanger Abbey.* 1818. Reprint. New York: Bantam Books, 1985.

———. *Pride and Prejudice.* 1813. Reprint. Ed. Mark Shorer. Boston: Houghton Mifflin Company, 1956.

Avery, Gillian. *Nineteenth Century Children.* London: Hodden and Stoughton, 1965.

Baker, Mark. *The Libraries of George Eliot and George Henry Lewes.* English Literary Studies Monograph Series No. 24. Victoria: University of Victoria, 1981.

Banta, Martha. *Imaging American Women: Idea and Ideals in Cultural History.* New York: Columbia University Press, 1987.

Barker, Juliet R. V., ed. *The Brontës: Selected Poems.* London: J. M. Dent, 1993.
Bauer, Dale, ed. *The Yellow Wallpaper.* Boston: Bedford Books, 1998.
Baym, Nina. *Novels, Readers, and Reviewers: Responses to Fiction in Antebellum America.* Ithaca: Cornell University Press, 1984.
Beecher, Catharine E., and Harriet Beecher Stowe. *The American Woman's Home.* New York: J. B. Ford and Co., 1870.
Benjamin, Walter. "The Work of Art in the Age of Mechanical Reproduction." In *Illuminations,* ed. Hannah Arendt, 217–51. Trans. Harry Zohn. New York: Schocken Books, 1976.
Bersani, Leo. Introduction to *Madame Bovary* by Gustave Flaubert, ix–xxii. Ed. Leo Bersani. Transl. Lowell Bair. New York: Bantam Books, 1989.
Bewick, Thomas. *History of British Birds.* 1797. Reprint. 2 vols. Newcastle: Edward Walker, 1804.
Bledstein, Burton. *The Culture of Professionalism: The Middle Class and the Development of Higher Education in America.* New York: W. W. Norton and Co., 1976.
Bodenheimer, Rosemary. *The Real Life of Mary Ann Evans: George Eliot, Her Letters and Fiction.* Ithaca: Cornell University Press, 1994.
Braddon, Mary Elizabeth. *The Doctor's Wife.* 1864. Reprint. Ed. Lyn Pykett. Oxford and New York: Oxford University Press, 1998.
Brantlinger, Patrick. *The Reading Lesson: The Threat of Mass Literacy in Nineteenth-Century British Fiction.* Bloomington: Indiana University Press, 1998.
———. "What Is 'Sensational' about the 'Sensation Novel'?" *Nineteenth-Century Fiction* 37, no. 1 (June 1982): 1–28.
Bratton, J. S. *The Impact of Victorian Children's Fiction.* London: Croom Helm, 1981.
Brontë, Anne. *The Tenant of Wildfell Hall.* 1848. Reprint. Oxford: Oxford University Press, 1992.
Brontë, Charlotte. *Jane Eyre.* New York: Random House, 1945.
———. *Jane Eyre.* 1847. Reprint. 2nd ed. Ed. Richard J. Dunn. New York: W. W. Norton and Co., 1987.
———. *Jane Eyre.* 1847. Reprint. 3rd ed. Ed. Richard J. Dunn. New York: W. W. Norton and Co., 2001.
Brontë, Emily. *Wuthering Heights.* 1847. Reprint. Ed. Linda H. Peterson. Boston: Bedford Books of St. Martin's Press, 1992.
Broomfield, Andrea, and Sally Mitchell. *Prose by Victorian Women: An Anthology.* New York and London: Garland Publishing, 1996.
Bunyan, John. *The Pilgrim's Progress.* 1678, 1684. Reprint. With an introduction by Louis L. Martz. New York: Holt, Rinehart and Winston, 1962.
Burnett, Frances Hodgson. *Editha's Burglar.* With illustrations by Henry Sandham. Boston: Jordan, Marsh and Company, 1888.
———. *Little Saint Elizabeth and Other Stories.* With illustrations by Reginald B. Birch. New York: Charles Scribner's Sons, 1890.
Butler, Marilyn. *Jane Austen and the War of Ideas.* Oxford: Clarendon, 1975.

Cadogan, Mary, and Patricia Craig. *You're a Brick Angela!: A New Look at Girls' Fiction from 1839 to 1975.* London: Victor Gollancz, 1976.
Caird, Mona. *The Daughters of Danaus.* 1894. Reprint. With an afterword by Margaret Morganroth Gullette. New York: Feminist Press, 1989.
———. "The Duel of the Sexes," *Fortnightly* 84 (July 1905): 112.
Carroll, Lewis. *Alice's Adventures under Ground.* With illustrations by Lewis Carroll. 1864. Reprint with an introduction by Martin Gardner, New York: Dover Publications, 1965.
———. *The Annotated Alice: Alice's Adventures in Wonderland and Through the Looking Glass.* 1865. Reprint. Ed. Martin Gardner. New York: New American Library, 1960.
Castagno, John. *American Artists: Signatures and Monograms, 1800–1989.* Metuchen, N.J.: Scarecrow Press, 1990.
Casteras, Susan. *Images of Victorian Womanhood in English Art.* Rutherford, N.J.: Fairleigh Dickinson University Press, 1987.
Chopin, Kate. *The Awakening.* 1899. Reprint. 2nd ed. Ed. Margo Culley. New York and London: W. W. Norton and Co., 1994.
Clarke, Edward H. *Sex in Education; Or, A Fair Chance for the Girls.* 1873. Reprint, Salem, N.H.: Ayer Company Publishers, 1972.
Clarke, George. "The Novel-Reading Habit," *The Arena* 19 (Jan.–June 1898): 670–79.
"Classic Movie Reviews." <http://www.geocities.com/Hollywood/5555/reefer.html>.
Cohen, Jane R. *Charles Dickens and His Original Illustrators.* Columbus: Ohio University Press, 1980.
Cohen, Morton N. *Lewis Carroll: A Biography.* New York: Alfred A. Knopf, 1995.
Conway, Jill. "From 'Stereotypes of Femininity' in a Theory of Sexual Evolution." In *The Captive Imagination: A Casebook on "The Yellow Wallpaper,"* ed. Catherine Golden, 71–82. New York: Feminist Press, 1992.
Copans, Ruth. "Dream Blocks: American Women Illustrators of the Golden Age, 1890–1920." In *Book Illustrated: Text, Image, and Culture 1770–1930,* ed. Catherine J. Golden, 241–76. New Castle, Del.: Oak Knoll, 2000.
Cott, Nancy F. *The Bonds of Womanhood: "Woman's Sphere" in New England, 1780–1835.* New Haven: Yale University Press, 1977.
Crisler, Jesse S. "Alcott's Reading in *Little Women*: Shaping the Autobiographical Self," *Resources for American Literary Study* 20, no. 1 (1994): 27–36.
Cruikshank, George. *The Bottle. In Eight Plates by George Cruikshank.* London: David Bogue, 1847.
Cruse, Amy. *The Englishman and His Books in the Early Nineteenth Century.* New York: Thomas Y. Crowell Company Publishers, n.d.
———. *The Victorians and Their Reading.* Boston and New York: Houghton Mifflin Company, 1935.

Cunningham, A. R. "The 'New Woman Fiction' of the 1890's," *Victorian Studies* (Dec. 1973): 177–86.

Cunningham, Gail. *The New Woman and the Victorian Novel.* London: Macmillan, 1978.

Curtis, Gerald. *Visual Words: Art and the Material Book in Victorian England.* Hants, England: Ashgate Publishing, 2002.

Darton, F. J. Harvey. *Children's Books in England: Five Centuries of Social Life.* Cambridge: Cambridge University Press, 1932.

David, Beverly R., and Ray Sapirstein. "Illustrators and Illustrations in Mark Twain's First American Editions." In *The Adventures of Tom Sawyer,* by Mark Twain. Ed. Shelley Fisher Fishkin, 20–23. New York and Oxford: Oxford University Press, 1996.

———. "Reading the Illustrations in *Huckleberry Finn.*" In *Adventures of Huckleberry Finn,* by Mark Twain. Ed. Shelley Fisher Fishkin, 33–40. New York and Oxford: Oxford University Press, 1996.

———. "Reading the Illustrations in *Tom Sawyer.*" In *The Adventures of Tom Sawyer,* by Mark Twain. Ed. Shelley Fisher Fishkin, 24–31. New York and Oxford: Oxford University Press, 1996.

Davidoff, Leonore. *The Best Circles: Women and Society in Victorian England.* Totowa, N.J.: Rowman and Littlefield, 1973.

Davidson, Cathy N., ed. *Revolution and the Word: The Rise of the Novel in America.* New York: Oxford University Press, 1986.

———, ed. *Reading in America: Literature and Social History.* Baltimore: Johns Hopkins University Press, 1989.

Defoe, Daniel. *The History of the Devil.* 1726. Reprint. With an introduction by Richard G. Landon. Totowa, N.J.: Rowman and Littlefield, 1972.

Delamar, Gloria T. *Louisa May Alcott and "Little Women": Biography, Critique, Publications, Poems, Songs, and Contemporary Relevance.* Jefferson, N.C.: McFarland and Co., 1990.

Dickens, Charles. *David Copperfield.* 1850. Reprint. Ed. Jerome H. Buckley. With illustrations by Hablot Knight Browne. New York and London: W. W. Norton and Co., 1990.

———. *Dealings with the Firm of Dombey and Son Wholesale, Retail, and for Exportation.* With illustrations by Hablot Knight Browne. 1848. Reprint. London: Chapman and Hall; and Henry Frowde, c. 1905.

———. *Dombey and Son.* 1848. Reprint. Ed. Alan Horsman. Oxford and New York: Oxford University Press, 1982.

———. *Hard Times.* Ed. David Craig. New York: Penguin Books, 1976.

———. *Oliver Twist.* 1838. Reprint. Ed. Kathleen Tillotson. With illustrations by George Cruikshank. Oxford and New York: Oxford University Press, 1982.

———. *Oliver Twist; or, The Parish Boy's Progress by 'Boz' Charles Dickens.* 3 vols. With illustrations by George Cruikshank. London: Richard Bentley, 1838.

———. *The Personal History of David Copperfield.* With illustrations by Hablot Knight Browne. London: Bradbury and Evans, 1850.

———. *A Tale of Two Cities.* With frontispieces by F. O. C. Darley; illustrations by Hablot Knight Browne. 1859. Reprint. Boston and New York: Houghton, Mifflin and Company, 1894.

———. *A Tale of Two Cities.* 1859. Reprint. With an introduction by Frederick Busch; illustrations by Hablot Knight Browne. New York: Penguin Books, 1997.

Dimock, Wai Chee. "Feminism, New Historicism, and the Reader." In *Readers in History: Nineteenth-Century American Literature and the Contexts of Response,* ed. James L. Machor, 85–106. Baltimore: Johns Hopkins University Press, 1993.

Docherty, Linda J. "Women as Readers: Visual Interpretations," *Proceedings of the American Antiquarian Society* 107, part 2 (1998): 338–88.

Douglas, Ann. "Mysteries of Louisa May Alcott." In *Critical Essays on Louisa May Alcott,* ed. Madeleine B. Stern, 231–40. Boston: G. K. Hall, 1984.

Du Maurier, George. "The Illustrating of Books from the Serious Artist's Point of View," *Magazine of Art* (August–Sept. 1890): 349–53, 371–75.

———. *Peter Ibbetson.* New York: Harper and Brothers Publishers, 1891.

Edel, Leon. *Henry James: A Life.* New York: Harper and Row, 1985.

Edel, Leon, and Adeline R. Tintner, eds. *The Library of Henry James.* Ann Arbor: UMI Research Press, 1987.

Eliot, George. *Middlemarch.* 1872. Reprint. Ed. W. J. Harvey. New York: Penguin Books, 1976.

———. *The Mill on the Floss.* 1860. Reprint. Ed. Gordon S. Haight. Oxford: Oxford University Press, 1980.

Ellis, Sarah Stickney. *The Mothers of England; Their Influence and Responsibility.* 1843. Reprint. New York: D. Appleton and Co., 1844.

Emerson, Ralph Waldo. *Essays: First and Second Series.* 1844. Reprint. With an introduction by Harold Goddard. New York: Macmillan, 1926.

Engelsing, Rolf. "Die Perioden der Lesergeschicte in der Neuzeit." In *Zur Sozialgeschicte deutscher Mittel-und Unterschichten,* 112–54. Gottingen: Vandenhoeck und Ruprecht, 1973.

Everitt, Graham. *The Illustrated Book.* Cambridge: Harvard University Press, 1938.

Feldstein, Richard. "Reader, Text, and Ambiguous Referentiality in 'The Yellow Wall-Paper.'" In *The Captive Imagination: A Casebook on "The Yellow Wallpaper,"* ed. Catherine Golden, 307–18. New York: Feminist Press, 1992.

Fetterley, Judith. "Little Women: Alcott's Civil War." In *Critical Essays on Louisa May Alcott,* ed. Madeleine B. Stern, 140–43. Boston: G. K. Hall, 1984.

———."Reading About Reading: 'A Jury of Her Peers,' 'The Murders in the Rue Morgue,' and 'The Yellow Wallpaper.'" In *The Captive Imagination: A Casebook on "The Yellow Wallpaper,"* ed. Catherine Golden, 253–60. New York: Feminist Press, 1992.

Flaubert, Gustave. *Madame Bovary.* 1857. Reprint. Ed. Leo Bersani. Trans. Lowell Bair. New York: Bantam Books, 1989.

Flint, Kate. *The Woman Reader, 1837–1914.* Oxford: Oxford University Press, 1993.

———. "Women, Men and the Reading of *Vanity Fair*." In *The Practice and Representation of Reading in England*, eds. James Raven, Helen Small, and Naomi Tadmor, 246–62. Cambridge: Cambridge University Press, 1996.

Geddes, Patrick, and John Arthur Thomson. *The Evolution of Sex*. London: W. Scott, 1889.

Gennari, Genevieve. *Le Premier voyage de Madame de Staël en Italie et la genèse de Corinne*. Paris: Boivin, 1947.

Gérin, Winifred. *Anne Brontë*. London: Thomas Nelson and Sons, 1959.

Gilbert, Sandra, and Susan Gubar. *The Madwoman and the Attic: The Woman Writer and the Nineteenth-Century Literary Imagination*. New Haven: Yale University Press, 1979.

Gilman, Charlotte Perkins (Stetson), ed. *Art Gems for the Home and Fireside*. Providence: J. A. and R. A. Reid, 1888.

———. *In This Our World*. 1893. Reprint. New York: Arno Press, 1974.

———. *Women and Economics*. 1898. Reprint. Amherst, N.Y.: Prometheus Books, 1994.

———. "The Yellow Wall-Paper," *New England Magazine* 5 (January 1892): 647–56.

———. *"The Yellow Wall-Paper" and Selected Stories of Charlotte Perkins Gilman*. Ed. Denise D. Knight. Newark: University of Delaware Press, 1994.

Glazener, Nancy. *Reading for Realism: The History of a U.S. Literary Institution, 1850–1910*. Durham: Duke University Press, 1997.

Goddard, Harold. Introduction to *Essays: First and Second Series*, by Ralph Waldo Emerson. New York: Macmillan, 1926.

Golden, Catherine J. *Book Illustrated: Text, Image, and Culture, 1770–1930*. New Castle, Del.: Oak Knoll, 2000.

———. "The Pictures on the Paper: 'The Yellow Wall-Paper' and its Original Magazine Illustrations." Forthcoming.

———. "Turning Life into Literature: The Romantic Fiction of George Du Maurier." *The CEA Critic* 58, no. 1 (Fall 1995): 43–52.

———. "The Writing of 'The Yellow Wallpaper': A Double Palimpsest." In *Charlotte Perkins Gilman: A Study of the Short Fiction*, ed. Denise D. Knight, 155–65. Boston: Twayne, 1997.

———. "'Written to Drive Nails With': Recalling the Early Poetry of Charlotte Perkins Gilman." In *Charlotte Perkins Gilman: Optimist Reformer*, ed. Val Gough and Jill Rudd, 243–66. Iowa City: University of Iowa Press, 1999.

———, ed. *The Captive Imagination: A Casebook on "The Yellow Wallpaper."* New York: Feminist Press, 1992.

Green, Harvey. *The Light of the Home: An Intimate View of the Lives of Women in Victorian America*. New York: Pantheon Books, 1983.

Gullette, Margaret Morganroth. Afterword to *The Daughters of Danaus*, by Mona Caird. New York: Feminist Press, 1989.

Gutworth, Madeleine. *Madame de Staël, Novelist*. Urbana: University of Illinois Press, 1978.
Haight, Gordon S. *George Eliot: A Biography*. Oxford: Oxford University Press, 1968.
———, ed. *The George Eliot Letters*. 9 vols. New Haven: Yale University Press, 1954–78.
Hall, David D. "Readers and Reading in America: Historical and Critical Perspectives," *Proceedings of the American Antiquarian Society* 103 (1994): 337–57.
Hall, James. *Dictionary of Subjects and Symbols in Art*. Rev. ed. New York: Harper and Row, 1974.
Hamilton, Susan, ed. *"Criminals, Idiots, Women, and Minors": Victorian Writing by Women on Women*. Peterborough, Ontario: Broadview Press, 1995.
Hannah, Donald. "'The Author's Own Candles': The Significance of the Illustrations to *Vanity Fair*." In *Renaissance and Modern Essays Presented to Vivian de Sola Pinto in Celebration of His Seventieth Birthday*, ed. George R. Hibbard. London: Routledge and Kegan Paul, 1966.
Harvey, John Robert. *Victorian Novelists and Their Illustrators*. London: Sidgwick and Jackson, 1970.
Hedges, Elaine R. "Afterword to 'The Yellow Wallpaper,' Feminist Press Edition." In *The Captive Imagination: A Casebook on "The Yellow Wallpaper,"* ed. Catherine Golden, 123–36. New York: Feminist Press, 1992.
Heffernan, James A. W. *Museum of Words: The Poetics of Ekphrasis from Homer to Ashbery*. Chicago: University of Chicago Press, 1993.
Heller, Lee F. "*Frankenstein* and the Cultural Uses of Gothic." In *Frankenstein*, by Mary Shelley. Ed. Johanna M. Smith, 325–41. Boston: St. Martin's Press, 1992.
Helsinger, Elizabeth K., Robin Lauterbach Sheets, and William Veeder. *The Woman Question: Society and Literature in Britain and America, 1837–1883*. Chicago: Chicago University Press, 1989.
Heywood, Christopher. "Miss Braddon's *The Doctor's Wife*: An Intermediary between *Madame Bovary* and *The Return of the Native*," *Revue de littérature comparée* 38 (1964): 255–61.
———. "A Source for *Middlemarch*: Miss Braddon's *The Doctor's Wife* and *Madame Bovary*," *Revue de littérature comparée* 44 (1970): 184–94.
Hibbard, G. R., ed. *Renaissance and Modern Essays Presented to Vivian de Sola Pinto in Celebration of His Seventieth Birthday*. London: Routledge and Kegan Paul, 1966.
Higgins, Aileen Cleveland. *Dream Blocks*. New York: Duffield and Company, 1908.
"The Higher Education of Women," *The Westminster Review* 129 (1888): 152–62.
Hochman, Barbara. "The Reading Habit and 'The Yellow Wallpaper,'" *American Literature* 74, no. 1 (2002): 89–110.
Holley, Marietta. *Samantha Among the Brethren*. 1890. Reprint. With illustrations by E. A. New York: Funk and Wagnalls, 1892.

Holman, Hugh C. *A Handbook to Literature.* 3rd ed. New York: Bobbs-Merrill, 1972.

Homans, Margaret. *Bearing the Word.* Chicago: University of Chicago Press, 1986.

Honderich, Ted, ed. *The Oxford Companion to Philosophy.* Oxford: Oxford University Press, 1995.

Howe, Julia Ward, ed. *Sex and Education. A Reply to Dr. E. H. Clarke's "Sex in Education."* 1874. Reprint, New York: Arno Press, 1972.

James, Henry. "The Art of Fiction." In *Critical Theory Since Plato,* ed. Hazard Adams, 660–70. New York: Harcourt Brace Jovanovich, 1971.

———. *The Portrait of a Lady.* 1881. Reprint. New York: Penguin Books, 1976.

———. *A Small Boy and Others.* 1913. Reprint. New York: Charles Scribner's Sons, 1914.

James, Louis. *Fiction for the Working Man, 1830–50.* London and New York: Oxford University Press, 1963.

Jespersen, Otto. *Essentials of English Grammar.* Tuscaloosa: University of Alabama Press, 1981.

Kelley, Mary. "Reading Women/Women Reading: The Making of Learned Women in Antebellum America," *The Journal of American History* (September 1996): 401–24.

Kellogg, John Harvey. From *The Ladies' Guide in Health and Disease.* In *The Yellow Wallpaper,* ed. Dale Bauer, 157–73. Boston: Bedford Books, 1998.

Kelly, Gary. "Reading Aloud in *Mansfield Park,*" *Nineteenth-Century Fiction* 37, no. 1 (June 1982): 29–49.

Keyser, Elizabeth Lennox. *Whispers in the Dark: The Fiction of Louisa May Alcott.* Knoxville: University of Kentucky Press, 1993.

Knight, Denise D., ed. "Charlotte Perkins Gilman's Lost Book: A Biographical Gap," *ANQ: A Quarterly Journal of Short Articles, Notes, and Reviews* 14, no. 1 (Winter 2001): 26–31.

———, ed. *The Diaries of Charlotte Perkins Gilman.* 2 vols. Charlottesville: University of Virginia Press, 1994.

Kucich, John. *Repression in Victorian Fiction.* Berkeley: University of California Press, 1987.

Lessing, Gothold Ephraim. *Laocoön; or On the Limits of Poetry and Painting.* Trans. William Ross. London: J. Ridgway and Sons, 1836.

Lister, Raymond. *Victorian Narrative Paintings.* New York: Clarkson N. Potter, 1966.

Long, Robert Emmet. *Henry James: The Early Novels.* Boston: Twayne Publishers, 1983.

Longfellow, Henry Wadsworth. *Evangeline.* 1847. Reprint. With illustrations by Howard Chandler Christy. Indianapolis: Bobbs-Merrill, 1905.

———. *Evangeline, A Tale of Acadie.* 1847. Reprint. With illustrations by F. O. C. Darley. Boston: Fields, Osgood, and Co., 1869.

Mailloux, Steven. "Interpretation." In *Critical Terms for Literary Study,* ed. Frank

Lentricchia and Thomas McLaughlin, 121–34. Chicago: University of Chicago Press, 1990.
Mason, James. "How to Form a Small Library," *Girl's Own Paper*, 2 (1881): part 1, 7–8; part 2, 122–23.
McKinney, Lauren D. "Mona Alison Caird." In *Prose by Victorian Women: An Anthology*, eds. Andrea Bloomfield and Sally Mitchell, 625–28. New York and London: Garland Publishing, 1996.
McMaster, Juliet. *Thackeray: The Major Novels*. Toronto: University of Toronto Press, 1976.
Meisel, Martin. *Realizations: Narrative, Pictorial, and Theatrical Arts in Nineteenth-Century England*. Princeton: Princeton University Press, 1983.
Melville, Louis. *William Makepeace Thackeray: A Biography*. London: John Lane, Bodley Head, 1910.
Miller, J. Hillis. *Illustration*. Cambridge: Harvard University Press, 1992.
———. "*Wuthering Heights*: Repetition and the 'Uncanny.'" In *Wuthering Heights*, ed. Linda H. Peterson, 371–84. Boston: Bedford Books of St. Martin's Press, 1992.
Miller, Nancy K., ed. *The Poetics of Gender*. New York: Columbia University Press, 1986.
Mitchell, Sally. *The Fallen Angel: Chastity, Class, and Women's Reading, 1835–1880*. Bowling Green: Bowling Green University Popular Press, 1981.
———. *The New Girl: Girls' Culture in England, 1880–1915*. New York: Columbia University Press, 1995.
———. "Sentiment and Suffering: Women's Recreational Reading in the 1860s," *Victorian Studies* 21 (1977): 29–45.
Mitchell, S. Weir. *Doctor and Patient*. 1887. Reprint. Philadelphia and London: J. B. Lippincott, 1904.
Modern Language Association of America. "Statement on the Significance of Primary Records," *Profession 95* (1995): 27–28.
Montgomery, Lucy Maud. *Against the Odds: Tales of Achievement*. Ed. Rea Wilmshurst. New York: Bantam Books, 1994.
Morawski, Stefan. *Inquiries into the Fundamentals of Aesthetics*. Cambridge: MIT Press, 1974.
Mudrick, Marvin. *Jane Austen: Irony as Defense and Discovery*. Princeton: Princeton University Press, 1952.
Mulvey, Laura. *Visual and Other Pleasures*. Bloomington: Indiana University Press, 1989.
Nead, Lynda. *Myths of Sexuality: Representations of Women in Victorian Britain*. Oxford: Oxford University Press, 1988.
Patten, Robert L. "Boz, Phiz, and Pickwick in the Pound," *ELH* 36 (1969): 575–91.
———. *George Cruikshank's Life, Times, and Art*. 2 vols. New Brunswick: Rutgers University Press, 1992, 1996.

Peterson, Carla L. *The Determined Reader: Gender and Culture in the Novel from Napoleon to Victoria*. New Brunswick: Rutgers University Press, 1986.

Peterson, M. Jeanne. *Family, Love, and Work in the Lives of Victorian Gentlewomen*. Bloomington: Indiana University Press, 1989.

Phelps, Elizabeth Stuart. "The Angel Over the Right Shoulder." In *Scribbling Women: Short Stories by 19th-Century American Women*, ed. Elaine Showalter, 17–25. New Brunswick: Rutgers University Press, 1996.

Poovey, Mary. *The Proper Lady and the Woman Writer*. Chicago: University of Chicago Press, 1984.

Porter, Laurence M., and Eugene F. Gray, eds. *Approaches to Teaching Flaubert's "Madame Bovary."* New York: Modern Language Association, 1995.

Pykett, Lyn. *Emily Brontë*. Savage, Md.: Barnes and Noble Books, 1989.

———. Introduction to *The Doctor's Wife*, by Mary Elizabeth Braddon, vii–xxviii. Ed. Lyn Pykett. Oxford and New York: Oxford University Press, 1998.

Qualls, Barry V. *The Secular Pilgrims of Victorian Fiction*. Cambridge: Cambridge University Press, 1982.

Radway, Janice. *Reading the Romance: Women, Patriarchy, and Popular Literature*. Chapel Hill: University of North Carolina Press, 1984.

Ray, Gordon N., ed. *The Letters and Private Papers of William Makepeace Thackeray*. 4 vols. Cambridge: Harvard University Press, 1946.

———. *The Uses of Adversity: 1811–46*. Vol. 1. *The Age of Wisdom, 1846–63*. Vol. 2. New York: McGraw Hill Book Company, 1955.

Reach, Angus. *Clement Lorimer; Or, The Book with the Iron Clasps. A Romance*. London: David Bogue, 1849.

Reed, Sue W. "F. O. C. Darley's Outline Illustrations." In *The American Illustrated Book in the Nineteenth Century*, ed. Gerald W. R. Ward, 113–35. Charlottesville: University Press of Virginia, 1987.

Reynolds, Kimberley, and Nicola Humble. *Victorian Heroines: Representations of Femininity in Nineteenth-Century Literature and Art*. New York: New York University Press, 1993.

Rich, Adrienne. "Jane Eyre: The Temptations of a Motherless Woman." In *Jane Eyre*, 462–75. 2nd ed. Ed. Richard J. Dunn. New York: W. W. Norton and Co., 1987.

Richter, David H., ed. *Falling into Theory: Conflicting Views on Reading Literature*, 119–28. Boston: St. Martin's Press, 1994.

Ridding, Lady Laura. "What Should Women Read?" *The Woman at Home* 37 (1896): 29.

Roosevelt, Theodore. *An Autobiography*. New York: Charles Scribner's Sons, 1920.

Rostenberg, Leona. "Some Anonymous and Pseudonymous Thrillers of Louisa May Alcott," *Biographical Society of America Papers* 37 (2nd quarter 1943): 131–40.

Ruskin, John. *Sesame and Lilies: Three Lectures*. New York: Mershon Company Publishers, 1871.

Salmon, Edward. "What Girls Read," *The Nineteenth Century* 20 (1886): 515–29.

Saxton, Martha. *Louisa May.* Boston: Houghton Mifflin, 1977.
Scharnhorst, Gary. *Charlotte Perkins Gilman.* Boston: Twayne, 1985.
Scholes, Robert. *The Rise and Fall of English: Reconstructing English as a Discipline.* New Haven: Yale University Press, 1998.
Schöpp-Schilling, Beate. "'The Yellow Wallpaper': A Rediscovered 'Realistic' Story." In *The Captive Imagination: A Casebook on "The Yellow Wallpaper,"* ed. Catherine Golden, 141–44. New York: Feminist Press, 1992.
Sekula, Allan. "The Body and the Archive," *October* 39 (1986): 3–64.
Shefer, Elaine. *Birds, Cages, and Women in Victorian and Pre-Raphaelite Art.* New York: Peter Lang, 1990.
Sherwood, Mary Martha. *The History of the Fairchild Family.* London: Wells Gardner, Darton and Co., 1902.
Shorter, Clement, ed. *The Brontës, Life and Letters.* 2 vols. New York: Haskell House Publishers, 1969.
Showalter, Elaine. *A Literature of Their Own: British Women Novelists from Brontë to Lessing.* Princeton: Princeton University Press, 1977.
Sicherman, Barbara. "Reading *Little Women:* The Many Lives of a Text." In *U.S. History as Women's History: New Feminist Essays,* ed. Linda K. Kerber, Alice Kessler-Harris, and Kathryn Kish Sklar, 245–66. Chapel Hill: University of North Carolina Press, 1995.
———. "Sense and Sensibility: A Case Study of Women's Reading in Late-Victorian America." In *Reading in America,* ed. Cathy N. Davidson, 201–25. Baltimore: Johns Hopkins University Press, 1989.
Sidgwick, Eleanor Mildred (Mrs. Henry). *Health Statistics of Women Students of Cambridge and Oxford and of Their Sisters.* Cambridge: Cambridge University Press, 1890.
Smith-Rosenberg, Carroll, and Charles Rosenberg. "The Female Animal: Medical and Biological Views of Women and Her Role in Nineteenth-Century America," *Journal of American History* 60 (September 1973): 339–42.
Solomon, Barbara. *In the Company of Educated Women: A History of Women and Higher Education in America.* New Haven: Yale University Press, 1985.
de Staël, Madame. *Corinne, or Italy.* 1807. Reprint. Trans. Avriel H. Goldberger. New Brunswick: Rutgers University Press, 1987.
Stafford, William T. *Perspectives on James's "The Portrait of a Lady."* New York: New York University Press; London: University of London Press, 1967.
Stedman, Jane W. "Charlotte Brontë and Bewick's 'British Birds.'" *Brontë Society Transactions* 15 (1966): 36–40.
Steig, Michael. *Dickens and Phiz.* Bloomington: Indiana University Press, 1978.
Stephenson, Glennis, ed. *Nineteenth-Century Stories by Women.* Peterborough, Ontario: Broadview Press, 1993.
Stern, Madeleine B. *Critical Essays on Louisa May Alcott.* Boston: G. K. Hall, 1984.
———, ed. *Behind a Mask: The Unknown Thrillers of Louisa May Alcott.* New York: William Morrow, 1975.

Sutherland, John. *Can Jane Eyre Be Happy?* Oxford: Oxford University Press, 1997.

———. Introduction to *Vanity Fair: A Novel Without a Hero*, by William Makepeace Thackeray. Ed. John Sutherland. With illustrations by Thackeray, vii–xxx. Oxford: Oxford University Press, 1983.

———. Introduction to *The Woman in White*, by Wilkie Collins. Ed. John Sutherland, vii–xxiii. Oxford: Oxford University Press, 1996.

Swan, Annie S. *Courtship and Marriage, and the Gentle Art of Home-Making.* London: Hutchinson, 1893.

Talmage, T. DeWitt. *The Wedding Ring, A Series of Sermons on the Duties of the Husband and Wife, and on the Domestic Circle.* New York: J. S. Ogilvie and Company, 1886.

Thackeray, William Makepeace. *Vanity Fair: A Novel without a Hero.* 1848. Reprint. With illustrations by Thackeray. 3 vols. New York: Charles Scribner's Sons, 1903.

———. *Vanity Fair: A Novel without a Hero.* 1848. Reprint. Ed. John Sutherland. With illustrations by Thackeray. Oxford: Oxford University Press, 1983.

Thomas à Kempis. *The Imitation of Christ.* 1426. Reprint. Ed. Howard Malcom. Trans. John Payne. With an introduction by Thomas Chalmers. Boston: Gould and Lincoln, 1856.

———. *Of the Imitation of Christ.* 1426. Reprint. London: Kegan Paul, Trench, Trubner and Co., 1892.

Tintner, Adeline R. "The Books in the Books: What Henry James's Characters Read and Why." In *The Library of Henry James.* Eds. Leon Edel and Adleline R. Tintner, 69–96. Ann Arbor: UMI Research Press, 1987.

Tompkins, Jane. "Masterpiece Theater: The Politics of Hawthorne's Literary Reputation." In *Falling into Theory: Conflicting Views on Reading Literature*, ed. David H. Richter. Boston: St. Martin's Press, 1994.

———. *Sensational Designs: The Cultural Work of American Fiction, 1790–1860.* Oxford: Oxford University Press, 1985.

Trilling, Lionel. "Jane Austen and *Mansfield Park.*" In *From Blake to Byron*, ed. Boris Ford. Vol. 5, *The Pelican Guide to English Literature.* Harmondsworth: Penguin, 1957.

Trollope, Anthony. "Higher Education of Women." 1868. In *Four Lectures.* Ed. M. L. Parrish, 67–88. London: Constable and Company; Toronto: Macmillan Company of Canada, 1938.

———. *Orley Farm.* 1862. Reprint. 2 vols. (bound as one). With illustrations by John Everett Millais. New York: Dover, 1981.

———. *Orley Farm. A Novel.* New York: Harper and Brothers, 1862.

———. *Thackeray.* New York: Harper and Brothers, 1879.

Truitt, W. J. *Know Thyself or Nature's Secrets Revealed: A Word at the Right Time.* Marietta, Ohio: S. A. Mullikin, 1911.

Twain, Mark. *Adventures of Huckleberry Finn.* With illustrations by E. W. Kemble. 1885. Reprint. New York: Charles L. Webster and Company, 1889.

———. *Adventures of Huckleberry Finn.* 1885. Reprint. With illustrations by Worth Brehm. New York and London: Harper and Brothers, 1923.

———. *Adventures of Huckleberry Finn.* 1885. Reprint. Ed. Shelley Fisher Fishkin. With illustrations by E. W. Kemble. New York and Oxford: Oxford University Press, 1996.

———. *The Adventures of Tom Sawyer.* 1876. Reprint. With illustrations by True Williams. Hartford: American Publishing, 1876; San Francisco: A. Roman and Company, 1877.

———. *The Adventures of Tom Sawyer.* 1876. Reprint. Ed. Shelley Fisher Fishkin. With illustrations by True Williams. New York and Oxford: Oxford University Press, 1996.

Vicinus, Martha. "Rediscovering the 'New Woman' of the 1890s: The Stories of 'George Egerton.'" In *Feminist Re-Visions: What Has been and Might Be,* ed. Vivian Patraka and Louise A. Tilly, 12–25. Ann Arbor: University of Michigan Women's Studies Program, 1983.

Vogler, Richard A. *Graphic Works of George Cruikshank.* New York: Dover, 1979.

Welter, Barbara. "The Cult of True Womanhood: 1820–1860," *American Quarterly* 18, no. 2, part 1 (Summer 1966): 151–74.

"What Is the Harm of Novel-Reading?" *The Wesleyan-Methodist Magazine* 78 (October 1855): 932–34.

Wheeler, Michael. *The Art of Allusion in Victorian Fiction.* London: Macmillan, 1979.

Whitney, Helen Hay. *Verses for Jock and Joan.* With illustrations by Charlotte Harding. New York: Fox Duffield and Company, 1905.

Williams, Merryn. *Women in the English Novel, 1800–1900.* New York: St. Martin's Press, 1984.

Winchell, James. "Reading (in) *Madame Bovary.*" In *Approaches to Teaching Flaubert's "Madame Bovary,"* ed. Laurence M. Porter and Eugene F. Gray, 98–105. New York: Modern Language Association, 1995.

Winter, Kate H. *Marietta Holley: Life with "Josiah Allen's Wife."* Syracuse: Syracuse University Press, 1984.

Wolff, Robert Lee. *Sensational Victorian: The Life and Fiction of Mary Elizabeth Braddon.* New York and London: Garland Publishing, 1979.

Wood-Allen, Mary. *What a Young Woman Ought to Know.* Rev. ed. Philadelphia and London: Vir Publishing, 1913.

Woolf, Virginia. *A Room of One's Own.* 1929. Reprint. New York: Harcourt Brace, 1981.

Yannella, Donald. *Ralph Waldo Emerson.* Boston: Twayne Publishers, 1982.

Yates, Margarita. "Do Our Girls Take an Interest in Literature? The Other Side of the Question," *The Monthly Review* (April 1906): 120–32.

Index

Page numbers in italics refer to illustrations.

Abbey Church (Yonge), 19, 47
Adams, W. H. Davenport, 24, 105, 249n.12
Adventures of Huckleberry Finn (Twain), 12; illustrations by Brehm, *171*, 171–73; illustrations by Kemble, 168–71, *169*
Adventures of Tom Sawyer, The (Twain), 12; illustrations by True Williams and, 153, *172*, 173–74
Agnes Grey (Anne Brontë), 19
Ainsworth, William Harrison, 44, 259–60n.4
Alcott, Louisa May, 44, 45, 51–52, 65–71, 157–61, *184*, 184–85, 188, 229, 238–39n.61, 242nn.25, 30, 254nn.26, 34
Alice's Adventures in Wonderland (Carroll), 46–47, 191, 193, 202, 229, 257n.6
Alice's Adventures under Ground (Carroll), 178–80, 188–93, *190*, 201, 234n.16, 257nn.6, 7
Altick, Richard, 18, 235n.4
American Woman's Home, The (Beecher and Stowe), 40–41, 142, 164
Amy Herbert (Sewell), 19, 47
Anderson, Elizabeth Garrett, 28
angel in the house, 13, 23, 30, 112, 141, 142–46, 148–53, 211
Angel in the House, The (Patmore), 141, 143
"Angel Over the Right Shoulder, The" (Phelps), 141–42
antifiction critics, 8, 30–40, 189, 197–98
Arabian Nights, The, 58

Armstrong, Nancy, 85
Arnold, Matthew, 22, 91
Art Gems for the Home and Fireside (Gilman), 225–29, 263–64n.2
"Art of Fiction, The" (James), 51, 64, 65, 78, 233n.3, 240n.1
Art of Illusion in Victorian Fiction, The (Wheeler), 3, 58, 249n.11
Ashton, Rosemary, 92, 122, 124, 248n.1
Auerbach, Nina, 66, 144, 160–61, 189, 242n.27
Austen, Jane, 46; *Mansfield Park*, 6, 118, 119–22, 183; *Northanger Abbey*, 119, 196; *Pride and Prejudice*, 119, 122; *Sense and Sensibility*, 119
Avery, Gillian, 42, 238–39n.61

Badger, Joseph, 167
Bainton, George, 118
Ballantyne, R. M., 44
Balzac, Honoré de, 61, 100, 101
Banta, Martha, 22, 41–42, 143, 185, 230, 238n.60
Barnicoat, Constance, 46
Baym, Nina, 3, 5
Bearing the Word (Homans), 74
Beecher, Catharine, 40–41, 142, 164, 169
Bell, Mary, 37
Belsham, Thomas, 163–64, 185, 254n.34
Benjamin, Walter, 54

Bersani, Leo, 116, 248n.12
Bewick, Thomas, 52, 54–59, *56*, *57*, 231, 240nn.8, 9, 240–41n.11, 241n.12
Bible, 8, 18, 19, 20, 21, 65, 66, 71–74, 90, 91, 97, 145, 153, 156, 158, 160, 164, 166–67, 168–69, 173–74, 189, 202, 230, 254n.28
biological argument, 30–31, 32, 34, 35, 80–81, 124, 168, 189, 200–201, 229
Birch, Reginald B., 164
Birds, Cages, and Women in Victorian and Pre-Raphaelite Art (Shefer), 10
Black Arrow, The (Stevenson), 43
Black Beauty (Sewell), 46
Bodenheimer, Rosemary, 92
Bo-Peep (Johnson), 24, *25*, 142
Bottle, The (Cruikshank), 97, 202
Boy's Own Paper, The, 42, 239n.64
Braddon, Mary Elizabeth, 6, 9, 44, 99–100, 246–47n.9, 247n.22, 248nn.24, 26; *The Doctor's Wife*, 106–16
Brantlinger, Patrick, 3, 53, 72, 76, 119, 205, 261nn.9, 12
Brehm, Worth, *171*, 171–73
Brend'amour, Franz Robert Richard, 225–29, 263n.1
Bride of Lammermoor, The (Scott), 110
Brighty, G. M., 82, *83*
Brontë, Anne, 54, 77, 236n.7
Brontë, Branwell, 54
Brontë, Charlotte, 44, 45, 51–59, 77, 82, 111, 188–89, 204, 231, 236n.7, 240nn.8, 9, 240–41n.11, 260n.5
Brontë, Emily, 45, 51–52, 54, 71–78
Browne, Hablot Knight (Phiz), 13, 109, 143–49, *144*, *145*, *147*, *149*, 150–52, *151*, 153, 156, *175*, 175–77, *176*, 188, 253n.19
Browning, Elizabeth Barrett, 61; *Aurora Leigh*, 61–62
Browning, Robert: "Fra Lippo Lippi," 11–12; *The Ring and the Book*, 62
Bulwer-Lytton, Edward, 44, 45, 99, 113
Bunyan, John, 44, 53, 66–68, 81, 242n.28
Burnett, Frances Hodgson, 46, 164, *165*, *180*, 180–81
Byron, Lord, 81, 86, 92

Caird, Mona, 30, 119, 248–49n.5, 249–50n.19, 250n.30, 251n.33
Campbell, Helen, 34
caricature tradition, 1–2, *2*, 11, 32–33, *33*, 204, 206–7, 211–12, *212*
Carlyle, Thomas, 44, 91
Carroll, Lewis, 44, 47, 178–80, 188–93, *190*, 204, 206, 229, 234n.17
Cassandra (Nightingale), 37
Casteras, Susan, 10
"Character" (Emerson), 130–33
Chateaubriand, François René de, 100
children's literature, 12, 42, 66–67, 229, 238–39n.61, 239n.62, 254n.26
Chopin, Kate, 134
Christian Year, The (Keble), 90, 128, 245n.24
Christy, Howard Chandler, 178, *179*
Civil War (American), 4, 67, 157, 159, 168
Clarke, Dr. Edward H., 34–35, 200, 233n.4, 237n.46
Clarke, George, 37
classical education, 81, 86, 119, 123–25, 132, 225, 226, 230
Cobbe, Frances Power, 27, 237n.31
Cohen, Jane R., 143
Cohen, Morton N., 189
Comic Almanack, The, 1–2, *2*, 229
Conduct of Life, The (Emerson), 131
Conway, Jill, 31
Copans, Ruth, 23–25, 155, 162
Copley, John Singleton, 167
Corelli, Marie, 46
Corinne (de Staël), 79, 85–90, 95, 231, 244nn.15, 16, 18, 244–45n.20, 245nn.22, 23
Cruikshank, George: *The Bottle* and *The Drunkard's Children*, 97, 202, 204; *Clement Lorimer*, 202–3, 204; "My Wife Is a Woman of Mind," 1–2, *2*, 27, 178, 225, 227, 229, 231, 233n.2; *Oliver Twist* and, 11–12, 203–4, 252–53n.14
Cruse, Amy, 26–27
Culture and Anarchy (Arnold), 22

Darley, F. O. C., 12, *166*, 166–67
Darton, Harvey, 189, 238–39n.61

Daughters of Danaus, The (Caird), 119, 129–34, 250n.27; Hadria's reading interests and, 130–32; mismatched reading interests and, 132–34
David, Beverly, 153, 170
David Copperfield (Dickens), 46, 109, 113–14, 123, 252nn.10, 11; angel in the house and, 13, 114, 142–48, 211, 252n.9; illustrations, 13, *144*, 144–46, *145*, *147*, *175*, 175–77, *176*, 252n.12, 253n.19, 256n.49
Davidoff, Leonore, 23
Davidson, Cathy N., 3, 4–5, 235n.6
Davies, Emily, 19, 181
Defoe, Daniel, 44, 79, 81–85, *83*, 93, 243n.8
de Quincy, Thomas, 91
de Saint-Pierre, Bernardin, 100
de Staël, Madame (Anne Louise Germaine de): *Corinne*, 79, 85–90, 244nn.15, 16, 18, 244–45n.20, 245nn.22, 23; *De l'Allemagne*, 86
Determined Reader, The (Peterson), 3, 5, 80, 243nn.10, 13, 247n.14
Dickens, Charles, 3, 4, 11–12, 44, 45, 109, 229, 247n.22; George Cruikshank and, 11–12, 148–50; *David Copperfield*, 13, 109, 113–14, 123, 142–48, *144*, *145*, *147*, *175*, 175–77, *176*, 211, 252nn.10, 11, 12; *Dombey and Son*, 109, 111–12, 142, 148, *149*; *Oliver Twist*, 11–12, 108, 148–50, *150*, 203–4, 252–53n.14; *Our Mutual Friend*, 43, 114, 142; *Pickwick*, 204; *A Tale of Two Cities*, 148, 150–52, *151*
Dimock, Wai Chee, 196, 199, 258n.18
Docherty, Linda J., 3, 8, 10–11, 12, 139–40, 167, 174, 233n.11, 251n.3
Doctor's Wife, The (Braddon), 6, 9, 106–16, 247n.10, 247–48n.23, 248nn.24, 26; *Madame Bovary* and, 99–100, 107–8, 110–16, 248n.24; novel as an imitation of life and, 108; obsessive novel-reading in, 107–14, 247n.17; reading illustrations and, 109, 111
Dombey and Son (Dickens), 109, 111–12, 148, *149*
Don Quixote (Cervantes), 92
Dream Blocks (Higgins), *161*, 161–62
Drunkard's Children, The (Cruikshank), 97
Dryden, John, 23, 247n.21, 249n.11
"Ducking a Witch" (Brighty), 82–85, *83*, 93, 95
Du Maurier, George, 12, 204, 231

East Lynne (Wood), 46
Edgeworth, Maria, 44, 206
Editha's Burglar (Burnett), *180*, 180–81
education argument, 18–21, 26–28, 81, 181, 230
Egerton, George, 119
ekphrasis, 10, 80, 132, 231
Eliot, George (Mary Ann Evans), 3, 4, 44, 60–61, 111, 230; *Daniel Deronda*, 61; George Henry Lewes and, 86, 128; *Middlemarch*, 6, 61, 115, 122–29; *The Mill on the Floss*, 61, 79–95, 187–88, 243n.14, 244nn.16, 18, 19, 244–45n.20, 245nn.22, 23; *Romola*, 126
Ellis, Sarah Stickney, 24–25, 53, 160–61
Emerson, Ralph Waldo, 62–63, 119, 130–33, 227, 248–49n.5, 249–50n.19
empowerment argument, 28–30, 74–78, 85–90, 130, 185, 189–91, 197–201, 213, 215, 224, 230
English Common Reader, The (Altick), 18, 235n.4
Evangelicalism, 19, 72–73, 86, 91–92, 94–95
Evangeline (Longfellow), 8, 11, 164–67, *166*, 178, *179*

fallen woman, 85, 94
family/family circle, 1–2, 2, 24–25, 28, 40, 66, 68, 142, *145*, 145–46, 149–50, 157–61, *158*, *159*, *161*, 187, 230
Family, Love, and Work in the Lives of Victorian Gentlewomen (Peterson), 19–20
"Fate" (Ralph Waldo Emerson), 130–33
femininity/domestic femininity: 13, 40, 89–90, 93, 117–18, 142, 143–46, 156–62, 178, 185, 205, 227, 229, 230
Fetterley, Judith, 197
Fish, Stanley, 6–7
Flaubert, Gustave, 6, 61, 99–106, 246–47n.9, 247n.10

Flint, Kate, 3–4, 29, 79, 88, 110, 116, 118, 200, 205, 215, 251n.4
Found (Rossetti), 38
"Fra Lippo Lippi" (Browning), 11–12
French novels, 27, 39, 205, 211, 228

Gaskell, Elizabeth, 44, 46, 77, 114, 230
Geddes, Patrick, 31, 80, 233n.4, 243n.5
gender, 6, 13, 23–26, 31, 84, 86, 111–12, 129, 178, 185, 198–99, 229, 231
gentility/gentility argument, 6, 13, 22–23, 29, 66, 75–78, 117–18, 120–22, 141, 143–45, 149, 155–56, 157–62, 185, 230
George III, king of England, 72
George Cruikshank's Life, Times, and Art (Patten), 148, 252–53n.14
Gilbert, Sandra, 5, 53, 71, 85, 200
Gillray, James, 32, 33
Gilman, Charlotte Perkins, 25, 28, 30, 229, 230, 237–38n.47; *Art Gems*, 225–28, 231, 263–64n.2; *In This Our World*, 228–29, 236n.26; "The Yellow Wall-Paper," 14, 31, 189, 193–201, *194, 195*, 252n.11, 258n.19
Girl's Own Paper, The, 42, 239n.64
Godey's Lady's Book, 26, 39, 235n.3
Golden Age, The (Grahame), 47
Goldsmith, Oliver, 68, 163
governess, 19, 209–11
Grahame, Kenneth, 47, 239–40n.73
Grand, Sarah, 119
Great Expectations (Dickens), 135
Green, Elizabeth Shippen, 12
Gubar, Susan, 5, 53, 71, 85, 200
Gullette, Margaret Morganroth, 134, 248n.1
Gulliver's Travels (Swift), 44, 58

Hall, David D., 3, 4, 6–7, 10, 17
Harding, Charlotte, 12, 154–56, *155*
Hard Times (Dickens), 192
Hassam, Childe, 178
Hatfield, Jo. H., 189, 193–96, *194, 195*
Hawthorne, Nathaniel, 45
Hedges, Elaine R., 193, 199
Heffernan, James A. W., 10, 233n.15
Heir of Redclyffe, The (Yonge), 46, 68
Heller, Lee F., 23, 38–39
Helsinger, Elizabeth K., 5

Henty, G. A., 43, 46
Higgins, Aileen C., *161*, 161–62
high art, 79, 90, 149, 184–85
History of British Birds (Bewick), 52, 54–59, 56, *59*, 208, 240nn.8, 9, 240–41n.11, 241n.14
History of the Devil, The (Defoe), 79, 81–85, 231, 243nn.8, 11
History of the Fairchild Family, The (Sherwood), 44, 191–92, 238–39n.61
History of Sandford and Merton, The (Day), 44,
Hochman, Barbara, 197, 258n.22
Hogarth, William, 11, 260n.5
Holley, Marietta, 153, 253–54n.22
Homans, Margaret, 74, 82, 90
home, 1, 23, 24, 40, 156, 160, 172, 177, 229
Homer, Winslow, 238nn.54, 55; *The Country School*, 142, 252n.6; *The New Novel*, 37–38, *38*, 107, 178
House Maid, The (Paxton), 41, 238n.60
Howe, Julia Ward, 35
Hughes, Thomas, 44
Humble, Nicola, 7–8, 123

illustration, xiii, 11, 140, 165–66, 168, 251n.2, 255n.42; caricature tradition and, 1–2, *2*, 11, 32–33, *33*, 204, 206–7, *207*, 211–12, *212*; "feminine" approach to, *161*, 161–62; gender and, 13, 168; golden age of, 12, 157
Imaging American Women (Banta), 22, 41, 143, 230, 238n.60
Imitation of Christ, The (Thomas à Kempis), 79, 90–95, 245nn.25, 26
Inchbald, Elizabeth, 121
industrialization, 4, 18, 30, 145, 156, 235n.4
Irving, Helen, 30
Iser, Wolfgang, 6–7
Ivanhoe (Scott), 89, 101

James, Henry: "Art of Fiction," 51, 64, 65, 78, 233n.3, 240n.1; *The Portrait of a Lady*, 51–52, 59–65, 68, 82, 211, 225, 231, 241n.23; *A Small Boy and Others*, 11–12
James, Louis, 18, 235n.4
Jane Eyre (Charlotte Brontë), 7, 19, 27, 46,

51–60, 109; *History of British Birds* and, 54–59, *56, 57*, 208; reading illustrations and, 54–59, *56, 57*, 102, 187–88, 196, 204, 208
Jespersen, Otto, 199
Johnson, Eastman, 24, *25*, 236n.24
Johnson, Samuel, 211, 219, 224, 231

Keats, John, 79, 187, 256n.1
Kelley, Mary, 21, 198
Kellogg, Dr. John Harvey, 37, 70
Kelly, Gary, 120
Kemble, E. W., 12, 168–71, *169*, 253–54n.22
Kenilworth (Scott), 101
Kingsley, Charles, 44
Kucich, John, 87, 94

Lady Audley's Secret (Braddon), 99, 247n.22
leisure, 41–42, 179, 238n.60, 238–39n.61
Lewes, George Henry: as editor of *Fortnightly Review*, 42, 200; relationship with George Eliot and, 86
library: formation of a personal, 22, 118, 134, 164; women in the, 60, *184*, 184–85, *283*, 225–29, *226*
literacy, 18, 75–76, 98, 205, 235n.4
Literature of Their Own, A (Showalter), 29
Little Saint Elizabeth and Other Stories (Burnett), 164, *165*, 255n.36
Little Women (Alcott), 9, 13, 14, 45, 46, 51–52, 65–71, 74, 82, 157–61, *158*, *159*, 162–64, *184*, 184–85, 204, 238–39n.61, 242n.25, 254nn.26, 27, 254n.28, 34; *Pilgrim's Progress* and, 67–68, 242n.27, 254n.28; sensation fiction and, 68–71, 188, 189
Long, Robert, 62
Longfellow, Henry Wadsworth, 44; *Evangeline*, 8, 11, 164–67, *166*, 178, *179*, 255n.37
Lovers' Vows (Inchbald), 121
Low, Florence, 45–46
Lucretia (Paget), 70
Lyall, Edna, 46

Madame Bovary (Flaubert), 6, 99–106; Emma Bovary's adultery, 101, 104–5; Emma Bovary's reading illustrations, 101–2; Emma Bovary's reading process, 101–4; Emma Bovary's addiction to romance novels, 100–106
Madwoman in the Attic, The, (Gilbert and Gubar), 5–6
Mailloux, Steven, 9
Mansfield Park (Austen), 6, 118, 119–22, 183
marriage, 26, 87, 117–18, 124, 126, 132–34, 146–47
Marryat, F., 43, 44
Mary Barton (Gaskell), 230
Mason, Charlotte, 34
Mason, James, 22, 118, 134, 164, 236n.19, 248n.4
McMaster, Juliet, 215
Meade, L. T., 46, 239n.65
medical argument, 31–36, 106, 129–30, 168, 173, 189, 200–201
Meisel, Martin, 216
Melville, Herman, 45
Merrill, Frank T., 12, 13, 157–58, *158*, 160–61, 163–64, *184*, 184–85, 256n.55
Merriman, Henry Seton, 46
Middlemarch (Eliot), 6, 115, 122–29, 196; Dorothea Brooke's education, 122–23, 225; Dorothea Brooke's misreading of Edward Casaubon, 118, 122, 123, 124–29
Millais, Sir John Everett, 181–83, *182*,185, 186
Miller, J. Hillis, 73
Mill on the Floss, The (Eliot), 61, 79–95, 242n.28, 243n.14; *Corinne* and, 85–90, 231, 244nn.16, 18, 19, 244–45n.20, 245nn.22, 23; "Ducking a Witch" in *The History of the Devil* and, 82–85, *83*, 93, 95; *The Imitation of Christ* and, 79, 90–95; *Pilgrim's Progress* and, 82, 243n.10; reading illustrations and, 82–85, 102, 187–88; Scott's novels and, 81, 89–90, 92
Milton, John, 22–23, 82, 83
Mitchell, Dr. S. Weir: *Doctor and Patient*, 31, 201, 237n.41; "The Yellow Wall-Paper" and, 31, 194; rest cure and, 194
Mitchell, Sally, 9–10, 20, 43, 238–39n.61
Montgomery, Lucy Maud, 44

moral argument, 38–40, 53, 59, 64, 69–71, 73, 99, 102, 104–6, 109–10, 116, 129–30, 178, 185, 189, 211, 229, 230
Morawski, Stefan, 58
More, Thomas, 91
"Mother's Charge, The" (Gilman), 25, 236n.26
Mothers of England, The (Ellis), 24, 53, 160–61
mother-woman/motherhood, 23–26, 30, 160–64, 167, 229
Museum of Words (Heffernan), 10, 234n.15
"My Wife Is a Woman of Mind" (Cruikshank), 1–2, *2*, 27, 178, 225, 227, 229, 233n.1, 255n.41

neurasthenia, 35, 193
New England Magazine, 193
New Girl, The (Mitchell), 9–10, 43, 238–39n.61
New Novel, The (Homer), 37–38, *38*, 107,
"New Woman"/"New Woman" novelists, 26–27, 119, 248–49n.5
Nightingale, Florence, 37, 70, 129
Nineteenth-Century Stories by Women (Stephenson), 6
Northanger Abbey (Austen), 119
Norton, Caroline, 45
Novels, Readers, and Reviewers (Baym), 3, 5

Oakley, Violet, 12
Oliphant, Margaret, 46
Oliver Twist (Dickens), 11–12, 108, 148–50, *150*, 203–4, 252–53n.14
"On First Looking into Chapman's Homer" (Keats), 187
Origin of Species, The (Darwin), 27
Orley Farm (Trollope), 22, 188, 204; Millais' illustrations, 181–83, *182*
Our Mutual Friend (Dickens), 43, 114, 142

Paget, Rev. Francis, 70
Paradise Lost (Milton), 71, 83
parlor, 42, 148–50, *149*, 160, 172
Patmore, Coventry: Mrs. Coventry Patmore and, 141, 251n.4

Patten, Robert L., 148, 252–53n.14
Paxton, William McGregor: *The House Maid*, 41; *The Yellow Jacket*, 227
penny dreadful, 68–71. *See also* sensation fiction
periodicals, 44
Peterson, Carla L., 3, 5, 80, 85, 87, 102, 243nn.10, 13, 247n.14
Peterson, M. Jeanne, 19–20, 117
Phelps, Elizabeth Stuart, 141–42
phrenology, 1, 225
pictorial types of women readers: antiquated reader, 140, 167–77, *169*, *171*, *172*, *175*, *176*, 255nn.40, 41; Docherty's categories, 10–11, 139–41, 167, 174; interrupted reader, 140, 141–56, *144*, *145*, *149*, *150*, *151*, *154*, *155*; isolated reader, 140, 178–85, *179*, *180*, *182*, *184*, 214; mind traveler, 188–201, *190*, *194*, *195*; revolutionary reader, 6, 14, 202–24, *203*, *207*, *210*, *212*, *214*, *218*, *221*; social reader, 140, 156–67, *158*, *159*, *161*, *163*, *165*, *166*
Pilgrim's Progress (Bunyan), 8, 53, 65, 66–68, 71, 74, 158, 160, 164, 242n.28, 254n.28
Pirate, The (Scott), 89, 91, 101
Poe, Edgar Allan, 45
Political History of the Devil, The (Defoe). *See History of the Devil, The*
Pope, Alexander, 23, 211, 215–17
Portrait of a Lady, The (James), 51–52, 59–65, 107, 241n.19; German philosophy and, 62–63; reading illustrations and, 60; novel as imitation of life and, 63–65, 241n.23
Potter, Beatrix, 204
Pre-Raphaelitism, 150, 153, 154, 163, 185, 263
Pride and Prejudice (Austen), 119, 122
propaganda, 96–98
Pullan, Matilda, 98
Punch, 1
Pykett, Lyn, 77, 99, 110, 247n.10, 247–48n.23
Pyle, Howard, 12

Radway, Janice, 28, 188, 200

Rape of the Lock, The (Pope), 205, 211, 215–17
Reach, Angus B., 202–3
reader-response theory, 6–7, 188, 200
reading habit, 17, 25, 37, 96–97, 99, 197, 201
Reading Lesson, The (Brantlinger), 3, 53, 205
Reading the Romance (Radway), 28, 188, 200
Reefer Madness, 97
repression, 93–95
rest cure, 35, 193–97, 237–38n.47
Revolution and the Word (Davidson), 3, 5, 235n.6
Reynolds, Kimberley, 7–8, 123
Richardson, Samuel, 54
Ridding, Lady Laura, 36, 70, 98
Rise and Fall of English, The (Scholes), 54, 79
Robinson Crusoe (Defoe), 42, 92, 189
Rob Roy (Scott), 101
romance novels, 39–40, 101–5, 108, 200
Romantic aspirations, 100, 106
Romola (Eliot), 126
Roosevelt, Theodore, 45, 239n.69
Rossetti, Dante Gabriel, 38, 204
Rostenberg, Leona, 69
Rousseau, Jean Jacques, 104

Salmon, Edward, 26, 42, 43, 44, 45
Samantha Among the Brethren (Holley), 153–54, *154*, 253n.21
Sand, George, 100, 101
Sandham, Henry, *180*, 180–81
Sandford and Merton (Day), 42
Sapirstein, Ray, 153, 170
Saxton, Martha, 69, 242n.30
Scholes, Robert, 54, 79
Schöpp-Schilling, Beate, 197
Schreiner, Olive, 119, 134
Scott, Sir Walter, 44, 45, 81, 92, 104; Waverley novels and, 27, 86, 89–90, 91, 92, 101, 110
Secret Garden, The (Burnett), 164
sensation fiction, 2, 32, 38–40, 68–71, 98–99, 200, 242n.31
Sense and Sensibility (Austen), 119
Sewell, Anna, 46

Sewell, Elizabeth Missing, 45, 47, 236n.7
Sex in Education (Clarke), 34, 200, 233n.4, 237n.46
Shakespeare, William, 22–23, 92, 189, 247n.21
Sheets, Robin Lauterbach, 5
Shefer, Elaine, 10
Shelley, Percy Bysshe, 108
Sherwood, Mary Martha, 44, 191–92, 238–39n.61
Showalter, Elaine, 29, 123
Sicherman, Barbara, 3, 20, 29, 53, 198, 235n.6
Sidgwick, Eleanor, 36
Small Boy and Others, A (James), 11–12
Smith, Jessie Willcox, 12, 157, 158–62, *159*, *161*
Smollett, Tobias, 211–12
social class, 6, 42, 74–75, 76, 140, 183, 209–11, 230–31, 235n.4
socialization argument, 23–26, 66–68, 73, 87, 91, 93–94, 95, 117–18, 120–22, 141, 143–46, 155–56, 157–62, 167, 230
Soulsby, Lucy, 23–24
Spectator, The, 60–61
Stanton, Elizabeth Cady, 34
Stedman, Jane, 55
Stephenson, Glennis, 6
Stern, Madeleine, 69, 242n.30
Stevenson, Robert Louis, 43, 46
Story of an African Farm, The (Schreiner), 43, 46
Stowe, Harriet Beecher, 128; *The American Woman's Home*, 40–41, 142, 164, 169; *Uncle Tom's Cabin*, 46, 68
Stretton, Hesba, 44, 46
Sue, Eugène, 100
Sutherland, John, 69, 74, 222, 262–63n.21, 263n.26
Swan, Annie S., 117, 133, 146
Swift, Jonathan, 44, 58

Tale of Two Cities, A (Dickens), 148, 150–52, *151*
"Tales of Wonder!" (Gillray), 32, *33*
Talmage, Rev. T. DeWitt, 40
Taylor, Jeremy, 82–83, 122

Tenant of Wildfell Hall, The (Anne Brontë), 54
Tennyson, Alfred, 112, 114, 247n.21, 248n.25
Thackeray, William Makepeace, 3, 4, 44, 245n.25, 247n.22, 259–60n.4, 260n.5; *Vanity Fair*, 6, 109, 152, 202, 203, 204–24, 260n.6; illustrations for *Vanity Fair* and, 152–53, 203, *203*, 206–24, *207*, *210*, *212*, *214*, *218*, *221*, *223*
Thomas à Kempis, 79, 90–95, 245nn.25, 26
Thomson, J. Arthur, 31, 80, 233n.4, 243n.5
Tom Brown's Schooldays (Hughes), 42
Tompkins, Jane, 188, 245n.21
transcendentalism, 62
Treasure Island (Stevenson), 43
Trimmer, Sarah, 47
Trollope, Anthony, 22, 24, 29, 141, 181–83, *182*, 188, 260n.5
tropes of consumption and addiction, 3, 36–38, 43–44, 96–99, 106, 116, 178, 181, 189, 197–98, 213, 229
Truitt, Dr. W. J., 30
Twain, Mark (Samuel L. Clemens): illustration and, 12, 153, 255n.42; *Adventures of Huckleberry Finn*, 12, 168–71, *169*, *171*, 173–74; *The Adventures of Tom Sawyer*, 12, 153, 168, *172*;

Uncle Tom's Cabin (Stowe), 46, 68
ut pictura poesis, 11, 234n.17

Vanity Fair (Thackeray), 260nn.6, 7; treatment of adultery and murder in, 205, 215–17, 219–21, 261n.14, 262nn.18, 19, 20, 21, 263n.28; angel in the house and, 152; governess in, 209, 210, 211; illustrations, 152–53, 203, *203*, 206–24, *207*, *210*, *212*, *214*, *218*, *221*, *223*; Johnson's *Dictionary* and, 206–9, *207*, 219, 224, 231; Napoleonic imagery in, 202, 203, 214, 224, 259n.2, 260n.8; novel without a hero/heroine and, 215, 222, 224, 261n.16; *The Rape of the Lock* and, 205, 211, 215–17; revolutionary reader and, 6, 14, 202, 204–24

Van Ghent, Dorothy, 59
Veeder, William, 5
Verses for Jock and Joan (Whitney), 154–56, *155*
Vicar of Wakefield, The (Goldsmith), 68, 163–64
Vicinus, Martha, xiii, 248–49n.5
Victoria, queen of England, 3, 234n.16
Victorian Heroines (Reynolds and Humble), 7–8
Victorians and Their Reading, The (Cruse), 26–27
Voltaire, 104, 105

Walker, Alexander, 200
Warner, Susan (E. Wetherell) 44; *The Wide, Wide World*, 45; *Queechy*, 45, 239n.68
Waterhouse, A. C., 82
Waverley (Scott), 89
Webster, Thomas, 156
Welter, Barbara, 143
Wesley, John, 54
Wesleyan Methodist Magazine, The, 40, 96–97
"What Is the Harm of Novel-Reading?," 40, 96–97, 246n.8
Wheeler, Michael, 3, 58, 125, 249n.11
Whitney, Helen Hay: *Verses for Jock and Joan*, 154–56, *155*
Williams, Merryn, 177
Williams, True, 12, 172, 173–74, 253–54n.22, 256n.46
Winchell, James, 103
Winter, Kate, 153
Woman and the Demon (Auerbach), 144
Woman Reader, The (Flint), 3–4
Woman Question, The (Helsinger, Sheets, and Veeder), 5
woman's sphere, 13, 30, 31, 40, 89–90, 93, 230
women's books and magazines, 26, 39, 103. See also *Godey's Lady's Book*
women's reading: addiction and, 37–38, *38*, 107; compatibility and, 26, 87, 117–18, 124, 126, 132–34, 146–47, 247n.19, 248n.4; empowerment and, 21, 28–30,

134; escapism/rejection of domesticity and, 60, 255n.41; gentility and, 6, 13, 20, 22–23, 29, 66, 75–78, 117–18, 120–22, 141, 143–45, 149, 155–56, 157–62, 185, 230; health consequences and, 30–38, *33*, *38*, 40, 96–97, 106, 107, 192, 201, 233n.4, 237n.44; imagination and, 41; immorality and, 32, 38–40, 96–97, 104, 105, 238n.55; independent reading/isolation and, 28, 37–39, *38*, 52–57, 59–63, 66, *180*, 180–81, *182*, 182, *184*, 184–85; reading of illustrations and, 53–60, *56*, *57*, 101–2, 104, 109, 111, 135, 184, 187–88, 196, 208, 231, 241n.20, 247n.20; self-fashioning and, 20, 21; staple fare and rules for selection and, 22–26, 60, 180–81, 191–92, 201, 211, 229

Wood, Mrs. Henry, 44, 46

Wood-Allen, Dr. Mary, 32–34, 233n.4, 237n.44

Woolf, Robert Lee, 116

Woolf, Virginia, 28, 237–38n.47, 250n.27

Wordsworth, William, 29, 229, 241n.12

"Work of Art in the Age of Mechanical Reproduction, The" (Benjamin), 54

Wuthering Heights (Emily Brontë), 7, 51–52: 71–78; marginal writing and, 71–74, 204; reading for empowerment and, 74–78

"Yellow Wall-Paper, The" (Gilman), 14, 31, 252n.11, 258n.19; illustrations, 193–97, *194*, *195*, 258n.20; mind traveler and, 193–201

Yonge, Charlotte Mary: *Abbey Church*, 19, 47; *The Daisy Chain*, 46; *Heartsease*, 46; *The Heir of Redclyffe*, 46, 68, 185

Catherine J. Golden is professor of English at Skidmore College. She has published widely on Victorian illustrated fiction and British and American women writers. She is editor of *Book Illustrated: Text, Image, and Culture, 1770–1930* (2000); *The Mixed Legacy of Charlotte Perkins Gilman* (2000), with Joanna Zangrando; *Unpunished* (1997), with Denise D. Knight; and *The Captive Imagination: A Casebook on "The Yellow Wallpaper"* (1992).

www.ingramcontent.com/pod-product-compliance
Lightning Source LLC
Chambersburg PA
CBHW021339230426
43666CB00006B/341